COPYRIGHT ©2012. BRAINTREE PUBLISHING, LLC. ALL RIGHTS RESERVED.

No part of this book may be produced, stored in a retrieval system, or transmitted in any form or by any means, electronic, mechanical, photocopying, recording or otherwise, without the prior permission in writing from the publisher.

FIRST EDITION
ISBN 978-0-9828824-5-0

Produced by Braintree Publishing, LLC
187 Western Gailes
Williamsburg, VA 23188
www.braintreepublishing.com

Printed in the United States

MESSAGE TO THE EXAMINEE

This invaluable study guide covers all of the critical, bottom line information necessary to pass the **ADEX/NERB for Dentists**. This guide was written for ADEX/NERB examinees by successful ADEX/NERB examinees, and contains all of the important information required to assess the periodontal cases and questions, and identify the correct answers when manipulating the exam's three-dimensional prosthodonic images.

Dental Board Busters is on your side. We strive to ensure that you are fully equipped and prepared to pass the challenging ADEX/NERB diagnostic skills exams. With the guide, there is no need to spend your precious time searching through old class notes, exams, and textbooks because Dental Board Busters has already done it for you!

At Dental Board Busters, we know what you need to know to pass the ADEX/NERB diagnostic skills examination (DSE), and are confident that this guide will help you pass the ADEX/NERB and achieve your professional dental aspirations.

Test with Confidence,

Dental Board Busters

TABLE OF CONTENTS

ORAL PATHOLOGY **4**
Metabolic & Genetic Diseases 5
Inflammatory Jaw Lesions 11
Connective Tissue Lesions 13
Benign Epithelial Tumors 17
Verrucal Papillary Lesions 19
Neoplasms 20
Odontogenic Abnormalities 29
White Lesions 35
Blood Diseases 41
Neurologic & Muscle Disorders 48
Non-Odontogenic Cysts 49
Odontogenic Cysts 52
Non-Odontogenic Tumors 55
Odontogenic Tumors 61
Pigmented Lesions 66
Red-Blue Lesions 69
Pseudocysts (No Epithelial Lining) 71
Salivary Gland Tumors 72
Ulcerative Conditions 79
Vesiculo-Bullous Diseases 82
Hepatitis 89

RADIOLOGY **91**
Osteoradionecrosis 92
Digital Radiography 93
Primary & Secondary Radiation 94
Collimnation 94
Filtration & E-Speed Film 95
Panorex 96
Cephalometrics & BWX 97
Submental-Vertical 98
Water's View 99

Towne's View 100
Developer Solution & Chemicals 101
Vertical Angulation 102
Horizontal Angulation 103
Bisecting Angle Technique 103
SLOB Rule 104
Focal Spot & Half-Value Layer 105
Kilovoltage (kVP) 105
Density, Contrast, & Accurate Images 106
Dental X-ray Tube Parts 106
Radiograph Prescriptions 107

DENTAL EMERGENCIES & MEDICALLY COMPROMISED CONSIDERATION **108**
Dental Emergency Protocol 109
Dental Considerations For Medically
Compromised Patients 110

PRE-MEDICATION & PHARMACOLOGY **113**
Standard Pre-Medication Regimens 114
Conditions Recommending Antibiotic
Prophylaxis 114
Conditions Not Requiring Antibiotic
Pre-medication 115
DEA Drug Schedule 116
Important Pharmacologic Agents 116
NSAIDS 116
COX-1 117
Salicylates 118
COX-2 118
Heparin, Warfarin, & PT 119
Acetaminophen 120
Opioids 121

TABLE OF CONTENTS

Xerostomia & Drugs 122
Oral Hypoglycemics 122
Asthma & Beta Blockers 123
Alpha Blockers 123
Potassium & Thiazide Diuretics 124
Loop & Osmotic Diuretics 125
Corticosteroids 125
Calcium Channel Blockers 125
Amide Local Anesthetics 126
EPI 127
Nitrous Oxide 127

PERIODONTICS 129
Periodontal Prognosis 130
Mobility, Pocket Depth, CAL 130
Bleeding on Probing 131
Furcation Involvement 131
Periodontal Screening & Recording (PSR) ...132
Vertical & Horizontal Bone Loss 132
Deriving a Periodontal Diagnosis ...132
Plaque-Induced Gingival Diseases ...133
Drug-Induced Gingival Diseases 136
System Diseases & Gingival Diseases ...136
Bacterial, Viral, & Fungal Infections ...137
Periodontitis 138
Periodontal Therapy Goals 139
Aggressive Periodontal Disease 139
Chronic Periodontitis 140
Refractory Periodontitis 141
Systemic Conditions & Periodontal Disease ..141
Periodontal Disease & Systemic Health ...142
Mucogingival Conditions 142
Attached Gingiva & Marginal Gingiva ...143
Periodontium 143
Acute Periodontal Diseases & ANUG ...144

Periodontal Abscesses 145
Acute Herpetic Gingivostomatitis ...147
Periodontal Surgical Treatments ...148
Suprabony Pockets & Vertical Bone Loss ...149
Osseous Defects (Infrabony Pockets) ...150
Bone Grafting, GTR, Free Gingival Grafts ...151
Periodontal Flaps 152
Occlusal Trauma 155
Periodontal Treatment Planning 157
Ultrasonic Scaling, SRP, Oral Hygiene ...158
Implants 159

PROSTHODONTICS 161
RPD & Kennedy Classification 162
Major & Minor Connectors 163
Mandibular RPD Major Connector ...163
Maxillary RPD Major Connectors ...166
Indirect Retainers (Rests & Proximal Plates) .168
Direct Retainers (Clasps) 171
RPD Stress Breakers (Wrought Wires) ...176
Surveying RPD Abutments on Casts ...177
Face Bow & Framework Try-In 178
Chromium-Cobalt Alloys, Altered
  Cast, Impressions 179
Complete Dentures 180
Custom Tray & Border Molding 181
Occlusal Rims 181
Mandibular Complete Dentures 182
Maxillary Complete Dentures 184
Inflammatory Conditions & Dentures ...186
Immediate Dentures 188
Relining 189
Overdentures & Occlusion 190
Working Side, Balancing Side, Protrusive ...191
Curve of Spee & Wilson 192

TABLE OF CONTENTS

Bilateral Balanced Occlusion &
   Group Function 192
Vertical Dimension of Occlusion 193
TMJ 194
Centric Relation & Centric
   Occlusion (MICP) 195
Condylar Guidance 196
Occlusal Plane, Cusp Inclination, & Canine
Guidance 197
Anterior Guidance, Supporting Cusps,
   Non-Supporting Cusps 198
Selective Grinding & Occlusal Adjustment ... 199
Denture Teeth Selection & Setting Teeth 200
Phoenetics 202
Temporary (Provisional) Restorations 203
Crowns Preparation Guidelines 204
Types of Crown Margins 205
Porcelain Shade Selection 206
Pontic Design 207
Cantilever Bridges & Pier Abutments 209
Maryland Bridge & Resin Bonded FPD 210
Bridge Abutments & Ante's Law. 212
Rigid Connectors & Bridgework Design 213
Posts (Dowels) & Core Build-Ups 214
Ferrule Effect 215
Porcelain Veneers 216
Impression Materials 217
Gypsum & Cements 220

ENDODONTICS 222
Vertical Fractures & Cracked Tooth
   Syndrome 223
Electric Pulp Tester (EPT) & SLOB Rule 224
Diagnostic Tests for Traumatized Teeth 225

Pulpotomy 225
Apexification, Calcium Hydroxide,
   & Pulp Capping 226
Access Preparation for RCT 227
Canal Debridement & Obturation 228
Chloroform & Irrigants 229
Chelating Agents, ZOE, & MTA 230
Apicoectomy & Acute Apical Periodontitis ... 231
Endodontic Instruments 232
Tooth Avulsion & Treatment 233
Root Resorption (Internal & External) 234
Types of Dentin & Pulp 235
Mandibular Root Anatomy for RCT 236
Maxillary Root Anatomy for RCT 237
Alternatives to RCT 238
Thermal Sensitivity & Diagnosing Need
   For RCT 238
Abscesses 239
Combined Perio-Endo Lesion 240
Reversible Pulpitis 241
Irreversible Pulpitis & Necrosis 242
Restorations after RCT 243

TREATMENT PEARLS 244
Oral Pathology Pearls 245
Pre-Med, Emergency, & Medical
   History Pearls 249
Oral Surgery Pearls 252
Periodontic Pearls 253
Endodontic Pearls 254
Orthodontic Pearls 255
Prosthodontic & Restorative Pearls 256
Radiographic Pearls 260

CHAPTER 1

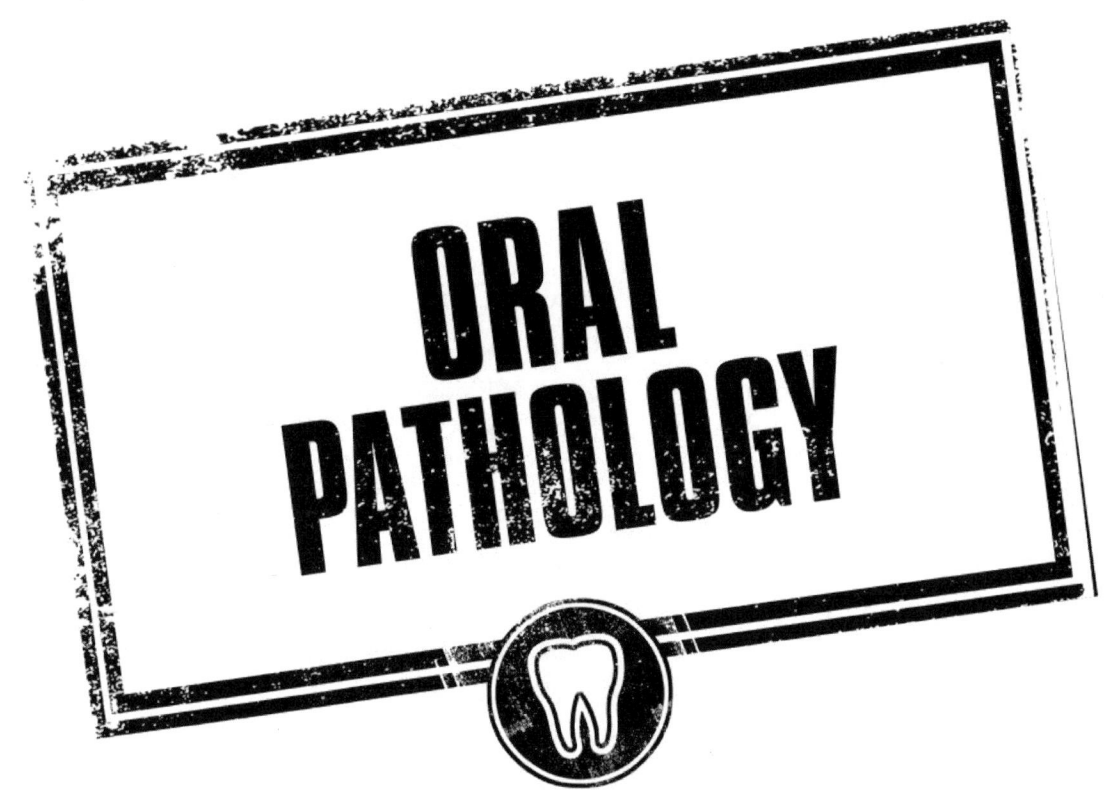

METABOLIC & GENETIC DISEASES

HYPERTHYROIDISM-caused by **excessive production of thyroid hormone (THYROXIN)**. Thyroxin's stimulates cellular metabolism, growth, and differentiation of all tissues. In excess, it **leads to high** basal metabolism, **fatigue**, **weight loss**, **excitability**, **elevated** temperature **(heat intolerance, sweating)**, generalized **osteoporosis**, **fine hair**, **diarrhea**, **tremor (shakiness)**, **tachycardia (rapid heart rate)**. Oral manifestations are not uncommon, but if the disturbance starts early in life, premature tooth eruption and loss of deciduous dentition are common. **GRAVES DISEASE & EXOPTHALMOS** (bulging eyes). Two types of Hyperthyroidism:

1. **Graves Disease (Toxic Diffuse Goiter)**-**most common** form that occurs mostly in WOMEN ages 20-40. Usually arises after an infection or physical or emotional stress. Typical signs of hyperthyroidism are present plus **GOITER & EXOPHTHALMOS** (bulging eyes).

2. **Plummer's Disease (Toxic Multinodular Goiter)**-caused by the presence of many toxic thyroid nodules (adenomas) within the thyroid gland. Plummer's is uncommon in adolescents and young adults, and increases with age. **Exophthalmos (bulging eyes) is rare**.

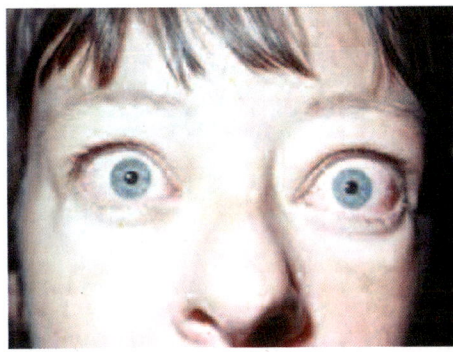
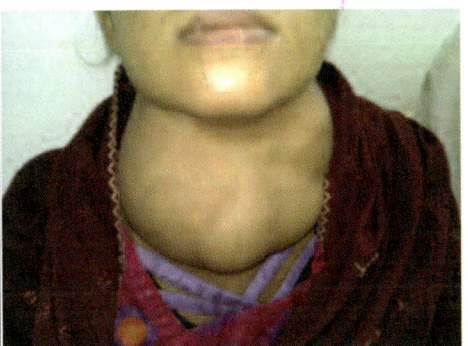

HYPOTHYROIDISM-a clinical feature is **WEIGHT GAIN**, **cold intolerance**, **lowered** pitch of **voice**, mental and physical **slowness**, **constipation**, **dry skin**, **coarse hair**, and **puffiness of face**, **eyelids**, and **hands**.

- **Myxedema**-very severe hypothyroidism in adults much more common in WOMEN than men. Characterized by **puffiness of face and eyelids, swelling of tongue and larynx**. The skin becomes **dry and rough**, and hair sparse. The individual has a **low** basal-metabolic rate and **low** body temperature, **poor** muscle tone, **low** strength, tires **easily**, and are mentally sluggish. Myxedema is alleviated by administering thyroid hormones.

- **Cretinism**-severe **hypothyroidism in a child** due to **lack of thyroid hormone** causing retardation of growth and abnormal bone development. **Severe mental retardation** is caused by improper CNS development. If recognized early, Cretinism can be improved with thyroid hormones.

- Dental findings in a child with hypothyroidism are a **LARGE TONGUE**, **under-developed mandible**, **over-developed maxilla**, **delayed teeth eruption**, and **deciduous teeth** are **retained longer**.

NOTES

↑ Ca²⁺, ↓ phosphate
↑ alkaline phosphate

HYPERPARATHYROIDISM-a common complication is **KIDNEY STONES** (renal calculi). Kidney stones form due to an increase in urinary excretion of calcium and phosphate. Osteoporosis, **GIANT CELL GRANULOMAS**, and metastatic calcifications are manifestations of hyperparathyroidism.

- The main cause is an **ADENOMA** (benign tumor of the gallbladder epithelium). **Laboratory findings** include hypercalcemia, decreased serum phosphorus, and increased serum alkaline phosphatase and serum PTH. <u>Clinical characteristics</u>: cystic bone lesions (osteitis fibrosa cystica or von Recklinghausen's Disease of bone), nephrocalcinosis, kidney stones (renal calculi), and peptic duodenal ulcers. *May find well-defined cystic radiolucencies on a panorex or peri-apical radiograph.*

- **EXCESS LOSS OF CALCIUM** in urine stimulates the parathyroid glands to undergo hyperplasia because the feedback mechanism that detects low serum calcium elicits growth of the gland. The resulting metabolic effects are identical to primary hyperparathyroidism effects.

HYPOPARATHYROIDISM-in rare instances, associated with congenital thymic hypoplasia (**DiGeorge's syndrome**). Hypoparathyroidism is most commonly caused by accidental surgery excision during thyroidectomy.

 ACROMEGALY – a hormonal disorder that occurs when the **PITUITARY GLAND** produces **EXCESS GROWTH HORMONE** (**HYPERPITUITARISM**) due to a **BENIGN TUMOR** after adolescence (fusion of long bone epiphyses). Most commonly affects **MIDDLE-AGED ADULTS** and can cause serious illness and premature death.

- In > 90% of acromegaly patients, GH overproduction is caused by a **BENIGN TUMOR** of the pituitary gland (ADENOMA). Whether or not the epiphyses of the long bones have fused with the shaft is the main determinant of whether gigantism or acromegaly will occur when there is over-secretion of GH by the pituitary gland.

- <u>Clinical Signs</u>: soft tissue swelling of the hands & feet (an early feature), with patients noticing a change in ring or shoe size. Gradually, bony changes alter the patient's facial features (i.e. brow & lower jaw protrude, nasal bone enlarges, and teeth spacing increases).

- <u>Oral Manifestations of Acromegaly & Gigantism</u>: enlarged tongue, mandibular prognathism, teeth are tipped to buccally or lingually due to an enlarged tongue, and roots may be longer than normal.

- **GIGANTISM**-caused by a benign tumor **BEFORE** adolescence (non-fusion of epiphyses).

DWARFISM (Pituitary Dwarfs) – characterized by arrested growth caused by undersecretion of GROWTH HORMONE. Dwarfs often have limbs and features not properly proportioned or formed.

- <u>Oral Manifestations</u>: delayed eruption rate & shedding of teeth, clinical crowns & roots appear smaller, dental arch is smaller causing malocclusion, and an under-developed mandible.

- The **MOST COMMON** type of Dwarfism is **ACHONDROPLASIA**. Child is very short (~50 inches), fingers are stubby, bowed legs, bulging forehead, bossing of frontal bones, saddle-like nose, and mandibular prognathism.

OSTEOGENESIS IMPERFECTA ("BRITTLE BONES") – a rare genetic defect/disorder that affects the **COLLAGEN PRODUCTION** (major protein of the body's C.T.). Person either has less collagen than normal, or poorer quality of collagen than normal causing **WEAK BONES THAT FRACTURE/BREAK EASILY** often from little or no cause.

- While the characteristics vary greatly, and not all are evident in each case, **the main clinical characteristic is EXTREME FRAGILITY & POROUS BONES** with a proneness to fracture due to the effects of inadequate osteoid production.

- <u>Additional Clinical Features</u>: **BLUE SCLERA**, deafness due to osteosclerosis, loose joints, low muscle tone, triangular face, and a tendency toward spinal curvature.

- Teeth have **bulbous crowns** with a cervical constriction, **partially or completely obliterated pulps**, and **narrower & shorter roots**. Deciduous (primary) teeth are more severely affected than permanent teeth. Teeth are poor and abnormal due to dentin malformation (Type 1 Dentinogenesis Imperfecta); may be linked to **DENTINOGENESIS IMPERFECTA**.

- <u>Treatment</u>: NO KNOWN CURE; treatment is directed toward preventing/controlling the symptoms.

HYPOPHOSPHATASIA – resembles **OSTEOGENESIS IMPERFECTA**. It's an inherited metabolic (chemical) **BONE DISEASE** that results from **LOW LEVELS of ALKALINE PHOSPHATASE** (enzyme essential the calcification of bone tissue). Loosening, hypocalcification, and premature loss of deciduous teeth are characteristic. Radiographically, large pulp chambers and alveolar bone loss are present.

Hypophosphatasia's severity greatly varies from patient to patient. Some have blue sclera that resembles osteogenesis imperfecta. Others have deformity of the arms, legs, and chest and/or frequent bouts of pneumonia and recurrent fractures. **Patients are classified as having either**:

→ **PAGET'S DISEASE OF BONE (OSTEITIS DEFORMANS)** – a common, chronic, non-metabolic bone disorder characterized by an **INCREASE in serum ALKALINE PHOSPHATASE** levels. Bones become **enlarged & deformed**, dense, but fragile due to excessive breakdown and formation of bone. Has potential to undergo "spontaneous" malignant transformation. There is excessive bone destruction and unorganized bone repair.

- <u>Radiographic Features</u>: **"COTTON-WOOL" APPEARANCE ON PANOREX** (skull and jaws). Hypercementosis of roots and loss of lamina dura around roots.

- Effects males & females, but rarely people under 40yrs (affects middle-aged & elderly people).

- Cause is hereditary. Patients are predisposed to developing **OSTEOSARCOMAS**.

- <u>Signs & Symptoms</u>: PAIN in affected area, bone deformity & susceptibility to fractures in the affected area, headache, and hearing loss if the affected area is the skull. Symptoms develop SLOWLY.

- <u>Clinical Features</u>: Patients may give a history of progressively **INCREASE IN HAT SIZE OR NEED FOR NEW DENTURES** being made more frequently due to bony changes.

- Bones are warm to touch due to **increased vascularity**.

Notes (handwritten):
- ↑ alkaline phosphate
- Fragile bone.
- Cotton wool appearance.
- Hypercementosts.

- Lab tests show highly **increased serum alkaline phosphatase, urinary calcium, & hydroxyproline**; with normal levels of SERUM PHOSPHATE & CALCIUM.

- <u>Treatment</u>: Administer anti-metabolites or **CALCITONIN** to decrease bone resorption, or treat with a high-protein & high calcium diet.

PAGET'S DISEASE (Enlarged Alveolar Ridges)

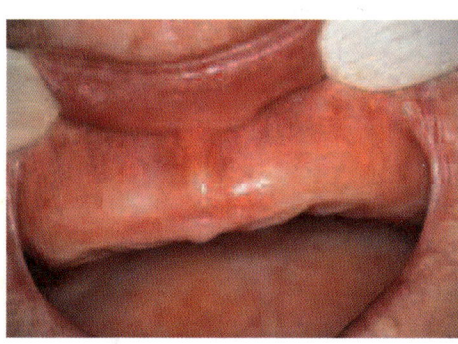
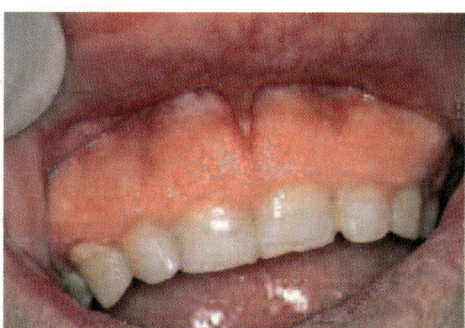

OSTEOMALACIA (Adult Rickets) – **SOFTENING of bones** in adults because osteoid tissue in bones failed to calcify due to **LACK OF VITAMIN D**. More common in women, and may be asymptomatic until a bone fracture occurs.

- <u>Steatorrhea</u>-one of the most common causes of Osteomalacia due to **FAT MALABSORPTION** where the **body cannot absorb fats**, so fats are passed directly out of the body in stool causing poor absorption of vitamin D (fat soluble) and calcium. Osteomalacia affects **ALL BONES**, specifically at their epiphyseal growth plates.

- <u>Signs & Symptoms</u>: pain in bones of the arms, legs, spine, and pelvis.

RICKETS (Child Osteomalacia) –causing skeletal deformities, and usually accompanied by irritability and generalized muscle weakness. Bowlegs, pigeon breast, and protruding stomach are signs. Teeth are affected by **delayed eruption, malocclusion, and developmental abnormalities of dentin and enamel, with a higher caries rate**.

CEREBRAL PALSY – a group of disorders affecting **body movement** and **muscle coordination** due to an insult or anomaly of the brain's motor control centers. This damage interferes with messages from brain to the rest of the body. The effects vary greatly among people.

- CP is mainly characterized by **SPASTIC PARALYSIS** or impairment of control or coordination over voluntary muscles. Often accompanied by mental retardation, seizures, & disorders of vision/communication.

NO ORAL PATHOLOGIC MANIFESTATIONS are present in people with cerebral palsy, but several conditions are more common, or more severe than in the normal population:
- Higher incidence of **periodontal disease, caries, bruxism, and malocclusion**.
- Prone to **gingival hyperplasia** if <u>Dilantin</u> is used to control seizures.
- More susceptible to trauma, especially maxillary anterior teeth.

DOWN SYNDROME – a congenital defect caused by a **chromosomal abnormality (TRISOMY 21)**, marked by various degrees of mental retardation and characteristic physical features (short, flattened skull, slanting eyes, thickened tongue/fissured, broad hands/feet, etc.)

NOTES
- mand prognathism.

- **Oral Manifestations**: mandibular prognathism (class III), increased periodontal disease, thickened or fissured tongue, delayed teeth eruption, higher incidence of congenitally missing teeth, malocclusion, & enamel dysplasia.

MUSCULAR DYSTROPHY – a group of genetic diseases marked by progressive **weakness & degeneration of skeletal or voluntary muscles** that control movement.

- **Oral Manifestations**: increase in dental disease if oral hygiene is neglected, weakness in muscles of mastication causing **decreased maxillary biting force**, higher incidence of mouth breathing, and open bite.

ECTODERMAL DYSPLASIA – hereditary condition characterized by abnormal development of the skin and associated structures (hairs, nails, teeth, & sweat glands). ED involves all structures derived from **ECTODERM**, affecting **MALES** more than females. **Manifests orally as reduced/missing teeth**.

- **Clinical Signs**: hypothrichosis (decrease in hair (fine sparse hair), anhidrosis (no sweat or sebaceous glands, causing heat intolerance), Anodontia (complete absence of teeth), Oligodontia (partial absence of teeth), no tooth buds of the primary or permanent dentition (edentulous), depressed nose bridge, lack of salivary glands, and child appears much older than their true age.

- Affects tooth bud development causing congenitally missing teeth (lack of permanent teeth) and/or peg-shaped or pointed teeth. Enamel may also be defective.

- **Treatment**: Dentures can be fabricated for young children, but they will need to be replaced periodically to accommodate the patient's jaw growth. Implants can be placed once the jaw if fully developed, or orthodontics to close spaces. Use a multi-disciplinary treatment approach as treatment is often complex.

ECTODERMAL DYSPLASIA

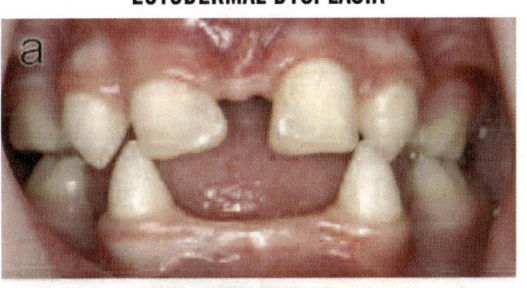
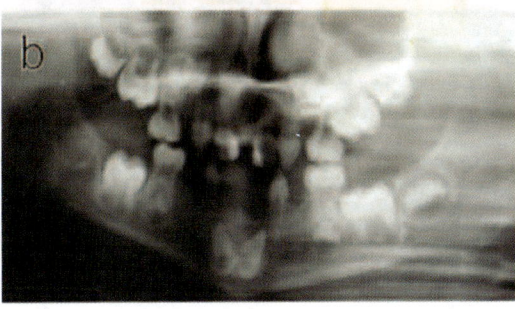

NOTES

CLEIDOCRANIAL DYSPLASIA (DYSOSTOSIS) - genetic disorder of bone development characterized by absent or incomplete formed **COLLAR BONES**, heavy protruding jaw, wide nasal bridge, and dental abnormalities (malaligned teeth, **multiple supernumerary teeth, and unerupted teeth**). Observing a panorex or FMX alone often suggests the diagnosis.

CLEIDOCRANIAL DYSPLASIA (DYSOSTOSIS)

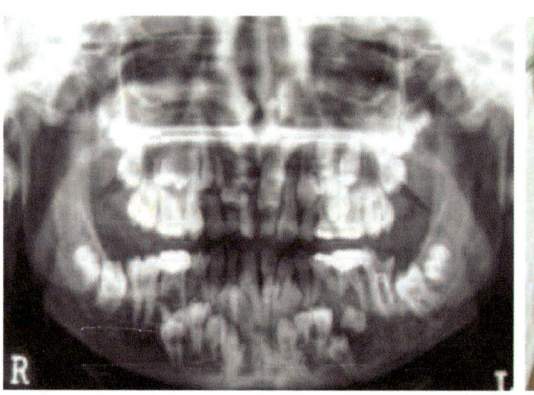
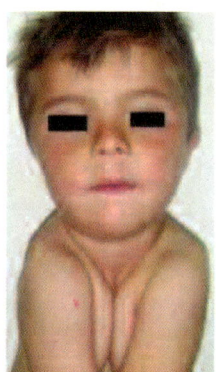

PIERRE-ROBIN SYNDROME – an inherited disorder with the **following findings in the NEONATE**:
- Micrognathia-smallness of the jaws.
- Glossoptosis-downward displacement or retracted tongue.
- Breathing problems & cleft palate.

LATERAL CLEFTING OF THE LIP – results from **failure of the MAXILLARY & FRONTAL NASAL PROCESSES TO MERGE**. Cleft lip occurs during the **5th-6th week of embryonic life**. It can be bilateral or unilateral, more common in males, and involves the LEFT SIDE more than the right side.

CLEFT PALATE – occurs in **6th-8th week of embryonic life**. Isolated cleft palates are more common in females characterized by a fissure in the midline of the palate due to failure of the two sides to fuse during embryonic development. The most severe handicap caused by cleft palate is an impaired mechanism **PREVENTING NORMAL SPEECH & SWALLOWING**.

Important: Speech problems associated with Cleft Lip & Cleft Palate are usually **due to the inability of the soft palate to close airflow** into the **nasal area**.

CHERUBISM – a **BENIGN** genetic autosomal dominant disease of the maxilla & mandible, typically in children by age 5 (affects males 2:1). Most cases occur in the **MANDIBLE**. The jaws are firm and hard to palpation, and regional lymphadenopathy may be present. **BILATERAL expansion of the jaws** gives the **child a very round face, reminding one of cherubs (cupids) in paintings**. The tumors stop growing shortly after puberty. As the patient's age and size increases, the deformity is less noticeable.

- **Histologically**, cherubism lesions **closely resemble** Central Giant Cell Granulomas. Histology shows a giant cell lesion with some reactive bone formation. However, perivascular collagen cuffing is pathognomonic for cherubism.

- **Radiographically**: lesions appear as multiple, well-defined, multi-locular radiolucencies of the jaw.

- No associated systemic manifestations. However, the deciduous dentition may spontaneously shed prematurely, starting as early as age 3. There is often **delayed eruption** of the permanent dentition, which is often defective with the absence of numerous teeth and displacement of those teeth present.

- <u>Treatment</u>: cautious waiting as Cherubism tends to regress in early adulthood. Do not treat with radiation therapy.

CYSTIC FIBROSIS – a congenital/genetic metabolic disorder that causes **EXOCRINE GLANDS** (glands that secrete fluids into a duct) to produce **ABNORMAL SECRETIONS** mainly affecting **GI and respiratory systems**. CF results in several symptoms (the most important symptom affects the digestive tract and lungs). In some glands (glands in the pancreas & intestines), the secretions are thick or solid excessively **viscous mucous** that can completely block a gland. Mucous-producing glands in the lung's airways produce abnormal secretions that clog the airways allowing bacteria to multiply. CF is **the MOST COMMON genetic disease** causing **death among white people in the U.S.** and is equally common in boys & girls.

- CF is usually characterized by COPD, exocrine pancreatic insufficiency, and abnormally high sweat electrolytes (sweat glands secrete fluids that have a high sodium & chloride content).

- <u>Oral Manifestations</u>: staining of teeth as patients with CF are usually subjected to large amounts of **tetracyclines** during childhood. A high % of children have **dark-colored teeth** (yellowish gray to dark brown). There is a greatly reduced caries rate in CF patients, probably due to saliva alterations and long-term use of antibiotics.

- <u>CF Signs & Symptoms</u>: poor growth despite good appetite, malabsorption, and foul, bulky stools (steatorrhea), chronic bronchitis (COPD) with cough, recurrent pneumonia with respiratory infections, clubbing of fingers/toes, & barrel-chested appearance.

INFLAMMATORY JAW LESIONS

OSTEOMYELITIS – inflammation or infection of the bone marrow and adjacent bone, usually caused by bacteria (Staphylococci) due to trauma or surgery by a direct extension from a nearby infection, or via the bloodstream.

- <u>Signs & Symptoms</u>: pain, redness, swelling in the infected area, fever, and general malaise. Radiographically, poorly circumscribed radiolucency with a central sclerotic nidus may be present.

CONDENSING OSTEITIS (CHRONIC FOCAL SCLEROSING OSTEOMYELITIS) (Non-vital tooth) – an unusual bone reaction to an infection (most often associated with a **long-standing periapical infection**), occurring in instances of extremely high tissue resistance or in cases of low-grade infection. There may be no signs or symptoms of the disease, other than mild pain associated with an infected pulp. **Mandibular 1st molar** is the tooth most commonly involved. Most often occurs in young patients.

- <u>Radiographic Findings</u>: periapical radiographs show pathognomonic, **well-circumscribed radiopaque mass of sclerotic bone surrounding and extending below the apex of one or both roots**. The entire root outline is always visible (important feature that radiographically distinguishes it from a **benign cementoblastoma**).

NOTES

- A tooth with a condensing osteitis lesion can be treated with RCT or extracted, since the pulp is infected, and the infection has spread past the immediate periapical area. The sclerosing bone constituting the osteomyelitis is NOT attached to the tooth, so it remains after the tooth is treated or removed.

PERIAPICAL ABSCESS – usually arises from **pulpal infection** of a tooth due to carious involvement of the tooth. The cellular debris and/or infection that caused the tooth pulp to become necrotic, slowly filters out of the root tip, producing an inflammatory reaction around the root tip. A periapical abscess can also occur after traumatic injury to a tooth, causing pulpal necrosis, and in cases of irritation of the periapical tissues (either by mechanical manipulation or application of chemicals) in endodontic procedures.

Clinical Features:
Acute Periapical Abscess: tooth is extremely painful to percussion (may feel slightly extruded from its socket), and is MOBILE. Radiograph presents only a slight thickening of the periodontal membrane (PDL).

Chronic Periapical Abscess: presents as a granuloma or cyst (radiolucent area at the root apex), but there are usually no clinical features or symptoms (asymptomatic).

- Treatment: establish DRAINAGE by opening the pulp chamber (RCT) or extracting the tooth. If not treated, it can cause serious complications (i.e. osteomyelitis, cellulitis, & bacteremia).

OSTEONECROSIS – bone death or necrosis; a rare complication of cancer patients (radiation and chemotherapy), patients with tumors or infectious embolic events, or with osteoporosis taking IV or oral bisphosphonates. May be caused by a defect in bone remodeling or wound healing (defect in osteoclast function).

BISPHOSPHONATE-OSTEONECROSIS (BON) - a dental phenomenon that may lead to surgical complications (bone necrosis) due to impaired wound healing after extractions, periodontal surgery, or RCT.
Caution with patients taking **IV bisphosphonates** (Zometa (zoledronic acid) & Aredia (pamidronate)) for osteoporosis and cancer treatment respectively.

Caution with patients taking **oral bisphosphonates** (Fosamax, Actonel, & Boniva). Occurs more common in patients taking IV bisphosphonates (20%) and less than 1% taking oral bisphosphonates.

OSTEONECROSIS

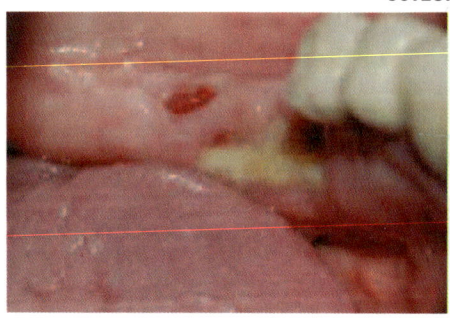 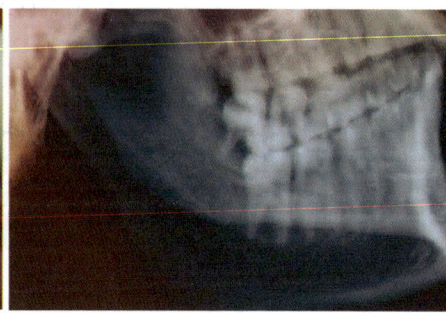

OSTEOPOROSIS – a reduction of total skeletal mass due to **INCREASED BONE RESORPTION**, causing predisposition to pathologic fractures caused by calcium or estrogen hormone deficiencies over a long time period. BONES BECOME LESS DENSE & BRITTLE.

- Osteoporosis is most common in THIN, ELDERLY WHITE WOMEN. <u>Treatment</u>: estrogen therapy, calcium & vitamin D supplements, bisphosphonates.

OSTEOPETROSIS ("Albers-Schonberg Disease" or "Marble Bone Disease") – an uncommon genetic disorder that manifests in infancy characterized by an **OVERGROWTH & DENSENESS OF BONES** due to a **DEFECT IN OSTEOCLASTS** which are needed for bone marrow formation. The long bones become dense and hard to the extent that BONE MARROW IS OBLITERATED (prevents bone marrow formation). **BONES BECOME HARD BUT BRITTLE & DENSE**.

- <u>Clinical Signs</u>: abnormal bone & dental development, fragile bones, stunted growth, anemia, spleen & liver enlargement, blindness, and progressive deafness.

CONNECTIVE TISSUE LESIONS

VON RECKLINGHAUSEN'S DISEASE (NEUROFIBROMATOSIS) – the most common feature is NEUROFIBROMATOSIS (multiple tumors of nerve tissue origin). VRD is a relatively common inherited autosomal dominant trait characterized by **multiple neurofibromas, cutaneous café-au-lait macules, bone abnormalities, & CNS changes**.

- <u>Clinical Signs</u>: 6 or more café-au-lait macules ≥ 1.5cm in diameter indicates VRD.

- <u>Treatment</u>: No satisfactory treatment. The lesions run a high-risk of becoming malignant.

- A single neurofibroma presents at any age as a **non-inflamed, asymptomatic nodule** on the **tongue, buccal mucosa, & vestibule**. This single nodule is removed by surgical excision, and rarely occurs.

SCLERODERMA – a relatively RARE autoimmune disease affecting the **blood vessels & C.T.** characterized by **hardness & rigidity of the skin and subcutaneous tissue**. The continuous deposition of collagen in major organs can cause dysfunction and potential organ failure.

- <u>Clinical Features</u>: systemic scleroderma usually appears during middle-age (30-50yrs), mainly in females (4:1). The skin is usually affected first and becomes indurated.

- <u>Oral Radiographs</u>: show **ABNORMAL WIDENING OF THE PDL AROUND ROOTS** (this is also found in osteosarcomas). The space is created by a thickening of the periodontal-membrane **due to an increase in size & number of collagen fibers**. The enlarged space is almost uniform in width, surrounds the entire tooth root, making the tooth appear as if it is being extruded rapidly from its socket. Other oral radiographic features may include **bilateral resorption of the angle of the mandible's ramus, or complete resorption of the mandibular condyles and/or coronoid process**.

- <u>Treatment</u>: No satisfactory treatment, other than palliative therapy.

SCLERODERMA

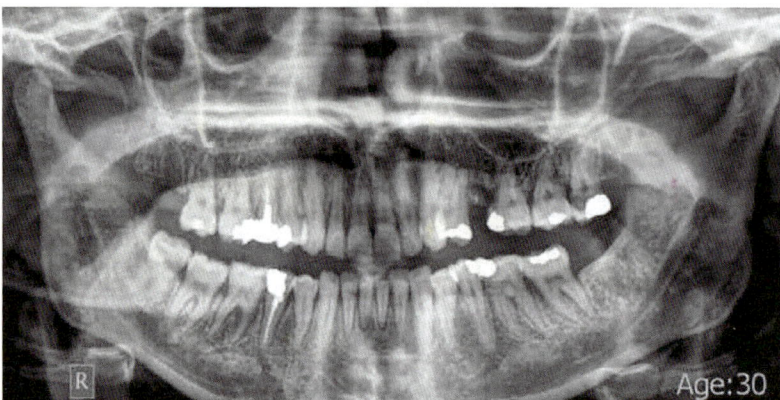

ORAL TRAUMATIC NEUROMA- a **SOFT TISSUE TUMOR** due to trauma to a peripheral nerve, usually appearing as a very small nodule/swelling (< 0.5cm in diameter) of the mucosa near/over the mental foramen on the alveolar ridge in edentulous areas, lips, & tongue. **MOST COMMON SITE IS OVER THE MENTAL FORAMEN IN EDENTULOUS PATIENTS**, but they can occur wherever a tooth has been extracted. Extraction sites in the anterior maxilla & posterior mandible are common sites.

- In the oral cavity, the traumatic neuroma may be due to trauma from a surgical procedure (i.e. tooth extraction, local anesthetic injection, or accident). A nodule or swelling PAINFUL WHEN PALPATED, as applied digital pressure elicits a response described as an "electric shock".

- Multiple neuromas on the lips, tongue, or palate may indicate the patient may have MEN III (Multiple Endocrine Neoplasia Syndrome).

- Treatment: surgical excision of the nodule with small proximal portion of the involved nerve. Recurrence is uncommon.

NEURILEMOMA (SCHWANNOMA) – a benign **SOFT TISSUE TUMOR** (encapsulated mass) of Schwann cells around the nerve that presents as an asymptomatic lump **most common on the TONGUE**. Bony lesions may cause pain or paresthesia. Derived from a proliferation of Schwann cells of the neurolemma that surrounds peripheral nerves. **Covered by normal mucosa, sessile** & does not metastasize but still do biopsy. Treatment: conservative excision. Recurrence is rare.

NEUROFIBROMA-may be derived from the Schwann cell or Perineural Fibroblast and can occur in two forms:

1. Solitary Neurofibroma-an asymptomatic nodule on the tongue, buccal mucosa, or vestibule treated by surgical excision.

2. Multiple lesions as part of the Neurofibromatosis syndrome. Removing the lesions is impractical, but monitor due to the high risk/rate of malignant transformation.

FIBROMA ("IRRITATION FIBROMA OR "TRAUMATIC FIBROMA")-the most common intra-oral **BENIGN** neoplasm of **CONNECTIVE TISSUE (soft tissue)** origin, that occurs in people of all ages and with equal frequency in both sexes. It's the most common tumor in the oral cavity and is reactive. Fibromas can arise from almost any soft tissue in the mouth, **but are most common on the buccal mucosa, lateral border of tongue, and lower lip**. NODBULAR PINK MORPHOLOGY (pink, fibrous nodule with smooth surface).

FIBROMA

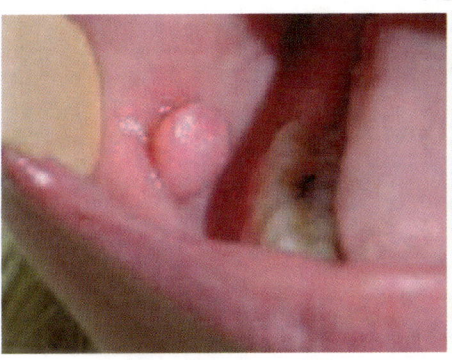
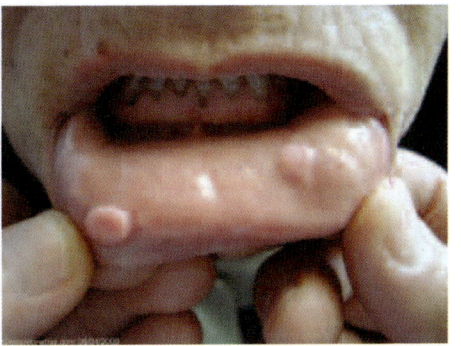

- **Clinical Features**: usually pink (same color or lighter than normal buccal mucosa, painless, smooth, elevated, well-demarcated masses). Smooth, sessile, soft-to-firm nodule on buccal mucosa, lips, and tongue.

- **Microscopic Features**: bundles of collagen interspersed (interlacing) with fibroblasts and small blood vessels.

- **Histogenesis**: fibrous C.T. (C.T. origin).

- In most cases, the tumor is reported present for months or years with a slow-growing behavior pattern.

- Some feel "true fibromas" of the oral cavity are rare and are merely localized hyperplasia due to long-standing irritation or trauma ("irritation fibroma or "traumatic fibroma"). These fibrous nodules are **comparable to hyperplasias from denture irritation ("epulis fissuratum")**. The only difference between a "true fibroma (a true neoplasm) and "irritation fibroma" (not a true neoplasm), is the hyperplastic tissue with an irritation fibroma can regress after removing the irritant, while a true fibroma will not regress. **Treatment**: conservative surgical excision. Recurrence is rare.

PERIPHERAL FIBROMA – a well-demarcated focal mass of hyperplastic tissue with either **a sessile or pedunculated base**. Similar in color to surrounding C.T., and may be ulcerated. **Treatment**: local excision & recurrence is **RARE**. **3 Forms of Peripheral Fibroma**:

1. **Peripheral Ossifying Fibroma**-a gingival mass with **visible characteristic calcified islands of bone and an ulcerated surface**. The **gingiva anterior to the permanent molars is most often affected**. Histologically, in its high degree of cellularity, it **exhibits bone formation** (in contrast to peripheral fibroma). **Vascularity is NOT a prominent feature** as it is with a pyogenic granuloma. It is a subtype or variant form of a peripheral fibroma. However, both **originate from an inter-dental papilla and both occur more frequently in young adult females** (but can occur at any age, although more common in children & young adults). Usually presents as **a well-demarcated focal mass of hyperplastic tissue on the gingiva with a sessile or pedunculated base**. It is usually the **same color as normal mucosa or slightly reddened**. May demonstrate bone radiographically and often demonstrates bone formation histologically. **Treatment**: Local Excision. POF lesions may recur (peripheral fibroma lesions rarely recur).

2. **Peripheral Odontogenic Fibroma**-gingival mass composed of well-vascularized, non-encapsulated fibrous C.T.

3. **Giant Cell Fibroma**-a fibrous hyperplasia composed of multi-nucleated C.T. cells.

GIANT CELL TUMOR – a bone tumor of multi-nucleated giant cells that resemble osteoclasts scattered in a matrix of spindle cells. May be benign or malignant, and can cause pain, functional disability, and sometimes pathologic bone fracture.

PAPILLARY FIBROMA – a benign neoplasm of C.T. origin.

LIPOMA – a **COMPETELY BENIGN** soft tissue tumor derived from **ADIPOSE (FAT) tissue** (C.T. origin). It is smooth or lobulated, sessile or pedunculated (foot-shaped), soft, movable, painless, **yellowish-white nodular mass.** Vessels are visible on the surface. **Locations: floor of mouth, buccal mucosa, and tongue.** YELLOWISH MASS covered by normal mucosa. A biopsy specimen will FLOAT in the formalin. Easier to diagnose than other tumors because it is yellowish, soft, smooth, & movable, and **FLOATS IN FORMALIN**.

- **Microscopic Features**: lobules of mature fat separated by delicate C.T. septae.

- **Treatment**: conservative excision. Recurrence is rare. Remove surgically only if it becomes painful, tender, infected, or enlarges to where it becomes bothersome.

LIPOMA

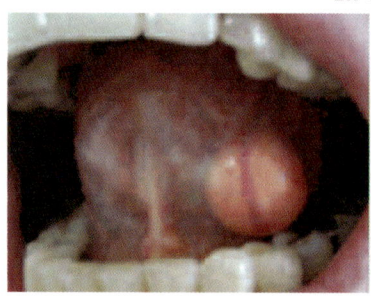
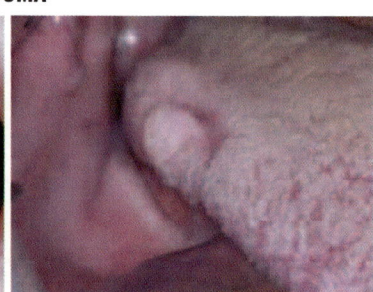

RHABDOMYOMA – a **RARE BENIGN** tumor of **SKELETAL MUSCLE. Tongue** is the most common place in the head & neck. Sessile, non-painful, and covered by normal mucosa.

LEIOMYOMA – an always benign tumor of **SMOOTH MUSCLE** (smooth muscle neoplasm). Non-painful, sessile, (covered by normal mucosa). Bundles of spindle-shaped smooth muscle cells.

LYMPHANGIOMA – a **BENIGN YELLOWISH-TAN TUMOR** composed of a mass of **DILATED LYMPH VESSELS**. Most common site in the oral cavity is the **TONGUE**, but can appear on the lips & neck. Derived from endothelial cells, C.T. origin. **Clinical Features**: painless, nodular, vesicle-like swelling that equally affects both sexes.

- Superficial lesions are manifested as grayish-red papillary lesions. On the tongue, considerable enlargement can occur (macroglossia). The papillary lesions may contain fluid, and are often present at birth or arise early in life, but are less common than Hemangiomas.

LYMPHANGIOMA (Dilated Lymph Vessels)

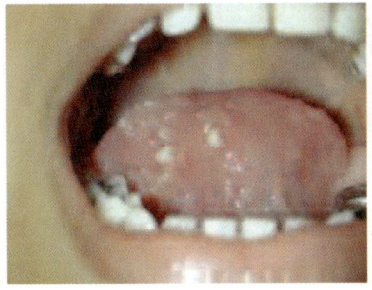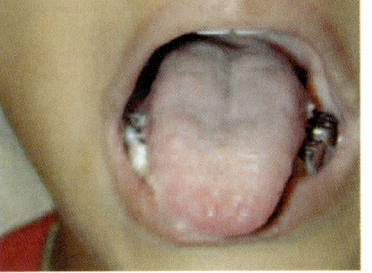

- **Microscopic Features**: can be simple, circumscriptum, or cystic (closely related to cystic hygroma, containing serous fluid).

- **Treatment**: SURGERY OR CRYOSURGERY. May recur due to their lack of encapsulation.

BENIGN EPITHELIAL TUMORS

PAPILLOMA

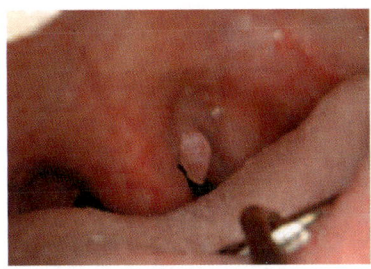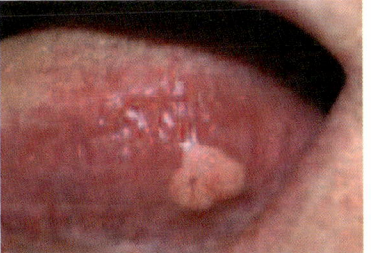

PAPILLOMA – the most common BENIGN neoplasm of EPITHELIAL TISSUE ORIGIN. It appears as a pedunculated (foot-shaped), or sessile WHITISH cauliflower-like mass on the tongue (posterior border), lips, gingiva, or soft palate. Papillomas are soft in the oral cavity, but on exposed areas of the lips, are usually rough & scaly.

- **Papilloma**-a vital benign cauliflower-like, white lesion with a verrucous & pedunculated (foot-shaped) surface. Easy to diagnose. VIRAL. Lesion is not covered by normal mucosa and is **a disease of epithelium**. Non-ulcerated, small, slow growing, usually non-painful. Lateral border of tongue, hard or soft palate are common areas. **MUST EXCISE SURGICALLY** and recurrence is rare.

- **Microscopic Features**: finger-like projections of stratified squamous epithelium supported by thin cores of vascular fibrous C.T. Epithelium may show hyperkeratosis or parakeratosis. **Histogenesis**: squamous epithelium.

Verruca (Warts)-similar to a papilloma, but is **NOT pedunculated caused by a viral infection**. Do excision & biopsy, especially children who have this on their finger and place their finger in their mouth and spread the infection orally.

Keratoacanthoma-a non-painful crater-formed lesion (VIRAL) growing for 2-3 months in the SKIN that looks like squamous cell or basal cell carcinoma, and can heal by itself, but **must still do biopsy**. Can last up to 6 months. It is usually only in the skin and very rarely inside the mouth.

MULTIPLE ENDOCRINE NEOPLASIA SYNDROMES (MEN SYNDROME) – groups of syndromes characterized by **tumors of various endocrine glands** that occur in association with a variety of other pathologic features. The most important aspect of MEN syndrome is **medullary carcinoma of the THYROID** due to its ability to metastasize and cause death. Thus, detecting mucosal neuromas may alert the clinician for early diagnosis and treatment. **MEN is classified into 3 groups**:

1. **Men I Syndrome**-tumors or hyperplasias of the **pituitary, parathyroids, adrenal cortex,** and **pancreatic islets** (pancreas).

2. **Men II (Sipple's Syndrome)**- parathyroid hyperplasia or adenoma, but **NO tumors of the pancreas**. Patients have pheochromocytomas of the adrenal medulla, and medullary carcinoma of the thyroid gland.

3. **Men III Syndrome**-mucocutaneous neuromas, pheochromocytomas of the adrenal medulla, and medullary carcinoma of the thyroid gland. **The most constant feature is neuromas (especially in the oral cavity),** most commonly on the lips, tongue, and buccal mucosa.

EPULIS GRANULOMATOSUM – soft, non-painful, bleed easily, most often caused by **RETAINED FOREIGN MATERIAL (i.e. bone or tooth fragment) due to an iatrogenic error**. Most commonly found in a **post-extraction socket**, almost always within 10 days of the extraction.

- **TREATMENT**: CURETTAGE.
- **Microscopic Features**: granulation tissue in bone, dentin, cementum, or foreign material.

CONGENITAL EPULIS OF NEWBORNS (CONGENITAL GINGIVAL GRANULAR CELL TUMOR) – composed of cells identical to a granular cell myoblastoma (granular cell tumor). Usually on the **ANTERIOR GINGIVA OF NEWBORNS** as a **PINK**, non-inflamed, pedunculated or broad-based mass. Maxillary gingiva is involved more than the mandibular gingival. Affects females more than males.

- **Treatment**: surgical excision with minimal recurrence.

CONGENITAL EPULIS OF NEWBORNS

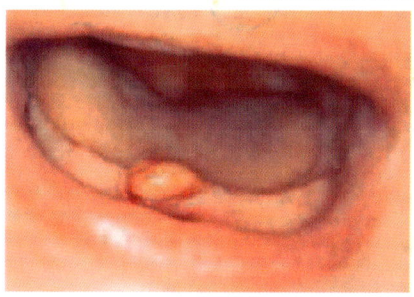
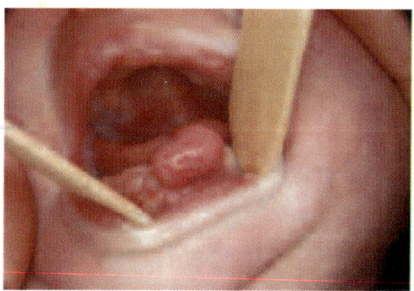

GRANULAR CELL MYOBLASTOMA (TUMOR) – an uncommon neoplasm of unknown etiology, presenting as an uninflamed, asymptomatic mass. **TONGUE is the most common location** in the head & neck region. Can affect any age group, but **affects females more** than males.

Congenital Epulis & Granular Cell Myoblastoma lesions are histologically identical as they both contain granular cells. However, Congenital Epulis of newborns does not exhibit pseudo-epitheliomatous hyperplasia of the overlaying epithelium, that is often seen in Granular Cell Myoblastoma.

GRANULAR CELL TUMOR (Tongue)

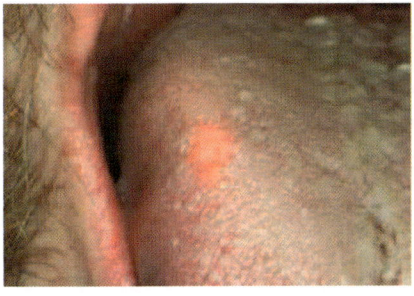
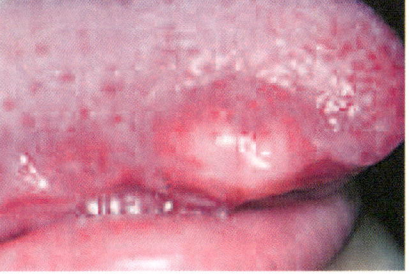

PYOGENIC GRANULOMA (PREGNANCY TUMOR) – an elevated ulcerated mass that bleeds easily, more common in females (pregnant women), and may recur. **Caused by minor trauma** that provides a pathway for non-specific organisms & calculus. Most commonly found on the gingiva, but also the lips, tongue, & buccal mucosa. **TREATMENT**: EXCISION (but may recur). Has exuberant granulation tissue microscopically.

PYOGENIC GRANULOMA (PREGNANCY TUMOR)

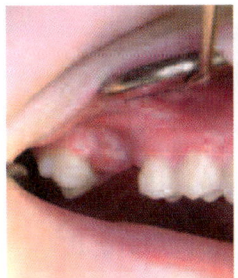
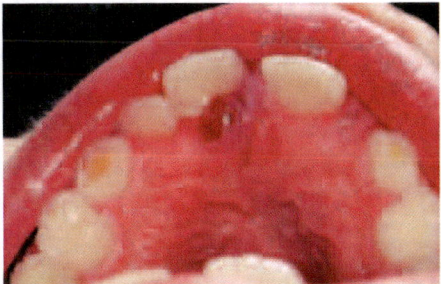
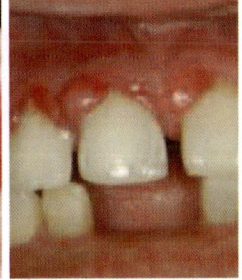

PYOGENIC GRANULOMA is BENIGN. The MOST common site is the INTER-DENTAL GINGIVA, but may also occur on the lower lip, tongue, & buccal mucosa. Rarely occurs on other areas of the oral mucous membrane. Arises due to minor tissue trauma (i.e. cementation of a crown or calculus) that provides a pathway for the invasion of non-specific types of microorganisms. Pregnant patients are prone to these lesions (**called a "Pregnancy Tumor" in a pregnant patient**). May be caused secondarily by an altered endocrine state (hormone changes) during pregnancy in the 1st trimester.

<u>Clinical Features</u>: soft, pedunculated (foot-shaped) broad-based growths with a smooth red surface due to the presence of hyperplastic granulation tissue that contains many capillaries. They are often ulcerated, bleed easily, and may look RASBERRY-LIKE.

<u>Treatment</u>: Surgical Excision after pregnancy. May occasionally recur.

VERRUCAL PAPILLARY LESIONS

VERRUCA VUGLARIS (SQUAMOUS PAPILLOMA) – the **common WART of VIRAL etiology** (caused by Papilloma virus) that is **a common skin tumor analogous to the oral papilloma**. It has an incubation period of 6 weeks to 1 year. Although it is a primary lesion of the skin, it **may occur in the oral cavity** (especially lips & palate). Clinically, it is **a sessile, soft, CAULIFLOWER-LIKE LESION**.

- <u>Microscopically</u>: is a papillomatous lesion where the epithelium is thrown into folds. The lesion shows alternating hyperkeratosis, parakeratosis, and long epithelial ridges. If excised, they usually do not recur, but autoinoculation is possible. Intra-orally, that is how most cases develop.

INFLAMMATORY FIBROUS HYPERPLASIA ("EPULIS FISSURATUM" OR "PALATAL PAPILLOMATOSIS") —found at the area of the denture borders, **more common in the maxilla (hard palate)** than mandible caused by ill-fitting dentures and poor oral hygiene.

- **Clinical Features**: rolls of soft-tissue in the muco-labial fold, RED-PINK, elongated, firm, ulceration, soft lesion.

- **Treatment**: SURGICAL EXCISION and re-evaluate the prosthesis or remake or reline the dentures.

INFLAMMATORY FIBROUS HYPERPLASIA

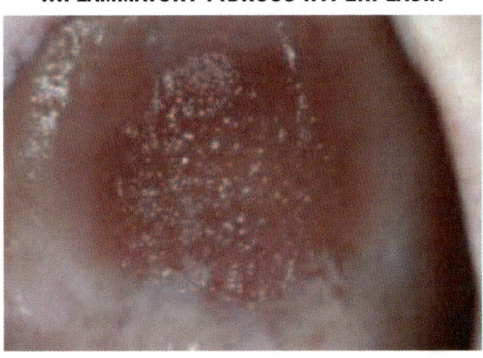

NEOPLASMS

LYMPHOEPITHELIOMA – a poorly differentiated **squamous cell carcinoma** involving lymphoid tissue in the tonsils & nasopharynx regions. It has a high frequency in young adults of East Asian decent. The primary lesion is usually very small (often completely hidden). **SWELLING OF THE LYMPH NODES is the most common** symptom, followed by sore throat, nasal obstruction, bloody nose, & headache.

- Lymphoepitheliomas are composed of squamous or undifferentiated cells, with a slight-to-moderate amount of fibrous stroma that contain numerous lymphocytes. **Lymphoepithelioma shows METASTASIS AT AN EARLY STAGE TO THE CERVICAL LYMPH NODES.**

- Treatment of choice is RADIATON, but the complicating factor is the relative inability to treat the widespread metastases in the various organs. **POOR PROGNOSIS** (30% 5-year survival rate).

METASTIC CARCINOMA—the **most common malignancy affecting SKELETAL BONES**. However, metastic disease of the mandible and maxilla is unusual (~1%). **Most important, a jaw tumor may be the first evidence of dissemination of a known tumor from its primary site.** *Metastases to the jaws most commonly originates from primary carcinomas of the BREAST, KIDNEY, LUNG, COLON, PROSTATE, & THYROID.* Metastatic carcinoma of the jaws is LEAST likely to originate from the brain.

- **Clinical Features of Metastic Jaw Lesions**: may be completely asymptomatic, but there is usually paresthesia or anesthesia of the lip or chin due to involvement of the mandibular nerve (patient is usually aware of slight discomfort or pain). Teeth in the area are loose or extruded (the molar region is mainly involved), there can be swelling or expansion of the jaw, and appears as an asymptomatic radiolucency. Although rare, metastic jaw tumors affect the mandible MUCH more than the maxilla.

Most common osseous malignancies are **OSTEOSARCOMAS** then Chondrosarcomas, Fibrosarcomas, & Ewing's Sarcoma.

OSTEOSARCOMA (OSTEOGENIC SARCOMA)–a **MALIGNANT BONE TUMOR** of anaplastic cells derived from mesechyme. **MOST COMMON PRIMARY MALIGNANT TUMOR OF BONE**, arising in **LONG BONES** which show the greatest longitudinal growth. Joint involvement is rare. Its **PEAK incidence is BEFORE epiphyseal fusion (ages 10-25yrs)**, but a later peak is associated with Paget's Disease, Chronic Osteomyelitis, and previous radiotherapy.

- **Radiographic Features**: most important **EARLY** radiographic feature of an osteosarcoma of the jaw is a **SYMMETRICALLY WIDENED PDL SPACE** around one or more teeth. Other radiographic features may be **"SUN-BURST"** or **"SUN-RAY"** appearance due to **excessive bone production**. Most osteosarcomas have a **MIXED** appearance radiographically (radiolucent + radiopaque).

OSTEOSARCOMAS (SUN-BURST APPEARANCE)

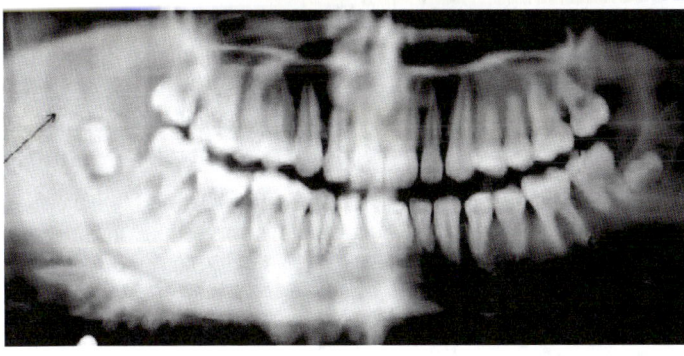
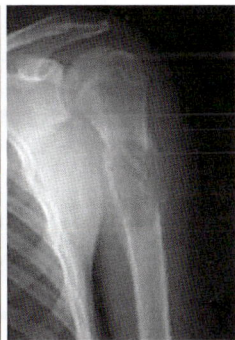

ERWING'S SARCOMA – a **MALIGNANT TUMOR** developing from **BONE MARROW**, usually in long bones or pelvis of adolescent boys **(peak ages 10-20yrs)**. It is an uncommon **HIGHLY LETHAL MALIGNAN NEOPLASM OF BONE** of uncertain origin. **PELVIS, THIGH, and BODY TRUNK**, are the most common sites.

- **Radiographic Characteristics**: **MOTH-EATEN** destructive radiolucencies of the medulla, with erosion of the cortex with expansion. A variable periosteal **"ONION-SKIN"** reaction may also be seen.

EWING'S SARCOMA (MOTH-EATEN APPEARANCE)

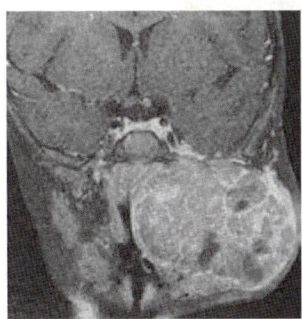
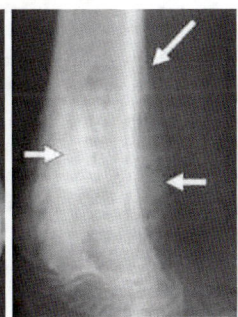
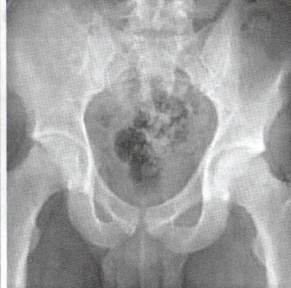

- **Intermittent pain and swelling** of the involved bone are the **earliest** clinical signs/symptoms. Fever & leukocytosis are also present.

- Histologically, ES is **difficult to distinguish** from a neuroblastoma or reticulum cell sarcoma, but **cells of ES contain GLYCOGEN**.

- When the jaws are involved, there is predilection for the **RAMUS OF THE MANDIBLE** with pain followed by **rapid swelling and loosening of the teeth**.

MULTIPLE MYELOMA ("PLASMA CELL MYELOMA") – a **FATAL** malignant neoplasm/lesion of bone marrow & plasma cells. Characterized by elevated blood levels of **Bence-Jones Protein** & **multiple radiolucent areas in the mandible** & skull. The tumor consists mainly of **PLASMA CELLS** that destroy osseous tissues (progressive bone marrow destruction occurs and is replaced with neoplastic plasma cells).

- Most patients are older than 40yrs (40-70yrs) affecting males 2x more than females (2:1). The vertebrae, ribs, and skull are most often involved. PAIN in the lumbar or thoracic regions of the spine is a common early symptom.

- Jaws are RARELY a PRIMARY site, but are involved in 70% of cases. **Mandibular molar-ramus area is the most common intra-oral site**. **Symptoms**: swelling, pain, loose teeth, and paresthesia.

- <u>Radiographic Features</u>: variable, slight demineralization to extensive bone destruction. Characteristic finding is **multiple, small, discreet "PUNCHED OUT" radiolucencies of involved bones**. A **LATERAL SKULL RADIOGRAPH best confirms a Multiple Myeloma diagnosis**.

<u>Treatment</u>: Chemotherapy/Radiation. Poor prognosis, with a median survival time of 2-3 years.

MULTIPLE MYELOMA

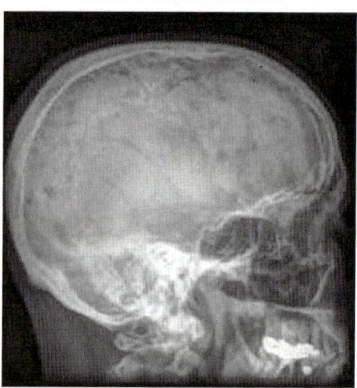

ODONTOGENIC MYXOMA–a RARE slow growing, usually asymptomatic MANDIBULAR TUMOR. Patients are usually < 35yrs of age. Causes localized jaw expansion. <u>Treatment</u>: Curettage. Not fatal.

ODONTOGENIC MYXOMA

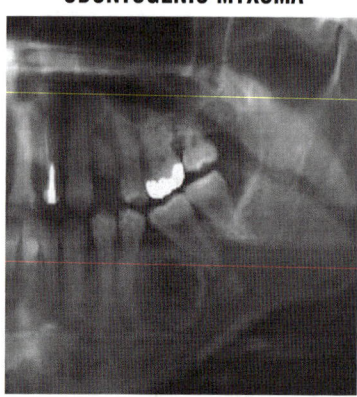

OSTEOCHONDROMA – a BENIGN tumor of bone & cartilage.

TNM–a method to clinically stage and assess the prognosis and therapy of **MALIGNANT NEOPLASMS (TUMORS)** based on the primary tumor's size (T), presence of regional lymph node involvement (N), and presence of distant metastases (M). Ex: a carcinoma of the oral cavity may have a TNM assessment of T2, N1, M0.
T = SIZE of the primary tumor.
N = Presence of regional LYMPH NODE involvement.
M = Presence of DISTANT metastasis

MELANOMA exhibits a "**radial**" (horizontal) or "**vertical**" growth phases in the skin:

- **Radial Growth Phase**-the **INITIAL** growth phase of melanoma just above & below the dermo-epidermal junction in a horizontal plane. It is clinically macular or only slightly elevated.
- **Vertical Growth Phase**-begins when neoplastic cells populate the underlying dermis. Characterized clinically by an increase in size, change in color, nodularity, & ulceration. **METASTASIS is possible when the melanoma reaches this phase**.

MALIGNANT MELANOMA —the **MOST SEVERE** and potentially serious type of **SKIN CANCER** mainly due to excessive exposure to UV sun radiation causing the tanning cells (melanocytes) in the skin that produce a dark-colored substance (melanin) to undergo uncontrolled growth. May suddenly appear without warning, but **often develops from or near a MOLE (NEVUS)**. Common in fair-skin white people, occurring anywhere on the skin.

- **SKIN CANCER IS THE MOST COMMON MALIGNANCY IN THE U.S.** 1 in 100 people in the U.S. develop this cancer in a lifetime. Without treatment, it can widely metastasize and cause death. Linked to excessive **SUN EXPOSURE & PAINFULL SUNBURNS during childhood**.

- Malignant Melanoma is an uncommon neoplasm of the oral mucosa but exhibits a definite predilection for the **HARD PALATE & MAXILLARY ALVEOLAR RIDGES**. Unfortunately, oral mucosa melanomas have a poor prognosis (5-year survival rate for oral melanoma tumors is ~7%). **The most common intra-oral site for melanoma is the hard palate**.

MALIGNANT MELANOMA (HARD PALATE)

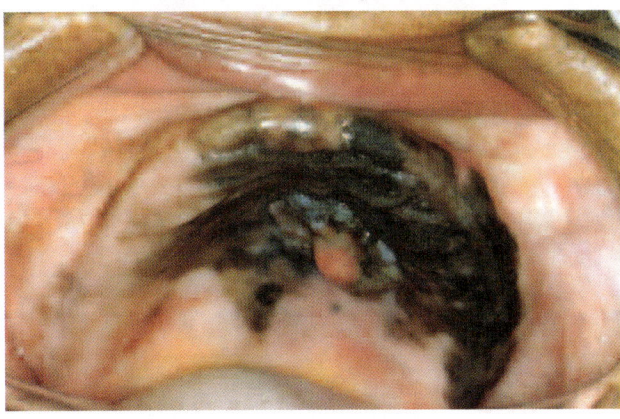

4 TYPES OF MELANOMA:

Superficial Spreading Melanoma-the **MOST COMMON form of malignant melanoma (65%)**, & most common cutaneous melanoma in Caucasians. The lesion is **TAN, BROWN, BLACK, or ADMIXED on sun-exposed skin (especially BLACK)**. The cancer begins at one focus in the skin at the dermo-epidermal junction (DEJ). It initially grows in a horizontal plane, along and just above & below the dermo-epidermal junction (this is the "radial" growth phase of melanoma which predominates), and is clinically macular or only slightly elevated. The "vertical" growth phase is characterized by an increase in size, change in color, nodularity, and at times ulceration.

Nodular Melanoma-much less common (~13% of cutaneous melanomas). **THERE IS NO "RADIAL" GROWTH PHASE** (it exists only in the "vertical" growth phase). NM presents as a sharply defined nodule with degrees of pigmentation (may be pink (amelanotic melanoma) or black, and occurs more often on the **back, head, and neck** of men.

Lentigo Maligna Melanoma-even less common (~10% of cutaneous melanomas), and is most common in the **ELDERY** population. The lesion may grow for years in the "radial" growth phase before developing into the more aggressive "vertical" growth phase. This radial growth phase is known as lentigo maligna (melanotic freckle of Hutchinson), while the vertical growth phase is known as lentigo maligna melanoma.

Acrolentiginous Melanoma-occurs on the **hands & feet** with a reputation for being ignored by the patient, resulting in the development of metastic disease.

NEVUS (MOLES)-almost all moles are normal. Atypical (Dysplastic) nevi-unusual moles are generally larger than normal moles, and are flat or have a flat part, with irregular borders with variable shades of color (especially brown, but can be a Blue Nevus). The presence of dysplastic nevi may mark a greater risk of malignant melanoma developing on apparently normal skin.

NEVUS

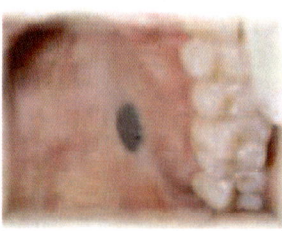 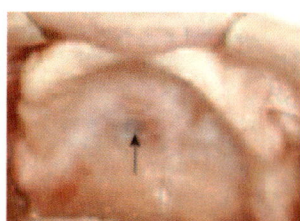 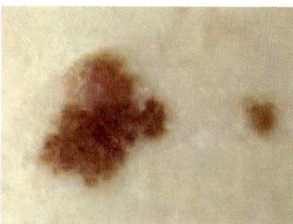

ACQUIRED NEVI (MOLES) — small, usually dark, skin growths that develop from pigment-producing cells (melanocytes) in the skin. Fairly common on the skin and intra-orally (much more common than congenital nevi both intra-orally and extra-orally). When present, they are usually on the **HARD PALATE**, or may be on the gingiva & lips. **Acquired nevi are microscopically classified into 5 subtypes**:

1. **Intramucosal Nevus**-the **MOST COMMON nevus in the oral cavity**. Nevus cells are located in the C.T. or lamina propria of the oral mucosa. Under palpation, these nevi appear **SOLID & SLIGHTLY RAISED** over the mucosa surface.

2. **Blue Nevus**-the **SECOND most common** acquired nevus in the oral cavity. Congenital, painless, color is based on the deep cutaneous or subcutaneous/submucosal deposits of melanin.

3. **Compound Nevus**-rare in the oral cavity. Nevus cells are located at the epithelium-lamina propria interface deep in the dermis. They are raised and solid.

4. **Junctional Nevus**-rare in the oral cavity. Nevus cells are located at the interface between the epithelium and lamina propria. They are flat and not detected by palpation. Some regard as pre-malignant, and may undergo transformation into malignant melanoma.

Intradermal Nevus (common mole)-the most common lesion of skin. Nevus cells lie exclusively in the dermis.

TREATMENT OF CHOICE FOR ORAL PIGMENTATIONS with unknown etiologies is **CONSERVATIVE, EXICIONAL BIOPSY** to rule out melanoma. Recurrence of oral nevi is very rare and malignant transformation has not been reported.

BASAL CELL CARCINOMA – a **MALIGNANT epithelial cell tumor** that begins as a papule that enlarges peripherally, forming a central crater that erodes, crusts, & bleeds. Only found on the skin, and **NEVER in the mouth due to EXCESSIVE SUN EXPOSURE** (UV radiation) or to x-rays. Metastasis is rare, but the local invasion by direct extension destroys underlying and adjacent tissues. Frequently develops on exposed skin surfaces, face (nose), & scalp in middle-aged or elderly people. **Treatment**: eradicate the lesion by electrodessication or cryotherapy. **BASAL CELL CARCINOMA IS THE MOST COMMON SKIN CANCER,** that usually appears as an ulcerated, crateriform lesion. It may look exactly like SCC, but **RARELY produces metastasis**.

- **BASAL CELL CARCINOMASA ARE NEVER FOUND IN THE MOUTH (INTRA-ORALLY)**.

- Common in adult Caucasians with fair complexions due to sun exposure or in patients with basal cell syndrome.

- Basal Cell Carcinoma has a much better prognosis than squamous cell carcinoma since it DOES NOT PRODUCE METASTASIS (it is invasive, so if you do not do surgery, the patient will die, but if treated, the patient will be cured). **Ex**: Frontal skin lesion in a 72-year male with two years of evolution.

SQUAMOUS CELL CARCINOMA (EPIDERMOID CARCINOMA-the **MOST COMMON MALIGNANCY IN THE ORAL CAVITY (90%)** & occurs more often in the oral cavity than any other type of cancer (90% of all malignant oral cavity neoplasms). SCC is a malignant EPITHELIAL TUMOR that is twice as prevalent in males (ages 40-65yrs).

- More common on the **LOWER LIP** than intra-orally. The most common intra-oral site is the lateral border & ventral surface of the **TONGUE** (from this site, it often metastasizes to cervical lymph nodes). *Dorsal tongue surface is almost never affected.* **FLOOR OR MOUTH is the second most common intra-oral site, with the WORST prognosis**.

- **Risk Factors**: smoking & smokeless tobacco (main risk factor), alcohol, painful & ill-fitting dentures, and chronic inflammation.

- **INVASION** is the most reliable histologic criterion for diagnosing oral SCC.

- **Treatment**: surgery & radiation to remove lymph nodes in neck.

NOTES

Squamous Cell Carcinoma can be **RED**, irregular, non-painful lesion, or a **WHITE** lesion caused by sun exposure. Lasts > 1 month.

Histology: hyperchromatism, pleomorphism, atypical mitosis, dyskeratosis, alteration of nuclei-cytoplasm ratio, acanthosis, but **NOT** sub-epithelial cleft.

Found **MAINLY** in **posterior LATERAL tongue border (can also be on the ventral surface)**, but can be on lower lip & floor of mouth. **NOT** common on dorsum of tongue.

SQUAMOUS CELL CARCINOMA

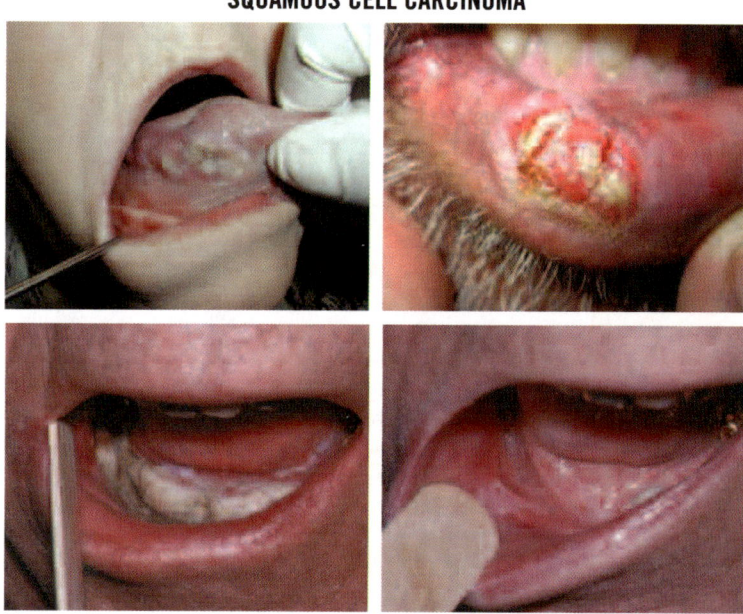

Metastasis of SCC occurs via **CERVICAL LYMPHATICS**. Risk increases with age.

Squamous Cell Carcinoma Occurs in these Head & Neck Locations:
Nasopharynx: caused by **tobacco & alcohol**. Represents **< 2%** of all cancers in U.S. (the least common SCC). Affects males ages 30-40yrs. Roof or lateral wall is the most common site. **Signs**: cervical mass, earache, sore throat, and nasal obstruction.

Palate: uncommon, but caused by **tobacco, alcohol, and denture irritation**. Represents **10%** of all oral carcinomas (soft palate is more common than hard palate). Affects men > 60yrs. **Signs**: painful ulcer, leukoplakia, exophytic mass.

Oropharynx: caused by tobacco & alcohol. Represents **10%** of all head & neck cancers, affecting men > 50yrs. **Signs**: sore throat, dysphagia, painful ulcer, cervical mass.

Maxillary Sinus: etiology unknown. Represents **30%** of all head & neck cancers. Affects men > 40yrs. **Signs**: chronic sinusitis, bulging palate, teeth loosening, paresthesia in the cheek.

Tongue: most common site is the **LATERAL BORDER**, but also occurs on the ventral surface (under the tongue) (dorsum is the least likely involved). **Tongue cancer causes more deaths than any other malignant lesion** in other regions of the head & neck because the tongue is the **MOST COMMON INTRAORAL SITE OF CANCER** because it is a highly mobile organ richly endowed with lymphatics & blood vessels that facilitate metastasis (**most commonly metastasizes to the CERVICAL LYMPH NODES**). It very **RARELY** gives rise to skeletal metastasis.

Etiology: tobacco, alcohol, syphilis, Plummer-Vinson Syndrome.

Mostly effects men > 60yrs. on the **posterior lateral border and middle third of the tongue**. Presents as a **painless ulcer** with **leukoplakia** and **erythroplakia**.

Lips: THE **MOST COMMON SITE FOR SCC** (more than intra-orally). **95% of all SCC** are found on the LOWER LIP (vermillion of the lower lip) of which 90-98% of lower lip cancers occurs in **MALES 60+** due to **chronic sun exposure & pipe smoking**. This location (lips) is etiologically related to race, complexion, pipe smoking, sunlight. It is a PAINLESS ulcer and keratotic plaque.

Floor of Mouth: **SECOND MOST COMMON INTRA-ORAL SITE FOR CANCER**, occuring mainly in the **ANTERIOR SEGMENT** on either side of the midline **near salivary gland orifices**. Caused by **tobacco & alcohol**. Pre-malignant lesions of squamous epithelium most often occur here. **VERY POOR PROGNOSIS**. Typically effects men 40-60yrs. It is a painless ulcer with leukoplakia and erythroplakia.

Buccal Mucosa: generally occurs along the **PLANE OF OCCLUSION**, midway anteroposteriorly. Represents **10% of all oral carcinomas**, caused by tobacco, alcohol, and denture irritation. A painless ulcer and **exophytic mass with leukoplakia**.

Gingiva & Alveolar Mucosa: more common in the **POSTERIOR MANDIBLE** than maxilla, with posterior sites affected more than anterior sites. Represents **10-15% of all oral carcinomas**, caused by tobacco and alcohol. Mainly effects **men 60+ years**. Common on the mandibular mucosa as a painless ulcer and plaque-like or exophytic mass.

Squamous Cell Carcinoma is **most easily managed** when found on the **LOWER LIP**. SCC is the most common malignant oral tumor, **representing >90% of all oral malignancies**. SCC is 9-10 times **more common in males** than females, and while it is seen in all ages, its **highest incidence is after age 40yrs**. SCC IS MORE COMMON **ON THE LIPS** than intra-orally.

- **95% of lip carcinomas** occur on the **LOWER LIP**, and are usually discovered early and only a small percentage show lymph node metastasis. The prognosis is very good.

- SCC of the **TONGUE** is the most common **INTRA-ORAL** malignancy. The most common location is the **posterior lateral border**, then the posterior 1/3 (tongue base). SCC is uncommon on the dorsum or tongue tip. These lesions metastasize early, and the prognosis is not as good as lip lesions.

- **MOUTH FLOOR** is the 2nd most common **INTRA-ORAL** location of SCC. It occurs mainly in older men (especially alcoholics and smokers). These lesions metastasize early with a **poor prognosis**.

- Treatment of choice for **ORAL CANCER** (SCC) IS **SURGERY**.

SQUAMOUS CELL CARCINOMA (3 TYPES):

VERRUCOUS CARCINOMA- RARE form of squamous cell carcinoma (**MALIGNANT**) that **DOES NOT METASTASIZE**, but occurs in oral cavity soft tissues (mandibular mucobuccal fold, alveolar mucosa, & palate), or laryngeal cavity due to tobacco chewing, smoking, or snuff dipping. **Mostly effects men 60+ years**. The tumor mass has a characteristic **WHITISH-CAULIFLOWER or CORAL-LIKE papillary appearance**. Typically, develops on the vocal cords of an elderly male who has been a heavy cigarette smoker. It is known for its **slow growth pattern** and well-developed hyperkeratotic epithelial boundaries.

NOTES

VERRUCOUS CARCINOMA

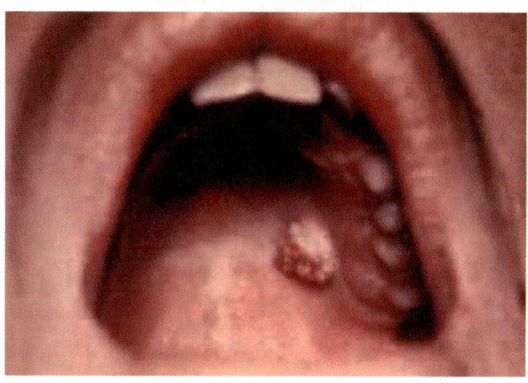

Pathologically, it is a well-differentiated squamous cell neoplasm that may invade or infiltrate the borders of adjacent structures, but **does not metastasize**. It can transform into an invasive form of carcinoma, or co-exist with other squamous cell carcinomas. Often misdiagnosed histologically as a benign lesion.

Treatment: SURGERY. Prognosis: 60-70% have 5-year survival rate.

Verrucous Carcinoma is a non-aggressive, very well-differentiated tumor that does not metastasize. A disease of OLDER PEOPLE. Can present as a diffuse, WHITE, well-demarcated, painless papillary surface mass on the **UPPER (MAXILLARY) ALVEOLAR RIDGE**, measuring 6x4 cm, and can be present 2-3 years before a definitive diagnosis is made. Better prognosis than carcinoma invasive. Can destroy the bone.

CARCINOMA IN SITU: located only inside epithelium (intra-epithelium), atypical mitosis, hyperchromatism, all epithelial layers are affected, **BUT IT DOES NOT INVADE C.T.** (basal membrane is intact). **Better prognosis than carcinoma invasive**, but must treat. **Carcinoma in situ is MALIGNANT, BUT CANNOT matastasize due to lack of blood or lymphatic vessels in epithelium. Located ONLY in the epithelium** which does not have blood or lymphatic vessels so it cannot produce metastasis. Ex: 60-year-old alcoholic female with red FLAT area in the mouth floor. Area is flat, asymptomatic, present for 4 months, increasing in size, but not painful. Her medical history is non-contributory.

CARCINOMA INVASIVE-Ex: 60-year-old alcoholic female with **red area in the mouth floor**. Area is flat, asymptomatic, present for 4 months, increasing in size, but not painful. Her medical history is non-contributory.

Characteristics of Lesions that may be Malignant:

Erythroplasia: lesion is **totally red or speckled red and white**. Red, non-ulcerated area on a mucous membrane. The texture can be **normal or rough, and its size varies** (some are so small and may go undetected, while large areas are conspicuous to casual inspection). There are **usually no symptoms**, being neither elevated nor depressed, presenting as quiet, unpretentious lesions The border may be sharp, or blend imperceptibly into surrounding normal mucosa. **Important**: **early carcinoma often appears as an area of erythroplasia**. There are certain areas of the oral mucosa that are more prone to malignancy. Additionally, **oral cancer is more often seen in people over age 40yrs**. Because of this, an area of erythroplasia in a cancer prone area in a patient over 40yrs is highly suspicious of malignancy and should be **biopsied on the day it is seen** (especially lesions whose duration exceeds 2 weeks).

Rapid growth, **ulcerated fixed lesion that bleeds on gentle manipulation**. The lesion and surrounding tissue is firm to touch. **On physical examination, PAINLESS induration of soft tissue suggests an invasive malignant lesion**.

ODONTOGENIC ABNORMALITIES

ABRASION – abnormal **PATHOLOGIC WEARING AWAY** of tooth structure. Pathologic loss of tooth structure.

1. **Toothbrush Abrasion** - most often results in **V-shaped wedges** at the cervical margins in canines & premolars. Caused by using a hard bristle toothbrush and/or horizontal brushing strokes with a gritty dentrifice.

2. **Occlusal Abrasion** - results in flattened cusps on all posterior teeth & worn incisal edges due to chewing or biting on hard foods or objects, and chewing tobacco.

ATTRITION physiologic wearing away of enamel & dentin due to **NORMAL** function or mainly excessive **GRINDING/GRITTING/CLENCHING** teeth together **(BRUXING)**. The most noticeable effects are **POLISHED FACETS** (flat incisal edges that usually develop on the linguoincisal of maxillary canines & central incisors, and facioincisal of mandibular canines). Discolored tooth surfaces, and exposed dentin.

ATTRITION (BRUXING/GRINDING)

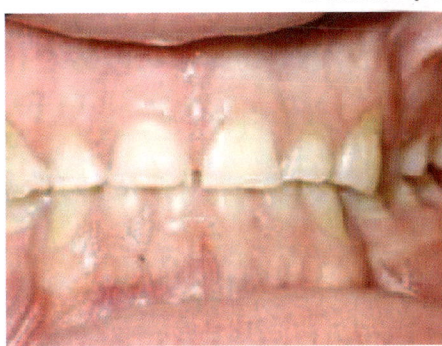
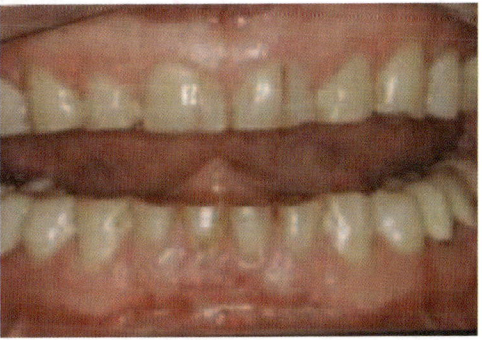

EROSION – **CHEMICAL** loss of tooth structure from **NON-MECHANICAL MEANS** such as drinking acidic liquids (soda) or eating acidic foods. Common in **BULIMCS** due to regurgitated stomach acids. Affects smooth surfaces and occlusal surfaces of teeth.

EROSION

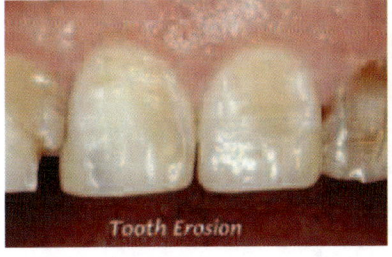
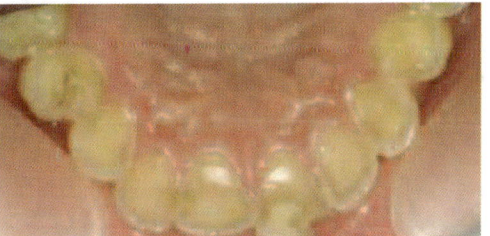

INTRINSIC STAINING: can be caused by the following except DIABETES MELLITUS.
- **Dentinogenesis imperfecta** - causes a translucent or opalescent hue, usually gray to bluish-brown.
- **Erythroblastosis fetalis** - causes intrinsic stain that is bluish-black, greenish-blue, tan, or brown.
- **Porphyria** - causes an intrinsic stain that is red or brownish.
- **Fluorosis** - causes white opacities, or light brown to brownish-black.
- **Pulpal injury** - intrinsic stain starts pink, then becomes orange-brown to bluish-black.
- **Internal resorption** - causes a PINKISH intrinsic stain.
- **Tetracyclines** - intrinsic stain varies from light-gray, yellow, or tan to darker shades of gray.

NOTES

ANKYLOSIS —fusion of surrounding alveolar bone to a tooth root. Ankylosis may be initiated by an infection or trauma to the PDL. The **ankylosed tooth has lost its PDL space**, and is actually fused to the alveolar process of bone. There is change in the continuity of the occlusal plane caused by the continued eruption of non-ankylosed teeth & growth of the alveolar process.

GEMINATION (TWINNING) – a division of a single tooth germ by invagination causing incomplete formation of two teeth (usually the incisors). Incomplete splitting of a tooth germ.

GOMPHOSIS – a type of fibrous joint where a conical process is inserted into a socket-like portion (i.e. styloid process in the temporal bone, or the teeth inserted into the dental alveoli).

FUSION – developmental joining of > 2 teeth (germs) where dentin & another dental tissue are united (maybe the root).

CONCRESCENCE – a condition where **only the CEMENTUM of two or more teeth are joined**.

TAURODONTISM ("Bull-Like") -found usually in **MOLARS**; the tooth body and pulp chamber are enlarged vertically at the root's expense **causing an apical shift of the pulpal floor and tooth furcation down the tooth root** (large pulp chambers and short roots) causing teeth to look "bull-like". Caused by failure or late invagination of **Hertwig's epithelial root sheath** that is responsible for root formation.

TAURODONTISM

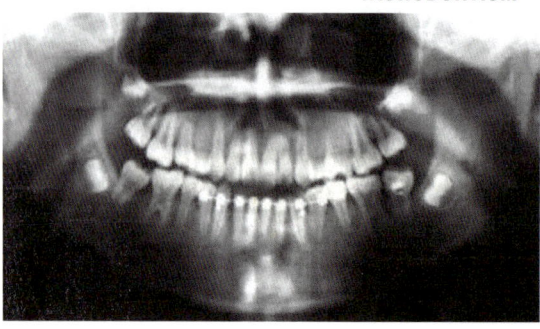
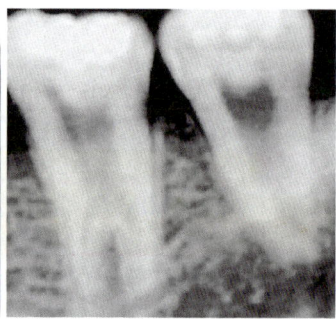

DENS-IN-DENTE (Dens Invaginatus)-"tooth within a tooth", caused by a deep invagination of the enamel organ **Hertwig's epithelial root sheath** during formation. Most commonly associated with a **MAXILLARY LATERAL INCISOR**.

DENS-IN-DENTE (TOOTH WITHIN A TOOTH)

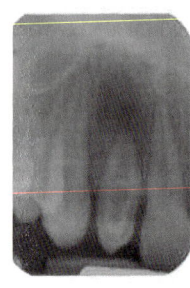
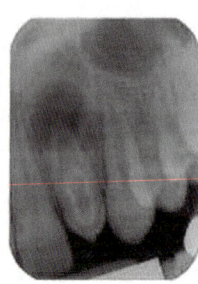
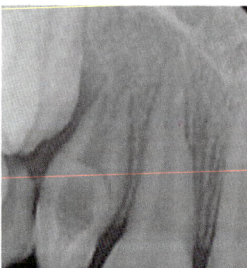

MESIODENS – the most common **SUPERNUMERARY TOOTH** (extra tooth) usually appearing singly, or in pairs as a **small tooth with a cone-shaped crown and short root visible between** vital **PERMANENT MAXILLARY CENTRALS** on a radiograph. It may be erupted, impacted, or inverted. Appears **situated in the maxilla** near the **midline and almost always posterior to normal central incisors**. Thus, many mesiodens are bypassed by the permanent incisors still erupt into their normal position in the arch regardless.

NOTES
- btw #8 & 9.

MESIODENS (SUPERNUMERARY)

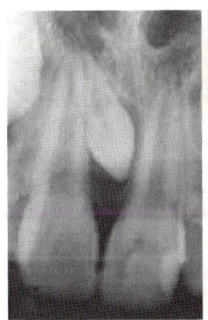
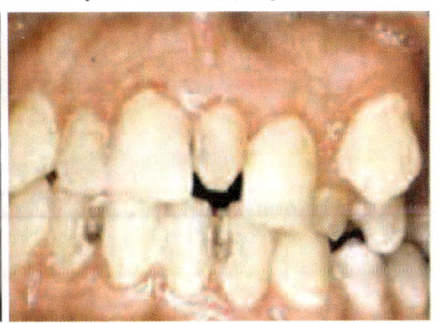

If the mesiodens does not interfere with the normal eruption of the permanent maxillary central incisors, you can wait until the child is 6-8 years old to extract the mesiodens non-surgically if it erupts, or surgically if it does not erupt.

HYPERCEMENTOSIS – **excessive (abnormal) CEMENTUM FORMATION** around or on root surface after tooth eruption (often confined to the apical half of the root, but may involve the entire root). **THICKENING OF CEMENTUM (ROOT TISSUE)**. Caused by trauma, metabolic dysfunction, chronic periapical inflammation, or when a tooth has lost its antagonist. Hypercementosis is merely a dental anomaly, but can be **seen in ACROMEGALY & PAGET'S DISEASE**.

- Mainly affects **VITAL** teeth (**MAINLY PREMOLARS**), then first & second molars.

- Produces no significant clinical signs or symptoms, but seen radiographically as a **BULBOUS ENLARGEMENT** with a surrounding **continuous/unbroken periodontal membrane space and normal lamina dura**. Radiographically, with Paget's Disease, there is complete absence of the periodontal membrane space & lamina dura that surrounds the hyperplastic cementum.

HYPERCEMENTOSIS

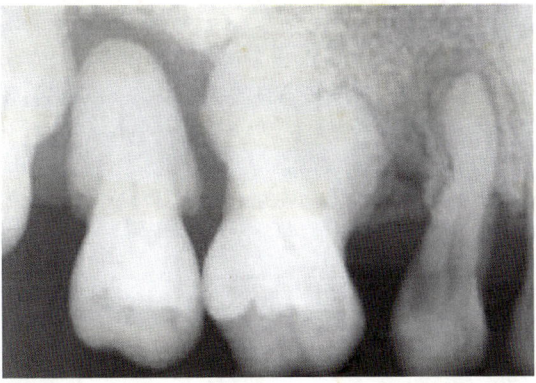

NOTES

ENAMEL HYPOPLASIA—enamel **developmental defect** due to **INCOMPLETE FORMATION** of the enamel matrix. **ENAMEL IS HARD, BUT, THIN & DEFICIENT IN AMOUNT**, resulting in incomplete formation of the enamel matrix with a deficiency in the cementing substance. EH affects deciduous (primary) and permanent teeth, and is **usually caused by illness or injury during tooth formation**, or due to a genetic disorder (genetic forms of EH are considered types of amelogenesis imperfecta). If only one permanent tooth is affected, it is usually caused by physical damage to the replaced primary tooth. **WHITE & BROWN DEFECTS ON TOOTH SURFACE**.

- **Clinical Features**: lack of contact between teeth, rapid breakdown of occlusal surfaces, yellowish-brown stain that appears due to **EXPOSED DENTIN**.

ENAMEL HYPOPLASIA

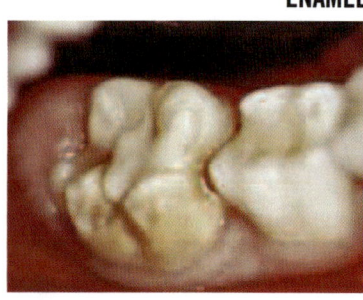 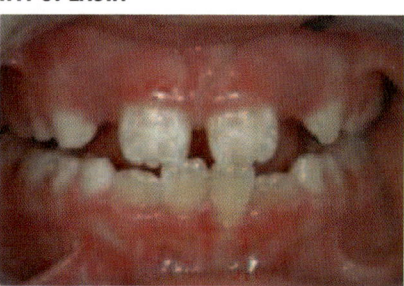

ENAMEL HYPOCALCIFICATION-a hereditary dental defect where the **ENAMEL IS SOFT & UNDERCALCIFIED, yet normal in quantity** due to **defective maturation of ameloblasts** (a defect in the mineralization of the formed matrix). Teeth are chalky, surfaces wear down rapidly, and a yellowish-brown stain appears due to underlying **EXPOSED DENTIN**. Affects deciduous & permanent teeth.

ENAMEL HYPOCALCIFICATION

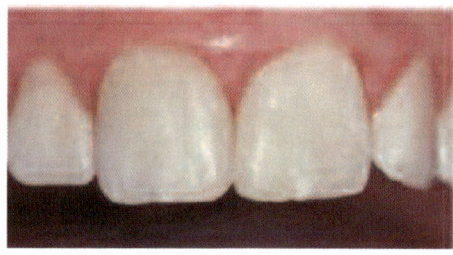 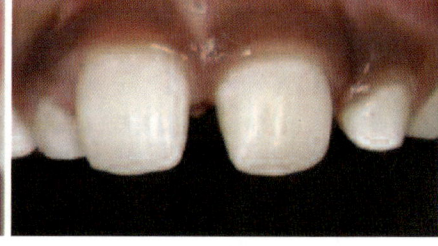

AMELOGENESIS IMPERFECTA  – an inherited hereditary **ECTODERMAL DEFECT** transmitted as a dominant trait that affects the deciduous & permanent dentition, causing **enamel to be soft, thin, and yellow due to EXPOSED DENTIN through the thin enamel layer**. Teeth are easily damaged and susceptible to decay. Crowns may or may not show discoloration. If discoloration is present, it varies depending on the type of disorder, ranging from yellow to dark brown.

- **Open contacts** between teeth and occlusal surfaces/incisal edges are often severely abraded.

- **Radiographic findings are often distinctive & pathognomonic**. When enamel is totally absent, the radiographic appearance makes the diagnosis obvious. When some enamel is present, thin radiopaque coverings on the proximal surfaces are visible. When anatomic crown forms are normal or near normal, the softness of the defective enamel may not be easily distinguished from dentin.

- **Dentin, pulp, & cementum are NOT affected by AI** (unlike dentinogenesis imperfecta). **Exception**: AI will only show pulp obliteration if there is advanced abrasion with secondary dentin formation.

AMELOGENESIS IMPERFECTA

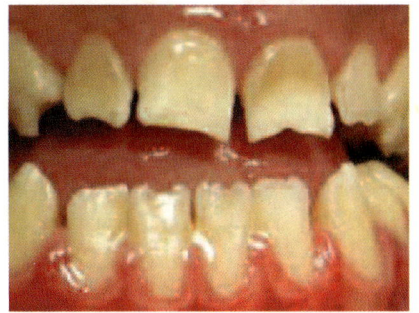

OPEN CONTACTS & SQUARE CROWNS (AI)

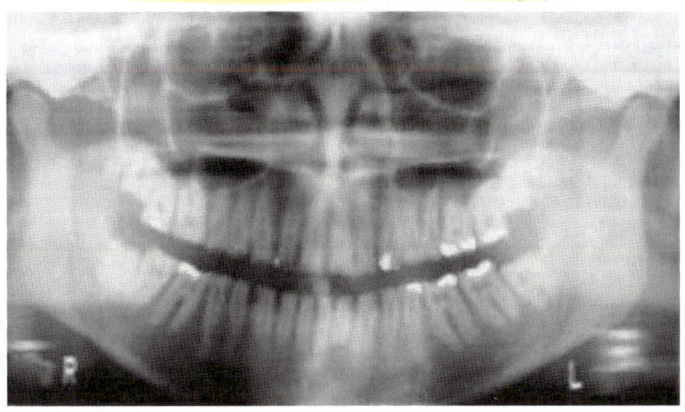

3 Types of Amelogenesis Imperfecta:
(Type 1) Hypoplastic AI: enamel has not formed to full normal thickness, or may be completely absent on newly erupted developing teeth due to **defective formation of the enamel matrix**.

(Type 2) Hypomaturation AI: enamel can be pierced by an explorer tip under firm pressure and chipped away from normal-appearing dentin. Characterized by **IMMATURE CRYSTALLITES**.

(Type 3) Hypocalcified AI: quantity of enamel is normal, but so soft it **can be removed** during a prophylaxis due to the **defective MINERALIZATION of the enamel matrix**.

DETINOGENESIS IMPERFECTA (HEREDITARY OPALESCENT DENTIN) – **RARE** disorder found in only 1:7,000 children. An inherited/hereditary **MESODERMAL DEFECT OF DENTIN** that only affects deciduous & permanent teeth. **Teeth have an OPALESCENT HUE.**

- **Clinical Features:** teeth have **amber, gray,** or **purple opalescence/translucence** or **discoloration, pulp chambers may be completely obliterated due to continued deposition of dentin,** crowns are short & bulbous, with narrow roots. Enamel can chip away within 2-4yrs after eruption, exposing the dentin which is soft and wears away rapidly. **Enamel is structurally and chemically normal.** DI is usually **easily detected and identified**, as teeth exhibit a **translucent** or **opalescent appearance**. Abnormal constriction at the CEJ is another clinical feature detected by exploration.

DENTINOGENSIS IMPERFECTA

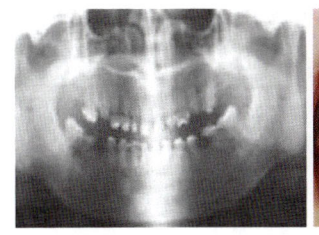
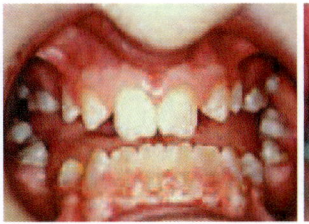
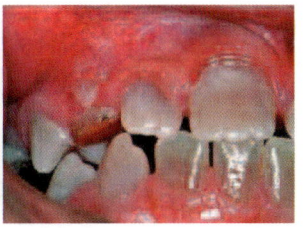

NOTES

3 Types of Dentinogenesis Imperfecta:
Type 1: dentin abnormality occurs in patients with **Osteogenesis Imperfecta**, characterized by **blue sclera** or history of **bone fractures**.

Type 2: the **most common**; only a dentin abnormality exists. **NO BONE INVOLVEMENT**.

Type 3 (Brandywine Type): like Type 2, only a dentin abnormally exists. There are clinical & radiographic variations that include **multiple pulp exposures in the deciduous (primary) dentition**.

DENTIN DYSPLASIA (ROOTLESS TEETH) – a hereditary disease transmitted as an autosomal dominant trait. **Clinical Features:** normal enamel, **atypical dentin, pulpal obliteration**, defective root formation, tendency toward **multiple periapical radiolucencies** and early exfoliation of teeth. Not associated with any systemic C.T. disorder. **2 Types of Dentin Dysplasia:**

Type I (Radicular)-the more common type involving both dentitions. Normal morphology and color (deciduous & permanent teeth). **Mobile teeth**, premature exfoliation, short roots (rootless teeth), obliterated pulp chambers (deciduous), crescent-shaped pulpal remnant (permanent), **periapical radiolucencies**, coronal dentin is normal, but **root dentin is disoriented**. **PULPAL OBLITERATION BY EXCESS DENTIN "chevron" shaped pulp chambers**.

Type II (Coronal)-involves both dentitions (but coronal dentin is normal). Deciduous teeth exhibit bluish-gray opalescent appearance, **obliterated pulp chambers**, amorphous & atubular dentin in the radicular portion of the teeth. Permanent teeth exhibit a normal clinical appearance, thistle-tube pulp chambers & stones, and true denticles. Pulpal obliteration of primary teeth, and pulp stones in permanent teeth.

ANODONTIA – a developmental abnormality characterized by **TOTAL ABSCENSE of teeth**. Two Forms:

Complete/True Anodontia-a rare condition where **ALL TEETH are missing**. May involve the primary & permanent dentitions, and is usually associated with **hereditary Ectodermal Dysplasia**.

Partial Anodontia (Congenitally Missing Teeth)-a common condition usually affecting maxillary & mandibular 3rd molars (affects mainly maxillary 3rd molars), maxillary laterals, & mandibular 2nd premolars. **Rule**: if only one or a few teeth are missing, **the absent tooth is the MOST DISTAL tooth** (if a molar, then the 3rd molar is missing; if a premolar, then the 2nd premolar).

OLIGODONTIA – congenital absence of **MANY (but not all) teeth**.

HYPODONTIA – absence of only a **FEW** teeth

WHITE LESIONS

ORAL CANDIDIASIS ("THRUSH" OR "MONILIASIS") – a **FUNGAL infection** of the oral cavity or vagina caused by a Candida species (usually Candida albicans) causing an inflammatory, pruritic infection with a thick, white discharge. Appears **diffuse, curly or velvety white mucosal plaques on the cheeks, palate, and tongue** that **CAN BE WIPED OFF**, leaving a red, raw, or bleeding surface. The most common symptoms are **discomfort and burning** of the mouth & throat, and altered taste.

- Candida is **a yeast-like fungi and normal inhabitant of the oral cavity** & vaginal tract, but is normally held in check by indigenous bacteria of these areas. Factors that stimulate Candida growth are **extended use of antibiotics** (antibiotics prescribed for a dental infection), **steroids, diabetes, pregnancy, or vitamin deficiency (iron, folate, B_{12}, zinc)**.

- Very common in patients on **long-term antibiotic** or **chemotherapy**, and immunosuppressed patients (AIDS).

- **Treatment**: topical with **LOZENGES** (Trouches) & mouth rinses (**NYSTATIN** is most widely used).

ACUTE PSEUDOMEMBRANOUS CANDIDIASIS – the **most common oral candidiasis**, usually found on the **buccal mucosa, tongue, and soft palate**. Oral cytology smears diagnose acute pseudomembranous candida by revealing **budding organisms** with **branching pseudohyphae**.

ANGULAR CHEILITIS (PERLECHE) – any chronic inflammatory lesion that **occurs at the labial commisure (corners of mouth)** due to **unknown cause**. Generally associated with **LOSS OF VERTICAL DIMENSION in elderly patients**. Mouth corners are painful, irritated, red, cracked, and scaly. Candida albicans fungus (Thrush) may grow in the corners of the mouth, keeping them sore.

- **Predisposing Factors**: Candida albicans infection, loss of inter-maxillary distance (decreased vertical dimension), trauma to the labial commissure due to prolonged dental treatment, & vitamin deficiencies (especially **riboflavin or thiamine**).

- **Treatment**: **NYSTATIN** will eliminate the **FUNGAL** infection only.

ANGUAL CHELITIS (PERLECHE)

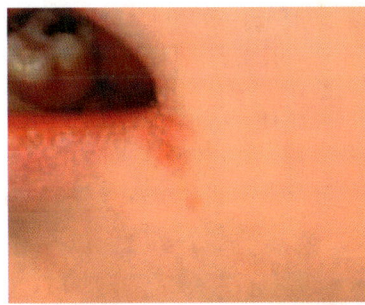
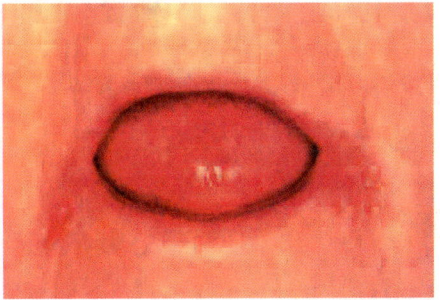

ACTINIC CHEILITIS (SOLAR CHEILITIS/FARMER'S LIP) – a **PRE-MALIGNANT condition** caused by chronic and excessive exposure to the **UV sunlight radiation**. **A counterpart of actinic keratosis of the skin, and can also develop into squamous cell carcinoma**. There is thick, **WHITISH** discoloration of the lip at the border of the lip and skin, and loss of the usually sharp demarcation between the red of the lip and normal skin (vermillion border). **May lead to SCC, so it must be treated**.

ACTINIC CHEILITIS

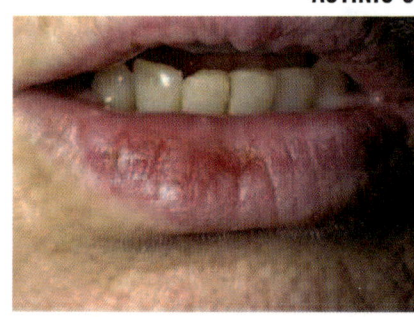
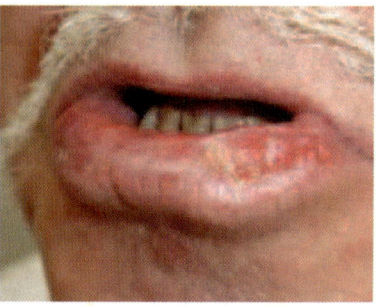

LEUKOEDEMA – a condition that mimics leukoplakia as it appears to be a **WHITE PATCH**, but is a just a **VARIANT OF NORMAL MUCOSA**. Varies from a filmy opalescence of the mucosa in the early stages, to a more definite grayish-white cast with a coarsely wrinkled surface in later stages. Usually occurs **BILATERALLY** and along the occlusal line in the bicuspid and molar region. Diagnostically, one can stretch the tissue and the white disappears (Important: Leukoplakia DOES NOT DISAPPEAR WHEN STRETCHED). **NO TREATMENT REQUIRED**.

LEUKOEDEMA

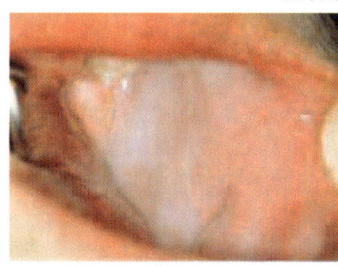
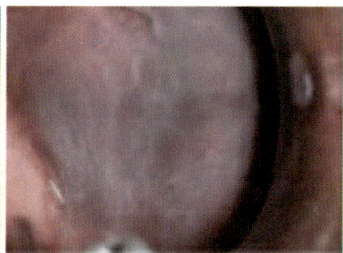

Leukoedem's white appearance is caused by water inside spinous cells, causing light to reflect back as whitish.

Differential Diagnosis: leukoplakia, white sponge nevus, & benign intraepithelial dyskeratosis.

WHITE SPONGE NEVUS (FAMILIAL WHITE FOLDED DYSPLASIA)—a **BUCCAL MUCOSAL ABNORMALITY (BENIGN)** often mistaken for leukoplakia, that follows a hereditary pattern as an autosomal dominant trait/condition with no sex preference. It is congenital in many instances, but may occur in childhood or adolescence. Most common location is the buccal mucosa (bilaterally), followed by the labial mucosa, alveolar ridge, and floor of mouth. Almost **NEVER** found on the gingival margin & dorsal of tongue.

- Clinical Features: soft, thickened, and corrugated folds of mucous membrane. Mucosa appears thickened and folded with a soft or spongy texture, and peculiar pearly white or opalescent hue.

- **NO TREATMENT**, but because the condition is benign, prognosis is excellent, with no serious clinical complications.

WHITE SPONGE NEVUS

LEUKOPLAKIA – a **PREMALIGNANT LESION WHITE PATCH** or plaque on the oral mucosa that **DOES NOT RUB OFF (UNLIKE CANDIDA)** and cannot be assigned as any specific disease. Possible etiologic factors are tobacco (**PIPE SMOKING**), alcohol, oral sepsis, and chronic irritation. Most often due to **TOBACCO** and chronic irritation (ill-fitting denture, rough filling, cheek biting). May be present for many months in a heavy pipe-smoker. **Pipe-smoking is the most important predisposing etiologic factor in leukoplakia**. More common in elderly men, and **DOES NOT DISAPPEAR WHEN STRETCHED**. Mouth floor, tongue, and lower lip are the regions at greatest risk for carcinoma occurring in leukoplakia.

- Leukoplakia is a slow developing change in a mucous membrane characterized by thickened, white, firmly attached patches, that are slightly raised & sharply circumscribed. Lesions on the mouth floor and base of the tongue are the most aggressive. Most display no dysplasia, but can be pre-malignant so **MUST BIOPSY**.

- Treatment: BIOPSY. Due to chance of malignant transformation, **ALL LEUKOPLAKIAS MUST BE BIOPSIED & COMPLETELY EXCISED** (if untreated, some progress to carcinoma). Although less common than leukoplakias, **erythroplakias have a much greater malignant potential**. Incisional Biopsy is indicated for a 3cm area of leukoplakia of the soft palate. Biopsy are not required for papillary fibroma, exostosis, Fordyce's granules, or Hemangiomas as these are benign.

- Any white or red lesion that does not disappear itself in 2 weeks must be re-evaluated and considered for BIOPSY to obtain a definitive diagnosis.

LEUKOPLAKIA

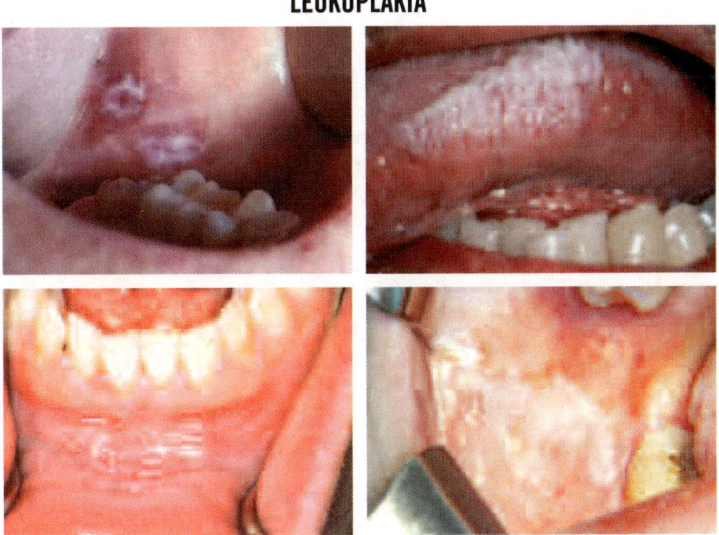

NOTES

- **Carcinoma in situ** is a term applied to mucosal lesions that resemble leukoplakia in all respects except dysplasia is very pronounced and involves almost all epithelial layers. It shows no tendency to invade or metastasize to other tissues. Exhibits all of the histologic characteristics of malignancy (pleomorphism, hyperchromatism, abnormal mitoses, anaplasia), but **DOES NOT show invasiveness or extension into adjacent structures**.

- **Clinical Differential Diagnosis of White Patch**: leukoplakia, lupus erythematosus, leukoedema, white sponge nevus, chemical or thermal burn, candidiasis, lichen planus, & migratory glossitis/stomatitis.

HAIRY LEUKOPLAKIA—an unusual BENIGN form of leukoplakia seen mainly in people with **HIV/AIDS or the immunocompromised caused by EPSTEIN-BARR VIRUS (HSV-4)**. Fuzzy, hairy white patches mainly on the tongue (may resemble THRUSH caused by Candida). **Treatment**: systemic anti-viral therapy (Acyclovir) or topical therapy with retinoic acids (tretinoin), or ablative therapy.

HAIRY LEUKOPLAKIA

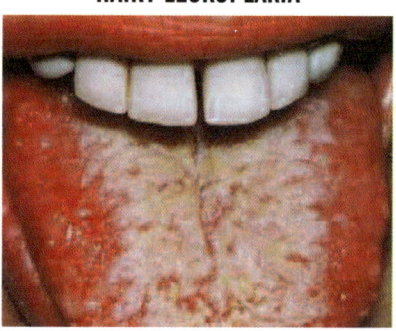

HAIRY TONGUE—**HYPERTROPHY** of **FILIFORM PAPILLAE (NO TASTE BUDS)**. A BENIGN condition of the tongue dorsum which is FURRY due to elongated filiform papillae. Color varies from yellowish-white to brown or black. This is not Hairy Leukoplakia, but is **just DISCOLORATION of the DORSUM tongue surface**, elongation & hyperkeratosis of FILIFORM PAPILLAE ON TONGUE'S DORSUM SURFACE. **4 Types of Tongue Papillae**: taste buds are present only on fungiform, circumvallate, & foliate papillae.

Filiform papillae-the most numerous. Small cones in "v"-shaped rows paralleling the sulcus terminalis, characterized by no taste buds and increased keratinization. **NO TASTE BUDS**.

Fungiform papillae-scattered among filiform papaillae. Flattened, mushroom-shaped, and found mainly at the tongue tip and lateral margins. **HAVE TASTE BUDS**.

Circumvallate papillae-the LARGEST, LEAST NUMEROUS papillae. Circular-shaped arranged in an inverted "v"-shaped row toward the **back of the tongue**. Associated with ducts of Von Ebner's glands. **HAVE TASTE BUDS**.

Foliate papillae-found on the lateral margins as 3-4 vertical folds. **HAVE TASTE BUDS**.

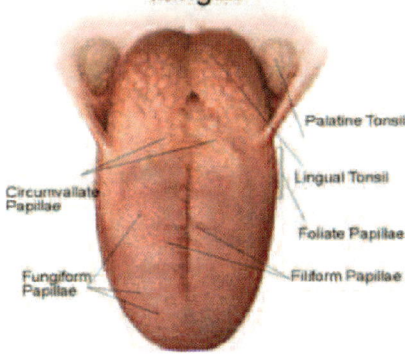

CIRCUMVALLATE PAPILLAE

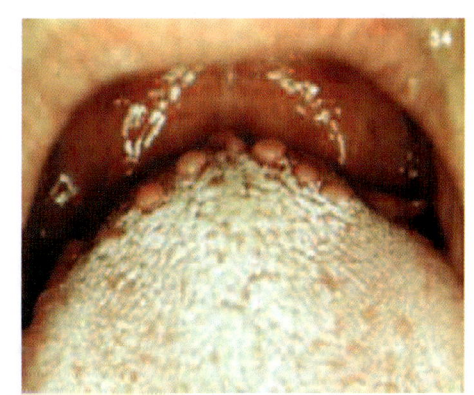

Hairy tongue can be **WHITE, GREEN, BROWN, OR BLACK** completely covering the tongue dorsum as filiform papillae are stained and **discolored with DEBRIS the patient eats or smokes**. Ex: dorsal surface of tongue of a smoker exhibits elongated, brownish filiform papillae. Can present as a bright green, flat area on the tongue dorsum, with very poor dental status & oral hygiene. The green area is probably DEBRIS. **Etiology**: overgrowth of fungal microorganisms due to smoking or poor oral hygiene (**brush tongue**).

HAIRY TONGUE

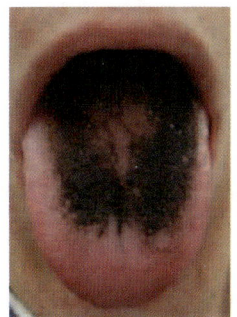

BENIGN MIGRATORY GLOSSITIS (GEOGRAPHIC TONGUE) OR (ERYTHEMA MIGRANS) A **HARMLESS, USUALLY PAINLESS** (maybe slight burning), **COMMON** condition due to **desquamation of FILIFORM papillae (no taste buds)**. One or more **irregular-shaped patches on the tongue exist**. The center area is redder then the rest of the tongue, and edges of the patch are whitish color. These patches appear and remain for a short time, heal, then reappear at another site. **The patches usually do not respond to treatment, but disappear spontaneously**.
Geographic Tongue often occurs with Fissured Tongue.

GEOGRAPHIC TONGUE

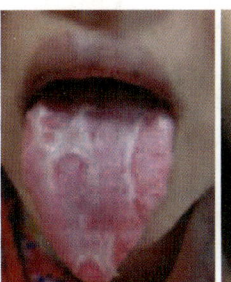 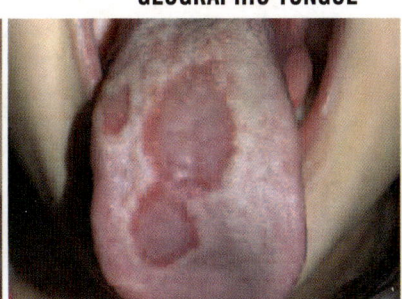 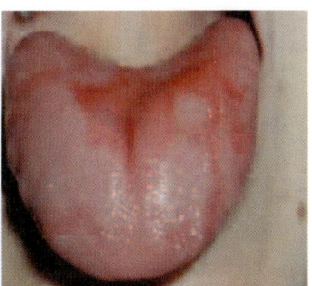

NOTES

FISSURED TONGUE ("SCROTAL TONGUE") – a DEEP, usually asymptomatic (maybe painful if infected with Candida Albicans) **MEDIAN FISSURE with laterally radiating grooves** that vary in number, but are usually symmetrically arranged **across the DORSUM (TOP) OF THE TONGUE**. Rare in children, but incidence increases with age. Found in **Melkersson-Rosenthal Syndrome** (along with **Cheilitis Granulomatosum** & Facial Nerve Paralysis).

FISSURED TONGUE

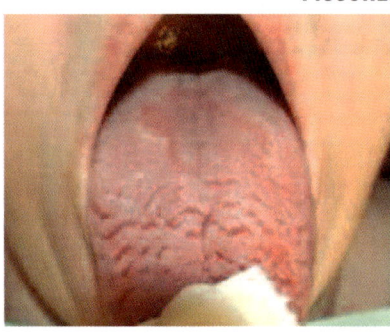
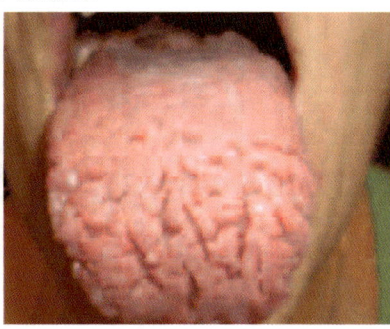

STOMATITIS NICOTINA ("PIPE-SMOKER'S PALATE" OR NICOTINIC STOMATITIS) Related to pipe smoking (tobacco), occurs **ONLY ON THE PALATE**, and mainly affects males. The palate is initially red & inflamed, then develops a diffuse, grayish-white, thickened, multi-nodular popular appearance with a small red "spot" in the center of each tiny nodule. This "spot" corresponds to orifices of palatal salivary gland ducts. **Treatment**: None, except to stop smoking. Not usually premalignant.

- Found ONLY in the palate (palate is leathery white and full of keratin (hyperkeratosis with RED DOTS (inflamed minor salivary glands). **The only lesion produced by tobacco that is not cancerous.** Usually a white, generalized area with red dots on the hard palate that are PAINLESS & non-indurated. **White areas with multiple red dots** (inflamed salivary glands in the palate).

NICOTINIC STOMATITIS (PIPE-SMOKER'S PALATE)

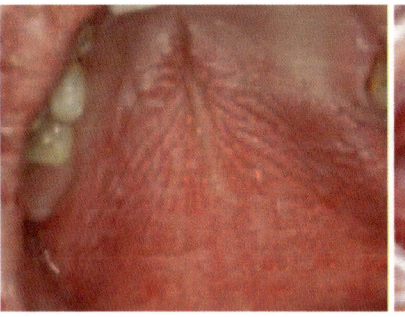
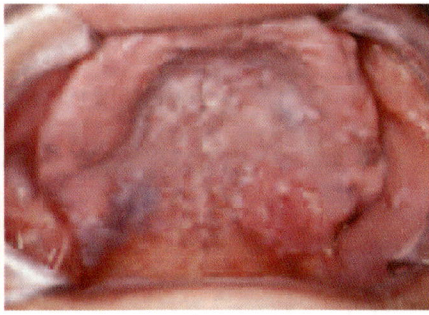

LICHEN PLANUS – oral lesion mainly on the **BUCCAL MUCOSA** appearing as **white or grayish-white striae arranged in a lace-like pattern (Wickman's Striae)** often bilaterally & symmetrically distributed, and usually asymptomatic, but may sometimes cause a burning sensation. A fairly common **inflammatory disease, of unknown cause**, but may be autoimmune. It usually affects the skin, mouth, or both. May also be on the tongue, lips, hard palate, & gingival, but **MAINLY BUCCAL MUCOSA**.

- **Microscopic Features**: hyperparakeratosis with thickening of the granular cell layer, development of a **"saw-tooth" appearance of rete pegs**, degeneration of the basal cell layer, and infiltration of inflammatory cells into the sub-epithelial layer of C.T.

LICHEN PLANUS

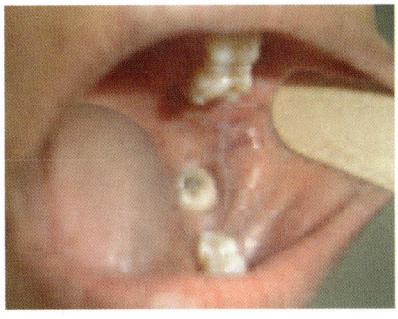
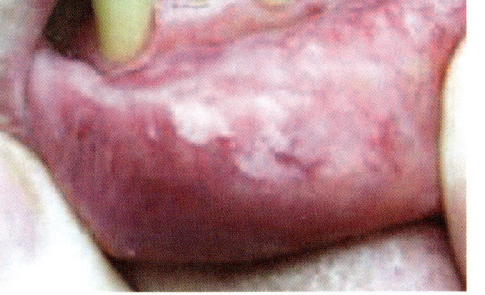

- Affects **women** slightly more than men, and occurs most often in **middle-aged adults**.

- Treatment: intra-oral lesions respond to **TOPICAL STEROIDS**.

Two Forms of Lichen Planus (in addition to the usual form):
  Bullous Lichen Planus-fluid-filled vesicles project from the buccal mucosa surface.

  Erosive Lichen Planus-intensely red or raw-appearing lesions that resemble desquamative gingivitis when they involve the gingiva.

FORDYCE'S GRANULES (ECTOPIC SEBACEOUS GLANDS)– found in the oral mucosa, present in > 75% of adults. Usually appear as **yellow or yellow-white submucosal clusters** that are normal. Rice-like or cauliflower-like whitish-yellow or white asymptomatic papules 1-3mm usually found **BILATERALLY on the buccal mucosa, upper lip vermillion, mandibular retromolar pad, and tonsillar area** (but can be on any oral surface). Surrounding mucosa looks normal, but they can remain constant throughout life.

FORDYCE GRANULES

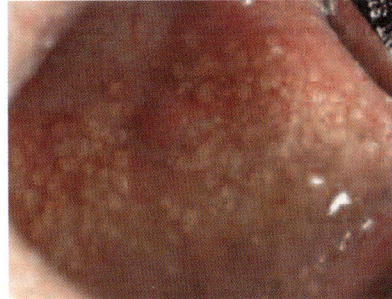
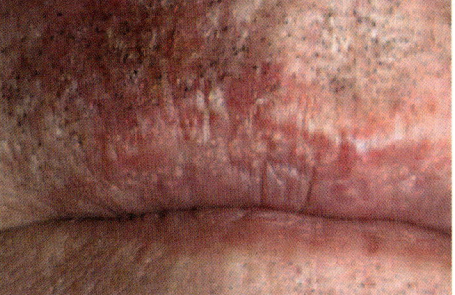

BLOOD DISEASES

PURPURA—HEMORRHAGES in the skin & mucous membranes that cause the appearance of **purplish spots or patches**. Tooth extractions are contraindicated due to potential excessive bleeding. **Two types**:

THROMBOCYTOPENIC PURPURA (Werlhof's Disease)-a bleeding disorder characterized by a **deficiency in the number of platelets**, resulting in multiple bruises, **PETECHIAE**, & hemorrhage into the tissues. May be caused by heparin (warfarin) therapy. Oral manifestations are severe/profuse gingival **hemorrhage, & palatal petechiae**. Petechie can also be caused by streptococcus.

NOTES

PETECHIAE

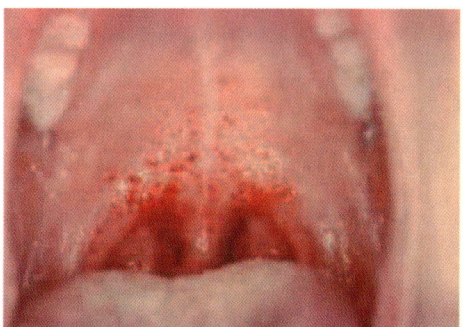

THROMBOCYTOPENIA-dominated clinically by **PETECHIAE cutaneous bleeding**, intra-cranial bleeding, and oozing from mucosal surfaces. Characterized by **decreased platelet count causing prolonged bleeding time**. **THE MOST COMMON CAUSE OF BLEEDING DISORDERS.**

IDIOPATHIC THROMBOCYTOPENIC PURPURA (ITP)-a bleeding disorder due to a deficiency in the number of platelets causing **multiple bruises, petechiae, & hemorrhage** into the tissues. **ITP is a common complication of Leukemia, Aplastic Anemia, & Aggressive Cancer Chemotherpy**.
Bleeding Time is abnormally prolonged in ITP.
THROMBOTIC THROMBOCYTOPENIC PURPURA (TTP)-a severe and frequently fatal form characterized by thrombocytopenia, hemolytic anemia, renal insufficiency, fever, and neurologic abnormalities. **Low platelet count in the blood** and thrombosis in the terminal arterioles and capillaries of many organs.
Purpura-a condition characterized by **hemorrhages in the skin and mucous membranes** that result in the appearance of purplish spots or patches.

Petechiae-small **pinpoint hemorrhages flush with the skin surface.**

Ecchymosis (bruise)-a **discoloration of an area of skin** or mucous membranes due to the extravasation of blood into the subcutaneous tissues due to trauma or hemorrhage.

PROLONGED BLEEDING TIME (Thrombocytopenia) CONDITIONS:
A patient taking **Dicumarol**-inhibits formation of prothrombin in the liver.
A patient taking **Heparin**-acts as an antithrombin by preventing platelet aggregation.
Idiopathic Thrombocytopenic Purpura (ITP)-often associated with leukemia; a decrease in the number of platelets.
Von Willebrand's disease-deficiency of vWF (von Willebrand's factor); results in impaired platelet adhesion.
Long-term treatment with aspirin; aspirin is a cyclooxygenase inhibitor; results in impaired production of thromboxanes, important in platelet aggregation.

AGRANULOCYTOSIS – an abnormal blood condition due to a **severe reduction in the number of granulocytes (NEUTROPHILS)** caused by **ingesting a drug**. It is an acute toxic effect/condition characterized by **pronounced LEUKOPENIA** with a severe reduction in the number of polymorphonuclear leukocytes (PMNs). It is a **toxic effect of certain anti-thyroid drugs** (propylthiouracil, methimazole, carbimazole). Can occur at any age, but is more common in adult females.

- **WBC count is < 2,000 with almost complete absence of PMN** neutrophils (polymorphonuclear leukocytes). Normal WBC count is 4,000-10,000 and neutrophils are usually 50-70%.

- Agranulocytosis begins with a **high fever, chills, and sore throat**. The patient suffers from **malaise, weakness, and prostration**. Skin appears pale and anemic. The most characteristic feature is the presence of an **INFECTION IN THE ORAL CAVITY**. Signs and symptoms develop very rapidly (within a few days), and death may occur soon after.

- Oral lesions (necrotizing ulcerations) are an important phase of the clinical aspects, appearing as **necrotizing ulcerations of the oral mucosa** of the **GINGIVA & HARD PALATE**. These lesions are ragged necrotic ulcers covered by a gray membrane. One important aspect is that there is little or no apparent inflammatory cell infiltration around the lesions. Histologically, the ulcerated lesions do not exhibit polymorphonuclear reaction due to the bacteria in the tissues.

- **Treatment**: **ELIMINATE THE CAUSATIVE DRUG**. Administer antibiotics to control the infection.

SICKLE-CELL ANEMIA (SICKLE-CELL DISEASE) — a chronic, usually fatal inherited form of anemia marked by **crescent-shaped red blood cells**, characterized by fever, leg ulcers, jaundice, and episodic pain in the joints due to the production of **abnormal hemoglobin (Hemoglobin S)** due to a genetic defect.

- Primarily affects **African-Americans** (especially females), and usually manifests before age 30yrs.

- **SCA Signs**: (patient is weak, short of breath, easily fatigued, and muscle and joint pain are common).

- Dental radiographs show **ENLARGED BONE MARROW (MEDULLARY) SPACES** because of loss of many bony trabeculae (but the trabeculae that are present are **abnormally prominent**). Occasionally, osteosclerotic areas are noted in the midst of **large radiolucent marrow spaces**. However, the lamina dura & teeth are unaffected.

SICKLE-CELL ANEMIA (ENLARGED BONE MARROW SPACES)

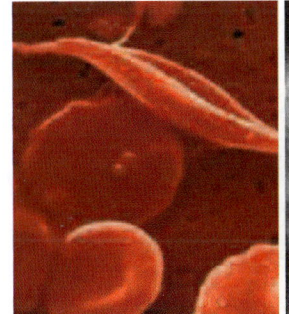 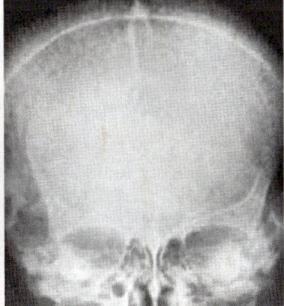 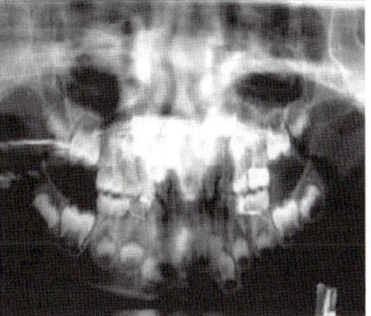

LEUKEMIAS - cancers of mainly **WHITE BLOOD CELLS** with most of unknown cause. LEUKEMIA involves uncontrolled proliferation of leukocytes causing a diffuse and almost **total replacement of the red bone marrow with leukemic cells**. Leukemia is classified by the dominant cell type and by duration from onset to death. It can modify the inflammatory reaction. While the cause is unknown, these **agents are closely associated with leukemia development**:

- **Ionizing radiation**: increased incidence of leukemia among atomic bomb survivors & radiologists, usually myelogenous.

- **Viruses**: shown to cause leukemia in fowl and rodents. Herpes-like viral particles have been cultured from patients with various types of leukemia and leukemic patients have high antibody titer to the Epstein-Barr Virus.

- **Genetic Mutations**: Philadelphia chromosome (translocation of chromosome material between chromosomes 22 and 9) is present in 90% of patients with Chronic Myelogenous Leukemia (CML). Also higher incidence of acute leukemia in patients with Down Syndrome (Mongolism) in which there is Trisomy 21.

- **Other**: chronic exposure to benzol, aniline dyes, and related chemicals.

All LEUKEMIAS occur in an **ACUTE or CHRONIC** form, but 50% are **ACUTE**. Acute Leukemia is the most common malignancies of the pediatric age group (under 20 years).

ORAL MANIFESTATIONS OF LEUKEMIA:
Acute and chronic leukemias of all types cause ORAL LESIONS. **The most common is seen in acute monocytic leukemia** (a subtype of acute myeloid leukemia), where 80% of patients exhibit **GINGIVITIS, GINGIVAL HYPERPLASIA, PETECHIAE, & HEMORRHAGE**. Spontaneous gingival bleeding in acute leukemia is due to **THROMBOCYTOPENIA**.

CLASSES OF LEUKEMIA: All Leukemia occurs in an **ACUTE or CHRONIC** form:

Myelogenous Leukemia-involves **granulocytes & megakaryocytes**. Philadelphia Chromosome and low levels of leukocyte alkaline phosphatase are common findings. **Massive splenomegaly** is characteristic. CML is one of a group of diseases called myeloproliferative disorders. Other diseases in this class are Polycythemia Vera, Myelofibrosis, & Essential Thrombocythemia. **CML is characterized by uncontrolled proliferation of immature granulocytes** (but is the least malignant leukemia). CML accounts for 20% of all adult leukemias (typically affects middle-aged individuals). Although uncommon, CML may occur in younger individuals.

- **CML Clinical Signs**: spongy bleeding gums, fatigue, fever, weight loss, moderate splenomegaly, joint/bone pain, and repeated infections.

- Leukemic cells in 95% of CML patients have a Philadelphia Chromosome which is the result of a reciprocal translocation between chromosomes 9 and 22 which result in a shortened chromosome 22.

- Mean survival time with CML is 4 years with death due to hemorrhage or infection.

Lymphocytic Leukemia-involves **lymphocytes**. Chronic Lymphocytic Leukemia runs a variable course (older patients may survive years even without treatment). **Lymph node enlargement** is the main pathologic finding. May be complicated by autoimmune hemolytic anemia.

Acute lymphocytic (lymphoblastic)-is largely confined to children (the most common leukemia in children). Lymph node enlargement is common. In 75% of cases, the lymphocytesare neither B nor T cells, but are called "null" cells. Bone and joint pain are common.

Monocytic Leukemia-involves **monocytes**. **ORAL LESIONS ARE COMMON** and may be the initial manifestations of the disease. Gingivitis, gingival hemorrhage, generalized gingival hyperplasia, petechiae, ecchymoses, and ulcerations. **Chronic Monocytic Leukemia is VERY RARE**.

Chronic Leukemia (Clinical Features):
- Insidious onset (slow) with weakness and weight loss. May be detected during an examination for another condition (i.e. anemia, unexplained hemorrhages, or recurrent intractable infections).

- Organ involvement is similar to acute leukemia: skin is often involved, and may manifest as petechiae or ecchymoses, recurrent hemorrhages and bacterial infections are common (anemia).

ACUTE LEUKEMIA — has an **abrupt onset** of a few months (not insidious) with fever, weakness, malaise, severe anemia, and generalized lympadenopathy. Untreated patients dies within 6 months (usually due to brain hemorrhage or superimposed bacterial infection). With intensive chemotherapy, radiation, and marrow transplants, **remissions lasting up to 5 years** may be obtained.

- **Clinical Features**: severe anemia, hemorrhages, and slight enlargement of the lymph nodes or spleen. Primary organs involved are bone marrow, spleen (splenomegaly), & liver (hepatomegaly). Petechiae & ecchymoses in skin and mucous membranes, hemorrhage from various sites, and bacterial infections are common.

- **Lab Findings**: leukocytosis 30,000-100,000/mm^3 with immature forms (myeloblasts & lymphoblasts) predominating; anemia and thrombocytopenia, prolonged bleeding and coagulation times, tourniquet test is usually positive.

ACUTE MYELOID/MYELOGENOUS LEUKEMIA (AML) - malignant **BONE MARROW** disease where hematopoietic precursors are arrested in an early stage of development (has an abrupt onset). AML is distinguished from other related blood disorders by the **presence of > 30% MYELOBLASTS** in the blood and/or bone marrow that contain **AUER RODS** in their cytoplasm. THE **MOST MALIGNANT LEUKEMIA**. More common in adults.

POLYCYTHEMIA VERA (PRIMARY ERYTHEMIA):
A **CHRONIC** myeloproliferative condition of **TOO MANY ERYTHROCYTES (RBC)** produced in the circulation due to tumourous abnormalities in tissues that make RBC, making **BLOOD TOO THICK** to pass easily through small blood vessels in the body. This leads to **CLOT FORMATION & BLOCKAGE** of vessels causing a **STROKE** (cerebrovascular accident). Usually accompanied by leukocytosis. **Splenomegaly**, due to vascular congestion, occurs in 75% of patients. Usually occurs within in ages 20-80yrs., with age 60yrs being the mean age of onset.

- **PV Clinical Features**: headache, weakness, weight loss, pruritis, hemorrhage and thrombosis.

- **PV Oral Manifestations**: oral mucous membranes (especially gingiva & tongue) appear deep purplish-red, gingiva is swollen and bleeds easily, and submucosal petechiae (purplish spots), ecchymoses (petechiae, but bigger), and hematomas are common.

- **Secondary Polycythemia** - an increase in the total number of erythrocytes (RBC) due to another condition (i.e. **chronic tissue hypoxia** of advanced pulmonary disease, high altitude (Osker's Disease), or **secretion of erythropoietins** by certain tumors.

NOTES

PLUMMER-VINSON SYNDROME - a rare disorder associated with severe and chronic iron-deficiency ANEMIA occurring mainly in women ages 30-40yrs. Due to the **predisposition to develop carcinoma of the oral mucous membranes**, it is essential to diagnose early, so treatment can be given ASAP (administer iron, vitamin B complex, and a high protein diet).

- **Systemic Symptoms**: weakness, pallor, difficulty swallowing (dysphagia) due to esophageal stricture or web, and difficulty breathing (dyspnea).

- **Oral Symptoms**: angular stomatitis, smooth, red, painful tongue with papillae atrophy.

APLASTIC ANEMIA – a form of anemia where **bone marrow's capacity to produce RBCs is defective. THE MOST SERIOUS & LIFE-THREATENING** blood dyscrasia associated with **drug toxicity**.

- **Primary Anemia**-unknown cause, affects young adults and is usually fatal. **Symptoms**: pallor, weakness, malaise, dyspnea (difficulty breathing), headache, and vertigo. **Oral symptoms**: **spontaneous bleeding, bruising (petechiae), and gingival infections**.

- **Secondary Anemia**-caused by **exposure to toxic agents** (i.e. radiation, chemicals, or drugs like Chloramphenicol). Occurs at any age, with the same symptoms as primary anemia. Prognosis is good after the cause is removed.

PERNICIOUS ANEMIA-a disease caused by an **inability to absorb adequate amounts of vitamin B_{12}** from the digestive tract. A relatively common, chronic, progressive megaloblastic anemia, caused by the **lack of secretion of INTRINSIC FACTOR in normal gastric juice** (intrinsic factor is necessary for adequate vitamin B_{12} absorption, which is required for erythrocyte maturation). As a result fewer than normal RBC are produced. **Lack of intrinsic factor, prevents poor B_{12} absorption leading to low RBC production**.

- **Characterized by a Triad of Symptoms**: weakness, **SORE PAINFUL TONGUE (ATROPHIC GLOSSITIS)**, and tingling of extremities.

ATROPHIC GLOSSITIS (PERNICIOUS ANEMIA)

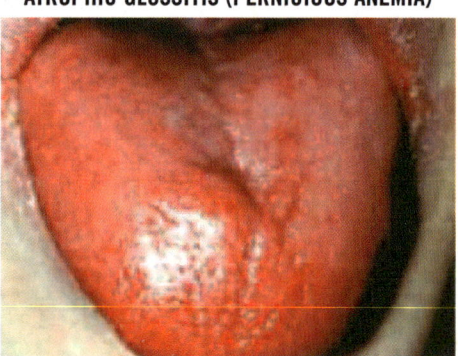

THALASSEMIA MAJOR & MINOR —hemolytic anemias caused by a genetic defect, characterized by a **low level of erythrocytes & abnormal hemoglobin**. **Oral Manifestations**: oral mucosa may exhibit anemic pallor, flaring of maxillary anterior teeth with malocclusion.

ERYTHROBLASTOSIS FETALIS (HEMOLYTIC DISEASE OF NEWBORN) – a severe **hemolytic disease** of the fetus or newborn caused by the production of maternal antibodies for fetal RBC. It usually **involves Rh factor incompatibility between the mother and fetus**. Characterized by excessive **destruction of erythrocytes** due to an antigen-antibody reaction in the infant's bloodstream resulting from the placental transmission of maternally formed antibodies against the incompatible antigens of the fetal blood. In Rh factor incompatibility, the **hemolytic reaction only occurs when the mother is Rh (-) and infant is Rh (+)**.

- Oral Manifestations: teeth have a green, blue, or brown hue due to deposition of blood pigment in enamel and dentin. ENAMEL HYPOPLASIA may occur, affecting the incisal edges of anterior teeth and middle portion of the deciduous canine and first molar crown.

ERYTHROCYTE SEDIMENTATION RATE (ESR) - a non-specific test that only monitors the PROGRESSION OF DISEASE. ESR is the rate at which RBC settle out in a tube of unclotted blood, expressed in mm/hour. Blood is collected in an anticoagulant and allowed to sediment in a calibrated glass column. At the end of one hour, the lab measures the distance the erythrocytes have fallen in the tube. The speed that the RBC fall to the bottom of the tube reflects the degree of inflammation

- Elevated sedimentation rates are not specific for any disorder, but indicate the presence of inflammation. Inflammation causing an alteration of blood proteins that make RBC aggregate, becoming heavier than normal. ESR rises during inflammation, tissue degeneration, suppuration, and necrosis. Certain non-inflammatory conditions (i.e. pregnancy) are also categorized by high sedimentation rates.

WISKOTT-ALDRICH SYNDROME – affects **ONLY BOYS** and causes eczema, low platelet count, and a combined deficiency of B and T lymphocytes that lead to **repeated infections**. Children who survive past age 10 usually develop cancers (lymphoma and leukemia).

EMBOLUS - a mass (**detached BLOOD CLOT = thrombus**), an air bubble or a foreign body that moves within a blood vessel to lodge at a site distant from its place of origin. The danger from an embolus is it can lodge in vascular beds of vital organs, occluding blood flow and causing infarction.
The most common source of a Pulmonary embolism is thrombophlebitis (a thrombus formed within a vein). Femoral vein is the common source of origin of the thrombus which then occludes a blood vessel in the lung.

GINGIVAL HYPERPLASIA: diffuse soft tissue overgrowth affecting both jaws with a pink-to-red color and firm consistency from the mucogingival junction to the free gingival margin.

- Local Factors: can be caused by poor oral hygiene, malocclusion, tooth malformations, caries, faulty restorations, allergens, chronic mouth breathing.

- Systemic Factors: diabetes, hormone changes (puberty and pregnancy), immunoincompetence, gingival fibromatosis, Wegener Granulomatosis, aplastic anemia, leukemia, scurvy, and drugs **PHENYTOIN (DILANTIN), VALPROIC ACID, CYCLOSPORINE, & CALCIUM CHANNEL BLOCKERS (CCBs)** (ex: **NIFEDIPINE** for hypertension and cardiovascular diseases). Other CCB that can cause gingival hyperplasia (Amlodipine, Felodipine, Verapamil, and Diltiazem).

- Develops 1-9 months after Calcium Channel Blocker administration.

- A **biopsy** of constant hyperplasia can rule out a **systemic disease** like **LEUKEMIA**.

- **Gingivectomy** can treat, but it will recur with continued use of most CCBs. **Discontinuing the CCB** usually restores the gingiva to normal size with in one month.

- **Histologic Examination**: epithelial hyperplasia with acanthosis, parakeratosis, and elongated, slender epithelial RETE PEGS and dense C.T. with foci of chronic inflammation.

NEUROLOGIC & MUSCLE DISORDERS

Trigeminal Neuralgia (Tic Douloureux) – an **excruciating, PAINFULL** illness where the person feels sudden stab-like pains in the face that usually last only moments, but **are among the most severe pain humans can feel**. This pain is provoked by touching a "trigger zone" near the nose or mouth, caused by **degeneration of the trigeminal nerve** or by applying pressure to the nerve. Can affect any of the trigeminal's three branches (V_1, V_2, or V_3). The momentary bursts of pain recur in clusters, lasting many seconds. Paroxysmal episodes of the pains may last hours.

- **Drug Treatment**: drug of choice is **Carbamazepine (Tegretol)** which is an analgesic and anticonvulsant that usually relieves the pain within 48hrs. Tegretol is also prescribed to treat certain seizure disorders.

MULTIPLE SCLEROSIS (MS)-a chronic, often disabling disease that randomly **attacks the CNS (brain and spinal cord)** due to an **autoimmune response** where the immune system attacks a person's own tissues. **Women are affected 2x more than men**, with the onset of symptoms occurring usually between ages 20-40yrs (tingling, numbness, paralysis, and blindness). Patients with MS may have **facial and jaw weakness, and Bell's Palsy & Trigeminal** Neuralgia may develop more frequently in MS patients.

GLOSSOPHARYNGEAL NEURALGIA – pain similar to trigeminal neuralgia that arises from the glossopharyngeal nerve (**CN 9**). It is not as common as trigeminal neuralgia, but the pain may be as severe. Occurs in both sexes (middle-aged or elderly). Sharp, sudden, shooting almost always **UNILATERAL** pain in the ear, pharynx, nasopharynx, tonsils, or posterior tongue.

POSTHERPETIC NEURALGIA-a persistent burning, aching, itching, and hyperesthesia along distribution of a cutaneous nerve **after an attack of HERPES ZOSTER**. May last a week or many months. Involves **FACIAL NERVE (CN 7) & geniculate ganglion** that produces Ramsey Hunt Syndrome (facial paralysis & otalgia/earache).

MYASTHENIA GRAVIS – a chronic condition of **EXTREME MUSCLE WEAKNESS** due to an **autoimmune disorder** where the body creates antibodies against its own nicotinic ACh (acetylcholine) receptors in the **neuromuscular junctions**. The muscles are quickly fatigued with repetitive use. It is typical for the patient to have a **flattened smile and DROOPY EYES** with slow papillary light responses (double vision). **XEROSTOMIA & RAMPANT CARIES** may be present because acetylcholine needed for proper transmission of nerve impulses is destroyed, so salivary glands do not receive adequate stimulation.

- Immune system produces autoantibodies that attack Acetylcholine receptors that lie on the muscle side of the neuromuscular junction causing dysfunction of the myoneural junction (the neuromuscular junction functions abnormally causing muscle weakness). **This decreases the responsiveness of the muscle fibers to acetylcholine** released from motor neuron endings. **Difficulty speaking and swallowing, and weakness of the arms and legs** are common (muscles of the face, neck, arms, and legs are affected).

- 10% of people develop a life-threatening weakness of the breathing muscles (a condition called myasthenic crisis).

- Drugs that increase the level of acetylcholine (e.g. **pyridostigmine or neostigmine**) may be given for treatment.

EATON-LAMBERT SYNDROME — similar to myasthenia gravis in that it is an autoimmune disease causing weakness, but due to the **inadequate RELEASE of acetylcholine** rather than by abnormal antibodies that attack acetylcholine receptors as in Myasthenia Gravis.

FREY'S SYNDROME (AURICULOTEMPORAL SYNDROME)—an uncommon phenomenon due to **damage to the auriculotemporal nerve** and subsequent reinnervation of the sweat glands by parasympathetic salivary fibers. **Can occur after surgery** (i.e. removal of a parotid tumor, ramus of the mandible, or infection of the parotid that has damaged the auriculotemporal nerve (branch of V_3). **Gustatory sweating is the chief complaint**. Patient exhibits flushing and sweating of the involved side of the face during eating.

BELL'S PALSY —**facial paralysis from damage to the FACIAL NERVE (CN7)**. Can occur at any age, but disproportionately **attacks pregnant women, diabetics, and people with influenza, cold, or other upper respiratory infection**.

- **Clinical Signs**: **unilateral paralysis of all facial muscles** with loss of eyebrow & forehead wrinkles, drooping of eyebrows, flattening of the nasiolabial furrow, sagging of the mouth corner, and inability to frown or raise the eyebrows. The upper and lower lips may also be paralyzed on the affected side. **Drooping mouth on one side with a watering eye, loss of taste sensation on the anterior portion of the tongue** may occur.

- Sudden onset, but **paralysis begins to subside in 2-3 weeks**, and gradual, complete recovery occurs in > 85% of patients.

- **Important**: While giving an inferior alveolar block, **if you inject anesthetic solution into the parotid gland capsule, you may cause a Bell's Palsy-like feeling by anesthetizing the facial nerve.**

NON-ODONTOGENIC CYSTS

CONGENITAL CYSTS:
- **Branchiogenic Cyst**-arises from the persistence of the **second branchial arch cleft**. This cyst is **located** along the **anterior border of the sternocleidomastoid muscle at any level in the neck**. The cyst is lined with ciliated and striated squamous epithelium, and contains a milky/ mucoid fluid. **Treatment**: complete surgical excision.

- **Dermoid Cyst**-relatively uncommon cyst in the oral cavity. This cyst often contains hair, sebaceous and sweat glands, and tooth structures. The most common site is the **MOUTH FLOOR**. **Treatment**: complete surgical excision.

- **Thyroglossal Duct Cyst**-may arise from any part of the thyroglossal duct. Found in a midline position and is usually **dark colored, and** may be vascular **resembling a hemangioma**. Hemorrhage into the mouth is a **common and important symptom** caused by rupturing of the overlying veins. **Treatment**: complete excision of the tract to the base of the tongue (often including part of the hyoid bone).

FISSURAL CYSTS (DEVELOPMENTAL CYSTS)

Non-Odontogenic Cysts: (Nasopalatine, Nasoalveolar, Median Palatal, and Globulomaxillary cysts).

NASOPALATINE DUCT CYST (Incisive Canal Cyst)-**OVAL** or **"HEART-SHAPED"** radiolucency in the **midline of the hard palate**. Most common **non-odontogenic/developmental/fissural cyst**. Usually asymptomatic (but patient may complain of tender swelling of the palate), or may produce an elevation in the anterior part of the palate. Teeth are vital. **Treatment**: surgical excision/enucleation. Prognosis is excellent. Occurs in bone (intra-osseous).

Radiographic Features: a circular (round) well-demaracated oval or heart-shaped radiolucency between and above the **MAXILLARY CENTRAL INCISORS** (rarely just lateral to the midline) on a radiograph clinically seen as a marked swelling in the region of the palatine papilla, situated distal to the roots of the central incisors. The pulps of the anterior teeth are vital. **The lesion crosses the midline**. Do not confuse with an enlarged palatine foramen.

Cysts that arise from epithelial remnants in the incisive canal are the most common type of maxillary developmental cyst. Histologically, it's walls are lined with vessels, nerves, and mucous glands (remnants of nasopalatine ducts within bone). They most often remain limited in size and are asymptomatic. Some however, become infected or have a tendency to grow extensively. When this occurs, surgical intervention is indicated.

NASOPALATINE DUCT CYST (INCISIVE CANAL CYST) = HEART SHAPED

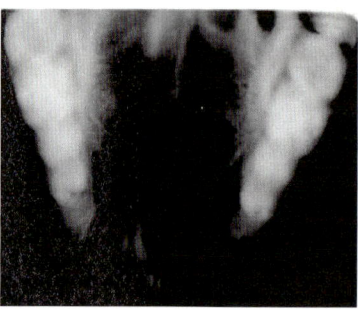
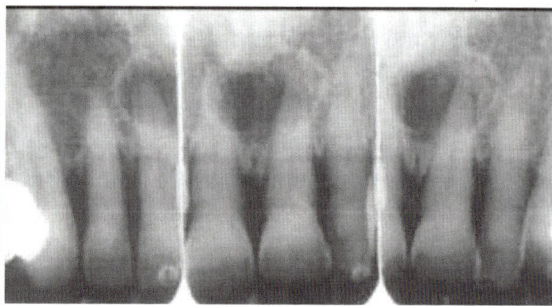

Palatine Papilla Cyst-the soft tissue (and much less common) variant of the Nasopalatine Duct Cyst.

NASOLABIAL CYST (Nasoalveolar Cyst)-a soft tissue cyst of the **UPPER LIP** (extra-osseous cyst) superficially located in soft tissue of the upper lip that histologically develops from epithelial remnants from the inferior and anterior portion of the nasolacrimal duct.

- **Clinical Characteristics**: swelling below or inside the **NOSTRIL** that may present in the canine region. **CANNOT SEE THIS CYST ON A RADIOGRAPH**, but may produce "cupping" of underlying bone. **NOT WITHIN BONE (extra-osseous)** so **cannot** be seen on a radiograph. **Treatment**: Enucleation (surgical excision). Excellent prognosis.

GLOBULOMAXILLARY CYST- an **inverted "PEAR-SHAPED" radiolucency** in bone between the roots of the maxillary lateral & canine (**often causes roots of the involved teeth to DIVERGE**).

- **Clinical Features**: usually **asymptomatic**, but occasionally produces **swelling** with or without pain. All regional **teeth are vital**. Occurs **within bone** (intra-osseous).

- **Histologic Features**: consists of epithelial remnants where the globular & maxillary processes are fused.

- **Radiographic Features**: inverted **PEAR-SHAPED radiolucency** between the maxillary lateral & canine roots. Teeth are **vital**, but roots may be **divergent**. Do **not** confuse with a **Lateral Periodontal Cyst**.

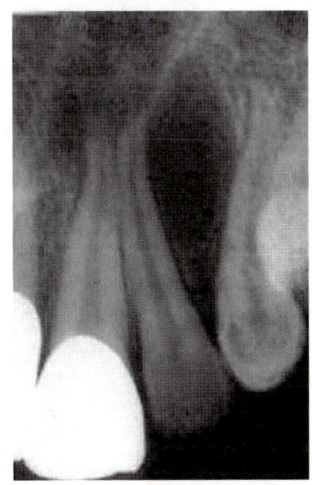

GLOBULOMAXILLARY CYST PEAR-SHAPED

Treatment: Enucleation without disturbing the teeth. Excellent prognosis.

MEDIAN PALATAL CYST- rare, but may occur anywhere along the **MEDIAN PALATAL RAPHE, usually in the HARD PALATE MIDLINE, posterior to the pre-maxilla** (occurs in bone; intra-osseous). May produce **swelling on the palate**. Clinically, this lesion presents as a **firm, painless swelling**. This cyst may represent a more posterior version of a Nasopalatine Duct Cyst, rather than a separate cystic degeneration of epithelial rests at the line of fusion of the palatine shelves.

Histologic Features: epithelial remnants in the line of fusion between the palatine processes. Appears as a **soft**, fluctuant or crepitant **swelling in the hard palate midline**.

Radiographic Features: well-demarcated radiolucency in the midline of the hard palate.

Treatment: Enucleation with an excellent prognosis.

Median Alveolar Cyst- rare, but occurs in the bony alveolus (intraosseous) between the central incisors. Distinguished from a periapical cyst by the fact that the adjacent teeth are vital. Treatment: enucleation.

ODONTOGENIC CYSTS

LATERAL PERIODONTAL CYST-inflammatory in origin. Forms **along the vital tooth's LATERAL surface** (95% form along the mandibular canine-premolar area). If it forms at the **root apex**, it is a **Radicular Cyst**. Apposition with the root of a vital tooth. Usually asymptomatic.

- **Radiographic Features**: well-defined, **round or tear-drop shaped radiolucency** with an **opaque margin** along the lateral surface of a tooth.

- **Histologic Features**: thin lining of non-keratinized epithelium.

LATERAL PERIODONTAL CYST

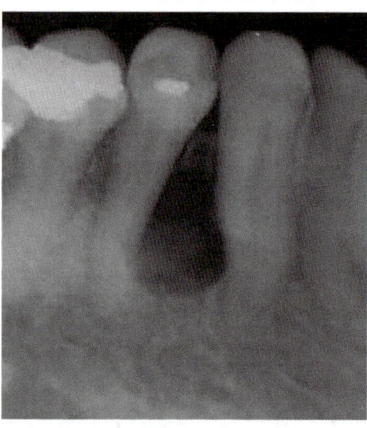

RADICULAR CYST (APICAL PERIODONTAL CYST OR PERIAPICAL CYST)-the **MOST COMMON ODONTOGENIC CYST**, mainly found at the **ROOT APEX**. It develops within a pre-existing periapical dental granuloma. Increased osmotic pressure in the cyst lumen is important in its pathogenesis. **Clinical Features**: asymptomatic, **tooth is NECROTIC**; can be **sensitive to percussion**.

- **Radiographic Features**: well-circumscribed radiolucency at the tooth apex.

- **Histologic Features**: exhibits a lumen (true cyst) invariably lined by stratified squamous epithelium. The cyst wall is condensed C.T. with plasma cells, lymphocytes, and PMN leukocytes.

- **Treatment**: RCT with apicoectomy, or extraction with socket curettage.

RADICULAR CYST

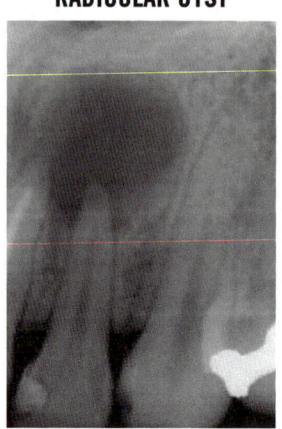

RESIDUAL CYST-occurs when a tooth with a radicular (periapical) cyst is extracted, but the radicular cyst is left undisturbed and persists within the jaw now as a residual cyst. To prevent a residual cyst, you must **CURETTE** the radicular cyst out of the tooth socket after extraction. Equally affects males and female at any age. Usually asymptomatic, and is found in **EDENTULOUS** areas. It is a radicular cyst left in the jaw after a tooth extraction.

- **Radiographic Features**: well-defined radiolucency not associated with a tooth. Usually solitary.

- **Histological Features**: same as a radicular cyst (apical periodontal cyst), of stratified squamous epithelium lining the lumen.

DENTAL GRANULOMA —the **MOST COMMON SEQUELAE OF PULPITIS AT THE ROOT APEX**. Only distinguished from a radicular cyst histologically.

- **Clinical Features**: asymptomatic, **NECROTIC TOOTH**, but may be percussion sensitive.

- **Radiographic Features**: circumscribed radiolucency at the tooth apex.

- **Histologic Features**: lined by stratified squamous epithelium. Cyst wall is fibrous C.T. with **macrophages, lymphocytes, cells, and capillaries**.

- **Treatment**: RCT or extraction of the involved tooth.

DENTIGEROUS CYST (FOLLICULAR CYST) – an odontogenic cysts always associated with the crown of an **UNERUPTED** or **DEVELOPING** tooth or dental anomaly (ex: odontoma). Most commonly found with a **developing 3rd molar**. Can cause marked displacement of teeth due to pressure of accumulated fluid that usually displaces the tooth apically. If a tooth with a dentigerous cysts begins to erupt, **the bulging the cyst produces on the ridge is an eruption cyst**.

- **Clinical Features**: found in **children & teenagers** in mandibular 3rd molar & maxillary canine area (70% in the mandible). Associated with impacted or unerupted teeth. **The 2nd most common odontogenic cyst**.

- **Radiographic Features**: well-defined, unilocular radiolucency.

- **Histologic Features**: lined by non-keratinized, stratified squamous epithelium with **NO** rete-pegs.

- An ameloblastoma is most likely to develop in the wall of a dentigerous cyst.

DENTIGEROUS CYST

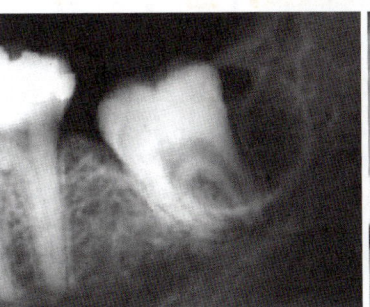
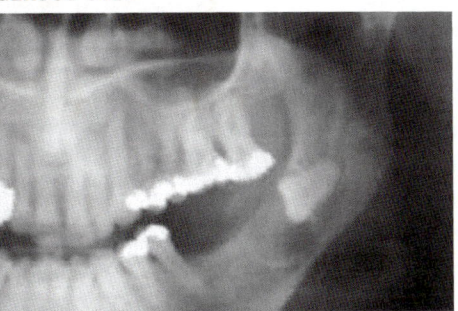

ERUPTION CYST – a **soft-tissue variant** of the dentigerous cyst, invariably associated with an erupting tooth (usually primary, but occasionally permanent teeth). Mainly effects overlying gingival tissues, not bone.

- **Clinical Features**: usually a smooth-surface lesion that is **REDDISH-PINK or BLUISH-PINK-BLACK**, fluctuant, localized swelling of the **ALVEOLAR RIDGE** over the crown of an erupting primary or permanent molar. The intense bluish color is due to accumulation of blood. Due to this appearance, it can be mistaken for a hemangioma or hematoma.

ERUPTION CYST

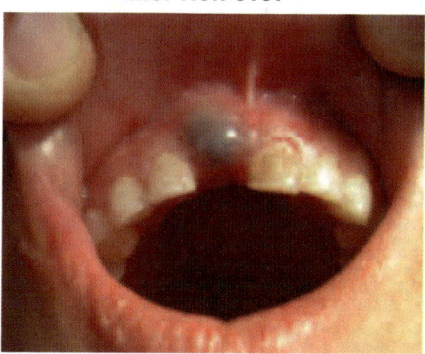

- **Treatment**: usually NO treatment is necessary. In rare cases, incision or removal of the overlying tissue may be required due to pain or tenderness associated with the cyst.

PRIMORDIAL CYST (FOLLICULAR CYST) – a **well-defined, oval radiolucent lesion** that differs from periodontal and dentigerous cysts since it **contains no calcified structures**. Located in the **MANDIBULAR 3rd molar space**. It may be locular, multilocular, or multiple. This cyst is **found in place of a tooth** rather than directly associated with a tooth. Equally affects males and females under age 25yrs.

- **Histologic Features**: lined by stratified squamous epithelium; no rete pegs (arises from epithelium of the enamel organ).

ODONTOGENIC KERATOCYST – follicular & dentigerous cysts that contain keratinizing material, and differs from other odontogenic cysts due to their microscopic appearance & clinical behavior. **Keratocysts may resemble periodontal, primordial, or follicular cysts, and usually CANNOT be distinguished radiographically.** The most remarkable feature is their **GREAT TENDENCY TO REOCCUR (over 30% reoccur)**. Usually occurs between ages 10-30yrs. Often associated with an impacted tooth. **50% are found in the mandibular 3rd molar area**.

- Keratocysts increase in size mainly by a process of epithelial cell multiplication.

- **Radiographic Features**: well-circumscribed radiolucency with smooth margins, and thin radiopaque borders.

- **Histologic Features**: thin layer of corrugated parakeratin. Uniform thin stratified squamous lining. Distinct cuboidal to columnar basal layer with varying amounts of keratin debris in the lumen.

- **Treatment**: excision of the overlying mucosa in the area where the cyst wall is adhered.

TRAUMATIC BONE CYST – may be completely devoid of solid or liquid material (but may contain blood, fluid, debris, or be completely empty). It is **most commonly found in younger people** with no sex predilection, in the **MANDIBLE BETWEEN THE CANINE & RAMUS**. Regional teeth are vital.

Clinical Case: a large radiolucent area on the mandible apical to the premolars and molars on a panorex. No clinical symptoms. Teeth are not carious and respond normally to vitality tests. Medical history is unremarkable. No fluid or tissue is evident.

GINGIVAL CYST – a rare, circumscribed **swelling** of the gingiva usually found in the **canine & premolar areas on the mandible**. Usually limited to the gingiva, but larger cysts may erode the bone. Gingival cysts are **easily excised**.

NON-ODONTOGENIC TUMORS

FIBROUS DYSPLASIA – a rare, GENETIC abnormal condition that affects young people (15-30 years) characterized by the fibrous replacement of the osseous tissues in affected bones. The cause is unknown. Demonstrates typical **"GROUND GLASS" appearance of bone**, thus if this appearance is seen, additional tests like a **skull radiograph & blood chemistries are performed** to help diagnose. Characterized by **normal bone replaced** by fibrous tissue. Three types exist depending on the extensiveness of bone involvement:

Monostotic-involves one bone.
Polyostotic-involves more than one bone.
Albright's Syndrome-involves more than one bone with endocrine disturbances. Pathologic fractures are the chief complaint.

FIBROUS DYSPLASIA (GROUND-GLASS)

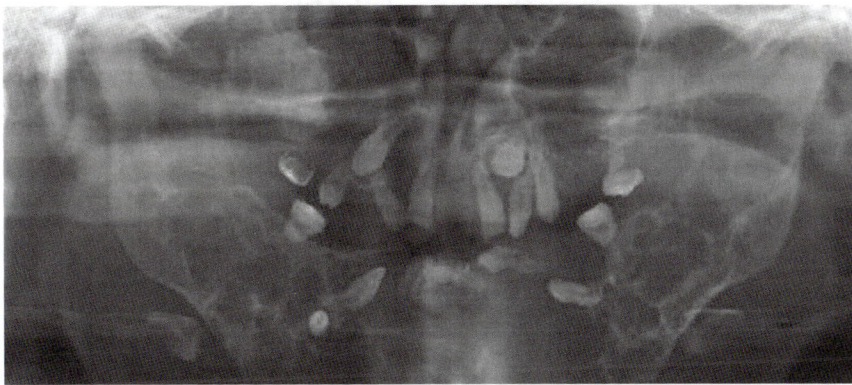

Fibrous Dysplasia is a **symptomatic alteration of bone (SWELLING MASS OF BONE OCCURS)**. Normal bone is **replaced by fibrous tissue & non-functional bony trabeulae (teeth may look like they are moving or displaced due to bone growing tissue)**. Panorex shows typical **"GROUND-GLASS" BONY APPEARANCE**. Thus, ground-glass is seen, perform additional diagnostic tests (skull radiograph & blood chemistries) to confirm the diagnosis.

- **Fibrous Dysplasia Treatment**: **SURGERY** to remove the area when the lesion stops growing. Benign osseous lesions were treated with radiotherapy, but this may produce osteogenic sarcoma (bone cancer), so do not want to radiate benign bone.

- **Radiographic**: when mature it has a **radiopaque "GROUND-GLASS"** appearance (diffuse/not well-defined, mixed radiopaque-radiolucent areas). **MAIN CHARACTERISTIC is you never see the lesion's borders (it blends with the bone).**

THREE TYPES OF FIBROUS DYSPLASIA:

1. **Monostotic Fibrous Dysplasia**-the most common form of fibrous dysplasia (80%) that affects children & young adults (both sexes equally). This form affects one bone (ribs & femur are common sites). The jaws are also commonly affected (mainly the maxilla, presenting as a painless swelling/bulge). A panorex reveals a radiopaque mass/lesion with irregular borders (poorly defined margins) with "ground/frosted glass" appearance. When several adjacent bones are affected, it is called "Craniofacial Fibrous Dysplasia".

   - A differential diagnosis of fibrous dysplasia of the jaws is Ossifying Fibroma. However, radiographically, an ossifying fibroma has a well-circumscribed appearance.

   - Often causes **expansion** and **deformity** of the **jawbone** and **tooth displacement**. There is radiographic characteristic **thickening at the skull base**. The lesion is usually **diffuse and radiopaque with "ground-glass" appearance radiographically**. Malignant transformation is possible if treated with radiation therapy, so **treatment usually consists of SURGICAL removal when possible**. However, since these lesions are not well-circumscribed, surgical recontouring is done to remove the portion of the lesion causing the **facial deformity**.

2. **Polyostotic Fibrous Dysplasia**-usually displays a **segmental distribution** of the involved bones (**multiple bones**). Occurs during childhood (mainly females who reach puberty prematurely). Affects **long bones, face, clavicles, and pelvic bones**. Initial signs may be a **limp, pain, or fracture** on the affected side.

3. **Albright's Syndrome (McCune-Albright Syndrome)**-a disease of **unknown cause** affecting the bones (bone disease), **skin pigmentation (irregular brown spots/skin pigmentation)**, and causing premature sexual development (endocrine problems). The extent of these problems varies depending on the individual. **Hallmark sign is FEMALE PREMATURE PUBERTY** (early sexual development in the male is less common). Affects young people (males & females equally). **Albright's is THE MOST SEVERE form of polyostotic fibrous dysplasia (involves multiple bones) with endocrine involvement**.

   - <u>Triad of Symptoms</u>: **polyostotic fibrous dysplasia, Café-au-lait brown skin spots, & endocrine abnormalities** (most common is **precocious sexual development in females**), and **pathologic bone fractures**. Malignant transformation potential of polyostotic (mainly) & monostotic fibrous dysplasias into osteosarcomas is an additional complication.

   - <u>Treatment</u>: No treatment. Drugs that **inhibit estrogen production** (Testolactone) have been used with some success.

GARDNER'S SYNDROME – a **polyposis syndrome** inherited in a **dominant** manner. The most serious complication of is **multiple (thousands) of POLYPS that affect the large intestine, duodenum, colon, and stomach**. The polyps usually appear around age 15yrs. and **eventually become malignant** eventually causing **COLON CANCER**.

- <u>Oral Findings</u>: multiple **ODONTOMAS**, multiple impacted & **supernumerary teeth** (like Cleidocranial Dysostosis), and **multiple jaw osteomas** giving a **"COTTON-WOOL" (LIKE PAGET'S DISEASE)** appearance to the jaws by appearing as dense, **well-circumscribed radiopacities**. Associated with **bony tumors** in the **jaw and skull**. When GS is suspected based on oral findings, **refer the patient to a Gastroenterologist**.

- Multiple desmoid tumors (fibromatosis), and epidermoid skin cysts may also occur.

GARDNER'S SYNDROME: MULTIPLE JAW OSTEOMAS WITH "COTTON WOOL" APPEARANCE

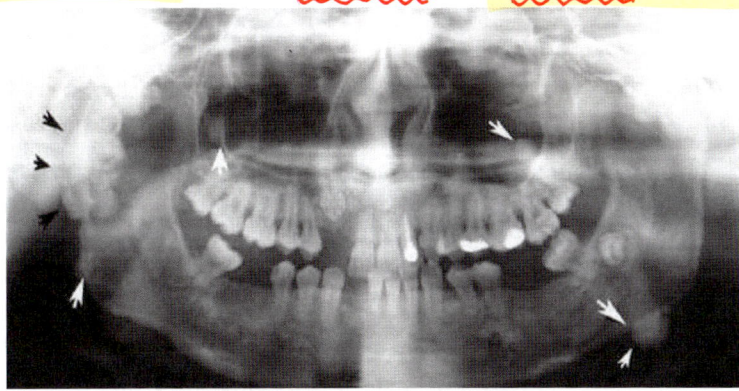

GARDNER'S SYNDROME (GI POLYPS)

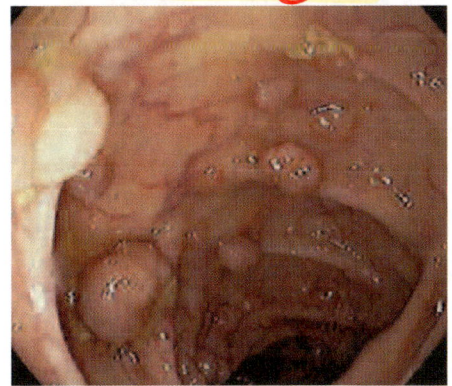

CENTRAL GIANT CELL GRANULOMA – a **BENIGN tumor** (accounts for < 7% of all benign jaw tumors). Occurs almost **exclusively in the JAWBONES** after **TRAUMA** (fall, blow, or tooth extraction). Occurs mainly in children or young adult ages **0-20yrs** (more common in **females**), and either jaw may be involved (but affects the mandible more).

- Most common in **ANTERIOR SEGMENT (SYMPHYSIS OF MANDIBLE)** of **females** during **0-20 years of age**. May sometimes cross the midline.

- Pain is not a main feature of this lesion. **Slight to moderate bulging of the jaw** due to expansion of the cortical plates occurs in the involved area depending on the extent of bone involvement.

- **Radiographic Findings**: unilocular or multi-locular radiolucencies of bone with well-defined margins (similar to ameloblastoma & odontogenic keratocyst).

- Histologically, has loose fibrillar C.T. Multi-nucleated giant cells are prominent throughout the C.T.

- **Treatment**: **Curettage or surgical excision**. These lesions fill in with new bone after excision.

NOTES

CENTRAL GIANT CELL GRANULOMA

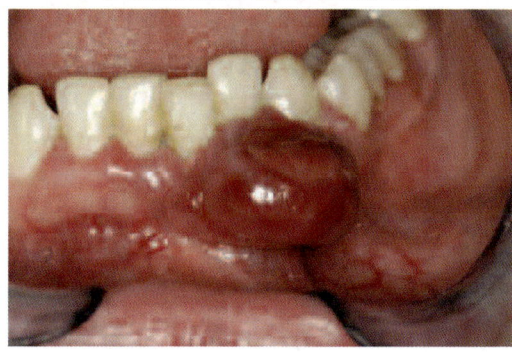

CENTRAL GIANT CELL GRANULOMA
WELL-DEMARCATED RADIOLUCENT LESION BETWEEN TEETH 22 & 23

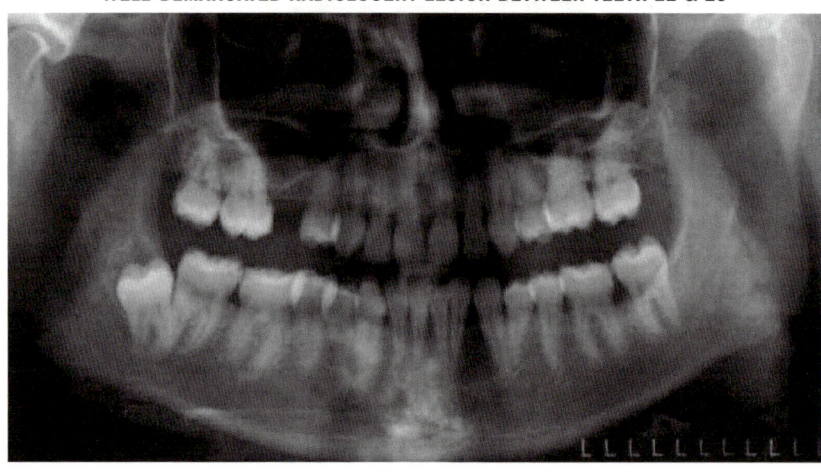

MANDIBULAR TORI (TORUS MANDBULARIS) —bony exophytic growths that occur along the lingual surface of the mandible, superior to the mylohyoid ridge. Mandibular tori most often appear on the **LINGUAL SURFACE** of the mandible, usually in the **PREMOLAR** REGION.

- Mandibular tori may occur singly, but there is a **marked tendency toward bilateral occurrence**, and the lesion is not always confined to the premolar region. Unlike palatal tori, **mandibular tori are more readily demonstrated radiographically**.

- Maxillary (palatal) & mandibular tori are **NOT** pathologic, and are rarely of clinical significance while teeth are still present. However, **if a complete denture must be made, tori should be carefully removed**.

EXOSTOSIS (TORI) – slow-growing, benign knots of bone on the hard palate (palatal or mandibular tori). Exostosis are the most common exophytic lesions.

TORI (EXOSTOSIS)

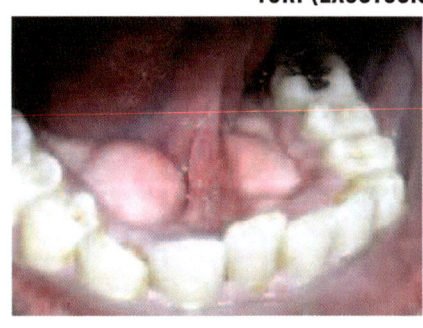 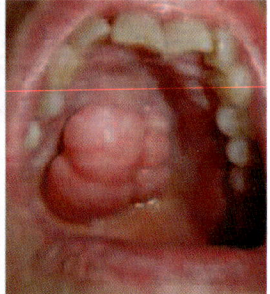

CONDYLAR HYPERPLASIA – a rare, **UNILATERAL enlargement of the condyle** of unknown cause. May be due to mild, chronic inflammation that stimulates the growth of the condyle or adjacent tissues. Afflicted patients usually exhibit a **unilateral, slowly progressive elongation of the face** with **deviation of the chin AWAY from the affected side**. The affected TMJ may or may not be painful, and there is usually **severe malocclusion**.

CONDYLAR HYPOPLASIA & APLASIA – can occur **unilaterally or bilaterally**. If unilateral, there is obvious **facial asymmetry**, which may **alter occlusion** and **mastication**. If unilateral, the mandible **shifts TOWARD the affected side** during **opening**. In bilateral cases, there is no shift.

CENTRAL OSSIFYING FIBROMA – **SLOW-GROWING, PAINLESS, BENIGN**, asymptomatic neoplasm (tumor)/lesion that **may occur in the MAXILLA or MANDIBLE**. Due to its slow growth, the cortical plates of bone and overlying mucosa or skin are almost **always** invariably intact. **Most commonly involves only ONE bone (Paget's Disease, however, involves multiple bones)**.

- May occur at any age, **but is far more common in YOUNG ADULTS**. It has an extremely variable radiographic appearance depending on its stage of development. However, despite the stage of development, the lesion **is always WELL-CIRCUMSCRIBED and demarcated from surrounding bone** (in contrast to fibrous dysplasia). **In its early stage, it is a RADIOLUCENT area, but as it matures, it becomes a uniform radiopaque mass**.

- **Early Clinical Feature**: **TEETH DISPLACEMENT**.

- Amazing similarity clinically exists between a Central **Ossifying** Fibroma & Central **Cementifying** Fibroma (a tumor of odontogenic origin). These are **two separate benign tumors**, identical in nature **except** for the cell undergoing proliferation (**the osteoblast with bone formation in COF, and cementoblast with cementum formation in the CCF**). **Treatment**: conservative excision. Recurrence is rare.

CENTRAL OSSIFYING FIBROMA

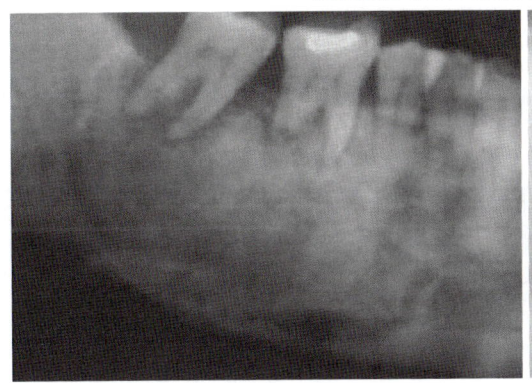
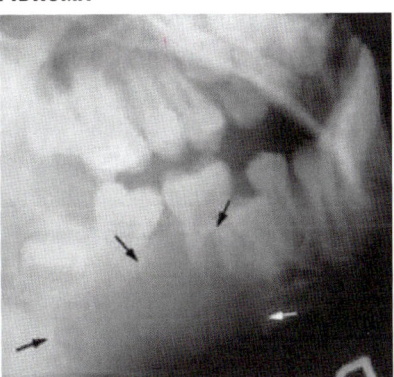

HISTIOCYTOSIS X—disorders where **abnormal scavenger immune system cells histiocytes (macrophages), and eosinophils proliferate in the bone and lungs, CAUSING SCARS TO FORM.** Three diseases are grouped under the generic term Histiocytosis, and occur **due to metabolic defects in the reticuloendothelial system**, and are characterized by proliferation of histiocytes (macrophages) of loose C.T.

1. **EOSINOPHILLIC GRANULOMA-** the **MOST BENIGN FORM** of Histiocytosis X more common in **males ages 20-40yrs**. It **may be totally asymptomatic, but there may be local pain or swelling, especially if a bone fracture occurs**. In the mouth, the mandible is most likely affected with **teeth on the affected side being loose and gingivitis**. When the LUNGS are affected, the symptoms may include coughing, shortness of breath, & weight loss. Pneumothorax is a common complication. <u>Radiographic Features</u>: lesion appears as irregular radiolucent areas involving superficial alveolar bone. Jaw lesions usually appear as single or multiple radiolucencies that may be so well-circumscribed, as to resemble cysts or periapical granulomas.

   - <u>Treatment</u>: bone lesions often resolve spontaneously, and do not require treatment unless they cause symptoms. Curettage provides diagnostic biopsy material and is curative.

2. <u>**LETTERER-SIWE DISEASE (Acute Disseminated Form)**</u>-starts before age 3yrs and is usually **FATAL** without treatment. Histiocytes damage the **lungs (pneumothorax may occur), skin, lymph glands, bone, liver, and spleen**. Oral lesions are uncommon.

3. <u>**Hand-Schuller-Cristian Disease (Chronic Disseminated Form)**</u>-usually begins in early childhood (more common in boys). <u>Triad of Symptoms</u>: exophthalmos, diabetes insipidus, & bone destruction (skull and jaws). <u>Oral signs</u>: bad breath, sore mouth, loose teeth.

<u>Treatment</u>: people with Hand-Schuller-Christian Disease or Eosinophilic Granuloma may recover spontaneously. **All three disorders may be treated with corticosteroids & cyto-toxic drugs** (ex: Cyclophosphamide). Use **radiation therapy if there is bone involvement**. Death usually results from respiratory or heart failure.

<u>**VERRUCIFORM XANTHOMA ("HISTIOCYTOSIS Y")**</u> – a **benign soft tissue tumor** that presents as a normal or white colored verrucous lesion. Its cause is UNKNOWN, as it is not associated with any systemic condition. In adults, the **alveolar and palatal mucosa are the common sites**.

- <u>Histologic Features</u>: verrucous, hyperparakeratotic surface with parakeratotic plugging. Large "foam" cells in C.T. papillae between elongated rete ridges.

- <u>Treatment</u>: simple excision; no recurrence.

ODONTOGENIC TUMORS

AMELOBLASTOMA-tumors of odontogenic epithelial origin and **MOST COMMON EPITHELIAL (ECTODERMAL) ODONTOGENIC TUMOR!** (its occurrence equals the frequency of all other odontogenic tumors combined). Consists entirely of odontogenic epithelium that shows the differentiation of the familiar, histologic layers of the enamel organ at sites. **Enlargement of the tumor may expand the buccal, lingua cortical plates of bone, or palatal bone plates.** Root resorption of teeth adjacent to the tumor is common, and in many cases an **UNERUPTED, MANDIBULAR 3rd MOLAR** is associated with the **radiolucent defect**. Ameloblastomas are slow-growing, locally invasive tumors that usually **run a benign course** (do not infiltrate). Often **asymptomatic, a painless swelling or expansion of the jaw is the usual clinical presentation**. Ameloblastomas occur in three different clinical-radiographic situations with different treatments & prognosis:

AMELOBLASTOMA

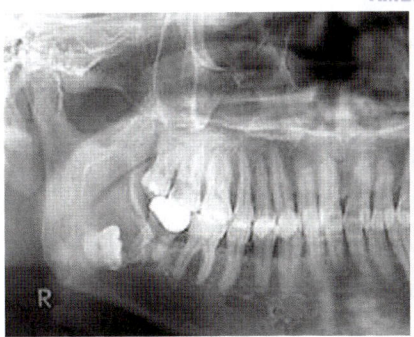
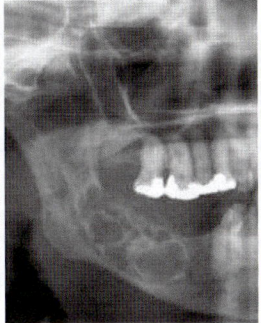

Ameloblastoma is **often associated with unerupted teeth mainly in the posterior body and angle of the mandible** (but can be in the maxilla). Looks like a multi-loculated "**SOAP-BUBBLE**" appearance on a panorex. **BENIGN TUMOR of ODONTOGENIC ORIGIN that is usually painless**. Can cause severe facial/jaw abnormalities due to its growth potential which destroys surrounding bone. **Treatment: SURGICAL EXICISION**.

- **Histogenesis**: may arise from rests of the dental lamina, epithelial lining of a dentigerous cyst, basal cells of the oral epithelium (mucosa), developing enamel organ, and possibly remnants of Hertwig's sheath. **Consists entirely of odontogenic epithelium** that shows the differentiation of the histologic layers of the enamel organ at sites.

- **Clinical Features**: most often seen in **adolescents** in the mandibular (retro) molar area. **THE MOST AGGRESSIVE ODONTOGENIC TUMOR that is usually benign**, but often shows a **highly expansive** and locally **invasive** mode of growth.

- **Ameloblastoma Radiographic Features**: multi-locular or uni-locular **RADIOLUCENT** lesion on **vital teeth** with a **"soap bubble" appearance** when the radiolucent loculations are large & honeycombed when the loculations are small. Has **irregular-scalloped margins**. Appears similar to a **Central Giant Cell Granuloma** in the mandible.

- **Microscopic Features**: various microscopic patterns of the tumor include the **follicular** (most common pattern of multiple islands with reverse polarity) & **plexiform** (also the most common pattern of large anastomosing cords), **cystic, acanthomatous** (extensive squamous metaplasia, keratin formation in central portions of epithelial islands), **granular cell** (cells with prominent granular cytoplasm), **desmoplastic** (thin cords), & **basal cell** (islands of hyperchromatic basaloid cells) patterns. **All are non-encapsulated**.

- **Treatment**: varies depending on the subtype. Recurrence is common (50-90%) if inadequately treated. Very rarely metastasizes.

ADENOMATOID ODONTOGENIC TUMOR (ADENOAMELOBLASTOMA) – a **BENIGN** tumor of **ectodermal origin (purely epithelial)** representing 3-7% of all odontogenic tumors. Limited to **CHILDREN & TEENAGERS** (10-19yrs), and **uncommon** in patients **older** than **30yrs**. Not a variant of ameoloblastoma (best classified as a **hamartoma; benign**, not a true neoplasm). Occurs mainly in the **ANTERIOR MAXILLA** (2x more common in maxilla than mandible) and **affects females 2x more** than males. Affects 2nd decade (teenagers). Asymptomatic or painless swelling.

- **Clinical Features**: most are **small** (< 3cm diameter). Clinically **looks like a gingival fibrous lesion**. Often **asymptomatic, circumscribed, unilocular radiolucency** associated with the crown of an **UNERUPTED** tooth (**mostly canines**). Radiolucency **sometimes extends apically along the root past the CEJ** (helps distinguish it from a dentigerous cyst). May be completely radiolucent, but often contains fine **snowflake calcifications** (tiny radiopaque foci).

- **Histology**: well-defined lesion surrounded by a thick, fibrous capsule. Enamel organ, lining of dentigerous cyst, reduced enamel epithelium, Rests of Malessez. Derived from ectoderm (epithelial) enamel organ and remanants of dental lamina. Tumor is composed of spindle-shaped epithelial cells that form sheets, strands, or whorled masses of cells in a scant fibrous stroma.

- **Treatment**: completely benign, and its capsule allows it to enucleate easily from bone (enucleation). Recurrence is rare, and is not aggressive.

CALCIFYING EPITHELIAL ODONTOGENIC TUMOR ("PINDBORG TUMOR") – a rare lesion/tumor (< 1% of all odontogenic tumors) derived **purely from ECTODERM (epithelial)**. Found in patients **mainly 30-50 years old**, no sex predilection (30% are 4th decade). Uncommon in children and adolescents. 2/3 of cases occur in **MANDIBLE (molar-premolar area). Painless, slow-growing swelling is the most common clinical sign**. Rarely extra-osseous. Radiolucent-radiopaque areas associated with an unerupted tooth and amyloid production.

- **Radiographic Features**: unilocular or more often multi-locular **radiolucent** defect. **Scalloped margin**. Tumor is often associated with an **impacted tooth (mandibular 3rd molar)**. Calcifications within the tumor are often most prominent around the crown of an impacted tooth.

- **Histology**: reduced enamel epithelium, has discrete islands, strands, or sheets of polyhedral epithelial cells in a fibrous stroma.

- **Treatment**: conservative **local resection** to include a narrow rim of surrounding bone. 15% recurrence rate (tumors treated by curettage have highest recurrence rate if inadequately treated). Good prognosis.

SQUAMOUS ODONTOGENIC TUMOR – rare benign odontogenic tumor/neoplasm derived purely from **ECTODERM** (epithelial). Found in patients ages 8-75yrs (average 38yrs). Randomly distributed throughout the alveolar processes of maxilla and mandible with no site or sex predilection. Most common complaint is **painless or mild painful gingival swelling associated with tooth mobility**.

- <u>Clinical Features</u>: may be asymptomatic, painless swelling associated with mobile teeth.

- <u>Radiographic Features</u>: triangular or circumscribed **radiolucency LATERAL to the roots** of an unerupted or erupted tooth. May be an ill or well defined area with sclerotic margins. Most are **small lesions** that rarely exceed 1.5cm diameter. <u>Histogenesis</u>: Rests of Malassez.

- <u>Treatment</u>: conservative local excision or curettage, and close follow-up. Recurrence is rare.

CEMENTOMA (PERIAPICAL CEMENTAL DYSPLASIA) – **BENIGN** odontogenic tumor that occurs most frequently in the **ANTERIOR MANDIBLE** (periapical region), and often **affects multiple VITAL teeth**. Cementoma is an unusual **response of the periapical bone to some local factor** (i.e. traumatic occlusion or infection). While it appears to arise from teeth, the **lesions arise within bone**. Age, gender, location, radiographic appearance, and tooth vitality are important diagnostic criteria. <u>Histogenesis</u>: PDL. Do **not** mistake this as a need to do **RCT** (it is not a periapical abscess). Do a pulp vitality test to diagnose. If the pulp is vital, then **NO TREATMENT IS REQUIRED**.

- <u>Clinical Features</u>: occurs at the **apex of vital anterior teeth**, affecting **women** over age 30yrs (especially **BLACK** women) more than men. Asymptomatic, usually **multiple, small periapical radiolucent areas** in the mandibular incisor area. Depending on its stage, a cementoma may appear radiolucent, mixed-radiolucent, or completely radiopaque. <u>Three Cementoma Stages</u>:

<u>Stage 1</u>: lesion is a periapical **RADIOLUCENCY**.
<u>Stage 2</u>: lesion begins to calcify and become more radioopaque (**MIXED**).
<u>Stage 3</u>: well-defined **RADIOPACITY** bordered by a thin radiolucent line.

<u>Radioraphic Features</u>: small sharply circumscribed radiopacity attached to, or adjacent to apices of teeth. Early lesions are radiolucent, then have a central opacity, and are densely radiopaque when mature. The opacities are not cementum, but are **BONE**.

PERIAPICAL CEMENTAL DYSPLASIA (STAGE 1)

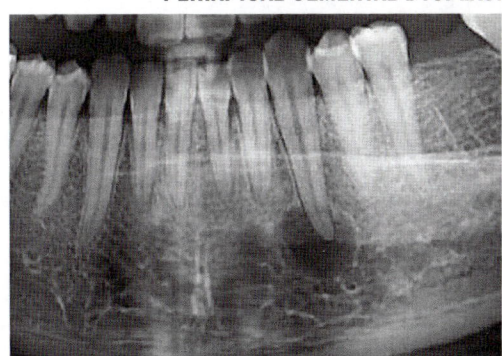
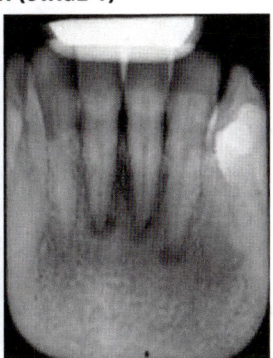

PERIAPICAL CEMENTAL DYSPLASIA (STAGES 2 & 3)

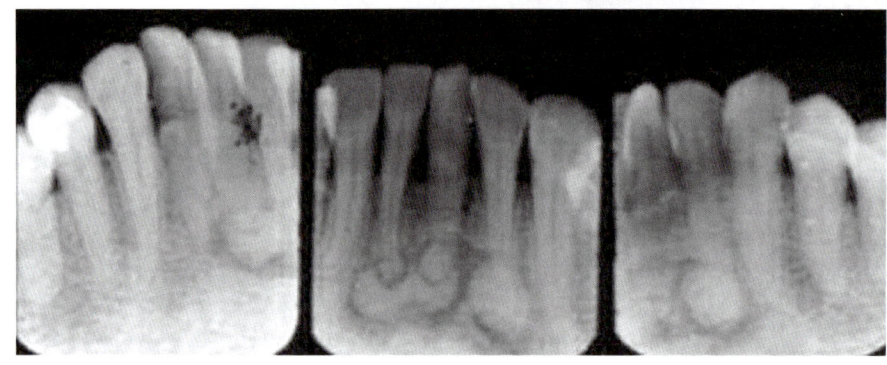

BENIGN CEMENTOBLASTOMA (TRUE CEMENTOMA)—usually affects males under 25yrs. Mandibular premolars or molars. Usually solitary, and may cause expansion of the cortical plates. Tooth is vital. **Histogenesis**: PDL.

- **Radiographic Features**: well-demarcated, mottled or densely radiopaque mass with radiolucent periphery attached to the root, causing the root resorption.

- **Microscopic Features**: cementum-like tissue with conspicuous reversal lines, variable amounts of fibrous C.T. with sheets of uncalcified "cementoid" especially at the periphery.

- **Treatment**: EXTRACT THE INVOLVED TOOTH.

GIGANTIFORM CEMENTOMA (FAMILIAL MULTIPLE CEMENTOMAS) —affects middle-aged black women. Multiple, often symmetrical, and may cause jaw expansion. **Histogenesis**: PDL.

- **Radiographic Features**: large, dense lobulated radiopaqe masses.

- **Microscopic Features**: large sheets of tissue that resemble secondary cementum.

- **Treatment**: conservative excision.

ODONTOGENIC MYXOMA – an AGGRESSIVE tumor derived from the papilla, dental sac, or PDL. Occurs in adults 30-40yrs as a painless swelling in the mandible.

- **Radiographic Features**: poorly-defined, multi-locular radiolucency that may be associated with an unerupted or displaced teeth.

- **Treatment**: curettage with cautery. High rate of recurrence if inadequately treated.

ODONTOGENIC FIBROMA – derived from dental papilla, dental sac, or PDL. Occurs as a painless swelling in the mandible of children & young adults. Radiographically, it is a multilocular or unilocular radiolucency that may be associated with unerupted or displaced teeth.

Treatment: Enucleation. Recurrence is rare.

CENTIFYING FIBROMA – a well-defined radiolucency with scattered radiopaque foci. Occurs in the mandible of adults as a painless swelling. **Histogenesis**: PDL. **Treatment**: curettage. Recurrence is rare.

ODONTOMA (Hamartoma)-ANY odontogenic tumor often associated with an unerupted tooth. The average age of people found with an odontoma is 14-years old. Remove with oral surgery.

ODONTOMA (HAMARTOMA)

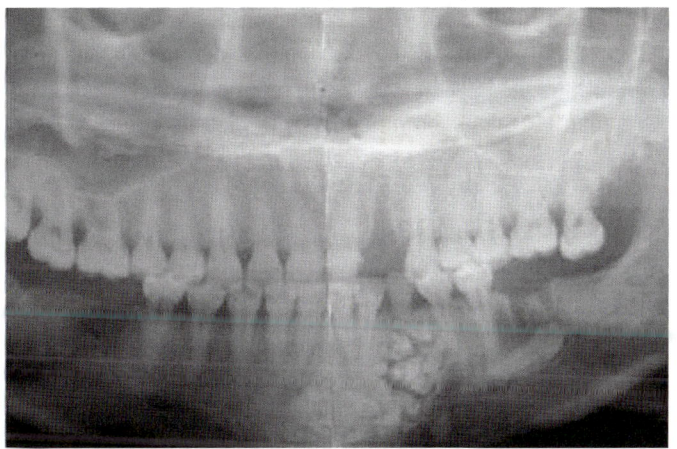

COMPLEX ODONTOMA-an amorphous **RADIOPAQUE** mass with a thin, radiolucent rim at the junction of surrounding bone (has varying densities). Most common in the **POSTERIOR** mandible. Derived from ectodermal & mesenchymal components of tooth germ. Affects **ages 20-30yrs**, and found in the **mandibular premolar-molar area**. Asymptomatic, but **may delay eruption of permanent teeth**.

- Radiographic Features: **well-defined, radiopaque mass surrounded by a narrow radiolucent zone**. May or may not be associated with an erupted tooth.

- Microscopic Features: conglomerate mass of dental tissues (dentin, enamel, cementum). Characterized by the formation of calcified enamel and dentin in an abnormal arrangement because of lack of morphodifferentiation.

- Treatment: Enucleation (Surgery), and does not recur.

COMPLEX ODONTOMA

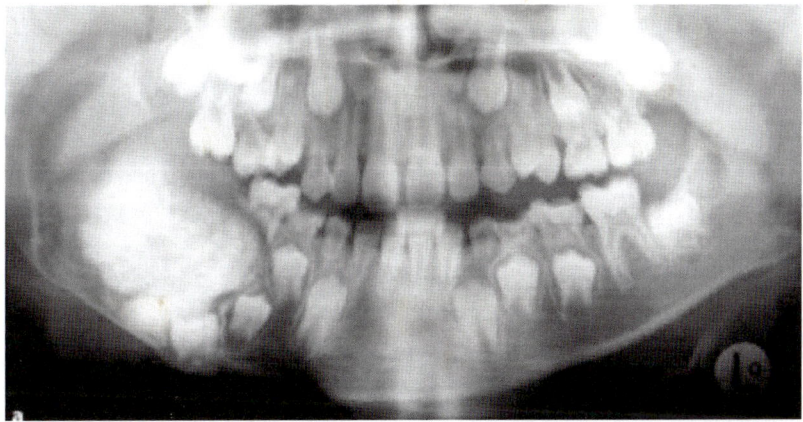

COMPOUND ODONTOMA – a **tumor of enamel and dentin common in the ANTERIOR MAXILLA** (incisor-canine area) derived from ectodermal & mesenchymal components of tooth germ. It is arranged in the form of anomalous **MINIATURE TEETH** (several small abnormal teeth). Affects **ages 20-30yrs**. May also appear in the **mandible canine-premolar area**, and can cause delayed eruption or prevent eruption of permanent teeth.

- **Radiographic Features**: groups of small radiopacities (multiple small tooth-like structures with a thin radiolucent rim at the junction with surrounding bone.) Common between the maxillary premolar and central incisor on a panorex.

- **Microscopic Features**: multiple, small malformed teeth of dentin, enamel, and cementum.

- **Treatment**: Enucleation (Surgery), and does not recur.

COMPOUND ODONTOMA (TOOTHLETS)

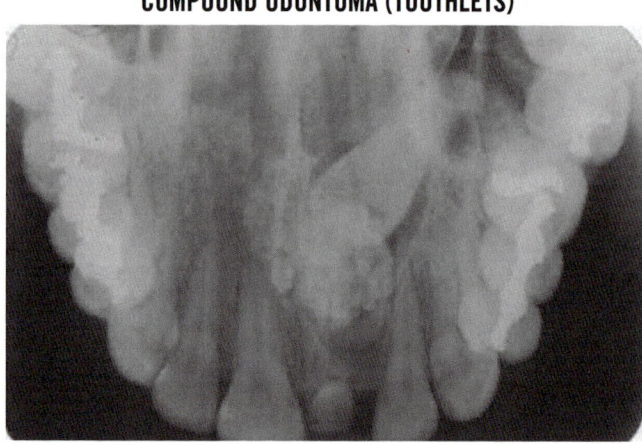

PIGMENTED LESIONS

PEUTZ-JEGHERS SYNDROME (HEREDITARY INTESTINAL POLYPOSIS SYNDROME) – an autosomal dominant inherited disorder, characterized by **MULTIPLE INTESTINAL POLYPS** distributed through the entire intestine (especially the jejunum) and intra-oral **MELANIN pigmentations** of the lips and oral mucosa at birth or early age (often during the first decade of life), and at this time is restricted to the oral region.

- Intra-orally, the pigmentations can be found anywhere on the mucosa, but are **most common on the BUCCAL MUCOSA, GINGIVA, and HARD PALATE.** The mucosal surface of the **LOWER LIP** is almost always involved. These spots or macules vary in intensity, and range in shades of **BROWN, BLUE, and BLACK**. The tongue seldom shows this melanin pigmentation. The oral pigmentations are harmless, but their presence is important to determine if multiple polyposis exist in the intestines and colon which may be harmful. There is a strong tendency for the multiple polyps of the colon to undergo malignant change.

- During succeeding decades of a patient's life, pigmentations may arise on the skin's extremities. **Pigmentations of Peutz-Jeghers Syndrome** may occur without polyps, and multiple polyps may be present without any pigmentations.

- When Peutz-Jegher Syndrome is suspected based on oral pigmentations, other conditions to consider in the differential diagnosis are **Addison's Disease & Albright's Syndrome**.

ADDISON'S DISEASE ("Chronic Adrenocortical Insufficiency" or "Hypocorticolism)-a rare endocrine disorder caused by **ADRNEAL CORTEX HYPOFUNCTION of CORTISOL (GLUCOCORTICOID)**—not enough cortisol is produced. The hyposecretion is either due to an adrenal gland disorder (primary adrenal insufficiency), or inadequate secretion of ACTH by the pituitary gland (secondary adrenal insufficiency). **CAUSES BRONZING OF THE ENTIRE SKIN**. Cortisol's most important function is to help the body respond to STRESS. Occurs in all age groups, affecting men and women equally. The **MAIN DENTAL CONCERN** during dental procedures is this patient's adrenal cortex has no capacity to produce extra cortisol in response to stress, which may result in Addison's Crisis.

Clinical Signs: usually start gradually and include **weight loss, loss of appetite, muscle weakness, low BP, darkening (hyperpigmentation) of the skin** in both exposed & unexposed parts of the body (most visible on scars, skin folds, pressure points like elbows, knees, knuckles, toes, and oral mucous membranes). Also nausea, vomiting, diarrhea.

Oral Signs: diffuse pigmentation of the **gingiva, tongue, hard palate, & buccal mucosa**. Although cutaneous pigmentation will usually disappear, after therapy, pigmentation of the oral tissues tends to persist.

Lab Tests: show low blood concentrations of Na+ and glucose, increased serum K+, and decreased urinary output of certain steroids.

ALBRIGHT'S SYNDROME (McCune-Albright Syndrome)-a severe form of polyostotic fibrous dysplasia that causes lesions of nearly all skeletal bones, brown patches of cutaneous pigmentation (café-au-lait spots), and endocrine dysfunction (especially precocious puberty in girls). There is also an increased incidence of osteosarcoma.

AMALGAM TATTOO — a common finding sometimes mistaken for a melanin-pigmented lesion. Most common on the **gingiva, buccal mucosa, and alveolar mucosa**.

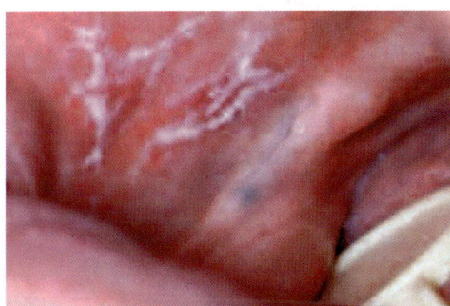
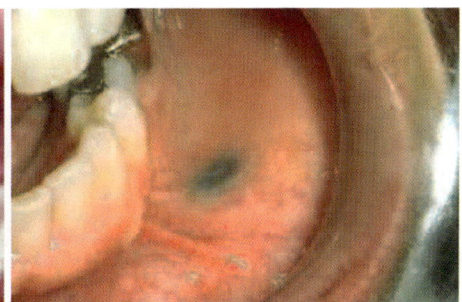

ASPIRIN BURN-occurs when patients place an aspirin tablet against an aching tooth, allowing the cheek or lip to hold it in position, while it dissolves slowly. Within a few minutes, a burning sensation of the mucosa is noted, and the surface becomes blanched or white (**ORAL MUCOSA NECROSIS**), with subsequent sloughing of the necrotic epithelium.

ASPIRIN BURN

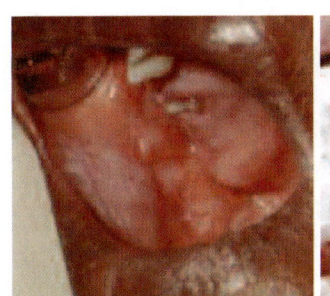
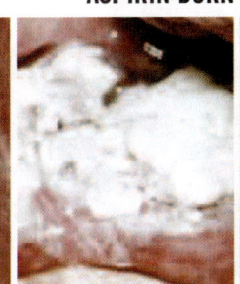
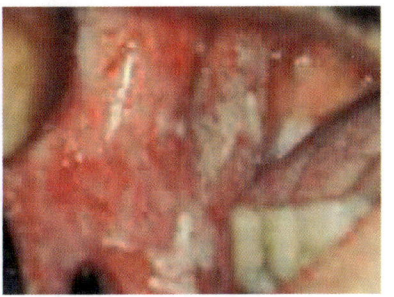

Heavy Metal Bismuth Ingestion-used to treat some dermatologic disorders and various other diseases. Bismuth pigmentation appears as a "bismuth line" (**thin, blue-black line in the marginal gingiva that is sometimes confined to the gingival papilla**).

Most pigmented skin tumors are composed of NEVUS cells due to a developmental anomaly of MELANOCYTES, and are RARE in the oral cavity. The initial flat, raised lesion can become nodular, with an increase in consistency. Spontaneous involution may occur, and malignant transformation is a rare complication. **When found intra-orally, pigmented skin tumors are most often on the HARD PALATE, but may appear on the gingiva and lips**. If a pigmented lesion shows ulceration, increase in size, color darkening, a biopsy is performed to determine if malignant transformation is occurring.

CONGENITAL NEVI (BIRTHMARK) – are usually larger (> 10cm) but as time passes, it can change from a flat, pale tan macules into elevated, verrucous, hairy lesions. ~15% occur on the head & neck skin. Have a **higher incidence of malignant transformation than acquired nevi**. Most common intra-oral location is the **HARD PALATE**.

FOCAL MELANOSIS – may occur at any age and presents as a single or multiple small, **FLAT BROWN** asymptomatic lesion found mainly on the **LOWER LIP**. Focal melanosis describes two similar lesions that differ in their location and size:

Labial Melanotic Macule-a lesion on the **lips (MAINLY LOWER LIP)**, and almost always near the midline. Most lesions are 5mm or less in diameter.

LABIAL MELANOTIC MACULE

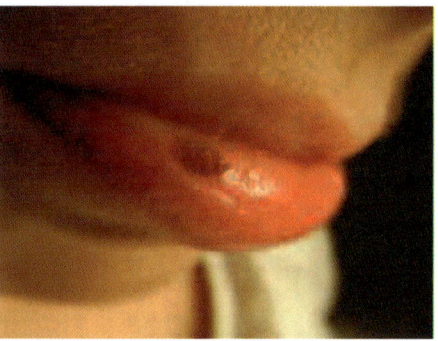

Oral Melanotic Macule-a intra-oral lesion found on the **gingiva, buccal mucosa, and palate**. Most lesions are under 1cm in diameter.

ORAL MELANOTIC MACULE

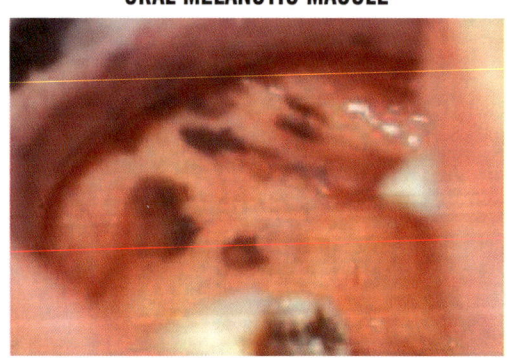

Treatment: melanotic macules with a short history are **EXCISED** and **BIOPSIED** to rule out the possibility of malignant melanoma. Lesions present > 5 years without a change in size or color, are followed unless the patient requests removal.

RED-BLUE LESIONS

MEDIAN RHOMBOID GLOSSITIS —often affects **MIDDLE-AGED ADULTS**. Once thought to be a congenital abnormality related to the persistence of the tuberculum impar, but is now believed to be a **permanent end result of a CHROINC CANDIDA ALBICANS INFECTION**. Diabetics, immunosuppressed patients, and patients on long-term antibiotic therapy are most susceptible.

- **Clinical Features**: smooth, denuded, **BEEFY-RED LESION** devoid of filiform papillae. Mainly found on the **MIDLINE of TONGUE DORSUM**, just anterior to circumvallate papillae. Generally asymptomatic, and **NO TREATMENT** is usually necessary.

MEDIAN RHOMBOID GLOSSITIS

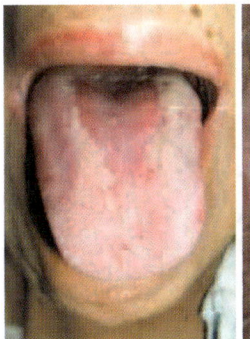
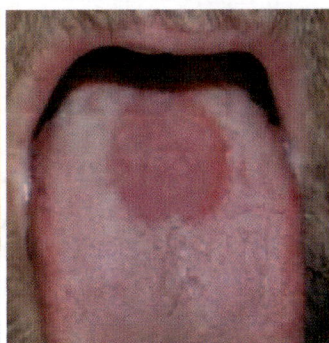
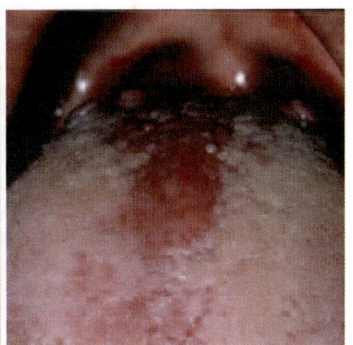

ERYTHROPLAKIA – a persistent, **VELVITY-RED PATCH** that cannot be characterized clinically as any other condition. Like "leukoplakia", it has no histologic connotation, but **most erythroplakias are histologically diagnosed as severe epithelial dysplasia, carcinoma in-situ, or invasive squamous cell carcinoma**. May be located anywhere in the mouth, but are **MOST** likely found in the mandibular mucobuccal fold, oropharynx, and floor of the mouth. Equally affects males and females, especially over 60yrs.

ERYTHROPLAKIA

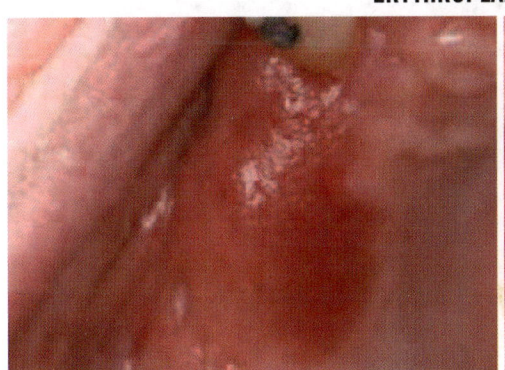
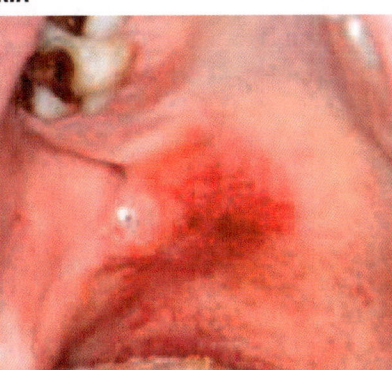

NOTES

BURNING TONGUE SYNDROME – patients usually do not exhibit clinically detectable lesions, but symptoms of intense pain and burning. BTS is frustrating for the patient and clinician because there is usually no clear-cut cause and no uniformly successful treatment. Typically affects MIDDLE-AGED FEMALES (it affects men too, but usually at an older age). Rare in children & teenagers.

- **Possible Etiologic Factors**: anemias (pernicious anemia & iron deficiency anemia), diabetes mellitus, gastric disturbances (i.e. hyperacidity or hypoacidity), psychogenic factors (emotional conflict, cancerophobia), trigeminal neuralgia, microorganisms (especially Candida Albicans & Streptococci), xerostomia (dry mouth) associated with Sjogrens Syndrome, anxiety, & drugs. Local irritation (tobacco, spices), and vitamin deficiency (especially B complex).

PERIPHERAL GIANT CELL GRANULOM-relatively uncommon, pedunculated broad-based growths with a smooth surface (usually). **Always on the GINGIVA (between 1st permanent molar & incisors) or ALVEOLAR PROCESS**. Mandibular gingiva is affected more than the maxillary gingiva. It represents an unusual hyperplastic C.T. response to injury of gingival tissues. **REDDISH-BLUE** in color, sometimes lobulated, and bleed easily. **Most patients are older than age 20yrs** (Central Giant Cell Granuloma occurs mainly before age 20yrs). Affects females 2x more than males.

- Radiographs are usually negative. Clinically, it **may resemble a fibroma or pyogenic granuloma**.

- Histologically identical to Central Giant Cell Granuloma. It consists of a non-encapsulated tissue mass composed of a delicate reticular & fibrillar C.T. stroma with multi-nucleated giant cells.

- **Treatment**: COMPLETE SURGICAL EXCISION.

PERIPHERAL GIANT CELL GRANULOMA

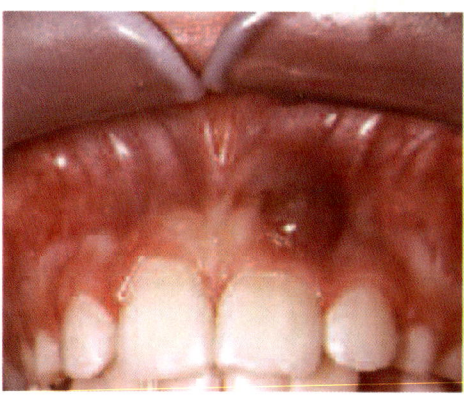
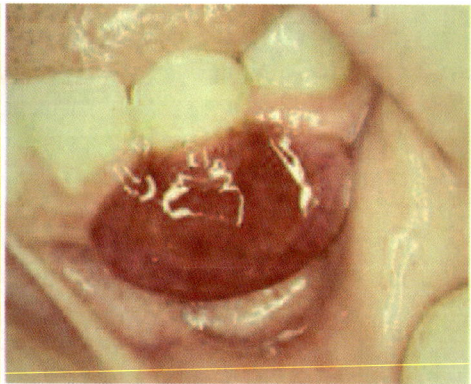

HEMANGIOMA – **BENIGN tumor** consisting of a **mass of BLOOD VESSELS**. It can range from a small mass, to very large sacs of unsightly red, purple, or blue blood vessels (they can enlarge to very alarming sizes). **Present at birth, childhood, or arise later in life** (enlarges as the child grows). In certain locations, large hemangiomas can interfere with proper organ development and function.

- **Clinical Features**: a common **BENIGN** tumor of a **PROLIFERATION OF BLOOD VESSELS**, affecting females 2x more than males (2:1). It is a soft, smooth, blue, red, purple, or purplish-red mass that most commonly affects the **TONGUE, BUCCAL MUCOSA, LIPS, PALATE**.

- **Microscopic Features**: capillary, cavernous, and a hemangioendothelioma of stratified squamous epithelium covering of loose, fibrous C.T. that contains many thin-walled engorged vascular spaces.

- **Treatment**: laser therapy or surgery. May regress spontaneously. **DO NOT INCISIONAL BIOPSY**.

HEMANGIOMA

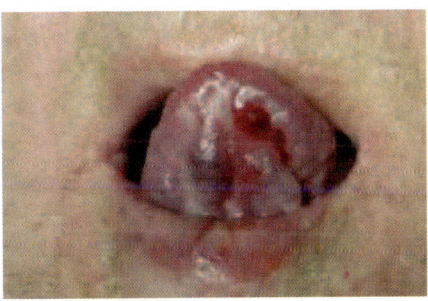
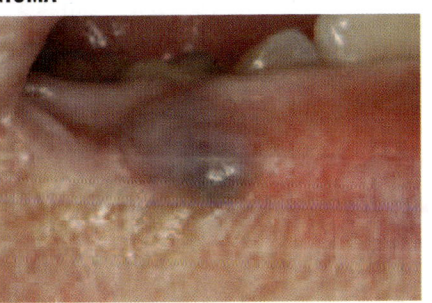

PSEUDOCYSTS ("NOT TRUE CYSTS")
NO EPITHELIAL LINING

TRAUMATIC BONE CYSTS (PSEUDOCYSTS) – non-cysts found in the MANDIBLE (between canine & ramus) of mainly **TEENAGERS** due to trauma. **PAINLESS, WELL-DEFINED SCALLOPED RADIOLUCENCY** between teeth. Although sometimes asymptomatic, it may produce jaw enlargement. Regional teeth are vital.

- **AKA**: simple bone cyst, hemorrhagic bone cyst, unicameral bone cyst, extravasation bone cyst, idiopathic bone cyst, and solitary bone cyst.

- **Treatment**: open the lesion, curettage, and suture. It may contain blood, serosanguineous fluid, debris composed mainly of a blood clot, or may be completely devoid of solid material.

ANEURYSMAL BONE CYST – a **BENIGN** bone lesion generally regarded as a "**reactive process**" (not a neoplastic or cystic process). A **RARE** expansile, osteolytic bone lesion consisting of a proliferation of vascular tissue that forms a lining around blood-filled cystic lesions. Most occur equally in males and females under age 20yrs, and is **UNCOMMON AFTER AGE 30yrs**.

- Involves the proximal humerus, femur, tibia, and pelvis (uncommon in jaws, but usually appears in the mandible). Lesions are usually tender or **PAINFULL** on motion of the affected bone. Upon entering the lesion surgically, excessive bleeding occurs, and the tissue often resembles a "**blood-soaked**" **sponge**.

- **Histology**: has no epithelial lining (thus is a "pseudocyst"). Consists of fibrous C.T. stroma with many cavernous or sinusoidal blood-filled spaces. Fibroblasts & macrophages (histiocytes) line the sinusoids. Multi-nucleated giant cells (similar to cells of a giant cell granuloma) are dispersed throughout.

- **Radiographic Features**: bone is expanded and appears **CYSTIC** with a "**HONEYCOMB** or **SOAP-BUBBLE**" appearance.

- **Treatment**: surgical curettage or excision, with little chance of recurrence.

ANEURYSMAL BONE CYST (BENIGN)

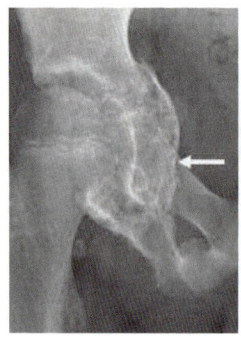
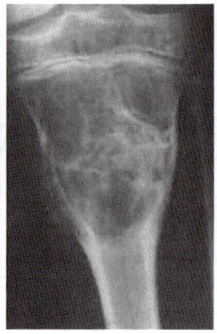
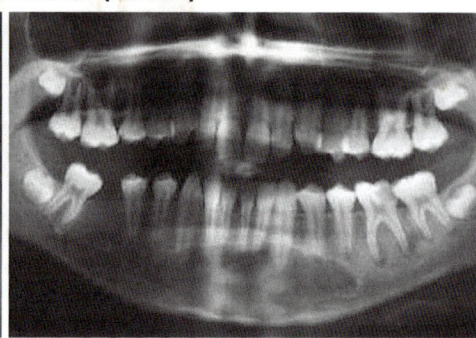

SALIVARY GLAND TUMORS

BENIGN SALIVARY GLAND TUMORS CLINICAL FEATURES —normal mucosa, painless, nodular, localized, movable, firm, slow-growing, well-differentiated, & encapsulated/well-circumscribed.

Radiographically, a benign neoplasm in bone may be distinguished from a malignant neoplasm in because with a **benign lesion, the CORTEX REMAINS IN TACT**, but may be thinned and the part involved may be expanded. Also, benign margins are usually defined and demarcated from surrounding bone.

PLEOMORPHIC ADENOMA (Mixed Tumor)- MOST COMMON BENIGN salivary gland tumor.

MONOMORPHIC ADENOMAS: Basal Cell, Canalicular, Myoepithelioma, Sebaceous, Papillary Cystadenoma Lymphomatosum (Warthin's Tumor), Onocytoma (oxyphilic/acidophilic adenoma).

The most common site of intra-oral **MINOR** salivary gland neoplasms/tumors is the **PALATE**. The most common site of intra-oral **MAJOR** salivary gland neoplasms is the **PAROTID GLAND**.

NECROTIZING SIALOMETAPLASIA – a benign lesion of **MINOR salivary glands**, characterized by necrosis of the glandular parenchyma with associated squamous metaplasia & hyperplasia of the ductal epithelium. Its etiology is unknown, but **may be related to vascular insufficiency and infarction** of the glands. **HARD PALATE** is the most common site.

- NS benign lesion shows no racial or sex predilection, with **most patients > 40yrs** of age. Clinically, it presents as a **tender deep ulcer with sharply demarcated margins**. Histologically, there is lobular necrosis of the glandular parenchyma, with squamous metaplasia & hyperplasia of the ductal epithelium. **Clinically and histologically, the lesion may stimulate a malignancy**. In the past, the lesion was **misdiagnosed** as a squamous cell carcinoma or mucoepidermoid carcinoma.
- After performing a BIOPSY and establishing a diagnosis, additional treatment is usually not recommended since healing usually occurs within 6-12 weeks.

MUMPS – most common **VIRAL DISEASE** of the **SALIVARY GLANDS** caused by **RNA-Paramyxovirus**. Clinically, 90% of cases occur before age 14yrs. A major sign is **sudden salivary gland swelling without purulent discharge from the duct. PAROITID GLAND is involved 90% of the time**, and is bilaterally involved in 2/3 of cases. Patient presents with **mild fever, malaise, and anorexia**. Most cases are self-limiting.

- **Complications**: orchitis (inflammation of the testis) and epididymitis can occur in post-pubertal males, and may cause sterility. CNS disturbances causing meningitis & encephalitis. Deafness, myocarditis, pancreatitis, oophoritis, and pyelonephritis.

- Serum amylase may be elevated during the acute phase. Prevent by administering a live, attenuated vaccine which is 95% effective for a least 5 years. However, in non-inoculated patients, it can still cause acute non-suppurative salivary adenitis.

MEASELES (RUBEOLA)-caused by RNA Paramyxovirus; characterized by the formation of **KOPLIK SPOTS in the oral cavity** (clustered white lesions on the buccal mucosa near each **STENSON'S DUCT** opposite maxillary 1st molars). They look like grains of salt on a wet background.

MEASELES (KOPLIK SPOTS)

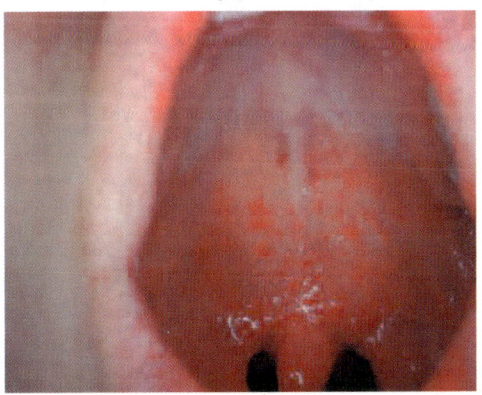

MUCOCELES (MUCOUS RETENTION CYST)- fluid-filled sac under the mucosa usually **on the LOWER LIP** (rarely on the upper lip) usually due to trauma (biting lip or tongue). It involves the **MINOR** salivary glands and their ducts (ex: trauma to the salivary duct by lip biting or pinching). A COMMON LESION that may also appear on the palate, cheek, tongue, and mouth floor. Treatment: Surgical Excision.

- **Clinical Features**: may lie deep in tissue or be very superficial. Depending on its location, its clinical appearance varies. **Superficial mucocele**- a raised, circumscribed vesicle, several millimeters to 1cm in diameter with a bluish-translucent cast. **Deeper mucocele**- appears as a fluctuant swelling also, but the tissue is normal in color.

MUCOCELES

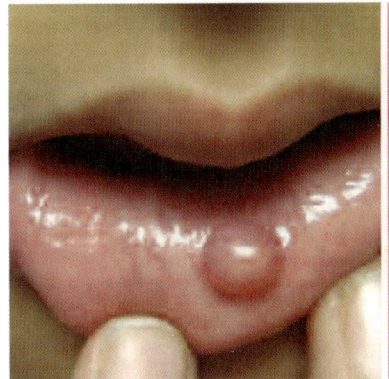
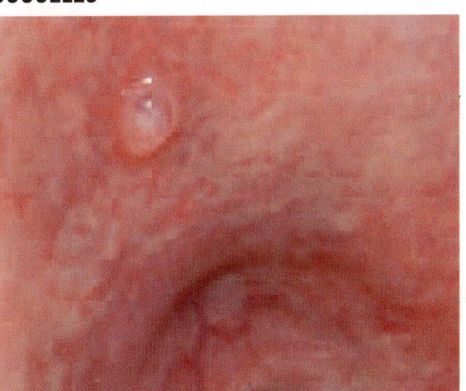

NOTES

RANULA ("TRUE RETENTION CYST") - a fluctuant & painless cyst (swelling) that presents as a translucent, bluish, well-rounded, smooth-surfaced bulge that protrudes from ONE SIDE of the MOUTH FLOOR. It characteristically occurs UNILATERALLY in the floor of the mouth. Caused by an obstruction of either the SUBMANDIBULAR or SUBLINGUAL GLANDS, due to a salivary stone or soft organic substance. A history of increased size just before or during a meal, and decrease in size between meals is of diagnostic significance.

- Treatment: COMPLETE SURGICAL EXCISION of the cyst roof. If it persists, excision of the gland may be needed.

RANULA

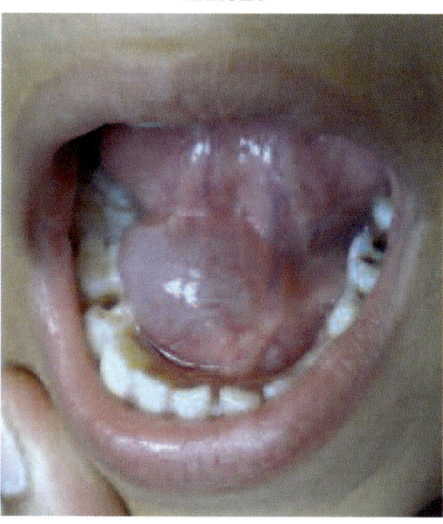

MIKULICZ'S DISEASE ("BENIGN LYMPHOEPITHELIAL LESION") —rare salivary gland lesion, closely related to Sjogren's Syndrome. A progressive, asymptomatic enlargement of the PAROTID & SUBMANDIBULAR glands. Appears initially unilateral, but over time becomes BILATERAL. Unknown etiology, but evidence suggests that both Mikulicz's & Sjogren's Syndrome are autoimmune diseases where the patient's own salivary gland tissue becomes antigenic. Occurs most often in MIDDLE-AGED WOMEN.

- Histologic Features: replacement of gland parenchyma by lymphocytic infiltrate that contains scattered epimyoepithelial islands within (this is the histologic cornerstone for the diagnosis).

- Most are BENIGN, but malignant transformation of the epimyoepithelial islands may occur.

MALIGNANT SALIVARY GLAND TUMORS

Clinical Features of MALIGNANT Salivary Gland Tumors: painful, ulcerated mucosa, nodular, firm, fixed, rapid growth, invasion, immovable, metastasis, and not well-differentiated (anaplastic). Metastasis is the most important characteristic that distinguishes a malignant tumor from a benign tumor. PARASTHESIA suggests metasatic disease.

- Histologic Features of Malignancy: anaplasia, abnormal mitosis, pleomorphism, hyperchromatism, increased nuclear-cytoplasmic ratio.

- Host response to a malignancy is best reflected by lymphocytic infiltration at the edge of a tumor. The most characteristic feature of a malignancy rather than an inflammatory lesion is the malignancy will grow after the causative agent is removed. The most important characteristic of malignant neoplasms that distinguishes them from benign neoplasms is their ABILITY TO METASTASIZE.

- **Histologic Grading of Malignant Neoplasms**: attempts to estimate the aggressiveness or degree of malignancy of a malignant neoplasm based on the degree of differentiation of the component cells and number of mitoses. Grading mainly applies to squamous cell carcinomas, and is of limited clinical use. Most pathologist use three grades, and designate SCC as well-differentiated, moderately well-differentiated, or poorly differentiated.

Grade 1 = well-differentiated.
Grade 2 = moderately, well-differentiated.
Grade 3 = poorly undifferentiated.
Grade 4 = undifferentiated.

ADENOCARCINOMA-affects MAJOR salivary glands (50%) & MINOR glands (50%). Its frequency is 25% minor glands, 5% submandibular glands, and 3% of parotid tumors. Usually presents as an asymptomatic mass. 80% survival rate for low-grade carcinoma, and 40% survival rate for high-grade carcinoma.

ADENOID CYSTIC CARCINOMA-a malignant salivary gland tumor that usually affects MINOR salivary glands of the PALATE (70%), parotid gland (15%), & submandibular gland (14%). Represents 31% of minor salivary gland tumors, 14% of submandibular gland tumors, and 2% of parotid gland tumors. Patient presents with pain and/or nerve dysfunction in 25%-33% of patients. Facial weakness or paralysis is common. A slow, but relentless tumor progression, with a 20% twenty-year survival rate.

ADENOID CYSTIC CARCINOMA

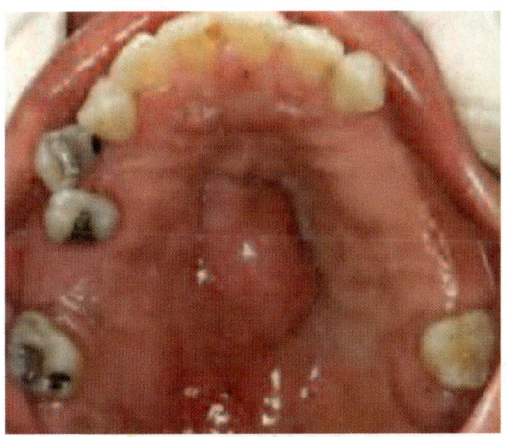

ACINIC CELL CARCINOMA-a malignant salivary gland tumor most likely associated with the parotid gland (96%), submandibular gland (2-3%), and minor salivary glands of the palate (1-2%). 2-4% of parotid tumors are acinic cell carcinoma. Patient presents with swelling, pain, or tenderness, and may have facial weakness or paralysis. 90% cure rate.

MUCOEPIDERMOID CARCINOMA - usually occurs in **the parotid gland (60%)**, palate (13%), & submandibular gland (6%). Represents 10% of minor salivary gland tumors, 6% of parotid tumors, and 5% of submandibular tumors. Patient usually has **asymptomatic swelling, with a peak incidence in the 3rd decade of life (30s)**. Patient may have **facial weakness or paralysis**. Low-grade carcinomas have an 85-100% 5-year cure rate, while high-grade carcinomas have a 20-45% 5-year cure rate.

Metabolic Conditions & Chronic Salivary Gland Enlargement: Diabetes Mellitus, chronic alcoholism, malnutrition (anorexia & bulimia), obesity, hypertension, & hyperlipidema. **PAROTID GLAND is most frequently enlarged** (either unilaterally or bilaterally).

Other Conditions Associated with PAROTID GLAND Enlargement:
1. Sjogren's Syndrome & Sarcoidosis
2. Warthin's Tumor (Papillary Cystadenoma Lymphomatosum)
3. Infections (mumps, actinomycosis, tuberculosis)
4. Benign Lymphoepithelial Lesion (Mikulicz's Disease)
5. Acute Epidemic Parotitis
6. Malnutrition

SJOGREN'S SYNDROME – a salivary gland disorder of **unknown cause**, but is **autoimmune**. Marked mainly by **chronic inflammation of the salivary and lacrimal glands**, that usually progresses to **fibrosis and atrophy** of these glands. Mainly affects **post-menopausal women** who present with **dry eyes, dry mouth**. ~50% of cases, have **BILATERAL enlargement** of the parotid & submandibular glands.

- **Symptoms**: rheumatoid arthritis, **xerostomia (dry mouth), & keratoconjunctiva sicca** (dryness of the eyes). However, **all 3 symptoms rarely occur in one patient**. The decrease in salivation may cause **rampant caries** reminiscent of **radiation caries**.

- **Histologic Features**: histological features of the salivary gland lesions in Sjogren's Syndrome & Benign Lymphoepithelial Lesion (Mikulicz's Disease) are identical.

- **Treatment**: treat the symptoms. Keratoconjunctivitis is treated with ocular lubricants, and **xerostomia is treated with saliva substitutes (artificial saliva).** Biopsy of the labial or palatal salivary glands, sialograms, salivary flow rate tests, and blood work may help establish a diagnosis. However, **radiation, surgical excision, and chemotherapy are NOT used as treatment**.

- Malignant lymphomas & "Pseudolymphomas" ("Atypical Benign Lymphoid Hyperplasia") develop in some patients diagnosed with Sjogren's Syndrome. Thus, close follow-up of patients is required.

XEROSTOMIA (DRY MOUTH) – not a disease, but **a SYMPTOM of certain diseases and medications**. Xerostomia is caused by **sialadenitis** (insidious inflammatory disease of the major salivary glands), **Sjogren's syndrome, medications** (anti-cholinergic drugs (Atropine & Scopolamine) & anti-psychotics (Phenothiazines: Chlorpromazine & Prochlorperazine), **cancer therapy, nerve damage**, Alzheimer's, stroke, bone marrow transplants, endocrine disorders, stress, anxiety, depression, and nutritional deficiencies. **Xerostomia is often caused by failure of the salivary glands to function normally, but it may also occur in people with normal salivary glands**. Xerostomia can cause health problems by affecting nutrition, and psychological health. **Extreme cases can cause rampant tooth decay and periodontal disease**.

SIALOLITHS (salivary calculus or stones) in **Wharton's Duct (Submandibular Duct)** are often found with **OCCLUSAL RADIOGRAPHS**. Calculus deposition in the salivary ducts and glands is more common in middle-age. The most common symptoms of duct obstruction are an increase and decrease in swelling of the gland (especially at mealtime). The swelling may or may not be painful, and may also occur in children. **Transillumination of the soft tissue** is useful to detect sialolithiasis in children.

- Rate of occurrence in the **SUBMANDIBULAR GLAND & DUCT** is much higher than in the parotid or sublingual glands due to the submandibular saliva's tenacity, and long, irregular duct shape.

- Treatment of choice is **surgical extirpation of the sialolith**. Salivary stones located in the glandular parenchyma also usually require surgical removal of the gland.

- OCCLUSAL RADIOGRAPHS are NOT useful for locating sialoliths in **STENSON'S DUCT**, identifying the mental foramen or hyoid bone.

SIALOLITHS

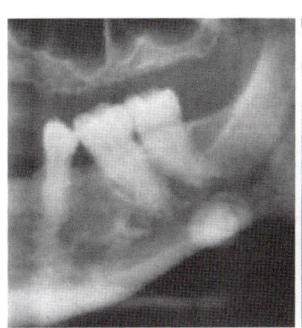
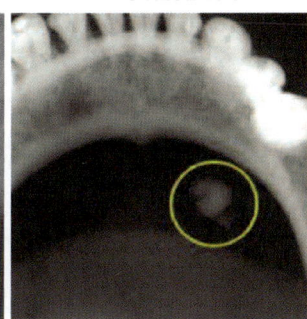
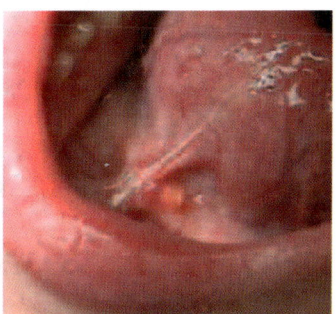

ONCOCYTOMAS ("OXYPHILIC/ACIDOPHILIC ADENOMA") – a **small, benign RARE glandular tumor** composed of large cells with a granular & eosinophilic cytoplasm due to the presence of many mitochondria. Can occur in the kidney, salivary glands, & endocrine glands. Its development may be related to the AGING PROCESS. **Treatment**: surgical excision; recurrence is rare.

- **Clinical Features**: most commonly seen in the **PAROTID GLANDS** of patients over age 50 (slightly more common in women). Slow growth, and they rarely reach any significant size.

- **Histologic Features**: the tumor is an encapsulated mass composed of relatively **large cells** (arranged in sheets, cords, or form tubular or acinar structures). The cells have **BRIGHT PINK CYTOPLASM** and small, round nuclei.

SIALOSCINTIGRAPHY-a simple, non-invasive procedure that SEPERATES BENIGN TUMORS (ex: Warthin's tumor & Oncocytoma) of the salivary glands from MALIGNANT TUMORS, and greatly affects the course of treatment.

WARTHIN'S TUMOR ("PAPILLARY CYSTADENOMA LYMPHOMATOSUM")-BENIGN PAROTID tumor (almost exclusively in the PAROTID GLAND), arising from heterotopic ductal epithelium within lymph nodes or near the parotid gland. **Strong association with cigarette smoking**.

- **Clinical Features**: most patients are older 60-70 years (affects males 5:1). 95% are unilateral. The tumor most often arises in the **tail of the parotid gland** as a painless, non-tender, slow growing, firm-to-fluctuant nodule over the **ANGLE or RAMUS OF THE MANDIBLE**.

NOTES

- **Histologic Features**: tumor is encapsulated and composed of **CYSTIC SPACES** surrounded by two uniform rows of cells with **centrally placed pyknotic nuclei**. The lining epithelium (papillary infoldings) of the cystic spaces protrude back into the spaces. The papillary foldings have lymphoid stroma aggregates with a geminal center formation that are interspersed.

- **Treatment**: **SURGERY**. Recurrence is uncommon and it is highly unlikely to become malignant.

PLEOMORPHIC ADENOMA ("BENIGN MIXED TUMOR") — the **MOST COMMON tumor of the major & minor salivary glands**. The term "mixed tumor" is used because it is of both ectodermal & mesenchymal origin.

- **Clinical Features**: **MOST COMMON SALIVARY GLAND NEOPLASM**. Affects more women than men (most patients between 40-60yrs). ~93% arise in **MAJOR** salivary glands (these are almost exclusively **PAROTID** tumors (84%), but can also affect the submandibular gland. Present as firm, painless lumps below and anterior to the ear. ~7% arise in the oral cavity with the **PALATE** being by far the most common intra-oral site (firm, painless swelling). In most cases, it does not cause ulceration of the overlying mucosa.

PLEOMORPHIC ADENOMA (BENIGN MIXED TUMOR)

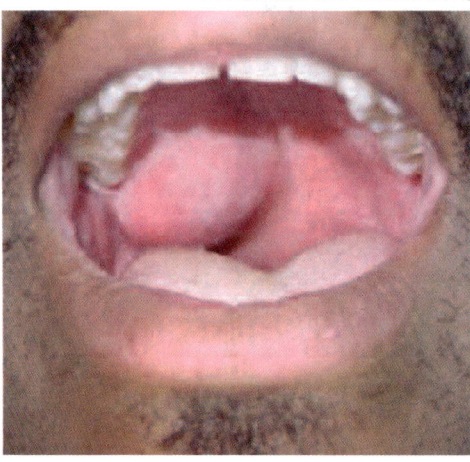 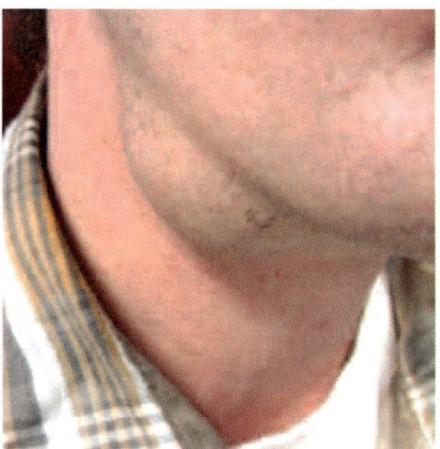

- **Histologic Features**: **epithelial (ectodermal)** component consists of round, polyhedral, elongated, or stellate cells that are relatively small and stain uniformly. The **mesenchymal** component varies from areas of myxomatoid tissue, to areas of dense, hyalinized C.T., pseudocartilage, or bone.

- **Treatment**: **SURGICAL EXCISION** with a generous margin of normal tissue is the treatment of choice. Inadequate initial removal of the mixed tumor in major salivary glands may cause recurrence. ~25% of benign mixed tumors undergo malignant transformation untreated for an extended period.

ULCERATIVE CONDITIONS

STEVENS-JOHNSON SYNDROME — a **SEVERE** bullous form of **ERYTHEMA MULTIFORME** where systemic symptoms are severe, and lesions are extensive, involving multiple body areas (especially mucous membranes). SJS is characterized by the **acute onset of fever, and eruptive, ulcerative lesion on the skin, oral mucosa, and eyes**. Frequently, genitalia, lungs, and joints are affected, and it can be fatal. Blindness can occur due to a secondary infection.

- **Clinical Features**: typical **"BULL'S-EYE-SHAPED" LESIONS** with the **classical triad of eye lesions, genital lesions, & stomatitis**. The lesions are severe and often vesicular or bullous, with hemorrhage after denudation.

- **Treatment**: **IV fluids, systemic sterolds, palliative rinses** and **antibiotics**.

ERYTHEMA MULTIFORME - allergic hypersensitivity reaction in response to **MEDICATIONS** (*sulfonamides, penicillins, barbiturates, & phenytoin*), **infections, or illness**. Associated infections include herpes simplex & mycoplasma infections. The exact cause is unknown, but is believed to involve **DAMAGED SKIN BLOOD VESSELS with subsequent damage to skin tissues**.

EM occurs mainly in **children and young adults**, and its diagnosis is based on the classic target OR **"BULL'S-EYE-SHAPED" SKIN LESION** that appears as a **central lesion** surrounded by concentric rings of pallor and redness over the **dorsal (top) of the hands** and **forearms**.

ERYTHEMA MULTIFORME

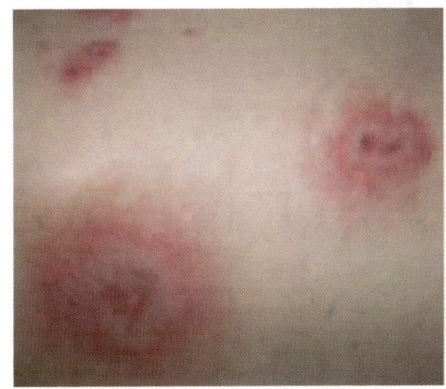
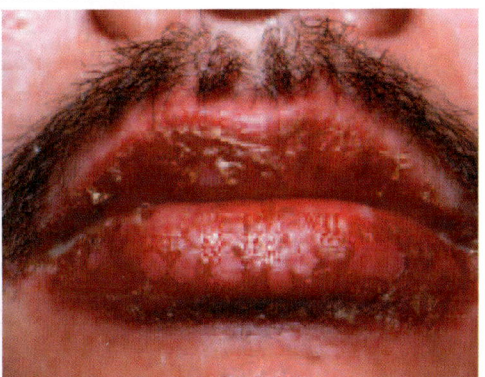

- **Low-grade fever, general malaise,** and **headache** usually precede the lesions by **4-7** days.

- Oral lesions appear as **red macules, papules,** or **vesicles** that may become **eroded and painful, covered by a yellowish-white membrane after rupturing**.

- **Treatment**: **topical palliative rinses** and sometimes low-dose systemic **steroids**.

RECURRENT APHTHOUS ULCERS (ULCERATIVE/APHTHOUS STOMATITIS "CANKER SORES") — may be associated with **STRESS, a bacterial infection, trauma** (self-inflicted, oral surgery procedures, routine dental procedures), endocrine conditions (menstrual cycle), **allergic factors** (certain foods or drugs), **immunologic abnormalities, iron, vitamin B, or folic acid deficiencies**. Cause is unknown, but they may be caused by an **autoimmune reaction**.

NOTES

Recurrent Aphthous Minor (Minor Aphthous Ulcer)-the MOST COMMON form ("canker sore"). Occurs more often in women, starting as a single or multiple superficial erosion covered by a gray membrane (1-5 lesions). Looks like an erythematous halo with yellow-grayish color with a red border). The lesion can be VERY PAINFUL, and varies from 2-10mm in diameter. Generally last for 7-14 days, and heal gradually with LITTLE OR NO SCARRING. Occurs on **cheeks, lips, tongue, roof of mouth**.

Recurrent Aphthous Major (Major Aphthous Ulcer) large, usually > 10mm, VERY PAINFUL ulcers that occur frequently. Patients usually get more than one ulcer at a time. Unlike minor aphthous ulcers, major aphthous ulcers can last up to 6 weeks and LEAVE A SCAR UPON HEALING. Occurs on non-keratinizing tissue (LIPS, TONGUE, CHEEKS), but their border can extend onto keratinized tissue.

Recurrent Herpetiform Ulcerations-the MOST SEVERE aphthous ulcer, characterized by crops of multiple, small, shallow ulcers, often in cluster of up to 100 (1-3mm lesions), and may occur in any area of the oral cavity. These lesions are present almost continuously for 1-3 years, with relatively short remissions. More common in adult FEMALES, and usually heal within a month and DO NOT LEAVE SCARRING.

MAJOR & MINOR APHTHOUS ULCERS (CANKER SORES)
ULCERATIVE/APHTHOUS STOMATITIS

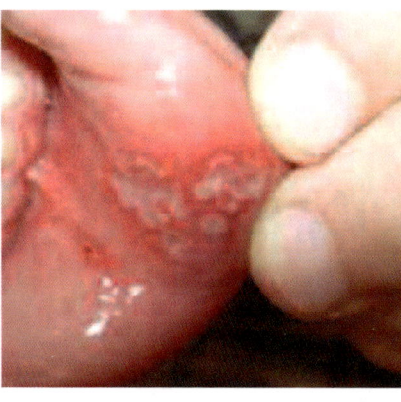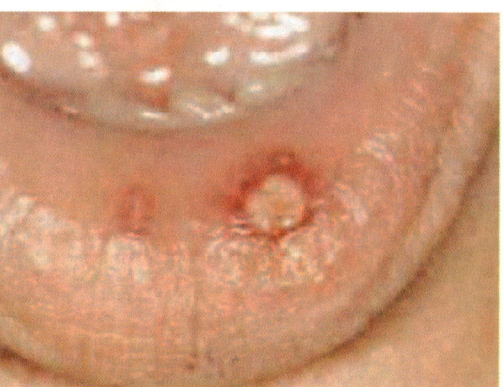

*Exact cause is unknown, but citrus, stress, allergies, immune reactions, and B_{12}, iron, zinc, and folic acid deficiencies may contribute (manifestation of Behcet Disease & Crohn's Disease)

Some Treatments: Non-alcoholic mouthwash, steroids.

Important: vesicular lesions (vesicles) DO NOT PRECEDE the formation of these ulcers. This is a distinctive diagnostic feature. When an ulcer heals, the epithelium that will eventually cover the defect is derived from intact epithelium at the ulcer margin.

ACTINOMYCOSIS — a subacute-to-chronic bacteria infection with Actinomyces (*A. israelii*) which are gram (+) filamentous bacteria that are normal inhabitants of the oral cavity and GI tract, characterized by contiguous spread, suppurative & granulomatous inflammatory reaction, and formation of multiple abscesses and sinus tracts that discharge SULFUR GRANULES. This infection is most likely to cause CHRONIC SUPPURATIVE LESION about the jaws. The most common clinical forms are cervicofacial actinomycosis (LUMPY JAW), thoracic, and abdominal actinomycosis.

CERVICOFACIAL ACTINOMYCOSIS ("LUMPY JAW") —the **most common manifestation of Actinomycosis**. Infection typically occurs in **patients with poor dental hygiene or after surgery**. In the **initial** stages, there is **soft tissue swelling of the perimandibular area**. Direct extension into the adjacent tissues occurs over time, along with the **development of fistulas that discharge purulent material** containing **yellow sulfur granules** (these granules are actually colonies of bacteria).

HISTOPLASMOSIS – disease caused by the **FUNGUS** Histoplasma Capsulatum. The symptoms vary greatly, but this disease **primary affects the LUNGS**. Sometimes affects other organs (Disseminated Histoplasmosis). Histoplasmosis infection is usually **asymptomatic**, but **may produce a benign, mild pulmonary illness** (the primary form of the disease).

- Oral Manifestations: nodular, ulcerative, or vegetative lesions on the **buccal mucosa, gingiva, tongue, palate, or lips** usually covered by a non-specific **Indurated gray membrane**.

SYPHILIS – a **sexually transmitted disease** caused by a spirochete **Treponema Pallidum** that occurs in 3 stages (*primary, secondary, & tertiary*). Syphilis is usually **treated with a PENICILLIN injection.**

Primary Syphilis-the first symptom is a **non-painful ulcer ("canker")** that **appears 2-6 weeks after exposure/infection.** Found on the body part exposed to the partner's ulcer (i.e. **penis, vulva, or vagina**). It can also develop on the **cervix, tongue, lips**, or other parts of the body. The **chancre** disappears within a **few weeks** even **without** treatment. If **not** treated during the primary stage, ~33% of people will progress to chronic stages.

PRIMARY SYPHILIS

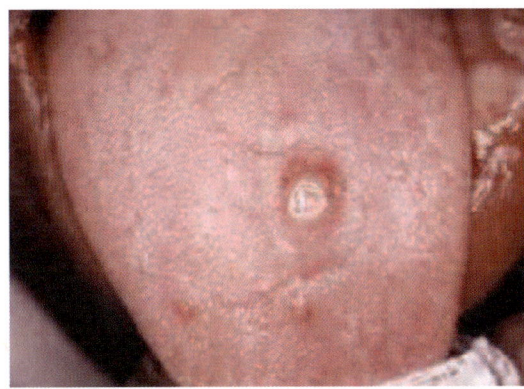
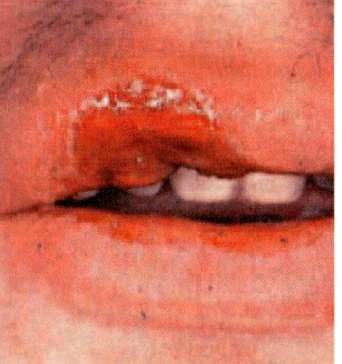

Secondary Syphilis-a **highly infectious** stage that **occurs 6 weeks after non-treatment of primary syphilis**. Often marked by a **skin** rash characterized by brown **"penny-sized"** sores. Widely disseminated spirochetes cause mucous membranes to **exhibit a reddish-brown maculopapular cutaneous rash** and ulcers covered with a **mucoid exudates** (mucous patches). **Condylomata lata** (elevated broad-based plaques) are also seen on the **skin** and **mucosal surfaces**.

Tertiary Syphilis-occurs in infected people **many years after non-treatment of secondary syphilis**. A **GUMMA** (a focal nodular mass) typifies this stage. Most commonly occurs on the **PALATE & TONGUE**. Bacteria damages the heart, eyes, brain, nervous system, bones, joints, or almost any other part of the body. In this **late stage**, untreated syphilis, although **not** contagious, **can cause serious heart abnormalities, mental disorders, blindness, other neurologic problems, and death.** Headache, stiff neck, and fever are symptoms of neurosyphilis.

NOTES

CONGENITAL SYPHILIS – caused by an infection by the **spirochete bacteria Treponema Pallidum** during the **fetal period**. Expectant mothers with syphilis can transmit the disease through the placenta to the unborn infant. **Nearly 50% of all infants infected during gestation die shortly before or after birth**. The severity of congenital syphilis depends on the time the organisms pass the placental barrier (protected up to the 16th week), the mother's stage of syphilis, and the fetus's immunologic response. If treated by the 4th or 5th month of pregnancy, 95% show no manifestations. However, if untreated, fetal sepsis may result in stillbirth or visceral & mucocutaneous manifestations.

CONGENITAL SYPHILIS & HUTCHINSON'S INCISORS

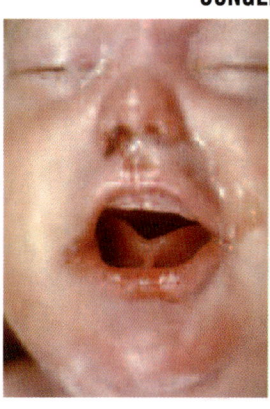
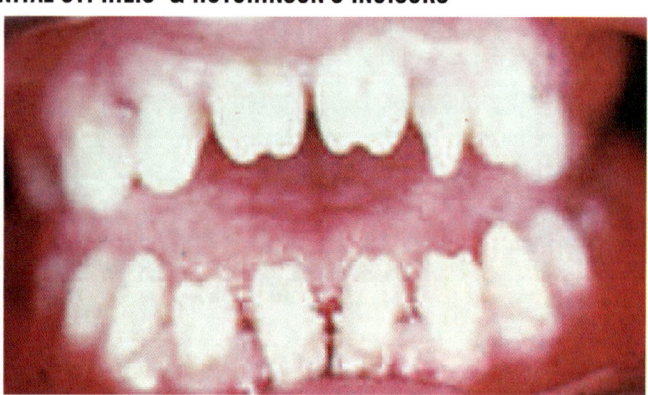

- **Newborn Symptoms**: irritability, blood discharge from nose, early rash (small blisters or flat or bumpy rash on the face, palms, and soles), failure to thrive, later rash (copper-colored vesicles on the palms and soles), **saddle nose, frontal bossing, short and high maxilla**.

- **Older Infant/Young Child Symptoms**: bone pain, joint swelling, abnormal teeth (**HUTCHINSON'S INCISORS**) *peg-shaped WIDELY SPACED permanent incisors, and notched at the end with a centrally placed crescent-shaped deformity*. Also gray, mucous-like patches on the anus and vulva (Condyloma lata), saber shins (bone abnormality of the lower leg), visual loss, CN VIII nerve deafness & intestinal keratitis, and scarring of the skin around earlier lesions of the mouth, genitalia, and anus ("rhagades").

- **Manifestations of congenital syphilis**: large frontal bone, Saddle nose, Hutchinson's teeth (very wide incisor crowns), & **MULBERRY MOLARS** (look like a mulberry). Not all people with mulberry molars have syphilis. There is **NO chancre in congenital syphilis**.

VESICULO-BULLOUS DISEASES

HERPES SIMPLEX VIRUS – always a vesicle (small virus filled with fluid) that breaks and the crust forms due to dried fibrin. Related to viruses that cause Mononucleosis, Chickenpox, and Shingles (not Mumps). **HSV is one of the most common viral diseases of man**.

HERPES SIMPLEX VIRUS TYPE 1 – **oral herpes** (affects outside of lips, face, skin, & oral mucosa) TRANSMITTED BY **DIRECT CONTACT**. HSV-1 includes **herpetic gingivostomatitis** (primary & secondary, and herepes labialis). It is **labial & intra-oral herpes** that are groups of small ulcerations in the hard palate, outside of lips, gingiva, or hands and fingers.

- **HSV Treatment**: "**SUPPORTIVE**" focused on relieving the acute symptoms so that fluid and nutritional intake can be maintained. Treatment involves **analgesics, topical anesthetics** before eating, maintaining electrolyte balance, and anti-viral agents. **NO CORTICOSTEROIDS** (contraindicated)!

PRIMARY HERPETIC GINGIVOSTOMATITIS (Acute Herpetic Gingivstomatitis)-the primary herpes infection (HSV-1) that mainly affects YOUNG CHILDREN (under age 5), but may also affect young adults (15-25yrs). It usually occurs in a child who has not had any contact with HSV-1, and who thus has no neutralizing antibodies. Nearly all primary infections are of the sub-clinical type that may only have flu-like symptoms, with 1-2 mild sores in the mouth that go unnoticed by parents. In other children, the primary infection may be manifested by acute symptoms (acute herpetic gingivostomatitis) these prodromal symptoms are (fever, malaise, irritability, headache, dysphagia, vomiting, cervical lympadenopathy) 1-2 days prior to local lesions. Then, fiery red gingival tissues and small yellowish vesicles form that rupture quickly, causing painful shallow, round, discrete ulcers with an erythematous (red) halo on the FREE & ATTACHED MUCOSA. Thus, the primary HSV-1 infection ranges from sub-clinical (asymptomatic) to severe systemic infections. Dehydration is the most serious potential problem due to the child not wanting to eat or drink because of the pain. A generalized marginal gingivitis may precede the ulcers.

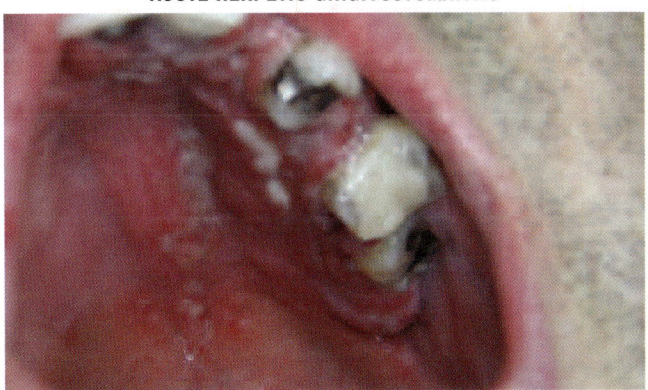

ACUTE HERPETIC GINGIVOSTOMATITIS

PRIMARY HERPETIC GINGIVOSTOMATITIS most commonly occurs in CHILDREN & YOUNG ADULTS. Patients develop FEVER, irritability, regional lymphadenopathy, and headache. Within days, the gingiva is intensely inflamed. Any part of the oral mucosa and lips may become involved. Vesicles then form and rupture shortly later to leave shallow VERY PAINFUL ulcers covered with a GRAY MEMBRANE and surrounded by a RED HALO. Ulcers heal on their own in 7-14 days.

- Treatment: fluid intake, good oral hygiene, and gentle debridement of the mouth. In healthy individuals, the lesions heal in 7-14 days, and the ulcers heal WITHOUT SCARRING.

- After recovery from primary HSV, the virus is not cleared from the body, but lies dormant in a non-replicating state in the sensory nervous system (trigeminal ganglion). Periodically, latency reactivates and allows the virus to return to the skin or mucous membranes, where it causes a recurrent infection.

- Primary herpes occurs only in YOUNG PATIENTS (baby, children, adolescents). Fever, malaise, pain, or could be CHICKENPOX (varicella zoster virus) in a 6yr old child. Multiple vesicles, sick for one week.

- AFTER the initial primary attack during early childhood, HSV-1 remains inactive in the TRIGEMINAL GANGLION (sensory nerve ganglia), but often reappears as the familiar "cold sore" on the OUTSIDE of the lips ("Recurrent Herpes Labialis"). Emotional stress, trauma, and excessive sun exposure may cause recurrent herpetic lip lesions. Acyclovir 5% ointment (Zovirax) can successfully reduce the duration and severity of these lip sores.

NOTES

SECONDARY (RECURRENT) HERPETIC STOMATITIS-generally occurs in **ADULTS**, triggered by trauma, fatigue, RTI (respiratory tract infection), stress, allergy, or UV exposure that causes the release/reactivation of the latent HSV-1 virus. This reactivation causes a recurrent infection (i.e. cold sores) on the lips (that is bound to periosteum), hard palate, attached gingiva, and alveolar ridge. Site-specificity is a characteristic manifestation.

- Recurrent Herpes Simplex Virus-**COLD SORES** on the lips are the most common manifestation of infection. Some factors often associated with a recurrent outbreak are sunburn, fatigue, emotional upset, trauma, upper respiratory tract infection, or menstruation. Often one day before the vesicles form, tingling or itching of the skin or mucosa occurs. Vesicles ulcerate and resolve just like in primary herpes.

- Remains **LOCALIZED** on the lower lip or inside the mouth. Lasts about 2 weeks then heals by itself, but recurrent herpes virus always lays dormant in the trigeminal nerve ganglion. May or may not have fever, malaise. May present with vesicles in hard palate.

HERPES LABIALIS (Fever Blisters/Cold Sores)-extremely common HSV-1 disease. Characterized by an eruption of small, usually **PAINFULL** blisters on the skin of the lips, mouth, gingiva, or skin around the mouth. The reason most patients suffering from Recurrent Herpes Labialis rarely give a history of having had acute herpetic gingivostomatitis is the primary infection was sub-clinical. HSV-1 lesions (cold sores) are found more forward in the mouth (tongue, gingiva, buccal mucosa) appearing as vesicles (small, clear, ulcerated, and crusty blisters) around the mouth and lips.

HERPES LABIALIS (COLD SORES/FEVER BLISTERS) HSV-1

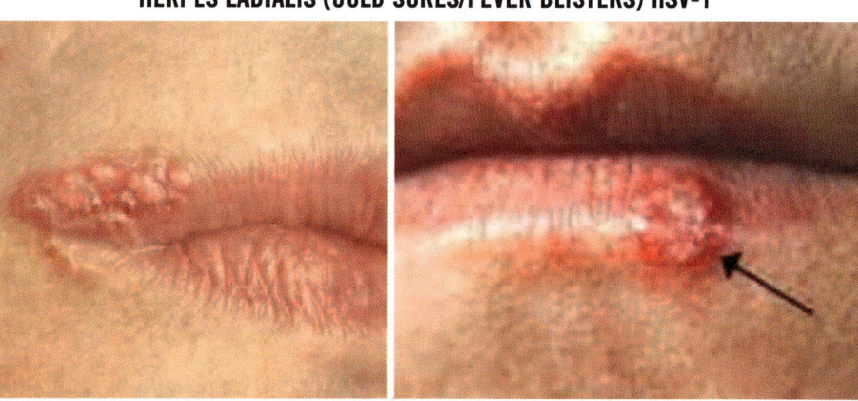

Histological Features: cytopathic effect (CPE) takes the form of **BALLOONING DEGENERATION** of epithelial cells with loss of cohesion to adjacent cells. The nuclei are often multiple, with margination of the chromatin around the intra-nuclear inclusions called Lipschultz Bodies. These changes are seen in Tzanck smear scrapings taken from an unroofed vesicle.

HERPES SIMPLEX VIRUS TYPE 2 ("HERPES GENITALIS" OR "GENITAL HERPES")– transmitted via **SEXUAL CONTACT**, and affects the mucosa of the genitalia and anal regions, but **may also occur in mouth**. Not as common as HSV1. "Genital Herpes" may have serious consequences in pregnant women because the virus **can be transmitted to the infant during vaginal delivery**, and can damage the infant's CNS and/or eyes.

HERPES SIMPLEX VIRUS TYPE 3 (HSV-3) —caused by **Herpes VARICELLA-ZOSTER virus** (**DOES NOT CROSS THE MIDLINE**). Produces recurrent herpes (adult shingles/herpes zoster), & chickenpox (primary herpes). Occurs after activation of varicella virus, the affected skin has **VERY PAINFULL ulcerated redicule vesicles**, and the lesion follows the path of the trigeminal nerve. May occur in an elderly patient with a history of leukemia (compromised immune system).

VARICELLA VIRUS — can cause Herpes Zoster lesions along sensory nerve roots in later life. It is a member of the herpes virus group that **causes chickenpox (varicella) & shingles (herpes zoster)**. Varicella virus is highly contagious and may be spread by direct contact or droplets. The histology of chickenpox and shingles shows the same cytopathic effect as herpes simplex.

- Chickenpox-primarily a disease of **CHILDREN** that peaks at school-age in winter and spring, characterized by the appearance on the skin and mucous membranes of successive crops of typical **pruritic vesicular lesions that break easily and scab**. Usually accompanied by mild constitutional symptoms (fever, malaise), and is **very contagious 1 day before the rash's onset and until all of the vesicles have crusted**. It is relatively benign in children, but adult infection may be complicated by pneumonia and encephalitis. ZIG (Zoster Immune Globulin) reaches morbidity in high-risk children.

- Shingles (Herpes Zoster)-caused by the **reactivation of a LATENT varicella-zoster virus** that may have remained in the body from a childhood chickenpox. The virus reaches sensory ganglia of the spinal and cranial nerves, producing an inflammatory response. Characterized by painful vesicles on the skin or mucosal surfaces along the distribution of the sensory nerve.

- Shingles (Herpes Zoster) Example: 16-yr old male with **fever & malaise, DOES NOT CROSS THE MIDLINE, and is very painful**. Can also be in a 65-year old male with a history of leukemia (weak immune system) who had chickenpox as a child. The affected skin shows vesicles and lesions follow the path of the nerve due to activation of varicella virus.

HERPES SIMPLEX VIRUS 4 (EPSTEIN-BARR VIRUS)

HERPES SIMPLEX VIRUS TYPE 4 —caused by **EPSTEIN-BARR VIRUS (EBV)** a member of the herpes virus group that **causes Infectious Mononucleosis (Kissing Disease)**, Hairy leukoplakia, Chronic Fatigue Syndrome, and two cancers (Burkitt's Lymphoma & Nasopharyngeal Carcinoma).

HAIRY LEUKOPLAKIA-this is NOT hairy tongue. **Appears 99% of time in HIV+ patients. ALWAYS white furry lesions on LATERAL tongue borders (bilateral) caused by EPSTEIN-BARR VIRUS.** Can usually diagnose without biopsy. Anti-viral medication removes the lesion, but it reappears when patients stops taking medications. **Only treat if the patient requests with anti-viral medication.** Presents as a WHITE extensive area in the LATERAL border of the tongue, present for 4 months, asymptomatic. The surface lesion is irregular, bluish areas on the gingiva, candida, and recurrent herpes infection may coexist. **99% occurs in HIV+ patients, so patient should get an HIV test**.

INFECTIOUS MONONUCLEOSIS-no specific oral manifestations, but secondary lesions occur and **neck swellings**, which are also characteristic of Hodgkin's Disease and Tuberculosis.

BURKITT'S LYMPHOMA-cancer caused by **EPSTEIN-BARR VIRUS**. High-grade **Non-Hodgkin's Lymphoma** (cancer)/neoplasm with a viral etiology **endemic in AFRICA**, but occurs sporadically in North America. There are significant differences between the African & Non-African forms, but **BOTH are histologically identical**. One manifests most often as a large osteolytic jaw lesion (African Form), the other as an **abdominal mass** (Non-African Form).

Jaw lesions usually present as expanding intra-oral masses with **mobility of the involved teeth**. Radiographically: **"MOTH-EATEN"** appearance with **poorly marginated bone destruction**.

Non-African Burkitt's Lymphoma patients are **generally older (ages 9-12yrs)**, with no gender predilection. Presents most often as an **ABDOMINAL MASS** involving mesenteric lymph nodes or Peyer Patches in the ileocecal region, often with **intestinal obstruction**. Involvement of the gonads, retroperitoneum, and other viscera are less common.

Burkitt's lymphoma is the **FIRST HUMAN CANCER WITH STRONG EVIDENCE OF VIRAL ETIOLOGY**. Epstein-Barr virus (herpes-type virus) as these patients have high titers of antibodies against EBV. <u>Important</u>: **Epstein-Barr is also associated with infectious mononucleosis, & orally hairy leukoplakia**.

BURKITT'S LYMPHOMA

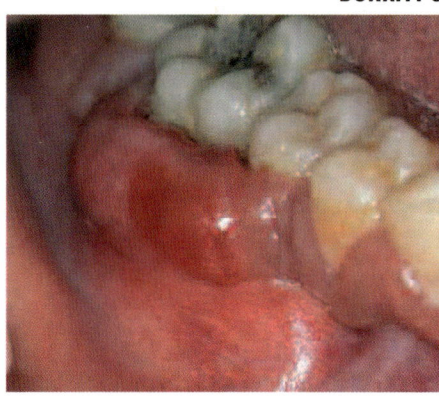
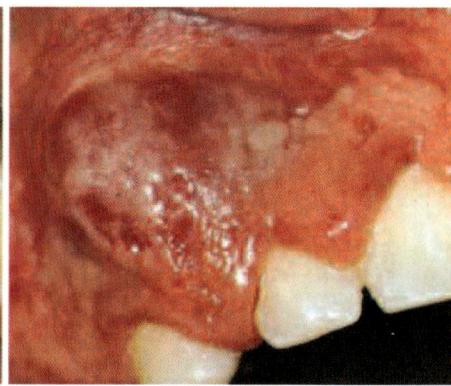

African Burkitt's Lymphoma (African Jaw Lymphoma)-affects younger patients (**age 3-8yrs**) than the non-African form. Affects males more than females (2:1), and typically involves the mandible, maxilla, & abdomen. Extra-nodal involvement of the retroperitoneum, kidneys, liver, ovaries, and endocrine glands may be affected.

HERPES SIMPLEX VIRUS TYPE 5 – cytomegalovirus that affects **salivary glands**.

HERPES SIMPLEX VIRUS TYPE 8—associated with **Kaposi's sarcoma-AIDS/HIV**. Kaposi Sarcoma: 34-year old male with AIDS, common on palate. Can have Kaposi Sarcoma without AIDS, but in U.S. it is usually with AIDS. It's a **superifical cancer on the skin, multiple, made of blood vessels, & is NEGATIVE to** pressure test (so don't confuse with Hemangioma which is pressure test positive +). Kaposi's Sarcoma is **very common on the PALATE**. Mostly associated with **HIV**, but can have Kaposi's sarcoma even without AIDS. (-) to pressure test. **RED LESIONS on the hard palate**.

KAPOSI'S SARCOMA—an oral manifestation most commonly associated with **AIDS**. It is a **MALIGNANT NEOPLASM** originating in the skin, characterized by **abnormal vascular proliferation (cancer of the lining of the blood vessels)**. It occurs on multiple sites, especially lower extremities. The initial lesions are small, red papules that enlarge and fuse to form **purple-to-brown spongy nodules**. It spreads to lymph nodes and internal organs.

- **HARD PALATE** is the most common intra-oral location of **KAPOSI'S SARCOMA**, followed by the gingiva and buccal mucosa.

- Important: **AIDS** is caused by an **RNA retrovirus** (HIV = HTLV-III) acquired by sexual contact (homosexual & heterosexual), or contaminated blood products.

Tests To Diagnose Herpetic Lesions:
Tzanck Smear-a **cytologic examination of fluid** harvested from an unopened vesicle stained with giemsa, and viewed by the **light microscope**. Pathologist looks for **LIPSHULTZ BODIES** (epithelial cells with intra-nuclear inclusions).

Fluorescent Staining-cells show (+) fluorescence when stained with fluorescent labeled HSV immune serum and globulin. **Used to distinguish between herpes zoster & herpes simplex**.

Isolation in Tissue Culture

Antibody Titers (Anti-HSV Ab Titers)-a test for complement fixing or neutralizing antibody in acute and convalescent sera, and on tissue sections (begins in 1 week, and peaks at 3 weeks).

Biopsy-shows **intra-epithelial cleft covered by an exudates of fibrin** & PMN leukocyte. The epithelium exhibits degenerative cells that include bizarre giant cells, and cells with displaced chromatin with perinuclear halos and inclusions. *Arthrogram is NOT a test to diagnose herpetic lesions.

HERPANGINA—an **acute** infectious disease (stomatitis/mouth inflammation) affecting **YOUNG CHILDREN** caused by a **Group A Coxsackie Virus**. It is differentiated clinically from HSV-1 (cold sore virus) as herpangina oral ulcerations/vesicles usually occur in the **BACK OF THE THROAT** around the tonsils and posterior palate. Herpangina may also appear on the tongue.

- **Clinical Features**: are mild and of short duration compared to HSV-1. Herpangina **begins with a sore throat, fever, headache, and sometimes vomiting & abdominal pain**. Papules or vesicles soon form in the pharynx, and evolve into shallow ulcers that heal spontaneously. Herpangina usually runs its course in less than 1 week. **Treatment**: **PALLIATIVE**.

HERPANGINA (GROUP A COXSACKIE VIRUS)

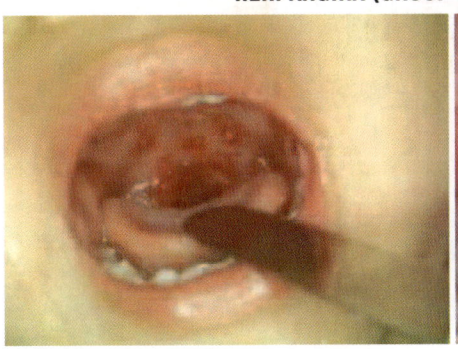
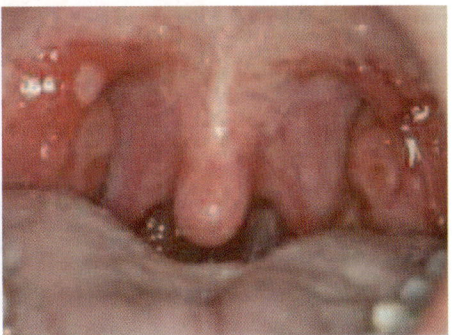

HAND, FOOT & MOUTH DISEASE (HFMD) - **VIRAL INFECTION** (usually Coxsackie A) that usually affects **infants and children**. Produces red-erythematous lesions/macules/vesicles areas in the **mouth, foot, & hands**. Oral lesions/vesicles appear on the **buccal mucosa, tongue, gingiva, & lips**.

- Patient has **fever, malaise, vomiting, fatigue** (may be confused with a cold). HFMD is self-limiting, disappearing by itself in < 15 days, & does not return. Erythematous macules develop central vesicles. A very mild disease that **is often not diagnosed**. No treatment, but symptoms may be eased with analgesics.

BENIGN MUCOUS MEMBRANE PEMPIGOID (BMMP) – a chronic self-limiting mucocutaneous autoimmune disease, usually limited to **oral** and **ocular** mucous membranes (conjunctival involvement may cause blindness). Usually effects **women over age 50yrs**. More common in the oral cavity, but much less severe **(better prognosis) than Pemphigus**. Occurs more often than realized due to improper diagnosis.

- A vesiculobullous disease where auto-antibodies act against basement membrane components (**below epithelium = subepithelial vesicle**), between epithelium & C.T. so **destruction is below the epithelium**. Usually shows nice epithelium since the epithelium is complete & C.T. is separated (not seen in Pemphigus).

- Oral lesions usually present as a **"desquamative gingivitis"** in which vesicles form, rupture, and leave **gingival erosions**. Found in all mucous membranes, but is less severe than Pemphigus.

- <u>Treatment</u>: Biopsy and systemic STEROID therapy. PAINFUL ORAL ULCERS.

<u>Important</u>: The MAJOR histological difference between BMMP & Pemphigus Vulgaris is **BMMP vesicles are subepidermal with no acantholysis**, while with Pemphigus Vulgaris, there is acantholysis and supra-basilar vesicle.

PEMPHIGUS VULGARIS – a chronic RARE SKIN DISEASE characterized by the formation of vesicles & bullae produced by dyhesion (**acantholysis**) of epidermal cells due to an autoimmune mechanism where antibodies attack the intracellular junction of epithelium. Usually occurs after age 30yrs (usually ages 30-50yrs), and **occurs more frequently in JEWISH people**.

- Oral lesions are often the FIRST MANIFESTATION. Intact bullae are rarely seen in the oral cavity, rather, **large areas of ulceration and erosions covered by a white or blood-tinged exudates**. Sometimes, areas of epithelium will slide off simply by rubbing of an apparently unaffected area (**Nikolsky's Sign** is an indication of Pemphigus vulgaris that may also be found in BMMP). This sign occurs when apparently normal epithelium may be separated at the basal layer and RUBBED OFF when pressed with a sliding motion. Pemphigus is often fatal without treatment, which includes high-dose systemic steroids or chemotherapy (Methotrexate).

PEMPHIGUS VULGARIS

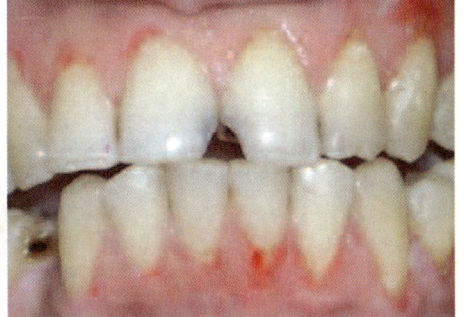
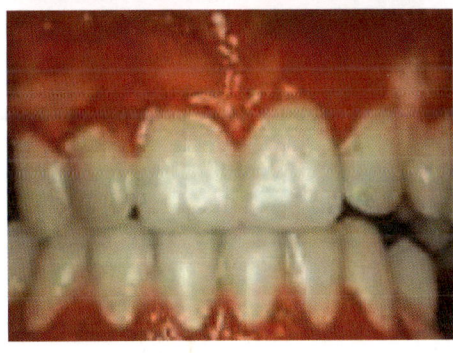
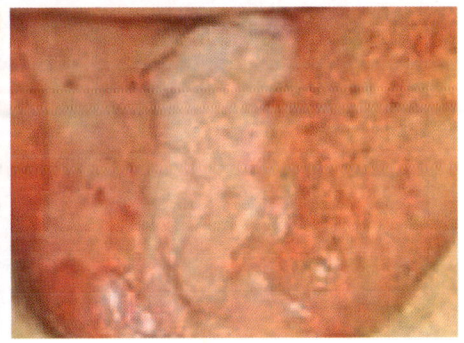

- **Histologic Features**: vesicles and bullae are formed entirely intra-epithelially, just **ABOVE** the basal layer of cells (**suprabasilar vesicles**). There is intercellular edema & loss of intercellular bridges with loss of cohesiveness (**acantholysis or dyhesion**). Clumps of cells are often found floating free in the vesicle space (**Tzanck cells**).

- Pemphigus Vulgaris is the most common form, and is more severe than Pemphigoid (**BMMP**). With Pemphigus, the patient has auto-antibodies produced against epidermal cell surface glycoprotein (a component of desmosomes that attaches epithelial cells together) causing painful oral ulcers. More common in older females (> 50yrs). Intraepithelial vesicle. A very bad disease whose only treatment is **STEROIDS**. Patient has vesicles on the skin. **GINGIVA** is red, inflamed and is the most common location in mouth.

- MUST DO **BIOPSY TO DIAGNOSE** using 2 small portions of tissue (one in a vile, the other goes into a vile of Michel solution (the fixative to do the **immunofluorsence**). If bullae is intraepithelial then its Pemphigus Vulgaris. If bullae are between epithelial & C.T. it is Pemphigoid. Produce Ab against desmosomes (attach one epithelial cell to another), so desmosomes are destroyed and the epithelium is broken causing gingival ulcerations. Tissue in the "Michel solution" shows yellowish fluorescence areas show where the antibodies are against desmosomes.

RUBELLA VIRUS—causes German Measles (Rubella). Characteristic **RASH** (flat, pink spots on the face that spreads to other body parts). Oral manifestations may include **swollen and congested tonsils, and red macules**.

HEPATITIS A (VIRAL OR INFECTIOUS HEPATITIS)—caused by an **RNA Enterovirus** usually transmitted by the **FECAL-ORAL ROUTE**. An infectious disease of the LIVER that most often occurs in young adults and is prevalent in areas with inadequate sewerage. **SHELLFISH** from contaminated waters is also a prime source. Initial symptoms (fever, abdominal pain, nausea, then jaundice) appear after an incubation period of 3-6 weeks. Vaccination exists.

- Damage to liver cells causes **increased serum levels of enzymes like transaminases**, normally active in liver cells. The detection of the increased serum levels of transaminases helps diagnose the disease. In most cases of Hepatitis A, the infection is self-limiting, and **recovery occurs within 4 months**.

HEPATITIS B ("SERUM HEPATITIS") – an infectious **LIVER DISEASE** caused by a **DNA virus** that produces **liver inflammation and necrosis**. Main method of transmission is exposure to **contaminated blood or serum** (but can be **transmitted sexually** or via **blood transfusions**). There is a **high rate of transmission** among **drug addicts** who may use **contaminated** needles. Vaccination exists.

- **Signs & Symptoms**: similar to Hepatitis A (fever, abdominal pain, nausea), but it **has a longer incubation period of 2-3 months**. Symptoms develop slower, but last longer. Most patients fully recover, but **some develop chronic liver disease**.

- Hepatitis B transmission is **a MAJOR CONCERN to the dental profession**, which have at least 3x higher risk than the general population to acquire this virus. Thus, **ALWAYS USE UNIVERSAL PRECAUTIONS**. Hepatitis D is found ONLY in patients with acute or chronic episodes of Hepatitis B.

- Hepatitis B vaccine is **recommended for all health care personnel**. A series of 3 doses is required (the 2nd and 3rd doses are given at 1 & 6 months after the 1st dose. The injection is given IM (in the deltoid muscle).

The presence of **SURFACE ANTIGEN (A or B)** in a patient's serum indicates the patient is potentially infected with Hepatitis ("carrier state"). Hepatitis viruses are **HIGHLY HEAT RESISTANT** (even more than AIDS virus). However, **autoclaving properly kills them**.

HEPATITIS C-an infectious liver disease that can cause liver scarring and cirrhosis. Spread mainly via **blood-to-blood contact associated with IV drug use, poorly sterilized medical equipment, and transfusions**. Hepatitis C virus persists in the liver and can be treated with medication (Peginterferon and Ribavirin). There is no vaccine, and liver transplantation may be required for severely damaged livers.

IMPORTANT DIAGNOSTIC TERMS

BIOPSY – the **MOST RELIABLE technique to diagnose soft tissue lesions**. Scalpel is the instrument of choice since it cleanly removes tissues without dehydrating them as cautery or a high-frequency cutting knife may. **FORMALIN (10%) is the fixative of choice**. The rationale for surgical removal and biopsy of a large periapical lesion suspected to be of inflammatory origin is that **a clinical diagnosis can be confirmed microscopically**. Biopsy is the only way to distinguish between a granuloma and a cyst.

EXCISIONAL BIOPSY –involves **TOTAL EXCISION** of a small lesion for microscopic study. This is preferred if the lesion size is such that it may be removed along with a margin of normal tissue, and the wound can be closed primarily (ex: a 1cm exophytic mass-a lesion that grows outward from an epithelial surface on the cheek).

INCISIONAL BIOPSY (DIAGNOSTIC BIOPSY) – **removes only a SMALL SECTION** of tissue for examination. Done when lesions are too large to excise initially without having established a diagnosis, or are of such a nature that excision would be inadvisable.

CHAPTER 2

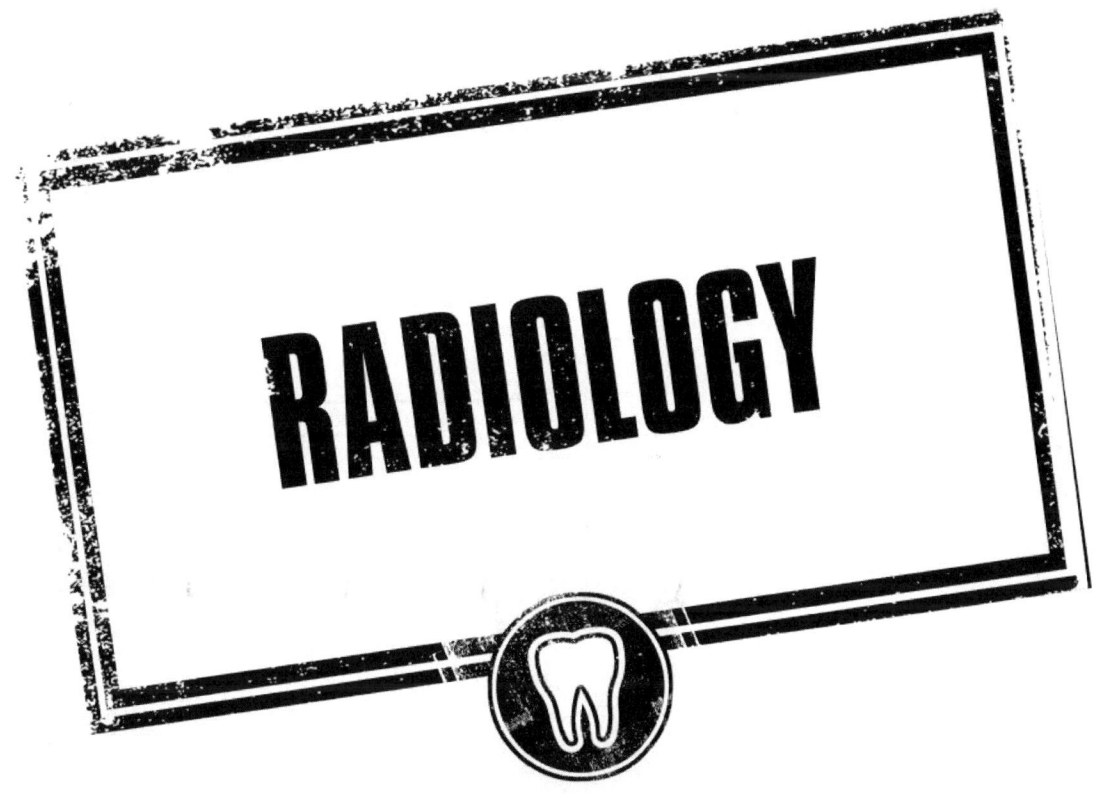

NOTES

Radiographs show shading from black to white (most radiolucent to most radiopaque). From least to most radiopaque: (PDL space, dentin, enamel, ZOE, and amalgam).

Radiopaque Structures & Dense Materials: metals, enamel, dentin, and bone that INHIBIT the passage of x-rays and appear WHITE on the processed film. Less radiation penetrates the structure and reaches the film.

RADIOLUCENT STRUCTURES AND MATERIALS – less dense materials like **soft tissue and air space** that appear gray to black on processed film) **ALLOWING RADIATION to pass through** by absorbing very little radiation. More radiation penetrates the structure and reaches the film.

- Radiolucent Lesions-appear every time bone is DESTROYED. **Unilocular & Multilocular are terms only used to describe radiolucent lesions**.

    1. **well-defined unilocular (one cavity)**: border is well-defined. Most benign lesions are unilocular, well-defined.
    2. **well-defined multilocular**: border is well-defined with several cavities.
    3. **well-defined honeycomb or soap bubble (multilocular)**:
    4. **diffuse**-cannot follow the border of the radiolucency: 90% of the time it is cancer. If loss of cortical plates, the first diagnosis is cancer.

OSTEORADIONECROSIS – the **necrosis of bone produced by ionizing radiation** that is more common in the MANDIBLE than maxilla due to the richer vascular supply to the maxilla, and because the mandible is more often irradiated. The most common factors precipitating osteoradionecrosis are **pre-irradiation & post-irradiation extractions, and periodontal disease**. Damage to blood vessels (not nerves or muscles) predisposes a patient to developing osteoradionecrosis. A complications that can occur with patients taking IV Bisphosphonates or oral bisphonates for more than three years orally (i.e. Fosamax).

Osteoradionecrosis is more common IN THE MANDIBLE probably because of the richer vascular supply to the maxilla and the fact that the mandible is more frequently irradiated. Caution with patients on IV bisphonates or if taking oral bisphonates (i.e. Fosamax).

- May occur after dental extractions.

- The most common factors precipitating osteoradionecrosis are pre and post irradiation extractions and periodontal disease.

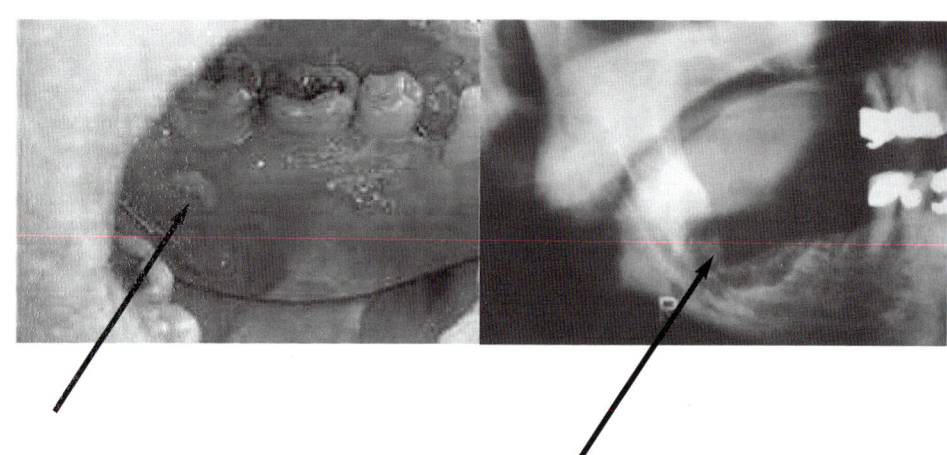

HAMULAR PROCESS — the **bony projection that arises from the SPHENOID BONE and extends downward and slightly posteriorly**. On the radiograph, it is seen in proximity to the posterior surface of the maxillary tuberosity. It varies greatly in length, width, and shape among patients. It usually exhibits a bulbous point, but sometimes the point is tapered.

CORONOID PROCESS — this image of the mandible often appears in the **periapical radiographs of the MOLAR REGION of the MAXILLA**. As the mouth is opened, the coronoid process moves forward, and thus comes into view most often when the mouth is opened to its fullest extent at the time the exposure is made. It is evidenced by a **tapered or triangular radiopacity** that can be seen below, or sometimes superimposed on the molar teeth and maxilla.

Dental Radiographs should be retained **INDEFINITELY**. The dental record must include documentation of informed consent and the exposure of radiographs (i.e. number and type of films, rationale for exposure and interpretation). **Legally, dental radiographs are the PROPERTY OF THE DENTIST**. However, patients have a right to reasonable access to dental radiographs, which includes having a copy forwarded to another dentist.

- **Patients may refuse dental radiographs**, but the dentist must decide whether an accurate diagnosis can be provided, and whether treatment can be provided.

- No document can be signed by the patient that releases the dentist from liability.

DIGITAL RADIOGRAPHY — requires **LESS radiation** than traditional radiography because **the sensor is more sensitive to x-rays**. Also, radiation exposure to the patient is **reduced 50-80%** with digital radiography. The **sensor is used in place of film** in digital radiography. Intra-oral, panoramic, & cephalometric images can all be obtained digitally.

Advantages:
- Superior gray-scale resolution. The human eye can only appreciate 32 shades of gray. The traditional radiograph differentiates 16-25 shades of gray, while the digital image uses up to 256 shades of gray.

- Less patient radiation and increased speed of image viewing.

- Decreased cost of equipment and film, image enhancement (this may also be a disadvantage in legal issues since the image can be manipulated), superior patient education tool. Although initial set-up costs for digital radiography can be significant, the elimination of film, darkroom chemicals, and equipment reduces maintenance costs.

- Each digital sensor costs between $5,000-$7,500 (initially expensive, but over the long-term, the office will save money due to savings in time, no film required, developing chemicals, etc.). Digital radiography is the absolute future in dentistry.

DIGITAL SENSOR

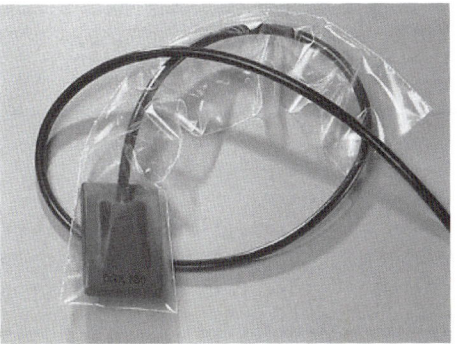

STORAGE PHOSPHOR IMAGING SYSTEM – a type of digital imaging system that uses a REVERSIBLE IMAGING PLATE rather than a sensor to record the image. The plates are more flexible, thus more comfortable for the patient.

DIRECT DIGITAL IMAGING SYSTEM – uses an intraoral sensor attached to a fiberoptic cable.

Indirect Digital Imaging System – scans an existing radiograph and digitizes the image.

Charge-Coupled Device (CCD) – currently **the most common digital image receptor**. It is a solid state detector with a silicon chip embedded in it (it is the electronic circuit in the silicon chip that is sensitive to x-rays). CCD technology is also used in home video cameras, fax machines, and telescopes.

PRIMARY RADIATION – the **radiation generated at the ANODE of the x-ray tube that is attenuated by the filter and object**. The amount of primary radiation follows the inverse square law measured from the focal spot. The attenuation of primary radiation is measured with a narrow beam geometry to include all secondary (i.e. scattered radiation).

SECONDARY RADIATION ("SCATTERED RADIATION") – arises from interactions of the primary radiation beam with atoms in the object being imaged. Since scattered radiation deviates from the straight line path between the x-ray focus and image receptor, scattered radiation is a major source of image degradation in both x-ray and nuclear medicine imaging techniques. When x-ray radiation passes through a patient, 3 interactions can occur (coherent scatter, photo electric absorption, and Compton scattering). Of these, **most scattered x-rays in diagnostic x-ray imaging arise from Compton scattering**. A LEADED, RETANGULAR cone (PID) best reduces the amount of scatter radiation to the patient as this greatly reduces the size of the beam.

- In performing normal dental diagnostic procedures, the operator receives the greatest hazard from secondary (scatter) radiation.

COLLIMATION – the **control of the SIZE & SHAPE of the x-ray beam** using metal plates, slots, or bars to confine and direct radiation (i.e. x-rays or gamma rays) to a specific region and/or to discriminate against radiation from unwanted directions (i.e. scattered radiation). In x-ray imaging systems, a collimator mounted to the x-ray tube is used to define the dimensions of the beam which is to be incident on the subject and detector. To minimize radiation dose and to comply with government regulations, a certain level of precision must be maintained.

- It is a basic rule of radiation hygiene that the **radiation beam be as small as practical**. For intraoral radiography, by state law, **the diameter of a circular beam of radiation at the patient's skin cannot be larger than 2.75 inches**. One can use a diaphragm or metal cylinders, cones, or tubes to collimate the beam.

- These devices reduce the amount of radiation received by the exposed tissues and the radiation to surrounding tissues due to x-ray beam divergence.

X-ray beam is composed of rays of different wavelengths and penetrating power (polychromatic) because the potential across the x-ray tube constantly changes as the kilovoltage changes:

- Short wavelength (high energy) x-rays: have great penetrating power (are useful). Short wavelength x-rays are produced at higher kilovoltages and penetrate objects more readily (**these form the image on the film**).

- Long wavelength (low energy) x-rays: are produced at lower kilovoltages (kVp) thus have low penetrating power (are easily absorbed), and do not reach the film in reasonable quantities because they are attenuated by the soft tissues. Low energy rays only add to the total amount of radiation the patient receives. Aluminum discs are used to "filter" out these USELESS long wave rays to increase the overall quality of the x-ray beam.

FILTRATION – the **removal of parts of the x-ray spectrum** using **absorbing materials in the x-ray beam**. The x-ray spectrum reaching the patient is filtered by attenuating material in its path. Filtering the beam is used to modify the spectral or spatial distribution of x-ray (or both). **Filtration reduces patient dose, contrast, & film density**.

1. **Inherent filtration**-the filtration of an x-ray beam by any parts of the x-ray tube or tube shield through which the beam must pass. The parts include the glass envelope of the x-ray tube and **OIL surrounds the x-ray tube to cool the tube to dissipate heat**, and the exit window in the tube housing. The inherent filtration corresponds to ~0.51mm of aluminum.

2. **Added filtration**-obtained by placing thin sheets of aluminum in the cone to filter the useful beam further.

3. **Total filtration** of the x-ray beam before it reaches the patient consists of the inherent filtration + added filtration. The recommended total is the equivalent of 0.5mm (below 50 kVp) and 2.5mm (over 70 kVp) of aluminum.

When taking radiographs, **the operator should STAND AT LEAST 6 FEET AWAY from the patient to reduce radiation exposure to the operator and should also stand behind a lead shield if possible**. The operator should **NEVER remain in the room holding the x-ray packet** in place for the patient. If a film must be held in place by someone else (i.e. for a child), drape the parent and have him or her hold the film. All dental personnel should wear film badges that monitor exposure dosages.

1. The operator must avoid the primary beam by positioning themselves at a 90°-135° angle to the beam.

2. Always maintain proper infection control when taking and processing dental radiographs!

EKTA-SPEED FILM – provides the **MOST EFFECTIVE way to REDUCE exposure time**, amount of radiation reaching the patient, and amount of scatter radiation (secondary radiation) to the dentist.

Additional Factors that Reduce Patient Radiation:
- **Lead apron & thyroid (cervical) collar**-is the most effective at stopping x-rays, so patient should always wear both. The cervical collar protects the thyroid gland.
- Increasing filtration using an aluminum disk.
- Lead diaphragms placed within the cone of an x-ray tubehead.
- Collimating an x-ray beam.
- Ekta-Speed Film
- Increasing the source-film distance.
- Intensifying screens-used for all extra-oral radiography (panoramics, cephalometrics).

Committee on Radiation Protection of National Bureau of Standards: recommends a **person who works near radiation be exposed in 1 year to a maximum dose of 5 REM (0.1 REM per week)**. Secondary (scatter radiation) is the greatest hazard to the dental team.

- **MPD (Maximum Permissible Dose of Radiation Exposure)**. The yearly MPD for a non-occupationally exposed person is 0.5 REM and 5 REM for people who work near radiation.

Sequence of Radiation Injury:
1. **Latent Period**-period of time between radiation exposure and onset of symptoms. It may be short or long, depending on the total dose of radiation received and amount of time it took to receive the dose.

2. **Period of Cell Injury**-comes after the latent period. Cellular injury may cause cell death, changes in cell function, or abnormal mitosis of cells.

3. **Recovery Period**-the last event in the sequence of radiation injury. Some cells recover from the radiation injury, especially if the radiation is "low level".

NOTES

Effects of radiation exposure are ADDITIVE, and the damage that remains non-repaired accumulates in tissues. The cumulative effects of repeated radiation exposure can lead to various serous health problems (i.e. **carcinogenesis**, which leads to various **carcinomas**, **genetic mutations** that cause birth defects, **different leukemias, and cataracts**).

Carcinogenesis & Genetic Mutations are important and serious effects of repeated exposure to low doses of x-radiation. The mechanisms involved are due to frame-shift mutations, synergism with chemical carcinogens, and altered DNA repair enzyme functions.

Cells in the body have different sensitivities to radiation. In general, the greater the rate of potential for mitosis and the more immature the cells and tissues, the more susceptible or sensitive these cells are to radiation.

- **Radiosensitive Cells**: small lymphocytes (immature blood cells), bone marrow, **reproductive** cells (sperm/ova), and immature bone cells.
  - Prostate gland is very sensitive to radiation.
  - Hemopoietic tissue is the most sensitive to radiation

- **Radioresistant Cells**: mature bone, muscle, and nerve (pulp).
  - Muscle cells are the most radioresistant.

RADIATION ABSORBED DOSE ("RAD") — a measure of the energy imparted by any type of ionizing radiation to a mass of any type of matter. The traditional unit of absorbed dose is the "rad".

EQUIVALENT DOSE ("DOSE EQUIVALENT") — the correct unit of measurement used by the dentist to compare the biologic-risk effects/estimates of different types of radiation damage to a tissue or organ.

EFFECTIVE DOSE — used to estimate the risk in humans.

EXPOSURE — a measure of radiation quantity, the capacity of the radiation to ionize air. Roentgen (R) is the traditional unit of radiation exposure measured in air. Roentgen only applies to x-rays and gamma rays.

X-rays have more energy than light. ~1% of the energy released in the x-ray tube is released as x-rays.

ELECTROMAGNETIC RADIATIONS — includes microwaves, x-radiation, visible light, and gamma radiation. X-rays & gamma rays are types of **non-particulate** radiation energy.

PANORAMIC RADIOGRAPH — an extra-oral radiograph where a bite piece is held between the patient's front teeth. This bite piece should either be sterilized after each use, or covered with a disposable plastic slipcover.

- **Indications**: diagnose oral pathology not visible on periapical radiographs, treating planning (especially orthodontic cases), evaluation of anomalies, as one part of the follow-up evaluation in surgical and trauma cases, edentulous patients prior to fabrication of full dentures, and in patients unable to tolerate intra-oral radiographs.

- **Advantages**: shows areas that may not be visible on a full-mouth series (and shows both arches on the same film). Greater patient comfort (eliminates gagging), and requires less time than a full-mouth series. **Panoramic radiograph is the screening x-ray for pathology of the jaws.** It is excellent for third molar pathology and to observe the TMJ, sinuses, and in sialography (a technique used in radiology that films the salivary gland after an opaque substance is injected into its duct). However, a sialolith that is located in Wharton's duct is best viewed with a cross-sectional occlusal radiograph.

- **Disadvantages**: **provides less image detail & definition than periapical radiographs** due to intensifying screens, movement of the x-ray tube and film, and increased object-film distance.
  - loss of image detail (making it difficult to diagnose early carious lesions). Bite-wing x-rays are required to diagnose carious lesions.
  - Image distortion due to increased object-film distance.
  - Inadequate for interproximal caries detection or detecting periodontal breakdown (bone loss).
  - Proximal overlapping (especially in posterior areas).
  - Added exposure to a large area of body tissue in addition to the oral tissues.

Poor definition of interproximal caries. However, by supplementing a panoramic with posterior or anterior bitewings, a more complete radiographic survey of the patient is obtained. The panoramic is NOT a substitute for intra-oral films.

Panoramic Positioning Errors:
1. **Chin Tilted too Far Upward**: a positioning error most likely to cause a **REVERSE OCCLUSAL PLANE** **CURVE** on a panoramic radiograph. A "**reverse occlusal plane curve**" is where mandibular structures look narrower and maxillary structures look wider (looks like a "frown").

2. **Chin Tilted too Far Downward**: occlusal plane shows an excessive upward curve (looks like a "big smile"), there is severe interproximal overlapping, and the anterior teeth appear highly distorted.

CEPHALOMETRICS ("LATERAL HEAD RADIOGRAPH)
— a technique employing oriented radiographs for the purpose of making head measurements used to study craniofacial growth, diagnosis, planning orthodontic treatment, and evaluation of treated cases. **Cephalometrics are useful to assess tooth-to-tooth, bone-to-bone, and tooth-to-bone relationships. Serial cephalometric films can show the amount and direction of growth.**

- Lateral head radiograph (cephalometric x-ray) must be compared with "normal" lateral radiographs from an accepted norm. **Linear and angular measurements are obtained using known anatomical landmarks in the lateral head radiography of the patient.** These measurements are then compared with those considered WNL, thus enabling the orthodontist to assess aberrations in the dentition and jaw structures that cause malocclusion.

- Cephalometric radiographic analysis includes **hard tissue structures** (bone & teeth), and measurements of **soft tissue structures** (nose, lips, soft tissue chin).

- Superimposition of longitudinal cephalometric studies is generally on a **reference plane and registration point** to best demonstrate the growth of structures farthest from the plane and point. The most stable area from which to evaluate craniofacial growth is the anterior cranial base due to its early cessation (stopping) of growth.

BITEWING RADIOGRAPHS
— an intraoral radiograph MOST useful to detect **INTERPROXIMAL CARIES** and demonstrate **alveolar bone resorption (periodontitis)**. Bitewings show the crowns of both maxillary & mandibular teeth, but NOT the root apices. **The main reason to take bitewings is to detect interproximal caries.**

- **Bitewings are most useful to monitor the progression of periodontal disease** as they show the crestal bone levels and interproximal areas of both arches. For the film to be of diagnostic use, the quality of the dimensional accuracy, open contacts, and optimum contrast and image clarity must be excellent. When taking bitewings, the film is placed in either a horizontal or vertical position.

- **Vertical bitewings**-provide more periodontal information (i.e. bony defects and furcation involvement). A fuzzy or indistinct image of crestal bone is often associated with early periodontitis. The vertical bitewing angulation should be between +8° and +10°. Vertical bitewings show more alveolar bone than traditional horizontal bitewings.

- **Adjust horizontal angulation** to direct the central ray toward the center of the film.

NOTES

- Two bitewings are usually taken on a child (one on each side). If the child only has the primary dentition, then #0 film is used. If the child has a mixed dentition, #1 film is used. Once the child has 2nd molars, two to four #2 films are used (if using 4 films, one film images the premolar area, while the other images the molar area). Sometimes two, long #3 films are used (one per side) rather then two #2 films on each side. This practice is not recommended due to the curvature of the arch, making it difficult to open all contacts on one film.

SUBMENTAL-VERTICAL (SUBMENTOVERTEX) – an x-ray designed to **diagnose BASILAR SKULL FRACTURES**, and provides some diagnostic information about the zygoma, zygomatic arches, and mandible. This film is taken with the **source below the mandible and the film above the head**. The submentovertex radiographic view is **used when you suspect a fracture of the zygomatic arch**.

SUBMENTOVERTEX IMAGE

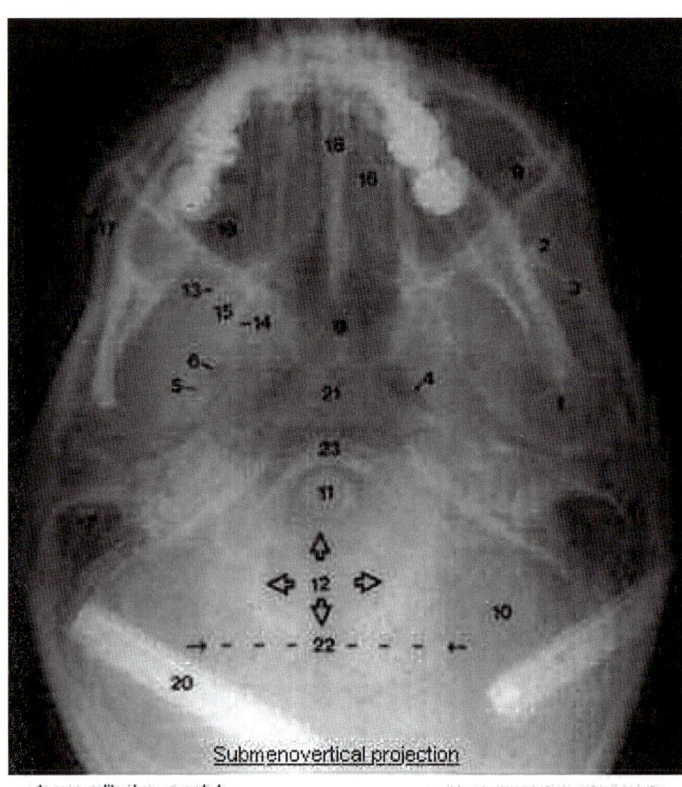

Submenovertical projection

1. mandibular condyle
2. coronoid process of mandible
3. anterior wall of middle crainial fossa
4. carotid canal
5. foramen spinosum
6. foramen ovale
7. mastoid air cells
8. sphenoid sinus
9. lateral wall of maxillary sinus
10. posterior cranial fossa
11. odontoid process of axis
12. foramen magnum
13. lateral pterygoid plate
14. medial pterygoid plate
15. pterygoid fossa
16. ethmoid sinus
17. zygoma
18. nasal septum
19. maxillary sinus
20. hair clip
21. pharynx
22. vertebrae
23. arch of C-1

WATER'S VIEW – the standard radiograph of choice for showing an ANTERIOR VIEW of the PARANASAL SINUSES and of the mid-face and orbits. This is a posterior-anterior projection with patient's face lying against the film and the x-ray source behind the patient's head. Water's is one of the best films for radiographic diagnosis of MID-FACIAL FRACTURES, sinus infections, and its view best demonstrates lesions of the maxillary sinus.

NOTES

WATER'S VIEW

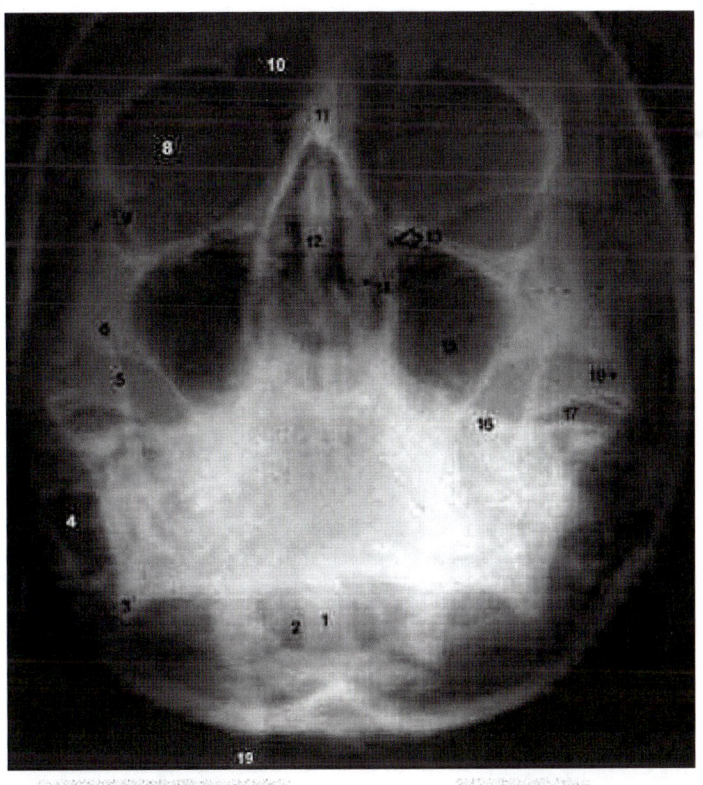

1. odontoid process of axis
2. foramen magnum
3. angle of mandible
4. mastoid air cells
5. coronoid process of mand.
6. body of zygoma
7. frontal process of zygoma
8. orbit
9. innominate line
10. frontal sinus
11. crista galli
12. nasal septum
13. ethmoid air cells
14. nasal turbinates
15. maxillary sinus
16. petrous ridge
17. mandibular fossa
18. zygomatic arch
19. cervical vertebra

TOWNE'S VIEW — the **best film to visualize the CONDYLES & NECK OF MANDIBLE from an AP** projection. The patient lies on his back with the film under his head. The x-ray source is from the front, but is rotated 30° from the Frankfort plane and is directed right at the condyles.

- Towne's view is **often of value to assess the status of the condyles, condylar neck, and rami** because superimposition of the mastoid and zygoma over the condylar neck region in the straight postero-anterior projection often makes interpretation difficult. Towne's view eliminates this superimposition to **give good visualization of the condylar area and rami**.

- Reverse Towne's View-used to identify fractures of the condylar neck and ramus area.

TOWNE'S VIEW

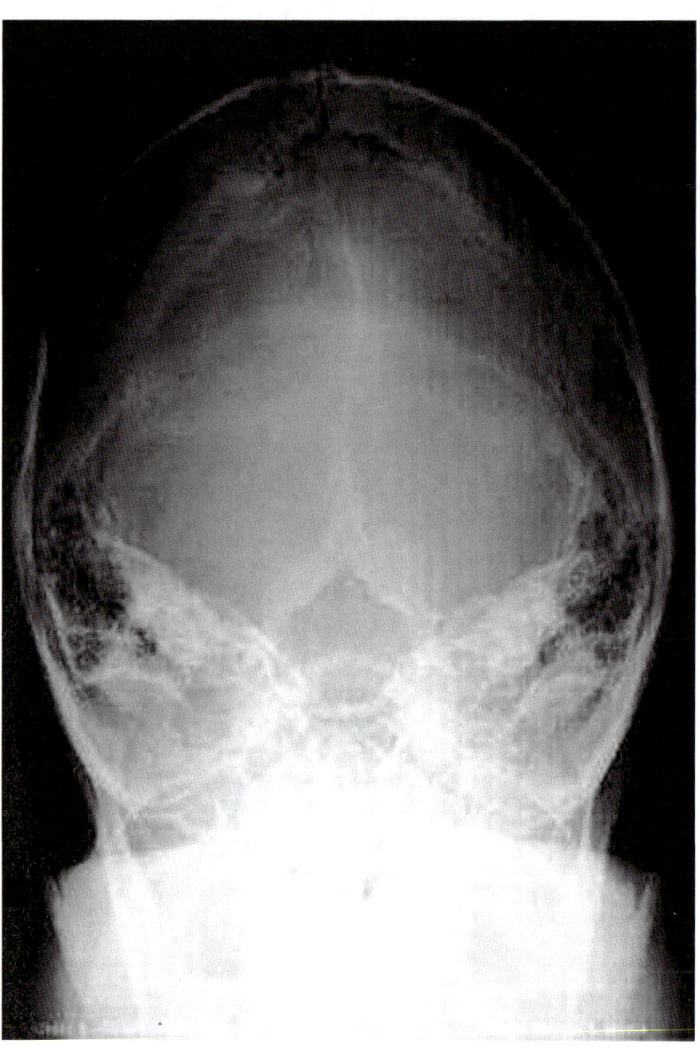

CONVENTIONAL TMJ RADIOGRAPHS — show the condyles position in the glenoid fossa, range of the condyles' antero-posterior movement, and areas of bone destruction on the condylar heads.

DEVELOPER SOLUTION — a chemical solution that converts the invisible image on a film into a visible image composed of minute masses of black metallic silver. Its function is to reduce silver halide crystals to black metallic silver.

X-ray Developing Solution Contains 4 Chemicals:
1. **Developing agent (hydroquinone)**-a chemical compound capable of changing the exposed silver halide crystals to black metallic silver, while producing no appreciable effect on the unexposed silver halide crystals in the immulsion. It gives details to the x-ray image. Elon, also quickly generates gray tones on the x-ray image.

2. **Antioxidant preservative (sodium sulfite)**-prevents the developer solution from oxidizing in the presence of air.

3. **Accelerator (sodium carbonate)**-an alkali that activates the developing agents and maintains the alkalinity of the developer at the correct value. It softens gelatin of emulsion.

4. **Restrainer (potassium bromide)**-is added to developers to control the action of the developing agent so it does not develop the unexposed silver halide crystals to produce fog.

When taking panoramic radiographs, if the films keep getting lighter & lighter after each development, to correct this problem simply replenish the developing solution. As the developing solution gets weaker, the films get lighter. Both the developing and fixing solutions should be replenished daily. These solutions need to be changed regularly and the tanks scrubbed and cleaned.

- **Factors that affect developing solution life**: cleanliness of tanks, size & number of films processed, and solution temperature.

- **Yellowish-brown film** is caused by insufficient fixing or rinsing.

- **Fogged film** may result from improper film storage or outdated films.

- **Low solution levels** will appear as developer cut-off (straight clear border) or fixer cut-off (straight black border).

X-RAY FIXING ("FIXER") SOLUTION — a chemical solution whose function of is to STOP development and remove remaining unexposed crystals. Fixing time is always at least twice as long as the developing time. **Fixer contains 4 chemicals:**

1. **Clearing agent (sodium or ammonium thiosulfate)**-commonly called "hypo" dissolves and removes underdeveloped silver halide crystals from the emulsion (one of the main functions of fixing solutions). The chemical clears the film so the black silver image produced by the developer is distinctly perceptible. When the film is improperly cleaned, the remaining unexposed silver halide crystals darken upon exposure to light and obscure the image.

2. **Antioxidant preservative (sodium sulfite)**-prevents the decomposition of the fixer chemical.

3. **Acidifier (acetic acid)**-necessary for the correct action of the other chemicals and also neutralizes any alkaline developer that may be carried over by the film or hanger.

4. **Hardener (potassium alum)**-shrinks and hardens the gelatin in the emulsion. It shortens drying time and protects the emulsion from abrasion.

If a dried radiograph were processed a second time, there would be no change in contrast or density.

After processing a film, if it appears the color BROWN, the most likely cause is the fixing time was not long enough. A film appears brown when it is not completely fixed.

Common Darkroom Errors:
- **Mounted films are improperly labeled** (wrong patient name): because racks are not labeled properly.
- **Fogged film (gray/lack of contrast)** due to faulty safelight in the darkroom. White light leaking into the darkroom.
- **Lost films** because films are not secured properly on the rack.
- **Static marks (multiple black lines)** due to friction when opening film packets causes static electricity.
- **Overdeveloped film (dark)** due to incorrect time (too long) and too hot a temperature.
- **Underdeveloped film (light)** due to incorrect time (too short), too cold a temperature, or weak solutions that are old or diluted.
- **Torn emulsion**: films were allowed to touch or overlap while drying.
- **Stained film (dark/white spots)** due to dirty work surfaces, person developing film was sloppy.
- **Scratched films (white lines)**: film emulsion removed by sharp object (fingernails/rack touching).
- **Clear films**: emulsion washed away, films left in water (wash) for over 24hrs.
- **Air bubbles (white spots)**: air trapped on the film surface while being placed in processing.
- **Overbent films**-causes crescent-shaped radiolucent marks due to cracked emulsion.

Common Errors When Taking Radiographs:
- **Light films (underexposed/image not dense enough)**: due to incorrect milliamperage (too low) or exposure (too short), incorrect focal-film distance, or cone too far from the patient's face, or film is placed backwards.
- **Dark films (overexposed/image too dense)**: due to incorrect milliamperage (too high), exposure (too long), incorrect kVp (too high).
- **Double exposure**: film was used twice.
- **Fogged films (gray/lack of contrast)**: exposed to radiation other than from the primary beam.
- **Poor contrast**: incorrect kVp (too high).
- **Poor film placement**: film is not placed far enough back or not forward enough in the mouth.
- **Blurred image**: patient movement or drifting of the x-ray arm.
- **Clear films**: were not exposed to radiation.
- **Artifacts**: patient did not remove eyeglasses, jewelry, or removable prosthetic appliances.
- **Herringbone ("Diamond Effect")**-a zig-zag pattern appears on the processed film when film is **placed backwards** in the mouth. Developing solution on the film. Double exposure of film.

RADIOGRAPHIC TECHNIQUES

VERTICAL ANGULATION – directing x-rays so they pass vertically through the part being examined. This is accomplished by positioning the tubehead and direction of the central ray in an **up-and-down (vertical)** plane. Foreshortening & Elongation are produced by INCORRECT VERTICAL ANGULATION.

- **Foreshortening**-a shortened image is caused by excessive vertical angulation. The teeth APPEAR TO SHORT due to either too much vertical angulation, or poor chair position.

- Elongation-an elongated image is caused by insufficient (too little) vertical angulation. Elongation is the MOST COMMON error when taking dental radiographs where the teeth APPEAR TOO LONG due to either too little vertical angulation, or the film not being parallel to the long axis of the teeth or the occlusal plane not being parallel to the floor.

VERTICAL ANGULATION

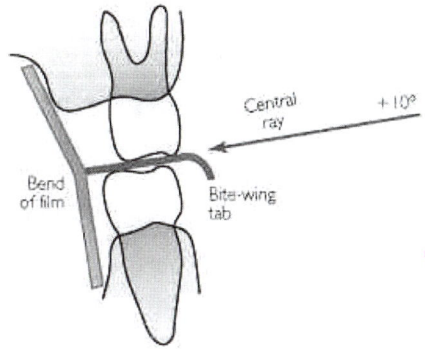

HORIZONTAL ANGULATION – maintaining the central ray at 0° as the tube is moved around the head. This is accomplished by positioning the tubehead and direction of the central ray in a **side-to-side (horizontal) plane**. The general rule for horizontal angulation is the central ray should be **perpendicular** to the mean antero-posterior plane of the teeth being x-rayed.

- **Overlapping-interproximal areas** are overlapped due to incorrect horizontal tube angulation (central x-ray was not directed perpendicular to the curvature of the arch and through the contacts). Overlapping **reduces** the **diagnostic quality** of **film to detect interproximal caries** since teeth images are superimposed on each other).

The central ray is at 0° when the x-ray tube is adjusted so the central ray is parallel to the floor. If the tubehead is directed at the floor, it is **positive angulation**. If the x-ray tubehead is directed toward the ceiling, it is **negative angulation**.

BISECTING ANGLE TECHNIQUE – a technique based on the **geometric rule of isometry** which states two triangles are equal if they have two equal angles and share a common side. **The image on the film is equal to the length of the tooth when the central ray is directed at 90° to the imaginary bisector**. A tooth and the radiographic image are equal in length when two equal triangles are formed that share a common side (imaginary bisector). The bisecting technique works as follows to produce a tooth image that is accurate if done correctly. **Advantage: decreased exposure time.**

- X-ray film is placed along the **lingual/palatal surface** of the tooth. At the point where the film contacts the tooth, an angle is formed by the plane of the film, and the long axis of the tooth.

- The person taking the x-ray must visualize a plane that bisects this angle (this plane is the **imaginary bisector** which creates two equal angles and provides a common side for the two imaginary equal triangles. The central ray is positioned **perpendicular** to the imaginary bisector.

- **Disadvantages**: x-ray film image may be dimensionally distorted (amount may vary); due to the use of a short cone (which causes divergent rays) the image is not a true reproduction of the object; may not be able to judge the correct alveolar bone height.

Paralleling Technique based on the concept of parallelism since the film is placed parallel to the long axis of the tooth being x-rayed, and the central x-ray beam is directed perpendicular or at right angles to the long axis of the teeth & plane of the film. A film holder (XCP) must be used to keep the film parallel to the long axis of the tooth.

- **Advantages**: little or no root superimposition on a maxillary molar view, accurate diagnosis of periodontal bone height (given minimal distortion), and the image formed is dimensionally accurate.

NOTES

- **Disadvantages**: film placement may be difficult in some areas (i.e. low palatal vaults), **increased exposure time is required due to the use of a LONG CONE**, and XCP holders/rings can be cumbersome to work with and may cause patient discomfort. **The object-film distance must be increased** to keep the film parallel, which results in image magnification and loss of definition. Also, the source-film distance must be increased to compensate for the image magnification, and to ensure that only the most parallel x-rays will be aimed at the tooth and film. Using a long cone to increase the target-film distance (16 inch target-film distance) is required to provide greater definition and less image magnification.

- **AKA**: XCP (Extension Cone Paralleling Technique), Right-Angle Technique, Long-Cone Technique.

BUCCAL OBJECT RULE ("TUBE SHIFT TECHNIQUE" OR "SLOB" RULE) – used to determine an object's special position within the jaws. This technique uses two radiographs of an object exposed with slightly different tube angulations, then compares the object's position on the radiograph with respect to a reference point (i.e. the tooth root).

- **SLOB (Same Lingual, Opposite Buccal)**: if the object in question appears to move in the **SAME** direction as the x-ray tube, then it is on the LINGUAL aspect. If it appears to move in the **OPPOSITE** direction as the x-ray tube, then it is on the BUCCAL aspect.

- If the x-ray tube is shifted and directed from a mesial direction/angualtion, and the object in question moves mesially from the reference point, then the object **lies lingual** to that reference point. The the x-ray tube was directed from a mesial angulation, the special position of the object lies LINGUAL. However, if the x-ray tube is shifted mesially and the object moves distally, it lies on the buccal aspect of the reference point.

CERVICAL BURNOUT – a phenomenon **caused by relatively low x-ray absorption** on the mesial or distal surfaces of teeth, between the edges of the enamel and adjacent crest of the alveolar ridge. Because of this diminished x-ray absorption, these areas appear relatively radiolucent will ill-defined margins. It is caused by the normal configuration of the affected teeth (CEJ) which results in decreased x-ray absorption in those areas. **These radiolucencies should be anticipated when viewing x-rays of almost any tooth, and must not be mistaken for a carious lesion.**

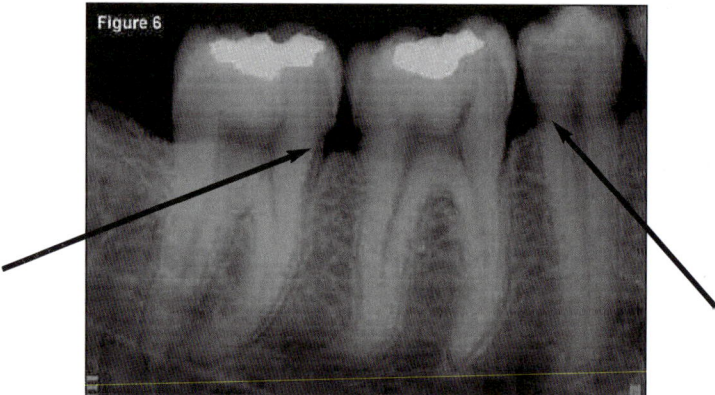

Inverse Square Law = $\dfrac{\text{original intensity}}{\text{new intensity}} = \dfrac{\text{new distance}^2}{\text{original distance}^2}$

Important: for a given beam of radiation, **the intensity is INVERSELY proportional to the square of the distance from the radiation source**. The intensity of an x-ray beam at a given point is dependent on the distance of the measuring device from the FOCAL SPOT. The reason for this decrease in intensity (the reason it is inversely proportional) is because the x-ray beam spreads out as it moves away from the source. The "spread out" beam is less intense.

FOCAL SPOT – the small area of tungsten on the anode (target) from which x-rays emanates and that receives the impact of the speeding electrons. **Focal spot is 1 of 3 factors that influences image sharpness**. **The size of the x-ray tube focal spot influences radiographic DEFINITION.**

- **Target (tungsten target)**-a tungsten wafer embedded in the anode face at the point of electron bombardment.

- **Target Film Distance (source-to-film distance)**-distance from the x-ray source (the focal spot on the tungsten target) to the film. It is determined by the length of the cone (position-indicating device = PID). Two standard target-film distances are used in intra-oral radiography.

    1. **20cm (8 inches)**: is the **short cone that exposes more tissue** by producing a more divergent beam.

    2. **41cm (16 Inches)**: is the **long cone that reduces the amount of exposed tissue** by producing a less divergent beam and a sharper image.

HALF-VALUE LAYER (HVL) – the **amount of material required to reduce the intensity of an x-ray beam to half**. For x-ray beams, this is **normally expressed in aluminum or copper thickness**, but may also be expressed in other materials or media (i.e. water). **HVL is an indicator of the QUALITY of an x-ray beam**.

Half-value layer is strictly defined for different quantities: photon fluence (# of photons/cm^2), energy fluence (# of photons x photon energy/cm^2) or absorbed dose. **Intensity**-a term commonly used, but is too vague, thus is avoided.

- Due to the spectral nature of x-rays, **HVL is not constant**. When measuring multiple half-value layers, the 2nd HVL is greater than the 1st HVL since the mean energy of the x-ray spectrum is increased following the passage of the 1st HVL that results in x-rays becoming more penetrating.

- In oral diagnostic radiography, **the HVL of the radiation beam is ~2mm of aluminum (this means 50% of the x-rays exiting the vacuum tube are absorbed by 2mm of aluminum. Doubling the thickness of aluminum will not absorb all of the x-rays, but one HALF of the remaining x-rays.**

INTENSIFYING SCREENS – devices used in extra-oral radiography that convert x-ray energy into visible light. The visible light then exposes the screen film. Thus, the radiation a patient receives is decreased. Used for all extra-oral radiography (panoramics, cephalometrics) films to decrease the amount of radiation exposure to patients.

CASSETTE HOLDER – a light-tight device used in extraoral radiography to hold film and intensifying screens.

Radiograph Operator Controls 3 Factors:
1. **Kilovoltage (kVp)**-the **quality or penetrating power of the x-ray beam that controls the speed of ELECTRONS**. The speed that electrons travel from the filament of the cathode to the anode's target depends on the potential difference between the two electrodes (kilovoltage). Thus, this has a very important effect on the x-rays produced at the focal spot. Kilovoltage has nothing to do with the number of electrons that compose the stream flowing from cathode anode. **The number of electrons (which determines the quantity of x-rays produced), is controlled by the temperature of the tungsten filament (milliamperage setting)**. The hotter the filament, the more electrodes are emitted and available to form the electron stream (x-ray tube current). In the x-ray tube, the number of **electrons flowing/sec is measured in millamperes**. The intensity of x-rays produced at a particular kilovoltage depends on that number. Suitable ranges of dental x-rays are 65-100 kVp

    - Important: **kilovoltage influences the x-ray beam and radiograph** by **altering contrast quality** (for patients with **thick jaws**, increase kilovoltage), **determining the quality of the x-rays produced**, and **determining the velocity of the electrons to the anode**.

NOTES

- **kVp** most directly affects radiographic **CONTRAST** and predominantly determines the penetrating ability of the x-ray beam.

- Setting the x-ray machine for a specific milliamperage actually means adjusting the filament temperature to yield the current flow indicated.

- To **increase film density**: **mA, kVp, & time**, and **source-object distance**.

- One effect of a change in kVp is a change in the x-ray's penetrating power. **Increasing kilovoltage (kVp)**: reduces subject contrast (and the longer scale of contrast) and produces new, more penetrating x-rays, while emitting less penetrating x-rays that were also produced at the lower kilovoltage. **Increasing kVp causes the resultant x-ray to have A LONGER SCALE OF CONTRAST. Decreasing** kilovoltage: increases subject contrast (and the shorter the scale of contrast).

2. **Milliamperage (mA)**-controls the number of x-rays produced (it's the quantity or number of x-rays produced). Suitable ranges for dental x-rays are 7-15mA.

3. **Exposure time**-the length of time x-rays are produced and the time the patient is exposed to them.

Some x-ray machines are calibrated in "impulses" (there are 60 impulses per second).

DENSITY – overall DARKNESS (blackness) of a radiograph that increases, as mA, kVp, or exposure time increases, and decreases as mA, kVp, or exposure time decreases.

CONTRAST – the difference in the degree of blackness (density) between adjacent areas on a radiograph. Only one exposure factor affects contrast (kilovoltage (kVp)). Filtration also plays a role. Higher kVp settings produce more shades of gray (low contrast).

- **High contrast**: very dark and very light areas.

- **Low contrast**: many shades of gray, and is preferred in dentistry. Produced by higher kVp settings.

5 Rules to Create Accurate Images when taking x-rays:
1. Use the smallest focal spot that is practical. The size of the focal spot influences radiographic definition or sharpness (they are inversely proportional, as focal spot decreases, image sharpness increases). The operator cannot control the size of the focal spot.
2. Use the longest source-film distance practical in the situation.
3. Place the film as close as possible to the structure being radiographed.
4. **Direct the central ray at as close to a right angle to the film** as anatomical structures allow.
5. Keep the film parallel to the structure being radiographed.

Image Magnification is minimized by USING a LONG CONE.

Dental X-Ray Tube Parts:
1. **Filament**-a coiled tungsten wire in the cathode (+) that when heated to incandescence, emits/produces the stream of electrons.

2. **Molybdenum cup**-houses the tungsten filament.

3. **Electron stream**-travels from the filament in the cathode to the tungsten target.

4. **Tungsten target**-located in the anode (-) to stop the stream of electrons.

5. **Focal Spot**-the portion of the tungsten target struck by the electron beam. It contains a small area "focal spot" that the electrons strike to produce x-rays. The focal spot's size directly influences x-ray definition (the larger the focal spot, the greater loss of image definition and sharpness).

6. **Copper sleeve**-located in the cathode.

7. **Vacuum**

8. **X-ray beam**-produced when the electron stream bounces off focal spot on the tungsten target

9. **Leaded glass housing**-houses the entire x-ray tube.

X-rays are generated when a stream of electrons (produced by the filament) travels from the **CATHODE ANODE** and is suddenly stopped by its impact on the tungsten target. The filament is located in the cathode and is made of tungsten wire. The small area on the target that the electrons strike is the **focal spot** (the x-ray source).

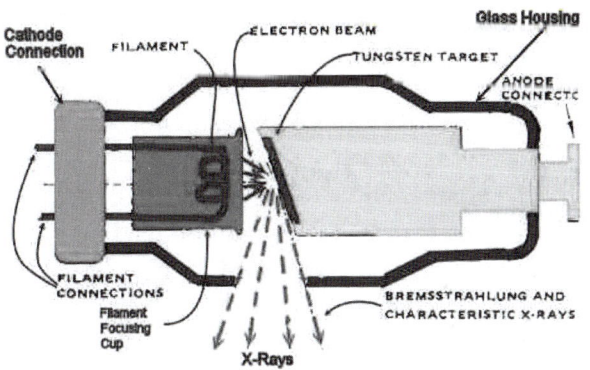

Prescribing Dental Radiographs:
- Dental radiographs are taken **ONLY** when needed as judged by each patient's needs. Decisions about the number, type, and frequency of dental x-rays are **DETERMINED ONLY BY THE DENTIST** based on each patient's needs. Every patient has a different dental condition, thus the frequency of x-rays differs as well. There are guidelines published by the ADA that assist a dentist in prescribing the number, type, and frequency of dental radiographs.

- Patients with tooth decay, periodontal disease, tooth mobility, pain in one or more teeth, or possible impacted teeth need more frequent radiographic examinations than patients without such problems. **A pediatric patient who is caries free and asymptomatic, the child's first bite-wing radiographs should not be taken until the spaces between the posterior teeth have closed.**

- <u>Occult Diseases</u>-includes **small carious lesions, cysts, & tumors** that <u>present no clinical signs or symptoms</u>. Because occult disease in the perioral tissues is <u>rare</u> (except for caries), **a radiographic examination of the jaws should NOT be done solely to look for it in an individual with teeth when there are <u>no</u> clinical signs or symptoms**. However, every x-ray taken must be evaluated for these lesions. **Remember: caries is <u>an exception</u>** to the above rule due to its <u>much higher prevalence</u> compared to <u>occult cysts or tumors</u>.

CHAPTER 3

DENTAL EMERGENCIES & MEDICALLY COMPROMISED CONSIDERATIONS

DENTAL EMERGENCY PROTOCOL

NOTES

ANAPHYLACTIC REACTION (allergic reaction develops in seconds or minutes) after local anesthetic, nitrous, or dental material exposure. **LIFE-THREATENING** causing **BRONCHOSPAM & DROP IN B.P.** (EPI pen bronchodilates and raises patient's BP):

EPI

1. Call 911 and position the awake patient in a comfortable position.

2. Get the preloaded EPI syringe in the emergency kit and inject EPI pen into patient's **DELTOID, TONGUE,** or **LATERAL THIGH.**

3. Re-administer EPI pen in 5 minutes ONLY IF SYMPTOMS PERSIST.

CHEST PAIN (ANGINA PECTORIS)—patient has tight, heavy, or constricted chest pain and may clench their fist against their chest.

Nitroglycerin

1. Call 911 and position patient so he/she is comfortable and ask if they have their nitroglycerin tablets or spray on them. If not, give **2 sprays of NITROGLYCERIN** (vasodilator) onto the patient's tongue.

2. Dental treatment can continue if patient and doctor are comfortable.

Important: do not give spray/tablets if the patient has chest pain and feels faint or dizzy (means BP is dropping), or if the patient took **VIAGRA** within 24hrs.

HEART ATTACK: after chest pain, patient says their pain is getting worse, patient has taken 3 doses of nitroglycerin at five minute intervals and pain continues, or the chest pain went away but comes back, or the patient has had no history of heart disease or chest pain. **CRUSHING, INTENSE, RADIATING PAIN** from the chest to the stomach or to the left side of the neck, jaw, left arm, and/or pinkie finger (tingles). SKIN TURNS **ASHEN GRAY** & PATIENT MAY **SWEAT PROFUSELY**.

Nitroglycerin + aspirin

1. Call 911 and position the patient so they are comfortable.

2. Administer 50% nitrous oxide & 50% oxygen (has same effect as IV Morphine) for pain and delivers more oxygen to the muscles/brain.

3. Give two sprays of nitroglycerin on patient's tongue and have the patient **CHEW 1 tablet of adult-dose ASPRIN (325mg)** EXCEPT if patient is allergic to aspirin, has a bleeding disorder, or gastric/peptic ulcer. ASPIRIN prevents clot from getting bigger.

CARDIAC ARREST (UNCONSCIOUS PATIENT):

1. Call 911 while dentist lays the patient flat in dental chair with their feet **ELEVATED**.

2. (CAB): Dentist **starts chest compressions, check airway** and open with the **HEAD LIFT/CHIN TILT** and then check for **breathing** and carotid pulse (in the groove under and to the side of the Adam's Apple). Follow CBA (compressions, airway, and breathing)-new AHA 2010 guideline.

3. Dentist **gives CPR** (30 chest compressions for every 2 breaths). 30:2 ratio.

DIABETIC SHOCK (HYPOGLYCEMIA = LOW BLOOD SUGAR). MENTAL CONFUSION, patient feels cold, sweaty, and shaky.

- Before treatment ask patient when did they take their insulin and eat last. If not recent, give patient third cup of **ORANGE JUICE** or **NON-DIET SODA** wait 5 minutes, then give another third cup. After 5 minutes, give last third cup. WITHIN 15 minutes signs should subside.

NOTES

- **Unconscious Diabetic**:
  1. **CALL 911** and lay patient flat with feet raised, check airway (head tilt/chin lift), check breathing (look, listen, feel) and check carotid pulse. **DO CPR if not breathing/no pulse** (15 compressions for every 2 breaths). **15:2**.

  2. **DO NOT ADMINSTER DRUGS!**

SYNCOPE (FAINTING): can occur due to **EMOTIONAL STRESS (nervousness)**. Occurs when there is a temporary decrease in blood flow to the brain due to sudden drop in BP, HR or blood volume change. Can happen to anyone, but the patient usually has an underlying medical condition like anemia or heart disease. **Signs a patient may faint: light-headed, nausea, heart palpitations**.
  1. Lay patient in dental chair with legs **ELEVATED**.
  2. Place a cold, wet towel over their forehead.
  3. Administer oxygen and **AROMATIC AMMONIA** held under patient's nose to stimulate blood flow to brain via movement.

SIEZURE (EPILEPSY): caused by signals in the brain are disrupted. GRAND-MAL is the most-common type (last 2-3 minutes; the body becomes rigid and relaxes). A seizure lasting more than 5 minutes is called Status Epilepticus and is life-threatening). Signs: **patient may have a visual, sound, or smell aura immediately before seizure starts** (so ask the patient with seizure history if they have a common aura or if they have taken their anti-epileptic medication.
  1. Call 911.

  2. Remove any sharp objects away from the patient and have one person gently hold the arms and the other the legs to protect patient from injury.

Handwritten note:
① Grand-mal: 2~3min
② Status Epilepticus: >5min

<u>Note</u>: if a minor has a seizure, call the parent into the room to help.

DENTAL CONSIDERATIONS FOR MEDICALLY COMPROMISED PATIENTS

CHRONIC OBSTRUCTIVE PULMONARY DISEASE (Asthma, Bronchitis, Emphyema):
- Sit patient upright in dental chair.
- No rubber dam in severe cases.
- No N_2O if severe emphysema.
- Avoid barbiturates, narcotics, anti-histamines.
- Avoid erythromycin, clarithromycin if patient takes theophylline.

ASTHMA:
- Have patient bring their inhaler to each appointment.
- Avoid Aspirin, NSAIDs, narcotics/barbiturates.
- Avoid Erythromycin if patient takes theophylline.
- Avoid sulfite-containing local anesthetics.
- Can use N_2O or Diazepam for anxious patient.
- Use pulse oximeter if necessary.

TUBERCULOSIS:
- **Active TB**: consult with physician before treatment and only treat emergencies.
- **Prior TB (Non-Active)**: Use caution, get good medical history, periodic chest-x-rays to rule-out reactivation. If patient is TB-free confirmed by physician, treat as a normal patient. May be taking ISONIAZID (INH) for 6 months to 1 year prophylactically.

VIRAL HEPATITIS (B,C,D,E):
- **Active Hepatitis**: Consult with physician and treat on emergency basis only.
- **Non-Active Hepatitis**: consult with physician, treat as normal.

DIABETES MELLITUS:
- In uncontrolled diabetics, they are prone to infection and poor-wound healing.
- Insulin patients: eat normal meal before appointment (schedule morning or mid-morning).
- Have sugar (OJ) available in case of diabetic shock.
- With well-controlled diabetics, no alteration of treatment plan is required unless. Treat as usual.

HYPERTHYROIDISM (Thyrotoxicosis):
- Avoid EPI and other vasoconstrictors in untreated patients.

HEMODIALYSIS:
- Delay treatment until off dialysis machine for at least 4 hours (because of heparin). Best to schedule dental appointment the day after hemodialysis.
- Pre-treatment screen for bleeding disorders.
- Avoid drugs metabolized by the kidneys.
- Consider antibiotic prophylaxis to minimize effects of bacteremia.
- Avoid BP cuff on arm containing the shunt.
- No routine dental care contraindications.

END-STAGE RENAL DISEASE:
- Check with physician for any hematologic disorders.
- Monitor BP during before and during treatment.
- Avoid drugs excreted by the kidney or nephrotoxic drugs.
- Extensive reconstructive crown and bridge not recommended.

PREGNANCY & LACTATION:
- Do not placed patient in supine position in late pregnancy for long periods.
- Avoid ASPRIN & NSAIDs.
- Pregnancy gingivitis common
- Consider use of fluoride or chlorhexidine.
- Major procedures (crown and bridge) are best until after delivery (unless emergency).
- Avoid elective care in first trimester. 2nd and 3rd trimesters are best for elective treatment.

SEIZURE (EPILEPTIC) PATIENTS:
- Get bleeding time for patients taking Valproic Acid.
- No aspirin and NSAIDs.
- No propoxyphene and erythromycin for patients taking Carbamazepine.
- Seizure is managed using a ligated mouth prop (bite block) at start of appointment.
- Use metal instead of porcelain when possible.
- **PROTECT THE PATIENT FROM HARMING THEMSELVES OR YOU.**

NOTES

RADIATION PATIENTS:
- Patients may develop mucositis, xerostomia, taste loss, trismus, candidiasis and other secondary infections, cervical caries, osteoradionecrosis.

- **Before Radiation**: extract teeth that cannot be repaired, restore large carious lesions, establish good oral hygiene, **start daily fluoride treatment**, treat RCT or extract non-vital teeth.

- **After Radiation**: do not extract teeth and treat diseased teeth with RCT if indicated. Most other dental procedures can be performed.

- Have patient come for frequent recall appointments (every 3-4 months) and continue daily fluoride treatment; chlorohexidine rinses for plaque and candidiasis control.

CHEMOTHERAPY PATIENTS:
- Eliminate all oral infections and treat advanced caries.
- Use topical fluoride for caries control and chlorohexidine for plaque/candidiasis.
- Rx: Rinses for mucositis and xerostomia.

HYPERTENSION: (normal <120/ and <80; pre-hypertensive 120-139 or 80-89; Stage 1: 140-159 or 90-99; Stage 2: >160 or >100).
- Send for medical evaluation if BP is ≥ 180/110 before any dental treatment.
- Avoid orthostatic hypotension (change chair position slowly; don't raise chair fast).
- Use minimal EPI (aspirate before injecting) no cord with EPI.
- Caution using EPI with patients taking non-selective beta blockers.
- Reduce dosage of barbiturates/sedatives whose action can be enhanced by anti-hypertensive agents.

STROKE HISTORY:
- No elective care for current transient ischemic attacks (**delay treatment for 6-months**).
- Consider panorex periodically to assess carotid artery patency.
- Short, morning appointments.
- No EPI in retraction cord.

PACEMAKERS & DEFIBRILLATORS:
- No antibiotic prophylaxis needed.
- Avoid ultrasonic scalers or electrosurgery.

THROMBOCYTOPENIA (Prolonged Bleeding):
- Do not use aspirin-containing drugs or NSAIDs.
- Use Acetaminophen/Tylenol and codeine if needed.

HEMOPHILIA (Congenital Coagulation Disorders)-excessive bleeding.
- No dental procedures until cleared with physician.
- Avoid aspirin and NSAIDs. Use acetaminophen (Tylenol) with or without codeine.

VON WILLEBRAND'S DISEASE:
- Avoid aspirin and NSAIDs.
- Use Acetaminophen (Tylenol) w/wo codeine or COX-2 inhibitors (Celecoxib, Rofecoxib).
- Screen prolonged bleeding time, PFA-100, or prolonged partial thromboplastin time.

ANTI-COAGULATION: (patients taking Heparin, Warfarin, Coumadin for clotting problems):
- No dental procedures until medical consult done (must achieve anti-coagulation levels). Check prothrombin time (PT).
- Can do most surgical procedures if **PT ratio is 2.5 or less or INR is 3.5 or less**.
- May have to delay procedure 2-3 days if anti-coagulation dose has to be reduced.

ALWAYS PRACTICE UNIVERSAL PRECAUTIONS!

CHAPTER 4

DENTAL PHARMACOLOGY CONSIDERATIONS

ANTIBIOTIC PROPHYLAXIS (PRE-MEDICATION)
GUIDELINES FOR DENTAL PROCEDURES TO PREVENT INFECTIVE ENDOCARDITIS
2007 AMERICAN HEART ASSOCIATION GUIDELINES

STANDARD REGIMEN	PENICILLIN ALLERGIC PATIENTS
AMOXICILLIN: **Adults**: 2g orally 1hr prior to appointment (4 capsules) **Children**: 50mg/kg (not to exceed adult dose) orally 1hr before appointment	**CLINDAMYCIN:** **Adults**: 600mg orally 1hr prior to appointment **Children**: 20mg/kg orally 1hr prior to appointment Each capsule is 300mg, so dispense 2 per appointment
	CEPHALEXIN: **Adults**: 2g orally 1hr prior to appointment **Children**: 50mg/kg orally 1hr prior to appointment Each capsule is 500mg, so dispense 4 capsules per appointment
	CEFADROXIL: **Adults**: 2g orally 1hr prior to appointment **Children**: 50mg/kg orally 1hr prior to appointment Each capsule if 500mg, so dispense 4 capsules per appointment
	AZITHROMYCIN: **Adults**: 500mg orally 1hr prior to appointment **Children**: 15mg/kg orally 1hr prior to appointment
*1kg = 2.20 lbs 22 lb child can Rx 500mg 44 lb child can Rx 1000mg (1g) 66 lb child can Rx 1500mg (1.5g) 88 lb child or more can Rx adult dose	**CLARITHROMYCIN:** **Adults**: 500mg orally 1hr prior to appointment **Children**: 15mg/kg orally 1hr prior to appointment

Bacterial Endocarditis Prophylaxis (Antibiotic Prophylaxis) is Recommended:
1. Prosthetic Cardiac Valves (i.e. biosynthetic (mechanical) & homograft (pig) valves)
2. Previous Bacterial Endocarditis.
3. Congenital Heart Disease of the following: (unrepaired cyanotic congenital heart disease, including those with palliative shunts and conduits); Completely repaired congenital heart disease with prosthetic material or device placed surgically or via catheter during the first 6 months after the procedure; repaired congenital heart disease with residual defects at the site or adjacent to the site of a prosthetic patch or device (which inhibits endothelialization); cardiac transplantation recipients with cardiac valvular disease. Complex Cyanotic Congenital Heart Disease (i.e. single ventricle states, transposition of great arteries, Tetrology of Fallot).
4. Surgically constructed synthetic **PULMONARY** shunts or conduits.
5. Hypertrophic Cardiomyopathy.

Dental Procedures: extractions, periodontal procedures (surgery, SRP, probing, and recall perio maintenance), implant placement, endodontic (RCT) instrumentation of surgery ONLY past the apex, subgingival placement of antibiotic fibers/strips, initial placement of orthodontic bands (**not brackets**), intraligamentary local anesthetic injections, **prophylactic cleaning of teeth or implants where bleeding is anticipated. ALL DENTAL PROCEDURES THAT INVOLVE MANIPULATION OF GINGIVAL TISSUE OR PERIAPICAL REGION OF TEETH OR PERFORATION OF ORAL MUCOSA NEED ENDOCARDITIS PROPHYLAXIS.**

Bacterial Endocarditis Prophylactic Antibiotic is NOT required:
- Isolated atrial or ventricular septal defects, or patent ductus arteriosus.
- Coronary Artery Bypass Graft Surgery (CABG).
- Mitral Valve Prolapse (with or without regurgitation).
- Rheumatic Heart Disease.
- Bicuspid Valve Disease
- Calcified Aortic Stenosis
- Congenital Heart Conditions (Hypertrophic Cardiomyopathy, Ventricular Septal Defect, or Atrial Septal Defect).
- Heart murmurs.
- Kawasaki Disease without valvular dysfunction.
- Cardiac Pacemakers (intravascular & epicardial) and implanted defibrillators.
- Restorative Dentistry: local anesthetic injections (non-intraligamentary), post & core placement, placing rubber dams, RCT not past the apex, post-operative suture removal, placement/adjustment of RPD and orthodontic appliances, impressions, fluoride treatments, radiographs, or shedding of primary teeth, or bleeding from trauma to the lips or oral mucosa.

NO antibiotic prophylaxis is required for patients who had a NON-VALVULAR devices placed unless it has been 2-3 weeks after surgery and healing is still occurring.

Non-Valvular Devices: PACEMAKERS, implantable cardioverter defibrillators, left ventricular assist devices (LVAD), total artificial hearts, ventriculoatrial SHUNTS, peripheral vascular STENTS, hemodialysis prosthetic vascular grafts, intra-aortic balloon counterpulsation CATHETERS, coronary angiography and percutaneous coronary artery intervention, CORONARY ARTERY STENTS, vascular closure devices, and vena cava filters.

Antibiotic Prophylaxis for TOTAL JOINT REPLACEMENTS:
- No scientific evidence currently supports antibiotic prophylaxis to prevent HEMATOGENOUS INFECTIONS before dental treatment in patients with total joint prosthesis.

- Antibiotic prophylaxis is NOT indicated for dental patients with PINS, PLATES, & SCREWS, nor is it routinely indicated for most dental patients with total joint replacements. BUT PREMEDICATION IS REQUIRED for ALL patients during the first 2 years after joint replacement. If more than 2 years after prosthetic joint replacement pass with no complications, then pre-medication is NOT required.

- If unanticipated bleeding occurs, administer an antimicrobial prophylaxis within 2 hours after the procedure!

- If a series of dental procedures is required: observe an interval of 9-14 days between procedures to reduce the potential for the emergence of resistant organisms, and allow the mouth to repopulate with antibiotic susceptible flora.

- If a patient is taking an antibiotic normally used for endocarditis prophylaxis then SELECT a drug from a different class rather than increase the dose of the patient's current regimen, or **delay the procedure for 9-14 days** after the patient completes the antibiotic.

Oral Contraceptive Precautions: the risk of cardiovascular side effects increases in women who smoke cigarettes, especially **women over age 35**. The risk of a thromboembolism also increases. Women with hypertension are encouraged to use a non-hormonal form of contraception. **The highest risk associated with use of oral contraceptives is thromboembolic disorders. Antibiotics have the potential to reduce the effectiveness of oral contraceptives.** Thus, advise patients to use additional methods of birth control when taking antibiotics and oral contraceptives concurrently.

DEA DRUG SCHEDULE

DEA Drug Schedule: prescriber must have a Drug Enforcement Agency authorization number (DEA#) to prescribe scheduled drugs.

- **Schedule I**: **not legitimate for medical use.** Among the substances classified by the DEA are Mescaline, LSD, Heroin, & Marijuana. Special licensing procedures must be followed to use these and other Schedule I substances. **These drugs CANNOT BE PRESCRIBED.** Only available for specific approved research projects.

- **Schedule II**: considered to have a **strong potential for ABUSE or ADDICTION, but have legitimate medical use.** Substances classified by the DEA like Amphetamines, Morphine, Cocaine, Pentobarbital, Oxycodone, Methadone, and straight Codeine. **Must have a written prescription** signed by a health professional (laws vary by state). **These drugs can be written prescribed, but cannot be refilled. A new prescription must be written for refills.** Prescriptions **CANNOT BE CALLED INTO THE PHARMACY.**

- **Schedule III**: have less potential for abuse or addiction than Schedule I or II drugs. These include various analgesic combination compounds containing codeine (i.e. Acetaminophen with codeine = Tylenol 3) and various analgesic combination compounds containing hydrocodone (i.e. hydrocodone and acetaminophen = Vicodin; Lorcet). **Must have a written prescription signed by a health professional** (laws vary by state). These drugs may be called into the pharmacy. The prescriber can authorize refills without writing a new prescription.

- **Schedule IV**: a category of drugs with less abuse or addiction potential then Schedules I-III. These substances include Diazepam (Valium), Lorazepam (Ativan), Triazolam (Halcion), Alprazolam (Xanax), and chloral hydrate.

- **Schedule V**: a category of drugs that have only a small potential for abuse and addiction. These substances include many commonly prescribed medications that contain only a small amount of Codeine.

FDA determines which drugs are to be sold by prescription only. The prescription must have the address of the patient and dentist, and the dentist's DEA number/license.

IMPORTANT PHARACOLOGIC AGENTS

NSAID's - have anti-inflammatory effects due to their ability to inactivate the enzyme "prostaglandin endoperoxide synthase" (cyclooxygenase). Enzyme inactivation inhibits the cyclooxygenase step of the arachidonic acid cascade, thus reducing local prostaglandin synthesis. NSAID's have anti-inflammatory, analgesic, & antipyretic actions.

- Prostaglandins are derived from the unsaturated fatty acids in cell membranes.

NSAIDs decrease production of inflammatory mediators possess anti-inflammatory, analgesic, & anti-pyretic effects. A "ceiling" effect exists for the analgesic properties. Most NSAIDs work best for mild to moderate pain, although efficacy varies between NSAIDs. Safer than corticosteroids for long-term use, but some NSAIDs have strong adverse effects, thus contraindicated in specific patient populations. Traditional NSAIDs "reversibly" reduce platelet aggregation (normal platelet function returns when the drugs leave the system).

- Aspirin, Cortisol, Ibuprofen (Motrin, Advil, Nuprin, Rufen), & Indomethacin have significant anti-inflammatory properties.

CYCLOOXYGENASE (COX) – enzyme producing prostaglandins that come in two forms (COX-1 & COX-2).

COX-1 Enzyme-produces prostaglandins in the GI tract. The prostaglandins formed act as a protective substance against the formation of GI ulcers. Traditional NSAIDs (Ibuprofen, Naproxen, Aspirin) inhibit the COX-1 & COX-2 enzymes to diminish the formation of the protective prostaglandins. They effectively reduce pain and inflammation, but can cause GI ulcers as a potential adverse effect. Since traditional NSAIDs (ibuprofen, naproxen, and aspirin) inhibit both COX-1 & COX-2 enzymes, they are "**Non-Selective COX inhibitors**:

- **Propionic Acid Derivatives**: **Ibuprofen (Motrin, Advil, Nuprin, Rufen)**-has anti-inflammatory properties by inhibiting prostaglandin synthesis/production in peripheral tissues at sites of pain and inflammation. Inhibiting prostaglandin production decreases the inflammatory response at sites of surgery, injury, or infection which results in a reduction of perceived pain. Ibuprofen is the MAIN INGREDIENT in OTC Advil, Nuprin, & Medipren (which contains 200mg of ibuprofen). Ibuprofen is also the main ingredient in Motrin (only sold via prescription) and contains at least 400mg of ibuprofen. More efficacious analgesics & anti inflammatory than aspirin. Better for moderate pain. One of the stronger NSAID analgesics. Patients intolerant to aspirin may not be able to tolerate ibuprofen. GI ulceration & upset, and drug interactions are common adverse effects. Fenoprofen, Suprofen, Naproxen, Naproxen Sodium, Ketoprofen, & Benoxaprofen are also NSAIDs propionic acid derivatives.
- **Ibuprofen (Motrin, Advil)** is a non-narcotic analgesic that may interact with Warfarin (Coumadin) to cause unnecessary bleeding because it inhibits platelet aggregation.

- Ibuprofen can be given to patients with a history of drug abuse since it has no addictive properties. Ibuprofen is an NSAID and non-narcotic analgesic which have no liability for abuse or addiction. They are not controlled substances.

- **Naproxen/Anaprox/Naprosyn (Aleve)**-potent anti-inflammatory & analgesic. Longer-acting than ibuprofen, better compliance, relieves pain longer. Does not interact with Warfarin or oral hypoglycemics, so better for Type II Diabetes Mellitus patients. Inhibit platelet aggregation.

- **Flurbiprofen (Ansaid)**-inhibits platelet aggregation.

- **Ketorolac (Toradol)**-a newer NSAID and more efficacious analgesic than aspirin. Sometimes used for moderate-to-severe pain after minor dental surgery or painful dental procedure. Suggested use for no > 5 days. Not for longer-term pain relief, as may be toxic with long-term use.

- **Acetic Acid Derivatives (NSAIDs)**: **Indomethacin** (Indocin), **Sulindac** (Clinoril), & **Tolmetin** (Tolectin). These NSAIDs can cause GI bleeding, ulcers, and possible stomach perforation.

- **Fenamic Acid Derivatives**: **Meclofenemate** (Meclomen) & **Mefenamic acid** (Ponstel).

Drugs that Increase Bleeding Times: aspirin, non-selective NSAIDs (Ibuprofen, Naproxen, Ketoprofen, Flurbiprofen), anti-platelet drugs (Clopidogrel (Plavix) & Ticlopidine (Ticlid), and anti-coagulants (Warfarin (Coumadin) & Heparin).
- **Ibuprofen & other "non-selective" NSAIDs** (inhibitors of COX1 & COX2 enzymes) inhibit platelet aggregation. This inhibition enhance/potentiates the anti-coagulant effects of Warfarin (Coumadin) to increase bleeding risk.

- **Clopidogrel (Plavix)**-inhibits blood clotting (increases bleeding time) by irreversibly inhibiting platelet aggregation. Thus, the effects on blood clotting are the same as with aspirin. Clopidogrel does not cuase gastric ulcers like aspirin, and is the **ANTIPLATELET AGENT OF CHOICE FOR PATIENTS WITH A HISTORY OF ULCERS**.

SALICYLATES: interfere with blood clotting mechanisms by **irreversibly reducing platelet adhesion** (stickiness or aggregation). Bleeding time is prolonged until new platelets are formed.

- **Aspirin (Acetylsalicylic Acid)-**prototypical non-selective COX inhibitors (NSAID) that **inhibits COX-1 & COX-2 (cyclooxygenase) to inhibit prostaglandin production** (prostaglandins are potent inflammatory mediators). **Aspirin's analgesic effects** are better if given to prevent prostaglandin production. Prevents worsening of pain. However, cannot reduce pain already caused by prostaglandin build-up. Aspirin **INACTIVATES** the cyclooxygenase enzyme that makes prostaglandins, thus **inhibits prostaglandin synthesis.** As a result, aspirin is an analgesic, antipyretic (reduces fever), and anti-inflammatory. Aspirin is an irreversible platelet inhibitor and can **reduce blood clotting, causing prolonged bleeding.** Aspirin may interact with Warfarin (Coumadin) to cause unnecessary bleeding.

- **Antipyretic** action of salicylates (aspirin) is explained in part by cutaneous vasodilation leading to increased heat loss.

- Aspirin is an anti-inflammatory, antipyretic, and analgesic used to relieve headaches, toothaches, minor aches and pains, and to reduce fever. The GI tract rapidly absorbs it.

- Low doses of aspirin taken regularly can have a cardioprotective effect. These low doses reduce thromboxane production of platelets to result in the inhibition of platelet aggregation. In this way, aspirin has the ability to inhibit the formation of life-threatening thrombi (blood clots).

- If a patient is taking ibuprofen, **ASPIRIN** is the analgesic that if given while the patient is taking ibuprofen will **DIMINISH** the analgesic effectiveness of the ibuprofen. When aspirin and ibuprofen are given together, the analgesic efficacy of both is less than that of aspirin or ibuprofen alone. Aspirin displaces ibuprofen from plasma protein binding sites, thus hastening its disappearance from the blood stream. It is then quickly eliminated from the body by the kidneys through urine.

- Aspirin inhibits blood clotting by inhibiting platelet aggregation in an irreversible manner. Inhibiting platelet aggregation prevents the activation of the coagulation pathway, thus no fibrin (clot) is formed. **Asprin does not affect the coagulation pathway.** Discontinuation of aspirin for 5-7 days allows for normal clotting time to reappear due to the synthesis of new platelets.

- **Aspirin (NSAIDs) Contraindications:**
  - Bleeding disorders (aspirin increases BT) & **ASTHMATICS.**
  - Children with viral infections with or without fever due to a potential association with Reye's Syndrome (a serious neurological defect).
  - Pregnancy, especially the 3rd trimester.
  - Peptic ulcers as aspirin may cause GI tract bleeding/ulcerations.
  - **Adverse effects:** GI upset, overdose causes hepatic & nephrotoxic. Death if overdose by respiratory acidosis.
  - **Salicylism-**describes all of the symptoms caused from ingesting extremely large doses of ASPIRIN (tinnitus/ringing in ears, vertigo/dizziness, nausea, sweating, vomiting, headache, and mental confusion).

COX-2 Enzyme-produces prostaglandins at sites of surgery, infection, and inflammation. When COX-2 enzyme is inhibited, less prostaglandins are produced, and there is less pain and inflammation. COX-2 selective inhibitors reduce pain and inflammation without any risk of GI ulcers. **COX-2 Selective Inhibitors-**newer NSAIDs that do not affect blood clotting (do not affect platelet function/aggregation) thus can be given to patients concomitantly taking **"blood thinners" like aspirin, warfarin (coumadin), & heparin.**

- **Rofecoxib (Vioxx) & Celecoxib (Celebrex) & Valdecoxib (Bextra)-**more efficacious analgesic than aspirin and ibuprofen with less GI side effects, and does not inhibit platelet aggregation, so **SAFER for bleeding disorders.** COX-2 selective inhibitors treat signs & symptoms or **RHEUMATOID OSTEOARTHRITIS, acute pain, and pain from dysmenorrhea.**

- COX-2 selective inhibitors are not salicylates because they are not aspirin drugs and are not opiates because they do not work like morphine, and are not steroidal anti-inflammatories because they are not corticosteroids like hydrocortisone.

HEPARIN-a high MW heteropolysaccharide found especially in the **LUNGS** and **inactivates thrombin** and other coagulation factors **to prevent blood clotting**. Heparin is **contained inside mast cells & basophils** found in C.T. and in extracellular spaces near blood vessels, especially in the lungs. *Heparin neutralizes tissue thromboplastin and blocks thromboplastin generation. Heparin inhibits blood clotting by affecting the coagulation pathway to **PREVENT FIBRIN FORMATION**.

- Administration of heparin causes **increased bleeding time** due to a potentiation of **Antithrombin III**, thus **inactivating thrombin**. This **prevents conversion of fibrinogen to fibrin**.

- Heparin acts as an **anticoagulant** by **enhancing** the inhibition rate of clotting proteases by Antithrombin III impairing normal hemostasis and **inhibiting factor Xa**. **Low MW heparins have a small effect on partial thromboplastin time (PTT), but STRONGLY inhibit factor Xa.**

- Heparin **inactivates thrombin** and **prevents** the conversion of **fibrinogen to fibrin (blood clot)**.

- Heparin is **used for prophylaxis and treatment of thromboembolic disorders**.

- Standard heparin consists of components with MW ranging from 4000-30,000 daltons (average is 16,000 daltons). Low MW heparins range from 2,000-8,000 daltons.

- **Low MW Heparin anticoagulant agents:** (Enoxaprin/Lovenox, Dalteparin/Fragmin, & Tinzaparin/Innohep) are used to **treat acute symptomatic deep vein thrombosis (DVT)** and to prevent deep vein thrombosis after knee or hip surgery. These are **administered subcutaneously** since they cannot be absorbed from the GI tract.

- **Thrombin-Inhibitor Type Anticoagulants:** administered IV to **prevent post-operative deep vein thrombosis (DVT) after** elective hip replacement surgery, and for prophylaxis or treatment of thrombosis in adults with **heparin-induced thrombocytopenia**. Their mechanism of action is directly **inhibiting thrombin** within the **coagulation pathway**, thus inhibiting fibrin formation. **Lepirudin (Refludan), Argatroban, Danaparoid (Orgaran)**.

WARFARIN (COUMADIN) & DICUMAROL-anticoagulants that **ANTAGONIZE VITAMIN K** to prolong blood clotting time, causing decreased liver synthesis of vitamin-K dependent factors (II, VII, IX, & X). Warfarin inhibits blood clotting by **affecting the coagulation pathway to PREVENT FIBRIN FORMATION**.

- Used after myocardial infarction to prevent coronary occlusion, treat pulmonary embolism, and venous thrombosis.

- **Enhanced** anticoagulant effects are seen when Warfarin or Dicumarol are **combined with aspirin**. Thus, use **acetaminophen (Tylenol)** for pain control rather than aspirin for patients **taking anticoagulants**.

- Warfarin interferes with the hepatic synthesis of vitamin-K dependent coagulation factors (II, VII, IX, X) resulting in the inability of the coagulation pathway to form fibrin (blood clot).

- **Vitamin K-**a group of fat-soluble vitamins **essential for the synthesis of coagulation factors II, VII, IX, X, & prothrombin in the liver**. Vitamin K **enhances (improves) blood clotting**.

Prothrombin Time (PT)-the **most valuable test** used to evaluate if a patient taking anticoagulants **is a surgical risk**. PT test is a one-stage test to **detect certain plasma coagulation defects** owing to a **deficiency of Factors V, VII, or X.** Thromboplastin and calcium are added to a sample of the patient's plasma and simultaneously to a sample from a normal control. The **length of time required for clot formation in both samples is observed.** Thrombin is formed from prothrombin in the presence of adequate calcium, thromboplastin, and the essential tissue coagulation factors. **A prolonged PT indicates a deficiency in one of the factors** (as in liver disease, vitamin K deficiency, or anticoagulation therapy with the drug Coumarin).

After prothrombin times (PT) are determined, they are **expressed as an INR value** (International Normalized Ratio). **INR is the ratio of the prothrombin time measured in the patient divided by a standard prothrombin time value, and multiplied by a constant.**

NOTES

Patients on anticoagulant therapy may have excess bleeding after dental treatment. Always check the patient's medical history. If the patient is on anticoagulants, have their physician provide documentation of their **INR (International Normalized Ratio)** values to assess anticoagulant effects. INR is the ratio of the prothrombin time measured in the patient divided by a standard prothrombin time value multiplied by a constant. **The higher INR, the greater the anticoagulant effect** (greater clotting).

- **INR value of 1**: means normal prothrombin times of ~12sec; normal blood clotting is present.
- **INR > 1**: indicates an anticoagulant effect exists.
- Many patients taking anticoagulants have INR values of 2, 3, 4, 5, and even 6.
- For surgical procedures, an INR of 1-1.5 indicates a normal prothrombin time (~12-18 seconds). This is within a safe range.

Conditions Managed by Anticoagulants (Warfarin/Coumadin) & Anti-platelet Agents (Aspirin & Clopidogrel (Plavix)):

1. **Coronary Artery Disease (CAD)** by helping prevent myocardial infarction in these patients.
2. **Angina Pectoris (Unstable Angina)** by preventing a thrombus from forming in the coronary arteries.
3. **Myocardial Infarction (MI)**: drugs that prevent blood clotting prevent threat of future infarcts.
4. **Stroke**: helps prevent a thrombus from forming, thus preventing threat of a cerebral embolism.

Hypertension IS NOT MANAGED with anticoagulants or anti-platelet drugs, unless it is accompanied by the above cardiovascular problems, as these drugs **DO NOT LOWER BLOOD PRESSURE**.

NSAIDs must be used cautiously in patients with **PEPTIC ULCER DISEASE**.
- **NSAID Adverse Effects**: GI upset (possible ulcers), prolonged bleeding time (due to reduced platelet aggregation).

- **NSAIDs Contraindications**: patients with impaired renal function, pregnancy, and GI disease (ulcers).

Drugs WITHOUT Anti-Inflammatory Properties:

1. **Acetaminophen (Tylenol)**- a WEAK inhibitor of prostaglandin synthesis in peripheral tissues, thus **DOES NOT GREATLY AFFECT INFLAMMATION**. Tylenol reduces pain by non-inflammatory mechanisms. It is unclear exactly how it works to reduce pain. Lacks anti-inflammatory effects of aspirin, but is a good analgesic when aspirin or ibuprofen are contraindicated. Better to use in GI, bleeding disorders, asthma, young children, and pregnancy. Less drug interactions than aspirin, but overdose can be hepatotoxic if mixed with alcohol. Acetaminophen is **NOT an NSAID**, but an alternative used for patients who cannot tolerate NSAIDS. **Disadvantage**: no peripheral anti-inflammatory effects since lacks anti-inflammatory properties.

   - **Pregnant or Nursing Women**: for mild-to-moderate pain, **acetaminophen is the accepted choice for short-term use** (long-term effects unknown in pregnant women), and safe for breast feeding, but acetaminophen lacks anti-inflammatory properties).

   - Acetaminophen does not hasten the elimination of ibuprofen. The analgesic efficacy of combining acetaminophen and ibuprofen is greater than either acetaminophen or ibuprofen alone. The combination provides effective pain relief.

   - **Acetaminophen is a non-narcotic analgesic that DOES NOT AFFECT PLATELET AGGREGATION or the coagulation pathway**. Thus, it does not affect the anticoagulant nature of Warfarin (Coumadin), so is safe in warfarin patients.

   - Acetaminophen has no effect on platelets nor the coagulation pathways, and does not affect bleeding times, even with high doses. Thus, a**cetaminophen is a non-narcotic analgesic that is the best choice to relive mild-to-moderate pain in a patient taking anti-coagulant medication (warfarin, heparin) because it does not effect blood clotting**.

   - **Acetaminophen's Two Major Pharmacological Actions**: **ANALGESIC & ANTIPYRETIC (fever reducer) effect**. While it is not effective enough to reduce severe pain, it is **effective in reducing mild-to-moderate pain**. Acetaminophen is a weak inhibitor of prostaglandin formation. Thus, for **mild-to-moderate pain, use acetaminophen** (never NSAID's aspirin or ibuprofen).

- Acetaminophen has little value in treating acute inflammation. Acetaminophen inhibits CENTRAL prostaglandin synthesis (it is an analgesic for low intensity pain and antipyretic). Because it is less effective than salicylates (aspirin) in blocking peripheral prostaglandin synthesis, it does not have anti-inflammatory activity and does not affect platelet function, thus does not affect clotting time. In large doses, acetaminophen can cause hepatic necrosis.
- Acetaminophen is a relatively safe ANTIPYRETIC drug with NO INFLAMMATORY ACTION.

OPIOIDS (NARCOTICS)-drugs WITHOUT ANTI-INFLAMMAOTRY PROPERTIES used as very effective analgesics to relieve moderate-to-severe pain, antitussives, antidiarrheals, preanesthetic medications, and as analgesic adjuncts during anesthesia.
- Opioids suppress the cough reflex (antitussive), cause constipation (antidiarrheal), and when used as preanesthetic medications, opiates reduce the amount of general anesthetic required for surgical anesthesia. Opiates are administered with caution to patients with HEAD INJURY or with a history of drug abuse and dependency.
- Common Side Effects: sedation and drowsiness (by depressing conscious centers of the brain), dizziness, & nausea. The MOST common side effect of the narcotic (opiate) analgesics is NAUSEA. Narcotic analgesics DO NOT cause peptic ulcers or Insomnia.
- Less Common Adverse Effects: vomiting, hypotension, irregular/labored breathing (dyspnea), lightheadedness, nightmares, and insomnia. *Respiratory depression is dose related and causes death in narcotic drug overdose. It can occur with any of the narcotics. Respiratory depression is the MAJOR disadvantage of using opioids and is the most significant and well-known adverse reaction. Death secondary to opioid overdose is usually always due to respiratory depression. When opioids are used correctly, the risk of severe respiratory depression is small as tolerance rapidly develops to this effect. The MOST SERIOUS side effect is respiratory depression. The cause of death from overdose of narcotics is respiratory depression and shut down of the respiratory system.
- Hydrocodone-similar potency as morphine. When combined with acetaminophen it is called (Vicodin, Lorcet, Lortab, Maxidone, & Zydone). Given orally it lasts 4-6hrs. Usually combined with acetaminophen. When combined with ibuprofen it is (Vicoprofen). Among the opiates available for dentistry, hydrocodone products are the drugs of choice. It is a mild-to-moderate agonist.

Narcotic analgesics DO NOT AFFECT BLOOD CLOTTING, thus do not enhance the anticoagulant effects of Warfarin (Coumadin). Narcotics with acetaminophen can be given safely to Warfarin patients
- Codeine + Aspirin (Empirin)-an analgesic/anti-inflammatory. Avoid in asthmatics and patients who cannot take aspirin as codeine precipitate acute asthma attacks.

Hydrocodone (Vicodin, Lorcet, Norcet, Lortab)-a combination analgesic more efficacious than codeine, but potentially greater abuse liability. Avoid in asthmatics. Has poor anti-inflammatory, but good analgesic (stronger than Tylenol).
- Hydrocodone + Ibuprofen-a strong analgesic for moderate-to-moderately severe pain, with good anti-inflammatory properties. Ibuprofen has similar contraindications to aspirin, with GI problems being the most common side effect (take with milk or food to limit). Better for patients who cannot take aspirin or ibuprofen.

Oxycodone-a combination analgesic that is more efficacious than codeine, but avoided in asthmatics. Treat moderately-to-severe pain. Oxycodone has the HIGHEST DEPENDENCY LIABILITY when compared to drugs like codeine, propoxyphene, and pentazocine. Oxycodone is contained in Percodan, Percocet.
- Oxycodone + Aspirin (Percodan)-good analgesic with anti-inflammatory properties. The strongest pain medication you can prescribe on an outpatient (ambulatory) basis. Do not take it on an empty stomach.

MORPHINE IS NOT USED IN DENTISTRY DUE TO ITS HIGH ADDICTIVE LIABILITY.

Drugs that cause XEROSTOMIA by INHIBITING SALIVA production & secretion: xerostomia produced by these drugs is reversible as normal salivary flow is regained after discontinuing the drug.

1. **Amitriptyline (Elavil)**-a tricyclic antidepressant (a drug class that causes significant xerostomia). They probably work through an anticholinergic action.

2. **Diphenhydramine (Benadryl)**-a sedating-type antihistamine (a drug class that causes significant xerostomia). They probably work through an anticholinergic action.

3. **Atropine**-a powerful anti-cholinergic that blocks saliva production in the salivary glands. Other anti-cholinergics have a similar action.

4. **Diazepam (Valium)**-a benzodiazepine tranquilizer that has moderate anticholinergic action to reduce the outflow of saliva.

Cholinergic drugs that TREAT dry mouth (Xerostomia) by INDUCING salivation:

1. **Pilocarpine (Salagen)**-a cholinergic agonist and alkaloid indicated to treat xerostomia caused by salivary gland hypofunction caused by radiotherapy for head and neck cancer by stimulating salivary flow. **Common side effects:** excess sweating, nausea, heartburn, and diarrhea due to the drug's cholinergic nature.

2. **Cevimeline (Evoxac)**-a cholinergic agonist indicated to treat xerostomia in patients with Sjogren's Syndrome. **Common side effects:** increased sweating, nausea, heartburn, diarrhea due to the drug's cholinergic nature. Specific for the M_3 receptor on the salivary glands.

ANTI-DIABETIC DRUGS (Oral Hypoglycemics): Glyburide (DiaBeta), Metformin (Glucophage), Pioglitazone (Actos), Chloropropamide (Diabinese), Tolbutamide (Orinase). These drugs are used as adjuncts to diet to treat non-insulin dependent diabetes mellitus (Type 2 Diabetes) that cannot be controlled by diet alone.

- **Glyburide & Chloropropamide**-stimulate insulin release from the pancreas, and work by reducing glucose output from the liver and by increasing insulin sensitivity at peripheral target sites.

- **Metformin & Pioglitazone**-increase insulin sensitivity at peripheral target sites.

- **Tolbutamide**-a sulfonylurea that stimulates the synthesis and release of insulin from the pancreas, increases the sensitivity of insulin receptors, and improves peripheral utilization of insulin.

Hypoglycemia-the most serious and common complication of insulin therapy. **Symptoms:** sweating, weakness, confusion, slurred speech, & blurred vision. Administration of a concentrated glucose source relieves mild hypoglycemia. **Humulin**-the brand name for the human form of insulin.

Insulin-a pancreatic hormone secreted by pancreatic beta-cells of ISLETS of LANGERHANS. Insulin is essential for glucose metabolism and for homeostasis of blood glucose. Insulin is usually administered by subcutaneous injection. Various insulin preparations are prepared from beef or pork pancreas, and differ mainly in their onset and duration of action. **Effects of Insulin:** gluconeogenesis & triglyceride storage, glycogen synthesis, & protein synthesis.

Insulin preparations mimic the activity of endogenous insulin, which is required for the proper utilization of glucose in normal metabolism. Insulin preparations are used in **Type 1 & Type 2 diabetes** that cannot be completely controlled by the oral anti-diabetic drugs or by diet alone. **Insulins differ in their onset and duration of action**:

ASTHMA-a respiratory disorder characterized by recurring episodes of paroxysmal dyspnea, wheezing on expiration, coughing, and viscous mucoid bronchial secretions. Asthma episodes may be precipitated by inhalation of allergens or pollutants, infection, vigorous exercise, or emotional stress.

- **Bronchodilators (b_2 adrenergic agonists that treat an acute asthma attack)**- **EPI**, **Albuterol** (Proventil), **Salmeterol** (Serevent), & **Metaproterenol** (Alupent). These drugs **stimulate beta receptors in the airway to cause bronchodilation**, thus are used to help reverse an acute asthmatic attack. They are taken via aerosol, inhalers, and nebulizer.

- **Aminophylline**-a **THEOPHYLLINE** compound administered orally as bronchodilators in reversible airway obstruction due to asthma or COPD (chronic obstructive pulmonary disease). Theophylline **RELAX bronchial smooth muscle** to **improve airway function**. A **CNS stimulant** that treats asthma.

Beta-Adrenergic Receptor Blockers (b Blockers): with all "selective" beta-blockers, selectivity for the b_1 is lost at high doses. As the dose is increased, they also block b_2 receptors, thus having effects on bronchial smooth muscle. The **most common adverse side effects of beta blockers are WEAKNESS & DROWSINESS**. Beta blockers **treat hypertension, angina, cardiac arrhythmias, MI, glaucoma**, and prophylaxis of migraine.

- **Propranolol (Inderal), Timolol, & Nadolol (longest-acting)**-lipid soluble drugs that blocks both b_1 & b_2 receptors (thus are "**non-selective**" beta-blockers). **Widely used to treat hypertension** (lower BP). **Non-selective beta blockers are absolutely contraindicated in patients with asthma** or other chronic obstructive airway disease as they **cause fatal bronchospasm**. Also, contraindicated in patients with insulin-dependent diabetes as they block hypoglycemia recovery. Propranolol exerts its major anti-anginal effect by **BLOCKING** beta-adrenergic heart receptors.
  - Propranolol is the **drug of choice for** adrenergically induced arrythmias.

- **Acebutolol (Sectral)**-a b_1 **cardioselective** antagonist that treats hypertension and controls ventricular arrhythmias. It has low lipid solubility which reduces is likelihood of producing adverse CNS effects, and has mild intrinsic sympathomimetic activity (partial agonist activity at b_2 receptors) similar to Pindolol.

- **Metoprolol (Lopressor)**-competitive b_1 **cardioselective** antagonist that blocks b_1 receptors to treat hypertension, acute angina pectoris, and may be helpful after a heart attack (very similar to Atenolol).

- **Atenolol (Tenormin)**-competitive b_1 **cardioselective** antagonist that blocks b_1 receptors to treat hypertension, **chronic angina pectoris**, or after a heart attack (MI recovery). Has a **long plasma life (long duration of action)**. Due to its low lipid solubility, it is **excreted by the kidneys**, minimally metabolized, and has a low potential for causing CNS side effects compared to lipid-soluble beta-blockers like Propranolol.

- **Metoprolol & Atenolol** are **longer-acting and more predictable** than Propranolol in producing therapeutic plasma levels. Since they are b_1 selective, they are **safer to use in patients with asthma or bronchitis**.

Alpha-Adrenergic Receptor Blockers (a Blockers)-pharmacological agents that can cause **tachycardia**, lower BP, vasodilation, and **orthostatic hypotension (postural hypotension)**-a fainting spell that occurs due to a rapid fall in BP when moving from the supine to the upright position when getting out of the dental chair. The symptoms are similar to simple fainting, but the condition is related to positioning. Alpha blockers are medications that act by **competitively inhibiting catecholamine actions at the alpha receptor site to CAUSE BLOOD VESSELS TO RELAX (DILATE)** and are used to reduce high BP and treat an enlarged prostate. While **HYPOTENSION** is the **major adverse effect** of alpha blockers, they cause relatively few adverse effects.

Orthostatic Hypotension (Postural Hypotension)-abnormally low BP occurring when an individual assumes the standing posture. **After vasovagal syncope, orthostatic hypotension is the 2nd most likely cause of transient unconsciousness in the dental office.**

Factors that can cause orthostatic hypotension: administration and ingestion of drugs, prolonged recumbency and convalescence, inadequate postural reflex, pregnancy, various defects in the legs, Addison's Disease, physical exhaustion, starvation, and chronic orthostatic hypotension (Shy-Drager Syndrome). The incidence of orthostatic hypotension increases with age. NSAIDs do not produce orthostatic hypotension as an adverse effect.

Drugs that can cause Orthostatic Hypotension:
1. **Antihypertensives**: (Guanethidine/Ismelin).
2. **Phenothiazines**: (Chlorpromazine/Thorazine & Thioridazine/Mellaril).
3. **Tricyclic Antidepressants**: (Doxepin/Sinequan, Amitriptyline/Elavil, Imipramine/Tofranil).
4. **Narcotics**: (Meperidine/Demerol & Morphine).
5. **Antiparkinson Drugs**: (Levodopa/Larodopa/Dopar & Carbidopa + Levodopa (Sinemet).

DIURETICS-anti-hypertensive agents used to **treat CONGESTIVE HEART FAILURE** by relieving edema and symptoms of dyspnea arising from pulmonary congestion. Diuretics also treat hypertension and manage edema associated with hepatic or renal disease. **Widely used Diuretics**:

Potassium (K+)-Sparing Diuretics- changes Na+ & K+ concentrations at the end of the distal convoluted tubules. Postassium sparing diuretics **act in the collecting tubule** to inhibit Na+ reabsorption, K+ secretion, & H+ secretion. **HYPERKALEMIA** is the most important toxic effect of potassium-sparing diuretics. Potassium-sparing diuretics conserve K+ while causing diuresis. Thus, no potassium is lost from the body as with other diuretics (i.e. Thiazides & Loops). **2 Types of Potassium-Sparing Diuretics**:

1. **Aldosterone Antagonists in Collecting Tubules**:
    - **Spironolactone (Aldactone)**-a pharmacologic antagonist of aldosterone in the collecting tubule. Treats **primary aldosteronism & heart failure** since hyperaldosteronism is common in heart failure patients. Spironolactone competes with aldosterone receptor sites in the renal tubules causing increased secretion of Na+, Cl, and H_2O, while conserving K+.

2. **Sodium Channel Blockers in Collecting Tubules**:
    - **Amiloride (Midamor)**-blocks Na2+ channels in luminal membrane of principal cells in the late distal tubule & collecting duct which decreases K+ excretion. It inhibits Na+ transport through ion channels in the luminal membrane causing a decrease in Na+K+ exchange.

    - 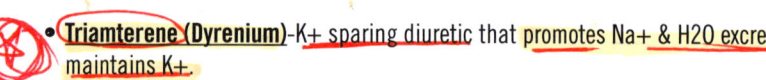**Triamterene (Dyrenium)**-K+ sparing diuretic that promotes Na+ & H2O excretion, but maintains K+.

Thiazides Diuretics-inhibit sodium reabsorption in the distal portion of the renal tubule within the kidney causing increased excretion of Na+ & H_2O (affects salt transport in the distal convulted tubule). Thiazide diuretics are the **most widely used diuretic drugs** used to treat hypertension, but may require supplemental administration of K+ (postassium). Inhibits Na+/Cl- symport. **Thiazides Treat**:
1. **Hypertension** (anti-hypertensive drugs) by decreasing systolic & diastolic BP.
2. **Edema of CHF** decreasing extracellular volume.
3. **Renal Edema (nephrotic syndrome)** if loop diuretics fail.
4. **Hypercalciuria** (increase uric acid in urine-inhibit urinary Ca2+ excretion). Treats patients w/ calcium oxalate stones in urinary tract (calcium nephrolithiasis).
5. **Nephrogenic Diabetes Insipidus** (lack of responsiveness to ADH)-thiazides **produce hyperosmolar urine** due to volume contraction causing **increased reabsorption at proximal tubule**. Thiazides treat this by substituting ADH.

Loop (High-Ceiling) Diuretics-inhibit Na+K+2Cl- symport or cotransport. Inhibit reabsorption of Na+ and chloride in the ascending Loop of Henle to cause increased secretion of H_2O, Na+, & Cl. **Furosemide (Lasix)** is the prototype loop diuretic. **Other loop diuretics**: Bumetanide, Torsemide, & Ethacrynic acid

1. **Mechanism of Action**: increase Ca^{2+} content of urine, while thiazide diuretics decrease Ca^{2+} concentration of urine.
   - Cause decreased renal vascular resistance and increased renal blood flow.
   - Acutely loop diuretics increase excretion of uric acid, where as chronic admin causes reduced uric acid excretion, and increases renal blood flow.

2. **Therapeutic uses**: acute pulmonary edema of CHF, loop diuretics are **DRUG OF CHOICE**. Useful in emergencies due to their rapid onset of action. Treats hypercalcemia by stimulating tubular Ca^{2+} secretion, and treat hypertension when other diuretics and antihypertensives do not produce a satisfactory response.

3. **Adverse Effects**: OTOTOXICITY as tinnitus, hearing impairment, deafness, vertigo, & sense of ear fullness.
   - Loop diuretics are toxic to the ear especially when used with aminoglycosides (antibiotics).
   - ETHACRYNIC is the most ototoxic.
   - Irreversible damage may result with continued treatment, and vestibular function is less likely to be distributed, but it too may be affected by prolonged combined treatment.
   - Hyperuricemia, acute hypovolemia (reduced blood volume), increase plasma LDL cholesterol and triglycerides, and decrease HDL.
   - Skin rashes, photosensitivity, paresthesias, K+ depletion, & bone marrow depression.

Osmotic Diuretics-highly filtered by the glomerulus and exerts a solute-induced diuresis in the proximal tubule. Osmotic diuretics are used to reduce excess edema associated with neurosurgery or trauma to the CNS. Mannitol (Osmitrol), Glycerin (Glyrol), Isosorbide (Ismotic), & Urea (Ureaphil). Must be given via injection.

- **Mannitol**-treats cerebral edema, increases delivery of Na^{2+} & water out of loop of Henle. Mannitol is NOT absorbed orally so it MUST be given intravenously.

- Osmotic diuretics are not useful in treating conditions where Na+ retention occurs, but are used to maintain urine flow after acute toxic ingestion of substances capable of producing acute renal failure.

- Osmotic diuretics treat patients with increased intracranial pressure, or acute renal failure due to shock, drug toxicities, and trauma.

CORTICOSTEROIDS (STEROIDS)-steroid hormones produced by the **ADRENAL CORTEX** that **DO NOT CURE** any disease (they supplement hormones (cortisol) as in Addison's Disease).
- Corticosteroids treat asthma, arthritis (if patient has peptic ulcer disease, do not use corticosteroids for arthritis), allergic reactions, Addisons, Lupus Erythematosus, Apthous Stomatitis, and TMJ pain

GINGIVAL HYPERPLASIA:
- Calcium Channel Blockers (Verapamil, Nifedipine, Diltiazem) have been associated with causing GINGIVAL HYPERPLASIA. Calcium Channel Blockers-include Amlodipine (Norvasc), Diltiazem (Cardizem), and Nifedipine (Procardia). These drugs inhibit calcium from entering into vascular smooth muscle, to cause vasodilation of the coronary and peripheral blood vessels, causing lower BP.

- **Phenytoin (Dilantin)**-anti-convulsant (seizure) drug that can induce gingival hyperplasia.

LOCAL ANESTHETICS, EPINEPHRINE, & NITROUS OXIDE

Amide Local Anesthetics: all are **metabolized in the LIVER** (except Articaine), and the **metabolites are then renally excreted**. All amides have an "amide" grouping within their chemical structure. An amide grouping is a bridge or link containing the $-CONHCH_2-$ **configuration**. Amides are **present in urine** as the parent compound in a **greater percentage** due to their more complex process of **biotransformation**. Amides are **the only local anesthetics presently available as dental injectables (Lidocaine (Xylocaine), Prilocaine (Citanest), Bupivacaine (Marcaine), & Mepivacaine (Carbocaine), Etidocaine, & Articaine)**. All drugs with two letter "i" in the name. Amides are metabolized by the "hepatic microsomal enzyme system", and the products formed to **not have anesthetic actions** and are excreted from the body by the KIDNEY. **Amides are used with caution**, or not at all in patients with **compromised liver function**. **AMIDES**-have a **longer duration of action**, and are **metabolized by P450 enzymes** in the liver so **toxicity is more likely if amides are given to individuals with liver dysfunction** or if given with other drugs that may alter hepatic metabolism. **Amides less likely to produce allergic reactions**.

1. **Articaine (Septocaine)**-the **only amide-type local anesthetic metabolized in the BLOODSTREAM**. It is **chemically unique** because it has an **ester group** attached to its molecule that can be acted upon by **plasma cholinesterase to** render it **ineffective**. Thus, it is the **only amide** metabolized in the **bloodstream**, and not the liver. Articaine is supplied as **articaine HCL 4% solution with EPI 1:100,000. It** is indicated for local, infiltrative, or conductive anesthesia in simple and complex dental and periodontal procedures. The onset of anesthesia after administration is **1-6min after injection**. Complete anesthesia lasts ~1hr. **Articaine is contraindicated in** patients with **hypersensitivity to local anesthetics of the amide type or to sodium bisulfite**.
   - Maximum dose of **Articaine (Septocaine)** recommended in one appointment is expressed as mg/kg body weight (not as total mg). **7mg/kg is the maximum recommended dose of Articaine in children and adults**. In a typical kg adult male, the 7mg/kg dose = **490mg**. Thus, the maximum recommended amount of Articaine that could be given to a 70kg adult in one appointment is **490mg**.

2. **Prilocaine (Citanest)**-a local anesthetic amide used for **nerve block, epidurals, and regional** anesthesia. It has an **intermediate** duration of action and is **longer** acting than Lidocaine, **produces less vasodilation than equal amounts of Lidocaine, and is somewhat less potent than Lidocaine**. Prilocaine is available as a **4% solution** with or without EPI, which **prolongs the** anesthetic effect. While Prilocaine is **50% as toxic as** Lidocaine, since **methemoglobinemia is a** possible reaction, **Prilocaine is not used for patient with hypoxic conditions** or patients with **Hepatic (liver) disease**. Prilocaine is **metabolized into orthotoluidine** (a product than can produce **methemoglobinemia**, a condition characterized by increased levels of **methemoglobin** in the blood which is **less effective** then hemoglobin in carrying oxygen in the blood.

3. **Bupivacaine (Marcaine)**-has the **longest duration** of action of any dental local anesthetic **available**. May be used with EPI. Appropriate for **extended procedures** although **long** duration of effect **increases risk of systemic absorption & toxicity**. *Radiotoxic in some patients and used with caution if **cardiovascular disease, elderly, or pediatric population***. Often used in **labor & procedures where motor control is essential** because exhibits strong preference for sensory fibers & is long-acting.

4. **Lidocaine (Xylocaine):** an **ANTI-ARRHYTHMIC AGENT** effective ONLY on the ventricle, often administered intravenously to **treat life-threatening ventricular arrhythmias**. When given IV to treat ventricular arrhythmias, it acts on the **fibrillating ventricles to decrease cardiac excitability and spares the atria**. It can effectively reverse a life-threatening situation.
   - Lidocaine and Mepivacaine are most likely to show **cross-allergy**.
   - Lidocaine is a **local anesthetic drug used topically in dentistry**.

4. **Mepivacaine (Carbocaine)**-equal to lidocaine in efficacy and used without EPI. **Ineffective for topical application**. Levonordeferin can be used as a vasoconstrictor. Duration of anesthesia in soft tissue is **shorter** than Lidocaine, thus **less useful for procedures lasting > 25 minutes**. **TOXIC TO NEONATES, so avoid for labor and infants**. Not best for **dental procedures more than 30 minutes (short effects)**.

EPI (Vasoconstictor) Therapeutic Indications:

- Alleviates symptoms of an acute asthma attack via its bronchodilator properties. EPI treats bronchospasm associated with hypotension (i.e. anaphylaxis). **EPI is the agent of choice to treat/reverse anaphylactic reactions (given sublingually or subcutaneously)** because it has desirable vasopressor activity, bronchodilator properties, and has a rapid onset of action. EPI has stimulatory effects on a & b adrenergic receptors. **EPI treats hypersensitivity reactions**.

- **The major reason that EPI vasoconstrictor is added to local anesthetics is to prolong the activity/duration of the local anesthetic** (anesthesia) by decreasing the rate of diffusion and absorption from the injection site.

- EPI also reduces systemic toxicity by **reducing** the rate of vascular absorption into the systemic circulation, & **provides hemostasis** by reducing/controlling local bleeding at the injection site. EPI also enhances the onset of action, decreases bleeding, and allergic reactions.

- EPI is used to restore cardiac activity in cardiac arrest relieves congestion of the nose, sinuses, and throat.

- Treats glaucoma by reducing internal eye pressure.

- Controls superficial hemorrhage/bleeding.

- EPI is administered IV, sublingually, subcutaneously, or intramuscularly. It has a **very rapid onset** of action when given via these routes.

- If **NE or EPI** stimulate or combine with eye **a-receptors**, they cause **MYDRIASIS (pupil dilation)**.

- EPI is ineffective in treating hypotension because of its alpha receptor stimulatory actions on the vasculature which could cause an even further elevation of BP. EPI does not reduce anxiety, but increases anxiety because it has CNS stimulatory effects.

- **EPI is a sympathomimetic agent** used in dentistry as the vasoconstrictor for anesthetic solutions to prolong the duration of local anesthesia, and is the vasoconstrictor component used in gingival retraction cords.

- **Contraindications**: patients with ANGINA conditions because EPI's cardiostimulatory effects aggravate this condition.

- **Common EPI side effects**: headaches, agitation (anxiety), and tachycardia. EPI is used with caution in patients with high BP and hyperthyroidism. These patients may have an increased sensitivity to EPI.

- **Norepinephrine (NE)**: $a_{1,2}$ & b_1 agonist.

- **Isoproterenol**: $b_{1,2}$ agonist (a synthetic catecholamine) and **MOST POTENT BRONCHODILATOR**.

Nitrous Oxide (N_2O)
-a slight sweet smelling, colorless, inert gas at room temperature and pressure that **cannot produce general anesthesia EXCEPT if administered at concentrations > 80%** (thus, it cannot be used as a single agent to produce general anesthesia). At these concentrations, the **lack of oxygen causes DIFFUSION HYPOXIA**. Inhalant anesthetics like halothane & isoflurane can produce general anesthesia at concentrations of 3-5%, thus are very useful in anesthesia. Nitrous oxide is stored under pressure in steel cylinders painted blue. Oxygen is stored in green tanks.

Important: ALWAYS TAKE VITALS BEFORE ADMINISTERING NITROUS OXIDE to determine if patient's vitals are stable to receive nitrous oxide and have the patient read and sign INFORMED CONSENT FORM.

- **Advantages of Nitrous Oxide Analgesia**: rapid onset of action, elevates pain threshold, produces euphoria, pleasant induction, titratable, rapid and complete recovery, virtually no adverse effects in absence of hypoxia, therapeutic for many medically compromised patients, and is suitable for all ages.

- Nitrous oxide is used to produce **SEDATION & MILD ANALGESIA**. Nitrous oxide's main therapeutic effect is **relaxation/sedation** (mild analgesia is a secondary effect). N_2O is usually used in 30-50% concentrations along with pure oxygen. It is a colorless, non-irritating gas at root temperature and pressure, and is non-flammable and non-explosive. Nitrous oxide delivery machines are pre-equipped with a failsafe mechanism that will not allow less than 20% oxygen to be delivered to the patient (nitrous oxide MUST be coupled with **AT LEAST 20% oxygen**). Nitrous oxide does not have local anesthetic (analgesic) properties. Thus, local anesthesia must be used in conjunction with nitrous oxide any procedure where pain is anticipated.

- Onset of sedation occurs **within 5 min** and the recovery is **just as rapid**. The **FIRST SYMPTOM** of nitrous oxide onset is **TINGLING OF THE HANDS**. It is excreted unchanged by the lungs. Most common complaint from patients taking N_2O is **mild nausea**. Always give the patient **100% oxygen after the procedure for 5 minutes to prevent diffusion hypoxia**.

- N_2O is quickly absorbed from the lungs and is physically dissolved in the blood. There is no biotransformation, and the gas is rapidly excreted by the lungs when the concentration gradient is reversed. It is recommended that the patient be maintained on oxygen for 5 minutes AFTER the sedation period. Nitrous oxide has a rapid onset (5min) and rapid recovery (5min).

- <u>Contraindications</u>: patients with **upper respiratory infections, emphysema, bronchitis, 1st trimester of pregnancy** (long-term exposure to low nitrous oxide doses can increase the incidence of spontaneous abortions), and in **patients where communication is difficult (i.e. autistic patients)**. Nitrous is **never used on patients with a contagious disease** as it is difficult to sterilize the entire tubing. Environmental contamination by nitrous oxide is kept to a minimum by employing a scavenger system.

- <u>Important</u>: Nitrous oxide is a **SEDATIVE**, NOT a general anesthetic because hypoxic levels are required to produce anesthesia. It is used alone to produce sedation or in combination with inhalation agents to supplement the anesthetic response. In dentistry always give at least 30% oxygen and no more than 70% nitrous.

CHAPTER 5

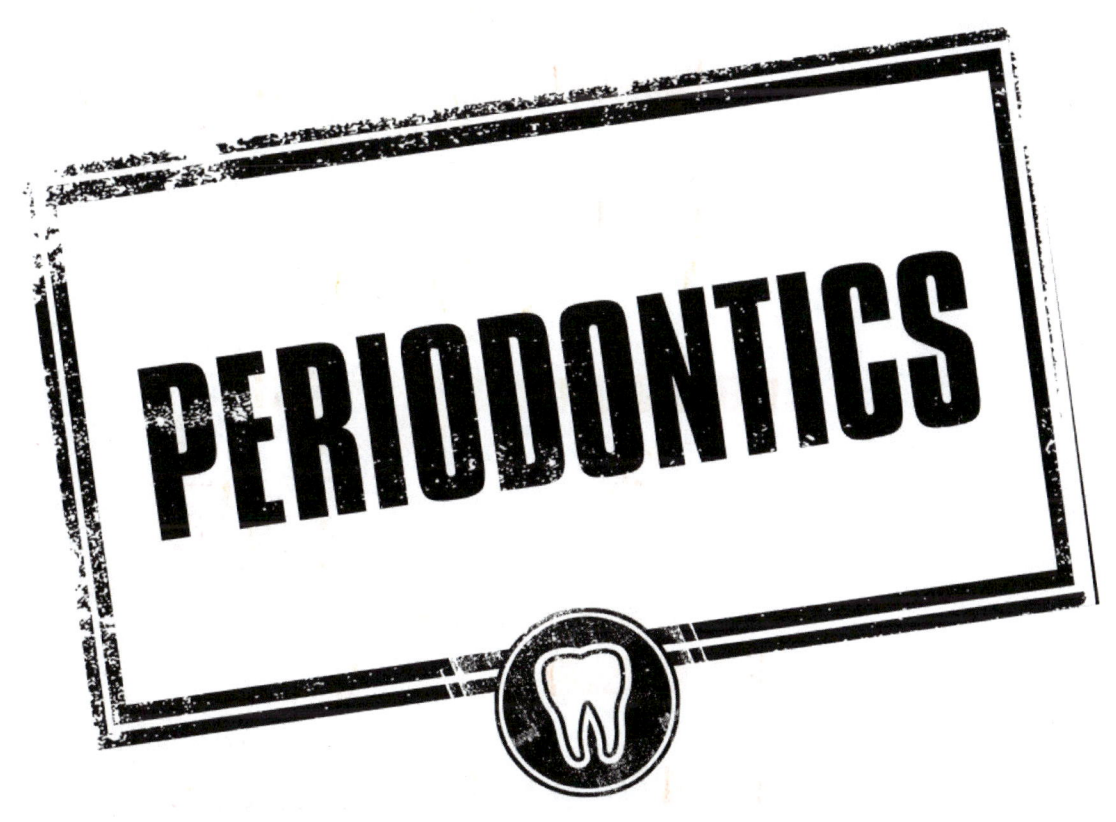

PERIODONTICS

The **two most critical factors** that determine the **PROGNOSIS** of a periodontally involved tooth are **MOBILITY** and **ATTACHMENT LOSS** (the most critical factor).

PERIODONTAL PROGNOSIS – a forecast of the possible response to treatment and long-term outlook for maintaining a healthy, functional dentition.

1. **Good Prognosis**: patient has at least 1 of these: healthy or slight CAL, adequate periodontal support, no mobility, no furcation, and control of etiologic factors to assure the tooth would be relatively easy to maintain under full patient compliance.

2. **Fair Prognosis**: patient has at least 1 of these: moderate or severe CAL and/or Class I mobility or furcation involvement. The furcation depth and location allows proper maintenance with full patient compliance.

3. **Questionable Prognosis**: patient has at least 1 of these: severe CAL (>5mm) causing a poor crown-root ratio, poor root form. Class II furcations not easily accessible to maintenance, or Class III furcations. Grade II or III mobility, significant root proximity.

4. **Hopeless Prognosis**: 1 or more of the factors under questionable prognosis with inadequate attachment to maintain the tooth in health, comfort, and function. **EXTRACTION is suggested** because active periodontal therapy (surgical or non-surgical) is unlikely to improve the tooth's status.

TOOTH MOBILITY – tooth movement in its socket due to an externally applied force. Measured by pushing the tooth gently in a F-L direction using the blunt ends of two metal instruments. A finger is not acceptable to assess mobility.
1. **Class 1 mobility**: total F-L tooth movement of < 1mm.
2. **Class 2 mobility**: total F-L movement 1-2mm with NO vertical/depressible movement.
3. **Class 3 mobility**: total F-L movement > 2mm and/or movement in a vertical/depressible direction.

POCKET DEPTH (PD) – each tooth has 6 measurements (B, L, MB, ML, DB, DL). Measured from sulcus base « GM.

CEJ«GM – distance in mm from the CEJ«gingival margin. Measurements are taken at the same six sites used to record probing depth.
- Gingival tissue above the CEJ is recorded as a **NEGATIVE** number.
- Gingival tissue below the CEJ is recorded as a **POSITIVE** number.

CLINICAL ATTACHMENT LOSS (CAL) – distance from CEJ in an apical direction to the pocket/sulcus base. CAL = (PD) – (distance from GM to CEJ). In disease, GM's location may be unrelated to the apically migrating sulcus base, its position is used only to calculate CAL. Health (Normal)-pocket depth is coronal to the CEJ with no CAL.
1. **Slight Periodontitis**-pocket depth is deepened, but the gingival margin is unchanged. CAL 1-2mm.
2. **Moderate Periodontitis**-greater attachment loss, but since GM is at the CEJ, CAL = PD. CAL 3-4mm.
3. **Severe Disease**-even greater attachment loss, and because of recession, the GM is below the CEJ. Thus, CAL = CEJ to the pocket base (or recession measurement + PD). CAL > 5mm.

Ex: If a probing depth is 4mm and recession is 3mm, total attachment loss = 7mm.

BLEEDING ON PROBING (BOP) – indicated on the patient's chart by a RED DOT for sites that bleed within 30 sec of probing. **BEST** way to evaluate SRP success is NO BLEEDING ON PROBING (BOP indicates active inflammatory periodontal disease). *BOP indicates crevicular epithelium is ulcerated due to active periodontal disease.* Bleeding scores (bleeding) is the **MOST RELIABLE** indicator of the gingival or periodontal inflammation.

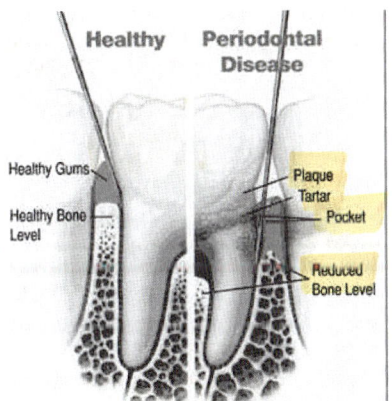

FURCATION INVOLVEMENT – noted in RED on the patients chart. Use a Naber's Probe to detect and clinically diagnose a furcation. Radiographs are helpful, but are ONLY an adjunct to the clinical examination.

1. **Class I: incipient involvement.** Tissue destruction extends **1-2mm** measured horizontally from the furcation's most coronal aspect. Probe tip feels the depression of the furcation opening. Incipient bone loss.

2. **Class II: Cul-de-sac involvement.** Tissue destruction is **deeper than 2mm** measured horizontally from the furcation's most coronal aspect, but **DOES NOT COMPLETELY PASS THROUGH THE FURCATION**. Partial bone loss. Probe tip enters under the furcation roof.

3. **Class III: Through-&-Through involvement.** Tissue destruction extends through the entire furcation so a blunt Naber's Probe can pass between the roots and emerge on the other side. Total bone loss, but the furcation entrance is not visible, but still covered by gingiva.

Grade I   Grade II   Grade III

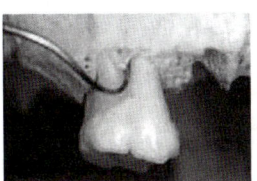 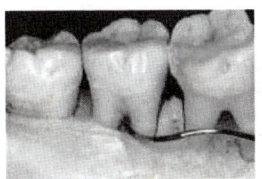 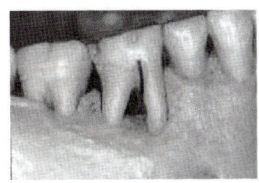

MAIN objective of treating furcations is to **ELIMINATE FURCATION INVOLVEMENT**, but some treatments only increas accessibility for plaque removal. Bone grafts are not effective to treat furcations. However, GTR successfully treats Grade II furcations. Furcation involvement of maxillary 2nd molars have the **POOREST PROGNOSIS** after therapy.

PERIODONTAL SCREENING & RECORDING (PSR) – a screening exam that promotes early detection and treatment of periodontal diseases. PSR **allows the dentist to rapidly assess and record a patient's periodontal status**, but does **NOT** replace the need to do a comprehensive periodontal exam and charting when warranted.
- PSR uses a special probe (**0.5mm ball tip** and **colored band from 3.5-5.5mm**) inserted into the gingival crevice under the contact until resistance is felt and is walked **DISTAL MESIAL**, watching the colored band relative to the gingival margin.
- Scoring system uses sextants. **6 sites per tooth are recorded**, but only **the HIGHEST score is recorded per sextant**. An (*) can be added for other clinical abnormalities.
- **Code 0**: colored band is completely visible, **no BOP, calculus, or defective margins**.
- **Code 1**: colored band is completely visible, **BOP present**. No calculus or defective margins.
- **Code 2**: colored band is completely visible, but calculus or defective margins are present.
- **Code 3**: colored band is **partly visible**.
- **Code 4**: colored band is **NOT visible**.
- **Code ***: furcation involvement, mobility, mucogingival defects, recession.

HORIZONTAL BONE LOSS – bone loss is parallel to an imaginary line from the CEJ to CEJ of adjacent teeth. **Measured from 2mm below the CEJ to the tooth's apex**, based on the normal bone crest position. Alveolar crest's normal position is no more than 2mm below the CEJ.

VERTICAL BONE LOSS – angular bone loss along the side of the tooth **from the most coronal aspect of the interproximal bone**. Common in Localized Aggressive Periodontitis around 1st molars and incisors in children.

DIAGNOSIS OF PERIODONTITIS is based on **RATE OF PROGRESSION & DISEASE SEVERITY**:
1. **Rate of Progression**:
   - **Chronic Periodontitis**-inflammation within supporting teeth tissues, **progressive attachment and bone loss, pocket formation and/or gingival recession. Most common in adults**, but begin to occur at any age.
     - If < 30% of sites are involved = Chronic **Localized** Periodontitis.
     - If > 30% of sites are involved = Chronic **Generalized** Periodontitis.
     - Chronic periodontitis is a SLOWLY progressive disease, but some patients may experience short periods of rapid progression. Thus, rates of progression is a criteria used to exclude people from being diagnosed with Chronic Periodontitis.
   - **Aggressive Periodontitis-rapid attachment loss & bone destruction**. Amounts of microbial deposits are *inconsistent* with the severity of periodontal tissue destruction. Classified as either Localized Aggressive Periodontitis or Generalized Aggressive Periodontitis.

2. **Severity of Periodontal Disease**:
   - **Gingivitis**-gingival inflammation with either changes in color, contour of gingival papillae/margins, or changes in tissue consistency.
   - **Slight Periodontitis**: **1-2mm CAL**.
   - **Moderate Periodontitis**: **3-4mm CAL**, possibly accompanied by tooth mobility and furcation involvement.
   - **Severe Periodontitis**: **at least 5mm CAL**, usually accompanied by tooth mobility, furcation involvement, & mucogingival defects.

✈ Bacteria associated with **PERIODONTAL HEALTH** are gram (+), non-motile, facultative anaerobes. In periodontal disease, the bacteria shifts to gram (-), motile, strictly anaerobic bacteria.

BACTERIAL PLAQUE – **KEY ETIOLOGIC AGENT** in causing gingivitis and periodontal disease. Plaque is an accumulation of a mixed bacterial community in a **DEXTRAN MATRIX** formed on a cleaned tooth surface within minutes composed of **80%** water & **20%** solids/bacteria. Plaque is most likely to accumulate on inter-proximal tooth surfaces first.

PLAQUE-INDUCED GINGIVAL DISEASES

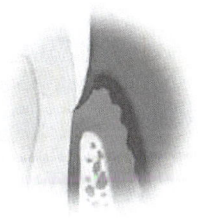
Sulcus

Pseudopocket (Gingivitis)

Pattern of dental plaque development is an early predominance of GRAM (+) FACULTATIVE bacteria, to a later domination of GRAM (-) ANAEROBIC bacteria (rods, fusiform, spirochetes), as the plaque mass accumulates and matures.

MOST abundant bacteria in a HEALTHY SULCUS are STREPTOCOCCUS & ACTINOMYCES species. Gram (+) cocci (Streptococci) & filamentous bacteria (Actinomyces) are the most abundant in a healthy sulcus.

PLAQUE-INDUCED GINGIVAL DISEASES – can occur on a periodontium without attachment loss or with attachment loss on a peridontium that is not progressing. Can be affected by local factors and may be modified by specific systemic factors found in the host. Gingivitis is the PREDOMINANT periodontal disease.

Gingival diseases are limited to GINGIVA, but the inflammatory response initiated in gingival diseases is a prerequisite condition for periodontitis. Gingivitis does not always lead to periodontitis, but periodontitis always progresses from gingivitis. IgG- the immunoglobulin most abundant in gingival exudates common in gingivitis.

There are NO radiographic features of gingivitis (radiographic appearance of bone is normal). But, there are radiographic features of periodontitis (loss of lamina dura, horizontal or vertical bone resorption, & widening of PDL space). GINGIVITIS DOES NOT CAUSE BONE OR ATTACHMENT LOSS.
- Bleeding, pocket depths > 5mm, and changes in tissue color and tone cannot lead to a diagnosis of periodontitis WITHOUT radiographic evidence of bone loss. Periodontal pockets CANNOT be determined from radiographs.

Characteristics of All Gingival Diseases:
1. Signs and symptoms confined to the gingiva.
2. Dental plaque to initiate and/or exacerbate the severity of the lesion.
3. Clinical signs of inflammation (enlarged gingival contours due to edema/fibrosis, color transition to red and/or bluish-red, elevated sulcular temperature, BOP, increased gingival exudates).
4. Clinical signs and symptoms are associated with stable attachment levels on a periodontium with no attachment loss or on a stable, but reduced periodontium.
5. Disease is reversible by removing the etiology.
6. Possible role as a precursor to attachment loss around teeth.

2 Categories of Plaque-Induced Gingival Diseases:
1. Gingival diseases affected by **local factors**.
2. Gingival diseases affected by **local factors, but modified by specific host systemic factors** via the **endocrine system, hematologic diseases, drugs,** or **malnutrition**.

PLAQUE-INDUCED GINGIVITIS – the **most common type** of plaque-associated gingival disease. It is gingival inflammation due to bacteria **at the gingival margin**. Occurs at all ages of dentate population and is **THE MOST COMMON FORM OF PERIODONTAL DISEASE**. Begins at the gingival margin and spreads through remaining gingival unit. Reversible with plaque removal.

- **Characteristics**: plaque at the **gingival margin (where it starts)**. Changes in gingival color (redness), edema, erythema, BOP, contour & consistency changes, sulcular temperature change, increased gingival exudates, BOP, histologic changes, sensitivity, tenderness, and enlargement. Presence of calculus and/or plaque.

- **Treatment Options**: goal is to **eliminate etiologic factors** (plaque, calculus, plaque-retentive features) through patient education & OHI, debridement of calculus, anti-microbial anti-plaque agents, correct plaque-retentive factors (over-contoured crowns, open/overhanging margins, narrow embrasures, open contacts, ill-fitting fixed or removable dentures, tooth malposition). Surgical correction may be required to correct gingival deformities that hinder plaque control. After active therapy is complete, evaluation is required to determine further course of treatment.

- **Treatment may be affected by systemic risk factors** (diabetes, smoking, periodontal bacteria, aging, gender genetic predisposition, stress, nutrition, pregnancy, HIV, substance abuse, medications. Other factors that may contribute to the condition not resolving (patient non-compliance, remaining calculus).

- If condition does not improve, additional OHI/education, medical/dental consultation, debridement, increasing prophylaxis frequency, microbial assessment and continuous monitoring and evaluation may be required.

PLAQUE-INDUCED GINGIVITIS ON A **REDUCED PERIODONTIUM** – after periodontal treatment and resolution of periodontal inflammation in periodontitis, the periodontal tissue is healthy, but with a reduced C.T. attachment and alveolar bone height. **Characterized by the return of bacteria-induced inflammation to the gingival margin on a reduced periodontium with no progressive attachment loss** (no indication of active disease). **Same clinical findings as plaque-induced gingivitis, but there is pre-existing attachment loss**.

CHLORHEXIDINE GLUCONATE (0.12%) – kills bacteria in situations when used for 30sec 2x/day. The most effective anti-microbial agent for reducing plaque and gingivitis over long-term.

Gingival diseases are affected by **local factors (plaque) but modified by specific host systemic factors via the ENDOCRINE SYSTEM, hematologic diseases, drugs, or malnutrition. THERE IS NO ATTACHMENT OR BONE LOSS WITH GINGIVITIS!**

Plaque-Associated Gingival Diseases modified by the ENDOCRINE SYSTEM:
1. **Puberty-Associated Gingivitis:** the **dramatic rise in STEROID HORMONE LEVELS during puberty in both sexes** has a transient effect on gingival inflammation. Gingival inflammation can develop with only small amounts of plaque during the circumpubertal period (this is what distinguishes this disease). **Characteristics**:
    - Plaque at the gingival margin, pronounced inflammatory response of the gingiva.
    - Must be circumpubertal (girls estradiol > 26; boys testosterone > 8.7).
    - Change in gingival color, contour, with possible changes in size.
    - Increased gingival exudates and BOP.
    - Reversible after puberty.

2. **Menstrual Cycle-Associated Gingivitis:** occurs **during the menstrual cycle** due to sex steroid hormones (estrogen & progesterone) causing gingival inflammation and an increase in gingival exudate (GCF) especially during ovulation. **Characteristics**:
    - Plaque at the gingival margin, modest inflammatory response of gingival prior to ovulation.
    - Must be at the ovulatory surge when luteininzing hormone levels are > 25mIU/ml and/or estradiol levels >200pg/ml.
    - Increase in gingival exudate by at least 20% during ovulation. Reversible after ovulation.

3. **Pregnancy-Associated Gingivitis:** plaque at the gingival margins, pronounced inflammatory gingiva response, **onset 2nd or 3rd trimester**. Change in gingival color (bright red), contour, increase in gingival exudates, BOP. Reversible at parturition. Main clinical finding is **gingival hemorrhage (bleeding) upon gentle pressure**.
    - If a women is in her **1st or 2nd trimester, scaling, polishing, & OHI can be performed.** If she is **well into her 3rd trimester, prudent treatment may be to just give OHI** and reappoint her after childbirth for scaling and polishing.

4. **Pregnancy-Associated Pyogenic Granuloma (Pregnancy Tumor)**-not a tumor (neoplasm), but **an exaggerated inflammatory response** during pregnancy to an irritation causing a solitary polyploidy capillary hemangioma that bleeds easily on provocation. May develop as early as the 1st trimester.
    - **Clinical Features**: painless protuberant, mushroom-like sessile or pedunculated mass at the gingival margin or inter-proximal space. Affects up to 5% of pregnant women. More common in **MAXILLA & INTERPROXIMALLY**.
    - **Characteristics**: plaque at the gingival margin, pronounced inflammatory response of gingiva. Can occur ANYTIME DURING PREGNANCY. Regresses or completely disappears after parturition.

NOTES

DRUG-INDUCED (Medications) Gingival Diseases:

1. **Drug-Induced Gingival Hyperplasia (Enlargement/Overgrowth):** caused by anti-convulsants (**Dilantin/Phenytoin**), immunosuppressants (**Cyclosporin** A-prevents organ transplant rejection), & calcium-channel blockers (**Nifedipine** (Procardia), **Verapamil, Diltiazem, Sodium Valproate**). Occurs more often in **ANTERIOR GINGIVA and in children**. **Onset within 3 months** of taking meds, **first observed in PAPILLA**. Not associated with attachment or bone loss.
   - **Phenytoin causes the highest gingival enlargement in 50% of patients**; Cyclosporin 25-30%; & Calcium-channel blockers cause overgrowth 20% of time.
   - Oral hygiene/plaque removal can **limit the severity** of enlargement, but **does NOT shrink the gingiva**. Plaque is not required to produce the enlargement.
   - **Characteristics**: variation in inter-patient & intra-patient pattern, change in gingival contour causing changes in size. **Enlargement is first observed at interdental papilla**, change in gingival color, increase exudates, BOP, found in gingiva with or without bone loss, but is **NOT associated with attachment loss**.

2. **Oral Contraceptive-Associated Gingivitis**- pre-menopausal women taking these hormones can develop plaque at the gingival margins, pronounced gingiva inflammatory response in the presence of little plaque, changes in gingival color, contour, and possibly size. Increased GCF (crevicular fluid), BOP. Reversible after discontinuing the oral contraceptive.

Plaque-Induced Gingival Diseases Associated with SYSTEMIC DISEASE:

1. **Diabetes Mellitus-Associated Gingivitis**-found in **CHILDREN** with **poorly controlled Type I DM (plasma glucose levels-insulin dependent)**. Similar features to plaque-induced gingivitis, **except controlling the diabetes is more important than plaque control in the severity of the gingival inflammation. Characteristics**: plaque at gingival margins, pronounced inflammatory response of gingiva, change in color/contour, increased exudates, BOP. **Most common in children with poorly controlled Type I DM**. Reversible if can control the diabetic state. Plaque reduction can limit the condition's severity.

2. **Leukemia-Associated Gingivitis (Hematologic Gingivitis)**-malignant blood disorder (blood dyscrasia-associated gingivitis) of abnormal leukocyte development and proliferation in blood and marrow. Acute leukemias can cause oral manifestations like cervical adenopathy, petechiae, mucosal ulcers, and **gingival inflammation & enlargement. Gingiva is swollen, glazed, and spongy tissues are red to deep purple. Gingival bleeding on probing is common and is the INITIAL ORAL SIGN**. Pronounced inflammatory response of gingiva in relation to the plaque present, but plaque is NOT required for the condition to occur.

GINGIVAL DISEASES & MALNUTRITION — nutritional deficiencies can significantly worsen the gingiva's response to plaque bacteria, and malnourished people have a compromised host defense system that may affect infection susceptibility. **Ascorbic Acid-Deficiency Gingivitis**: vitamin C (ascorbic acid) deficiency (Scurvy) especially in infants, institutionalized elderly, & alcoholics are at risk. Causes the gingiva to appear bright red, swollen, ulcerated, and susceptible to bleeding.

NON-PLAQUE INDUCED GINGIVAL LESIONS

NON-PLAQUE INDUCED GINGIVITIS – is caused by **specific** bacterial, viral, and fungal infections. This gingival inflammation may also be caused by **allergic reactions** or **toxic reactions, foreign body reactions, or mechanical and thermal trauma**.

INFECTIOUS GINGIVITIS:

1. **Bacterial Infections** that cause gingivitis. Infective stomatitis & gingivitis in **immunocompetent and immunocompromised individuals**, occurring when non-plaque pathogens overwhelm host resistance. Gingival lesions may occur due to infections by ***Neisseria gonorrhea, Treponema pallidum, & Streptococci***. Gingiva may appear as fiery red, edematous painful ulcerations, as asymptomatic cancres or mucous patches, or as atypical non-ulcerated, highly inflamed gingiva. Oral lesions may or may not be accompanied by lesions in other body sites.

2. **Viral Infections** that cause gingivitis. Mainly **Herpes Simplex 1 & 2 and Varicella-Zoster** when reactivated from their latent periods due to trauma, UV light, or fever. HSV-1 usually causes ORAL manifestations, while HSV-2 in mainly anogenital, but may also cause oral infections. HSV has been found in the gingiva, ANUG, & periodontitis. Immunocompromised patients are at increased risk of acquiring the infection.
   - **Primary Herpetic Gingivostomatitis**-classic manifestation of **HSV-1 infection**. Mainly in young children, but also adults. Painful, severe gingivitis with ulcerations and edema accompanied by stomatitis. **Classic Features: VESICLES THAT RUPTURE, coalesce, & leave fibrin-coated ulcers, fever & lymphadenopathy**.
   - **Recurrent Intra-oral Herpes**-cluster of small painful ulcers in **ATTACHED GINGIVA**. Less severe than primary herpetic gingivostomatitis. Diagnosis is made by cultures, enzyme-linked assays, PCR methods.
   - **Varicella-Zoster Virus**: latent in the dorsal root ganglion of trigeminal until it is reactivated in adults to cause SHINGLES. **Both chickenpox and shingles can affect the gingiva** and initiate as **VESICLES THAT RUPTURE** to leave fibrin-coated ulcers that coalesce to irregular forms. In immunocompromised patients (HIV), the infection can cause severe tissue destruction, tooth exfoliation, and alveolar bone necrosis. Initial intra-oral symptoms may be pain and paresthesia before the **UNILATERAL LESIONS OCCUR**.

3. **Fungal Infections** that cause gingivitis. Diagnosed by culture, smear, and biopsy. But since C. Albicans is common in healthy individuals, quantitative assessment and noticing clinical changes are needed for a reliable diagnosis.
   - **Candidosis (C. Albicans)**-opportunistic infection due to reduced host defenses, usually a superficial infection of the oral mucosa. May occur in HIV and other immunocompromised patients as erythema of attached gingiva
   - **HIV-Associated Gingivitis = Linear Gingival Erythema**. LGE is a gingival manifestation of immunosupression appearing as a distinct linear red band limited to the FREE GINGIVA. LGE lesion does not respond to plaque removal.
   - **Pseudomembranous Candidosis (Thrush)**-white patches that wipe off leaving a slightly bleeding surface. Usually no major symptoms.
   - **Histoplasmosis**: a granulomatous disease. Oral lesions affect any area of the oral mucosa, initiating as nodular or papillary and later ulcerate and are painful. Clinically may resemble a malignant tumor.

4. **Hereditary Gingivofibromatosis**-a rare **GENETIC DISEASE**. A progressive proliferation of the gingiva (genetic-derived fibrotic gingival enlargement). Clinically, **generalized diffuse gingival enlargement, often extensive enough to cover the teeth**. Tissue is dense and firm, with considerable distortion of normal contour. Gingival color is normal, but erythematous changes are a result of secondary bacterial involvement.

NOTES

5. **Dermatological Diseases**: may present gingival manifestations in the form of **DESQUAMATIVE lesions (peels away) of the gingiva** or **gingival ulceration**. Lichen Planus, Pemphigoid, Pemphigus Vulgaris, Erythema Multiforme, Lupus.
   - **Desquamative Gingivitis**-a chronic gingival disease characterized by erythematous, erosive, vesiculobullous, and/or desquamative involvement of **FREE & ATTACHED GINGIVA**. Most patients are postmenopausal **FEMALES ages 40-70yrs**. DG is a painful condition where the outer gingiva layer **desquamates (peels away)**, exposing an **acutely red surface**. Many diseases and conditions are associated with DG, but most are dermatologic. Plaque's role is vague. DG usually occurs due to an allergic reaction or is associated with skin diseases (lichen planus, BMMP, bullous pemphigoid, & pemphigus). DG generally resolves when the allergic reaction or skin disease is treated and clears up. **Treatment**: Topical corticosteroids.
6. **Allergic Reactions**: oral mucosa reactions are either **Type I** (immediate) mediated by IgE or **Type IV** (delayed) mediated by T-cells due to dental restorative materials, toothpastes, mouthwash, and food.
7. **Toxic Reactions**: chlorehexidine induced mucosal desquamation, aspirin burn.
8. **Foreign Body Reactions**: allows entry of a foreign material into the gingival C.T. via abrasion or cutting (i.e. amalgam tattoo). "Foreign Body Gingivitis".
9. **Mechanical Trauma**: self-inflicted lesions "**gingivitis artefacta**" caused by excessive brushing force, scratching the gingiva with a fingernail. Most **common in children and young people** (2/3 are females).
10. **Thermal Trauma**: thermal burns of oral mucosa are rare (hot beverages). Palatal & labial mucosa are the most common sites. Painful, red, and may slough the coagulated surface. Coffee, pizza, dental treatment with improper handling of hot hydrocolloid impression materials, hot wax, etc.

PERIODONTITIS

To **diagnose periodontitis**, radiographic evidence of bone loss **MUST** be evident. Bitewings are the **MOST** accurate tool to assess **BONE LOSS (RESORPTION)**. If extensive bone loss occurred, vertical bitewings should be taken as they reveal more of periodontium. **> 30% of the bone mass at the alveolar crest must be lost for a change in bone height to be evident on radiographs**.

A **REDUCTION IN NUMBER OR FUNCTION OF PMNs** (polymorphonuclear leukocytes) results in an **increased rate and severity of periodontal destruction**. Periodontal disease may be an **AUTOIMMUNE DISORDER** where the body's immune factors (cytokines) attack the person's own cells and tissues.

Radiographic Changes in Periodontal Disease:
1. **Early periodontitis**-areas of **localized erosion of the alveolar bone crest** (blunting of the crest in anterior regions, and rounding of the junction between the crest and lamina dura in posterior regions).
2. **Moderate periodontitis**- alveolar bone destruction **extends beyond early changes in the alveolar crest**, and may include buccal or lingual plate resorption, generalized horizontal erosion, or localized vertical defects and possible tooth mobility.
3. **Advanced periodontitis**-bone loss is so extensive that remaining teeth show **excessive mobility and drifting**, and are in danger of being lost. **Extensive horizontal bone loss or extensive bony defects**.

A reduction of only 0.5-1.0mm thickness of cortical plate is sufficient to allow radiographic visualization of destruction of the inner cancellous trabeculae. The crest of alveolar bone is affected in periodontal disease. **In health, the alveolar crest is 1-2mm below the CEJ of adjacent teeth**.

Factors that contribute to **Periodontitis**: smoking, stress, drugs, sex hormones, etc. Chronic gingivitis often leads to Periodontitis. Factors that can increase Periodontal Disease risk:
- Down's syndrome, HIV/AIDS, hormone imbalances (pregnancy), uncontrolled Type 1 & II Diabetes mellitus.
- Rare WBC disorders (Neutropenia, Agranulocytosis, Leukemias), genetic predisposition, medications, smoking (major preventable risk factor), & osteoporosis, **Crohn's Disease, RA, lupus erythematosus.**

PERIODONTAL THERAPY GOALS – to alter or eliminate microbial etiology and contributing risk factors for periodontitis, thus arresting the disease progression and preserving the dentition in comfort, function, and esthetics to prevent recurrence. Regeneration of attachment apparatus may be attempted. When control of the disease is not possible due to systemic factors, immune defects, & microbial flora, a reasonable treatment objective is to "slow the disease progression".

AGGRESSIVE PERIODONTITIS – can be localized or generalized. Patients are clinically healthy except for the periodontitis. Rapid attachment loss & bone destruction. May be of familial aggregation/nature.
- **Secondary Features**: amounts of microbial deposits are inconsistent with the severity of periodontal tissue destruction, elevated levels of AA & P. gingivalis. Phagocyte abnormalities and hyper-responsive macrophage phenotype (elevated levels of PGE_2 & IL-1b). Progression of attachment and bone loss may be self-arresting.
- **Localized Aggressive Periodontitis (formerly Juvenile Periodontitis)**-circumpubertal onset with a robust serum Ab response to infecting agents is detected. **Localized to 1st molars & incisors (vertical bone loss)** with inter-proximal attachment loss on at least 2 permanent teeth (one is a 1st molar, and involves no more than two teeth other than 1st molars & incisors). Caused by AA. One outstanding negative feature is the relative absence of local factors (plaque) to explain the severe periodontal destruction present. Possible etiologic factors: **genetic predisposition** or **neutrophil dysfunction** (a chemotactic defect). **SUDDEN DRIFTING OF TEETH IN CHILDREN.**
- **Generalized Aggressive Periodontitis**-usually affects people **under 30yrs** (but patients may be older). Poor serum Ab response to infecting agents is detected. Pronounced episodic nature of destruction of attachment and alveolar bone. Generalized inter-proximal attachment loss affecting **AT LEAST 3 PERMANENT TEETH OTHER THAN 1st MOLARS & INCISORS.** Caused by Actinobacillus A., P. gingivalis, & neutrophil function abnormalities.
- **Aggressive Periodontitis Treatment**: OHI, reinforcement and evaluation of patient's plaque control, SRP, control of other local factors (occlusal therapy, periodontal surgery and maintenance).
- **Additional treatment considerations**: general medical evaluation to determine if systemic disease is present in children & young adults, especially if initial therapy is unsuccessful. Adjunctive antimicrobial therapy combined with SRP, and/or evaluation and counseling of family members due to its potential familial nature.

Localized Aggressive Periodontitis

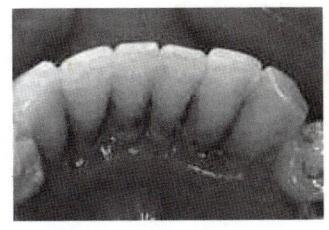

Desired Outcomes: significant reduction of gingival inflammation and probing depths, stabilization or gain of clinical attachment, radiographic evidence of resolution of osseous lesions, progress toward occlusal stability, and reducing detectable plaque to levels compatible with periodontal health.

CHRONIC PERIODONTITIS – gingival inflammation extending into the adjacent attachment apparatus. Clinical attachment loss due to destruction of the PDL and adjacent supporting bone. **MOST COMMON FORM OF DESTRUCTIVE PERIODONTAL DISEASE IN ADULTS**, but covers a wide range of ages. **Slow-to-moderate rates of progression,** but may have periods of rapid progression.
- **Clinical Features**: edema, erythema, BOP and/or suppuration. **MOST COMMON FORM OF PERIODONTITIS**. Its prevalence & severity increases with age.
- **Localized** if < 30% of sites are affected. **Generalized** if > 30% of sites are affected.
- Patient can simultaneously have areas of health and chronic periodontitis with slight, moderate, and advanced destruction

CHRONIC PERIODONTITIS WITH SLIGHT-TO-MODERATE DESTRUCTION – loss of **up to 33%** of supporting periodontal tissues. In molars, if the furcation is involved, clinical attachment loss should not exceed Class I (incipient). **Probing depths up to 6mm with clinical attachment loss up to 4mm**. Radiographic bone loss and increased tooth mobility may be present. **May be localized** (involving one area of the tooth's attachment) **or generalized** (involving several teeth or entire dentition).
- **Initial Treatment**: eliminate, alter, or control risk factors that contribute to Chronic Periodontitis (diabetes, smoking, aging, stress, pregnancy, systemic diseases, nutrition). OHI, SRP, & anti-microbial agents, remove local contributing factors (reshaping restorations, correcting ill-fitting prosthesis, odontoplasty, tooth movement, restoring open contacts, or treating occlusal trauma). If initial treatment is effective, **PERIODONTAL MAINTENANCE is SCHEDULED**. If initial therapy does not resolve the chronic periodontitis, **PERIODONTAL SURGERY** is considered:
  - **Surgical Treatments**: gingival augmentation, regenerative therapy (bone grafts, GTR), resective therapy (flaps with or without osseous surgery), & gingivectomy.

CHRONIC PERIODONTITIS WITH ADVANCED-TO-MODERATE DESTRUCTION – same clinical features as slight-to-moderate but with **advanced loss of > 1/3 of supporting periodontal tissues**. Loss of clinical attachment in the furcation if present is Class II or III. **Probing depths > 6mm with attachment loss > 4mm**. Radiographic evidence of bone loss, and possible increased tooth mobility. Can also be localized or generalized.
- In certain cases due to the severity and extent of the disease and patient age/health, treatment may not be intended to attain optimal results, so initial therapy may become the end-point which include timely periodontal maintenance.
- **Periodontal Surgery Considered**: gingival augmentation, regenerative therapy (grafts, GTR), resective therapy (flaps, root resective therapy, gingivectomy).

REFRACTORY PERIODONTITIS – applies to **all forms of destructive periodontal disease** that are non-responsive to treatment (Refractory Chronic Periodontitis & Refractory Aggressive Periodontitis). Diagnosed in patients previously diagnosed with periodontitis, who have additional attachment loss at one or more sites despite well-executed therapy and patient efforts to stop the progression. Primary clinical feature is *additional attachment loss after repeated attempts to control the infection with conventional therapy*.
- "Refractory" diagnosis is **ONLY** made in patients who satisfactorily comply with OHI and who followed a rigorous periodontal maintenance program, and is diagnosed AFTER conventional active therapy has concluded.

- **Refractory Periodontitis is NOT diagnosed in patients**: who received incomplete or inadequate conventional therapy, who have identifiable system conditions that increase their susceptibility, have localized areas of rapid attachment loss related to root fracture, pulpal disease, foreign body impaction, or root anomalies, or patients with recurrence of progressive periodontitis after many years of successful periodontal maintenance.
- **Treatment Goal**: arrest or slow the disease progression. Once the refractory diagnosis is made, collect subgingival microbial samples to analyze, administer antibiotics with conventional periodontal therapy, control risk factors (i.e. smoking), with an intensified periodontal maintenance program with shorter intervals between appointments.

SYSTEMIC CONDITIONS THAT AFFECT PERIODONTAL DISEASE

SYSTEMIC CONDITIONS MAY AFFECT THE PERIODONTIUM AND TREATMENT OF PERIODONTAL DISEASE – Physical disabilities, pregnancy, xerstomia, mucocutaneous lesions, gingival overgrowth, excessive gingival bleeding, drugs (anti-convulsants, calcium channel blockers, cyclosporine), smoking, history of recent chronic diseases (Diabetes Mellitus I & II), psychological factors, family history of disease.
- Request laboratory as needed and refer or consult with other healthcare providers when warranted.
- The treatment outcome of the periodontal therapy may be directly affected by controlling the systemic condition.
- Diabetic should take their medication and maintain an appropriate diet on the day of periodontal therapy.

For pregnant patients with periodontal disease, consult with their physician, consider postponing treatment during the 1st trimester. Can perform emergency periodontal treatment any time during the pregnancy. Perform periodontal maintenance as needed. Administer antibiotics with caution and local anesthesia is preferred to general anesthesia or conscious sedation.

HEMORRHAGIC GINGIVAL ENLARGEMENT – a common early manifestation of ACUTE LEUKEMIA where chemotherapy or bone marrow transplant therapy may adversely affect the gingiva.
- **Treatment considerations**: coordinate with patient's physcian, minimize periodontal infections by providing treatment prior to treatment of leukemia or transplantation. Avoid elective treatment during periods of exacerbation of the malignancy or during active phases of chemotherapy. Consider antibiotics for emergency periodontal therapy when granulocyte counts are low. Monitor for host-vs.-graft disease and drug-induced gingival overgrowth after bone marrow transplantation. Periodontal therapy and surgery is fine for patients with stable, CHRONIC LEUKEMIA.

GENETIC DISORDERS ASSOCIATED WITH PERIODONTITIS (BONE LOSS) – Down's Syndrome, Chronic Granulomatous Disease, Leukocyte Adhesion Deficiency Syndrome, Hypophosphatasia (decreased blood alkaline phosphates and bone loss), Papillon-Lefevre Syndrome (skin lesions, palmar-plantar keratosis), Chediak-Higashi Syndrome (neutrophil chemotaxis abnormal), Ehlers-Danlos Syndrome, glycogen storage disease, Cohen's Syndrome.

PERIODONTAL DISEASE AFFECTING SYSTEMIC HEALTH

The periodontium is a reservoir for bacteria that produce inflammatory and immune mediators that interact with body organ systems besides the oral cavity. **Periodontal infections may increase the risk of certain conditions (Diabetes, Pregnancy, & Cardiovascular Disease).** The dentist should inform the patient of possible interactions and establish periodontal health to minimize periodontal negative influences on systemic health.

- **Diabetes Mellitus**: periodontitis can affect glycemic control and increased the risk of cardiovascular complications associated with diabetes.

- **Pregnancy**: increased risk of pre-term low birth weight delivery.

- **Coronary Artery Disease**: individuals with periodontal disease may have increased risk of heart disease, angina pectoris, & MI. Periodontal pathogens may contribute to atherogenic changes and thromboembolic events in coronary arteries. May also increase the risk of cerebral ischemia and non-hemmorhagic stroke.

- **Infective Bacterial Endocarditis**: bacteremias are intensified in cardiovascular disease patients with periodontitis. Patients with MVP with regurgitation require pre-medication prior to probing and SRP. Usually 2g Amoxicillin 1hr prior to treatment in non-penicillin allergic patients.

MUCOGINGIVAL CONDITIONS

MUCOGINGIVAL DEFORMITIES – deviations from the normal anatomic relationship between gingival margin & mucogingival junction (MGJ). May be congenital (missing teeth), developmental (tooth eruption in a F or L position, cleft palate, cysts), or acquired defects (neoplasms). These deformities occur around teeth, implants, and in edentulous ridges. Infections associated with mucogingival deformities: periodontitis, peri-implantitis, & periapical infections.

- **Mucogingival Conditions**: gingival recession, lack of keratinized tissue, aberrant frenum positions, probings beyond the MGJ, gingival excess (pseudopockets, gummy smile, gingival hyperplasia), abnormal color.

- **Mucogingival**-oral mucosa covering the alveolar process, gingiva (keratinized tissue) and adjacent alveolar mucosa.

- **Gingival Recession (Atrophy)**-occurs when the gingival margin is apical to the CEJ.

- **Gingival Excess**: pseudopockets, inconsistent gingival margin, excessive gingival display, gingival enlargement.
  - **Pseudopocketing ("gingival pocket" or "relative pocket")**-condition where pocketing occurs **WITHOUT ATTACHMENT LOSS** due to expansion of the marginal tissue **CORONALLY**.
  - **Inflammatory Gingival Enlargement**-a form of gingivitis easily differentiated from simple gingivitis. Clinical findings are increase gingival size, distortion of normal form, and tissue tone change. There is significant increase in sulcus depth with pocket formation (pseudopocket or relative pocket). The pseuodpocket is caused by expansion of the marginal tissue coronally, rather than apical movement of epithelial attachment beyond its physiological level.

- **Anatomic variations that may complicate treating mucogingival conditions**: tooth position, frenulum insertions, and vestibule depth. Variations in ridge anatomy may be associated with mucogingival conditions.

- Mucogingival deformities are **NOT DETECTED ON RADIOGRAPHS**, but radiographs may help when combined with a medical/dental history, probing depths, and clinical examination.
- **Treatment**: non-surgical & surgical correction to help maintain the dentition or its replacements in health with good function and esthetics, and to reduce the risk of progressive recession via **root coverage, gingival augmentation, pocket reduction, crown lengthening, ridge augmentation, vestibuloplasty, papilla regeneration, odontoplasty, tooth movement, and controlling etiologic factors & inflammation via plaque control, SRP, and/or antimicrobials.**

ATTACHED GINGIVA (KERATINIZED) – measured from sulcus base (periodontal pocket) onto the gingiva surface to the mucogingival junction (MGJ). Calculated by **subtracting sulcus/pocket depth** from the **width of gingiva** from the **free gingival margin** to the **mucogingival margin**.

- Attached to underlying periosteum of alveolar bone and cementum by C.T. fibers and epithelial attachment. **Firmly joined to underlying** tooth structure, periosteum, & bone. **ATTACHED GINGIVA is normally CORAL PINK**. Its color varies depending on the degree of keratinization, thickness of epithelium, presence of melanin, and number of blood vessels.
- **NARROWEST BAND** is on **FACIAL SURFACES** of mandibular canine & 1st premolar, and lingual surfaces adjacent to mandibular incisors & canines. Narrow zones may also occur at **MB root of maxillary first molars** (associated with prominent roots and sometimes bony dehiscences), and at **mandibular 3rd molars**.
- Width of **FACIAL** attached gingiva ranges from **1-9mm. WIDEST** on facial of maxillary lateral incisor, & narrowest on facial of mandibular canine & first premolar.
- Attached gingival boundaries extend from the **MGJ** to the **free gingival groove** (sulcus base).
  - Mucogingival Junction (MGJ)-separates attached gingiva from alveolar mucosa.
  - Free gingival groove (base of sulcus)-separates free gingiva from attached gingiva.

All oral mucosa is **STRATIFIED SQUAMOUS EPITHELIUM** regardless if it is keratinized or nonkeratinized.

- Non-Keratinized Oral Mucosa: buccal & alveolar mucosa, tongue's inferior (ventral) surface, soft palate, floor of mouth, and lining mucosa, gingival col, and crevicular epithelium.
  - Alveolar Mucosa-a **LINING TISSUE**, located **APICAL** to attached gingiva on facial & lingual surfaces. Consists of thin, **NON-KERATINIZED** epithelium, loosely textured, **contains elastic fibers** and is loosely bound to periosteum of alveolar bone. **Well-adapted to permit movement, but cannot withstand frictional stresses**.
- Keratinized Oral Mucosa: hard palate & attached gingiva.

FREE GINGIVA (Marginal gingiva) – non-keratinized collar of tissue not attached to tooth or alveolar bone that extends from the free gingival groove (sulcus base) to the gingival margin. It is composed of:
1. gingival margin-the most coronal part of the free gingiva.
2. free gingival groove-separates free gingiva from attached gingiva. The beginning of the attached gingiva.
3. gingival sulcus-shallow groove between the marginal gingiva & tooth surface, bound by sulcular epithelium laterally, and JE apically.
4. interdental gingiva-occupies inter-dental spaces coronal to the alveolar crest.

NOTES

PERIODONTIUM – tissues that surround and support the teeth. Consists of the gingiva, PDL, cementum, alveolar & supporting bone. Main functions are to support, protect, and nourish teeth. Attachment apparatus-consists of alveolar bone proper, PDL fibers, & cementum that attaches the root to alveolar bone.

 In health, the JE is on enamel or at the CEJ. In disease, the JE migrates apically along the root surface. It is measured from an established reference point (CEJ or restoration margin) to the attachment with a periodontal probe.

ACUTE PERIODONTAL DISEASES

ACUTE PERIODONTAL DISEASES – clinical conditions of RAPID ONSET that involve the periodontium or associated structures, characterized by PAIN, DISCOMFORT, & INFECTION that may or may not be related to gingivitis or periodontitis. May be localized or generalized, with possible systemic manifestations. Acute Periodontal Infections:
- Necrotizing Periodontal Diseases (NUG & NUP)
- Gingival Abscess
- Periodontal Abscess
- Pericoronal Abscess (Pericornitis)
- Herpetic Gingivostomatitis
- Combined Periodontal-Endodontic lesions.

NECROTIZING ULCERATIVE GINGIVITIS (NUG) "VINCENT'S INFECTION"
 "TRENCH MOUTH" – an acute infection of the gingiva. Necrosis of gingival tissue (interdental & marginal). All 3 characteristics MUST be present to diagnose as NUG. An infection characterized by gingival necrosis presenting "punched-out" papillae with gingival bleeding and pain. Fetid breath and pseudomembrane formation may be secondary diagnostic features.
1. **INTENSE PAIN** (hallmark of NUG), usually rapid onset.
2. Inter-dental gingival necrosis "punched-out" ulcerated papillae (yellowish-white or grayish slough pseudomembrane formation of gingiva). Papillae tips are blunted and cratered.
3. Gingival bleeding (least distinctive clinical sign) that occurs with or without provocation. Bright red marginal gingiva.

Predominant factor in NUG development is IMMUNOSUPRESSION, which may be associated with all of its predisposing factors: pre-existing gingivitis, smoking, psychological stress, immune suppression (HIV), malnutrition, gross neglect (poor oral hygiene), fatigue, and trauma. NEUTROPHIL is the dominant WBC in the inflammatory infiltrate of ANUG.

ADDITIONAL NUG SIGNS & SYMPTOMS – lymphadenopathy, fetor ex ore (fetid breath), fever, malaise; are not pathognomonic symptoms as they often occur in many other forms of periodontal disease. Fever & malaise may also suggest Primary Herpetic Gingivostomatitis or Mononucleosis.
- NUG Etiology: Fusiforms, Spirochetes, & Prevotella intermedia.
- Loss of attachment and bone is uncommon, but can occur after multiple recurrences of the disease.
- Occurs most often in adults 18-30yrs.

NUG TREATMENT – Debride necrotic areas & tooth surfaces, water or warm saline rinses/irrigation, and antibiotic therapy (Penicillin V) if systemic involvement (fever, malaise, lymphadenopathy). Patients with HIV-associated NUG require gentle debridement & antimicrobial rinses. NUG resolves within a few days after treatment with debridement and anti-microbial rinses, but patients remain at risk for recurrences. Patient counseling on nutrition, oral care, fluid intake, smoking cessation.

NECROTIZING ULCERATIVE PERIODONTITIS (NUP) – a severe and rapidly progressive infection with a distinctive erythema and necrosis of free and attached gingiva, PDL, and alveolar bone. There is **severe loss of attachment and alveolar bone**. NUP has many of the clinical & etiologic factors of NUG, except there is loss of clinical attachment and bone at affected sites.
- **Treatment**: oral hygiene measures (SRP) combined with systemic antibiotics (**Metronidazole**).
- Commonly observed in individuals with systemic conditions, (i.e. HIV), severe malnutrition, and immunosuppression.

ABSCESSES OF THE PERIODONTIUM

Classifying periodontal abscesses is primarily based on **location of the infection**. Abscesses may be associated with pain, swelling, color change, mobility, teeth extrusion, purulence, sinus tract formation, fever, lymphadenopathy, and radiolucency of the affected alveolar bone. However, all of these clinical features are not always present.

GINGIVAL ABSCESS – a localized, painful swelling with purulent exudate **infection of the marginal gingiva or interdental papilla** with a red, smooth, shiny surface. Lesion may be painful and appear pointed. **Treatment**: eliminate the acute signs and symptoms ASAP via **DRAINAGE (irrigation/debridement)**. If the abscess does not resolve, it can become a chronic condition.
- It is usually an acute inflammatory response to foreign substances forced into the gingiva, appearing as a red, smooth shiny swelling in its early stages. Within 24-48hrs, it is fluctuant and pointed, with purulent exudates. If it progresses, the lesion ruptures spontaneously. Pulpal hypersensitivity may be a symptom. **If the abscess is limited to marginal gingiva or interdental papilla with no previous disease, and a foreign material or trauma exists, the lesion is usually a gingival abscess**.

PERIODONTAL ABSCESS – THE **MOST COMMON ABSCESS**, usually associated with a **pre-existing periodontitis**. A localized infection/accumulation of pus in the **gingival wall** of a periodontal pocket that may **destroy PDL & alveolar bone**. Smooth, shiny gingival swelling; pain with the area of swelling tender to touch, and purulent exudates and/or increase in probing depth. Tooth may be **sensitive to percussion and mobile**. **Rapid loss of attachment may occur**. Caused by gram (-) anaerobic rods (SPIROCHETES).

- **Signs & Symptoms**: swelling, suppuration, redness, extrusion of the involved tooth, loosening, tenderness to percussion, and slight temperature elevation.

- **MAY BE ASSOCIATED WITH ENDODONTIC PATHOSIS**. Can be a common clinical feature in patients with moderate or advanced periodontitis. **Strep. viridans is the most common isolate in the exudates of periodontal abscesses** (gram (-) anaerobic rods). Usually results from pre-existing cases of **CHRONIC** periodontitis. Can be a **common clinical finding in moderate-to-advanced periodontitis patients**.

- Factors associated with the formation of acute periodontal abscesses: occlusion of pocket orifices due to food impaction or foreign bodies prevents drainage of exudate, furcation involvement, systemic antibiotics, diabetes, or due to incomplete removal of calculus or instrumentation forces bacteria into the tissues.

- May become chronic if its purulent contents drain through a **FISTULA** into the outer gingival surface or into the pocket. A chronic abscess is **usually asymptomatic**, but some patients feel a dull pain, slight elevation of the tooth, and desire to bite tightly and grind. Chronic periodontal abscess can become acute if the sinus tract orifice is blocked.

- Appears as an **OVOID GINGIVAL ELEVATION ALONG THE LATERAL ROOT**. Feeling "**pressure in the gum**" is a common complaint. Abscesses are also often found in **furcations**. Most **periodontal abscesses occur in MOLARS**.

NOTES

- Rare in children, but if it occurs, it is usually due to a foreign body into previously healthy tissues.

- Systemic antibiotics taken by a patient with untreated advanced periodontal disease cause a **super-infection** by opportunistic organisms causing a periodontal abscesses.

- **Poorly controlled diabetics are prone to acute periodontal abscesses** due to lowered host resistance (impaired cell immunity). Diabetics also have vascular changes and altered collagen metabolism that may increase their susceptibility.

- Tooth trauma via perforation of the lateral wall during RCT, anatomic anomalies (enamel pearls in molar furcations & invaginated roots) can also cause an acute periodontal abscess.

- Treatment: **ESTABLISH DRAINAGE** by **debriding the pocket and removing plaque, calculus, and other irritants and/or incising the abscess.** Other treatments: pocket irrigation, limited occlusal adjustment, antibiotics, and managing patient comfort. Surgical procedure for access to debridement (flap) may be considered. Tooth extraction may be necessary in some cases. A comprehensive periodontal evaluation should follow resolution of the acute condition. **If the periodontal abscess is not localized, patient is placed on antibiotics (Penicillin V) and instructed to rinse with warm saline. Clindamycin** is used in penicillin allergic patients.

- Radiographic findings associated with the periodontal abscess are **NOT specific.** There may be no change radiographically in the early acute lesion. However, **there is often a localized discrete radiolucency lateral to the root or in a furcation** which can cause rapid alveolar bone destruction.

- **MOST COMMON symptom** a patient will report with a **periodontal abscess is ACUTE PAIN that is constant, severe, and dull throbbing.** Thermal changes do not cause or change the discomfort. Onset of discomfort is rapid and progressively intensifies. Patient may also notice an increase in tooth mobility, and say it is **difficult to close their teeth together without striking the involved tooth first, causing increased pain.**

- **PROBING** reveals **DEEP POCKETS** associated with the **periodontal abscess.** EPT and thermal tests exclude the pulp as the unlikely cause as **the tooth with a periodontal abscess is usually VITAL.** Methods to distinguish a periodontal abscess from a pulpal (peri-apical) abscess is done via **probing, EPT, thermal testing.** A periapical radiograph is not a good diagnostic method to distinguish a periodontal and pulpal abscess.

- **NEUTROPHILS** are the **MOST NUMEROUS** cells in the **inflammatory exudates** of an acute periodontal abscess.

PERICORONAL ABSCESS (PERICORONITIS) – a localized accumulation of pus within the overlying gingival flap surrounding a crown of a partially or fully erupted tooth (**USUALLY MANDIBULAR 3rd MOLAR AREA**).
- Clinical Features: **tissue flap is localized, red, swollen lesion, painful to touch.** Purulent exudates, trismus, lymphadenopathy, fever, malaise, and leukocytosis may be present. Infection can spread into the oropharyngeal area and to the tongue base and involve regional lymph nodes. **Patients may have DIFFICULTY SWALLOWING.** Caused by gram (-) anaerobes.
- Treatment: **DEBRIDEMENT & IRRIGATION** of the flap's undersurface, antibiotics, tissue recontouring, or extraction of the involved and/or opposing tooth. Home care instructions. Goal is to relieve inflammation and infection and restore tissue to healthy function.

COMBINED PERIODONTAL-ENDODONTIC ABSCESS (LESION) – localized, circumscribed areas of infection that originate in the periodontal and/or pulpal tissues. **INFECTION ARISES MAINLY FROM PULPAL INFLAMMATION OR NECROSIS** expressing itself through the PDL or alveolar bone to the oral cavity. May also arise mainly from a periodontal pocket communicating through accessory canals of the tooth and or apical communication and secondarily infect the pulp. May also arise from a fractured tooth.

- **Clinical Features**: **smooth, shiny swelling of the gingiva or mucosa**. Pain with swelling tender to touch and/or purulent exudate. Tooth may be sensitive to percussion and mobile. **FISTULOUS TRACK MAY BE PRESENT**. Rapid loss of the PDL attachment and periradicular tissues may occur. FACIAL SWELLING and/or CELLULITIS may be present.

- **Radiolucency of the periodontium and root apex, significant probing depths, and pulpal sensitivity**. *A "combined" abscess is one where an endodontically induced periapical lesion exists on a periodontally involved tooth*. A pulp infection/inflammation can communicate and spread into the peridontium through the root apex, LATERAL CANALS, accessory foramina, crestal extensions of granulomatous lesions along lateral roots, and through dentinal tubules. Periodontally derived endodontic lesions can also occur through **lingual grooves, root/tooth fractures, cemental hypoplasia, trauma-induced root resorption**.

- If the tooth is NON-VITAL, it is most likely a **PERIAPICAL ABSCESS**. Usually periapical abscesses occur singly, it may be extruded, tender to percussion, hypermobile, marked lymphadenopathy, and facial swelling, fever, malaise.

- Acute exacerbations of chronic periapical infections are often associated with P. gingivalis & P. endodontalis.

- **Treatment**: **ESTABLISH DRAINAGE** by debriding the pocket and/or incising the abscess. RCT, pocket irrigation, limited occlusal adjustment, and antibiotics. Extraction may be required in some cases. **PULP IS TREATED FIRST**, then the **periodontal condition is re-evaluated 2-3 months after RCT is complete**. Periodontal surgery can be done if needed for access, but is performed 2-3 months after completing the RCT.

- **EPT is essential for a differential diagnosis**. If the pulp is vital, but a pocket exists, then the periodontal tissues are most likely the origin of infection. If the pulp is NECROTIC, the inflammation that passes through a lateral canal or apical foramen into the periodontium is of endodontic origin.

Spontaneous **VERTICAL ROOT FRACTURE** of a non-RCT tooth can appear as **combined endodontic-periodontal lesion**. **Pain during occlusion or mastication is the main symptom**. Thermal sensitivity, gingival swelling, and periodontal abscess or sinus tracts are also common. Pulps may or may not respond to EPT, but deep pockets are usually detected on probing. Widening of the PDL space and periapical radiolucency and/or periodontal radiolucency may help with the diagnosis.

- Vertical root fractures often occur with RCT teeth and are associated with a deep pocket on the tooth surface which may or may not be abscessed. **PAIN ON THE LOADING CUSPS MAY INDICATE A ROOT FRACTURE**.

ACUTE HERPETIC GINGIVOSTOMATITIS – a HERPES VIRUS INFECTION of the oral mucosa causing generalized pain in the gingiva and oral mucous membranes, inflammation, vesiculation, and ulceration of the gingiva and/or oral mucosa, lymphadenopathy, fever, & malaise. The condition is self-limiting and contagious at certain stages. **Treatment**: palliative. Goal is pain relief to facilitate maintenance of nutrition, hydration, and basic oral hygiene. Treat with gentle debridement and topical anesthetic rinses for pain relief. Patient counseling and possible anti-virals.

- **EX**: A 6-year old boy complains his mouth has hurt for 4 days. 3 days before the onset of local symptoms, he had palpable, **tender, submandibular lymph nodes, and oral temperature of 101.2°F**. Oral exam reveals **generalized inflammation of the attached gingiva and alveolar mucosa**. Loose, white debris covers free gingival margins and fills inter-proximal embrasures. **Discrete areas of ulcerations** within rings of intense inflammation on the facial mucosa and palate. Interdental papilla are in tact, and salivary flow is heavy and viscous. **ACUTE HERPETIC GINGIVOSTOMATITIS**.

PERIODONTAL SURGICAL TREATMENTS

 GINGIVECTOMY – surgical procedure to **ELIMINATE POCKET DEPTHS** (periodontitis that does not respond to initial treatment) **by removing tissue coronal to the pocket base**. Bevel (contour) the wound's coronal margin **to provide the most physiological shape and marginal thickness so adequate oral hygiene techniques can be performed**.
- **Indications**: treat pseudopockets, hereditary gingival enlargement, suprabony pockets, and gingival hyperplasia. Corrects gingival contours for Hereditary Gingivofibromatosis & drug-induced inflammatory gingival enlargement.
- **Contraindications**: infra-bony pockets (defects) and lack of attached tissue. Limitations include compromised esthetics with longer teeth, lack of access to bony defects, and having a broad, open wound post-surgically.
- **Factors to consider when electing to perform a gingivectomy rather than a flap**: pocket depth (if the pocket base is at the MGJ or apical to the alveolar crest, do not perform a gingivectomy); need for access to bone; and amount of existing attached gingiva.

GINGIVOPLASTY – surgical procedure to **RESHAPE the gingiva & papilla to correct deformities and provide the gingiva** with **normal & functional form**. Objective is **NOT** to eliminate periodontal pockets, but **to provide a more physiological tissue contour**. While portions of the gingiva are excised during a gingivoplasty, **RESHAPING is the purpose. Commonly used to correct tissue contours from ANUG**.

OSTEOPLASTY – **reshaping or recontouring alveolar bone that does not provide attachment for periodontal fibers (non-supporting bone) without removing supporting alveolar bone**. Similar to a gingivoplasty since it is **not directed toward eliminating pocket walls, but RECONTOURING & RESHAPING underlying osseous structures**. Osseous reduction does not reduce the bone that the PDL is attached (supporting bone).
- **Non-supporting bone**-alveolar bone not directed related to tooth support (bony exostoses, edentulous ridges, tori, flattened inter-dental contours & ledges). **Walls of some osseous defects may consist of non-supporting bone**.

OSTECTOMY – **removes osseous defects or infrabony pockets (pockets below the crest of bone) by eliminating bony pocket walls**. REMOVES SUPPORTIVE BONE because eliminating the pocket is worth the price of the loss in attachment apparatus. After removing the osseous pocket walls, some re-contouring is done to provide optimal osseous architecture for the overlying gingival tissues to conform to and be maintained.
- **Major contraindication of removing crestal bone: if the removal will weaken an adjacent tooth's bony support.**

OSSEOUS DEFECTS – pattern of bone loss from periodontitis can be horizontal or vertical:

HORIZONTAL BONE LOSS – the pattern of inter-proximal **bone loss parallels the CEJ of adjacent teeth**. Usually generalized by involving multiple teeth in a segment.

SUPRABONY POCKETS – the pattern of HORIZONTAL bone loss and not intra-osseous. Transseptal fibers are usually normally arranged, but form at a more apical level, and the pocket base (epithelial attachment) is CORONAL to the crest of alveolar bone. Suprabony pockets may be further classified as a:
- Gingival pocket ("relative or "pseudopocket")-a condition where there is expansion of the marginal tissue coronally (not apical movement). Pocketing occurs WITHOUT attachment loss.
- Periodontal pocket ("true pocket")-a deepened gingival sulcus where epithelium undergoes ulceration. Characterized by APICAL MIGRATION of the epithelial attachment beyond its physiological level which is normally at or near the CEJ.

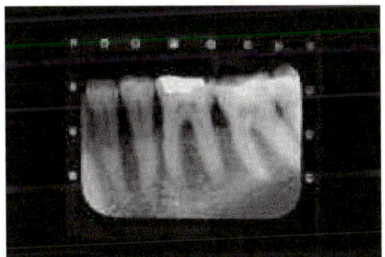

This radiograph illustrates horizontal bone loss in the posterior sextant. The crestal bone margin is horizontal and parallel to CEJ. The bottom of pocket is coronal to the adjacent alveolar bone. Note the "crater-like" interproximal defect common to the mandibular arch.

VERTICAL BONE LOSS – inter-proximal bone loss does not parallel the CEJ, but occurs around ISOLATED teeth. Bottom of pocket is apical to the adjacent alveolar bone.

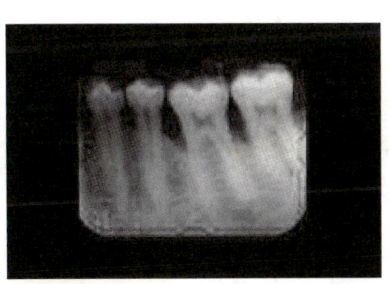

PERIODONTAL OSSEOUS DEFECTS (INFRABONY POCKETS) – classified by the number of bony walls remaining that surround the tooth. The pocket base (epithelial attachment) is APICAL to the crest of bone so there is a defect or hole in the bone (intra-osseous). For a defect to have a bony wall, it must be intra-osseous (i.e. partially or completely within alveolar bone; i.e. ramps, hemiseptums, interdental craters, intrabony defects, & moat defects). Infrabony pockets are associated with VERTICAL (ANGULAR) BONE LOSS that creates holes/defects within the bone, and are classified as follows:

1. **1-wall defects:** Hemiseptum- only the proximal wall is present. Ramp-only a facial or lingual wall is present.
2. **2-wall defects:** inter-dental crater.
3. **3-wall defects:** an intrabony pocket; offers the best opportunity for bone graft containment and periodontal regeneration procedures.
4. **4-wall defects:** circumferential or moat defects. Four-walled moat defects also offer the best opportunity for bone graft containment and periodontal regeneration procedures.
5. **Zero-wall defects:** alveolar dehiscences & fenestrations. Do not treat with osseous surgery.

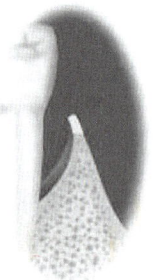
1 Wall Defect

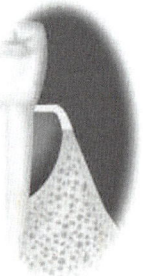
2 Wall Defect

3 Wall Defect

INFRABONY DEFECTS/POCKETS ARE CONTRAINDICATIONS FOR MUCOGINIGVAL SURGERY. With infrabony pockets, interproximally the transseptal fibers run in an angular direction not horizontally. Transseptal fibers extend in a sloping configuration from the cementum below the pocket base along the bone and down over the crest of bone to the cementum of the adjacent tooth.

OSSEOUS CRATERS – concavities in the crest of inter-dental bone confined within facial & lingual walls. Craters comprise 1/3 (35.2%) of all defects, (62%) of all mandibular defects. MORE COMMON in posterior segments, and are best treated with OSSEOUS SURGERY (recontouring).

Periodontal osseous defects are classified by the number of osseous walls present/remaining at the time of their surgical exposure, and may have 1, 2, 3, or 4 walls. When evaluating an osseous defect, the ONLY WAY TO DETERMINE the number of REMAINING osseous walls surrounding the tooth is by EXPLORATORY SURGERY. Radiographs DO NOT SHOW the number of walls left surrounding the tooth, the exact configuration of the defect, or location of epithelial attachment because a dense buccal and/or lingual plate of bone masks the defect and blocks it on the radiographs.

Bone grafting is MOST successful with a 3-Walled Defect. Success of periodontal bone grafting *varies directly* with the number of bony walls of the defect (vascularized, osseous surface area), and *inversely* with the surface area of the root against which the graft is implanted. A **narrow 3-walled infrabony defect yields the greatest success**, then a 2-walled defect, then a 1-walled defect (infra-bony defect/hemiseptal defect = least successful). Three-wall defects occur mainly in the **INTERDENTAL REGION. Success is best with a 3-walled infra-bony pocket and LEAST successful with a through-&-through furcation defect on a maxillary molar.**

ROOT RESORPTION – the most common side effect of an autogenous bone graft in managing an infrabony pocket and often extends into dentin and pulp. Other postoperative problems that sometimes occur after osseous transplants: **infection, graft exfoliation,** various and sometimes **prolonged healing rates, and rapid defect recurrence.**

GUIDED TISSUE REGENERATION (GTR) – placing non-resorbable barriers or resorbable membranes & physical barriers (bovine, calcium sulfate) over a bony defect. **GTR BLOCKS** re-population of the root surface by **long JE & gingival C.T.** to allow **PDL** and **bone cells** to re-populate the periodontal defect (this technique assumes only PDL cells can regenerate the tooth's attachment apparatus). **GTR Indications**:
1. patient exhibits exemplary plaque control both before and after regenerative therapy.
2. patient does not smoke.
3. there is occlusal stability of the teeth at the regenerative site.
4. osseous defects are **VERTICAL**. The more walls of bone remaining, the greater regenerative success.

FREE GINGIVAL GRAFT – an autogenous graft of gingiva placed on a viable C.T. bed where initially buccal or labial mucosa were present. The **donor site from where the graft is taken is an edentulous region or palatal area**. The graft epithelium degenerates after it is placed, then sloughs. Epithelium is reconstructed in 1 week by the adjacent epithelium and proliferation of surviving donor basal cells. In 2 weeks, tissue reforms, but **maturation is not complete until 10-16 weeks**. Healing time required is proportional to the graft's thickness. The greatest amount of shrinkage occurs within the first 6 weeks.

FGG removes a section of attached gingiva from another area of the mouth (hard palate or an edentulous region) and sutures it to the recipient site. FGG success depends on the graft being immobilized at the recipient site. **FGG is used to increase the zone of attached gingiva and possibility of gaining root coverage during recession.** The difficulty in getting complete root coverage lies in the fact that an avascular graft is placed over a root surface also devoid of blood supply.

- FGG retains **NONE** of its own blood supply and is totally dependent on the bed of recipient blood vessels. FGG receives its nutrients from the viable C.T. bed. **MAIN reason a FGG fails is disruption of the vascular supply before engraftment.** Infection is the 2nd most common reason of FGG failure.

FGG Indications:
- Prevent further recession and successfully increase the width of attached gingiva.
- Cover non-pathologic dehiscences & fenestrations.
- Performed with a frenectomy to prevent reformation of high frenal attachments.
- Cover a root surface with a narrow denudation. FGG may or may not yield a successful result when used to obtain root coverage (**FGG result is not highly predictable in root coverage cases**).

NOTES

- Used **to widen attached gingiva after recession occurs**, and prophylactically prevent recession where the band of attached gingiva is narrow and thin.
- **Correct localized narrow recessions or clefts**, but **NOT DEEP WIDE RECESSIONS**. In such cases, the laterally repositioned flap (pedicle graft) is more predictabe. **FGG is rarely used on facial or lingual surfaces of mandibular 3rd molars (especially facial)**.

FGG HEALING – involves graft revascularization. Graft's top layers are re-vascularized last. Thus, the epithelium dies off (degenerates), producing the necrotic slough. During healing, epithelium of FGG degenerates (necrotic slough), and re-epithelization occurs by proliferation of epithelial cells from adjacent tissue and surviving basal cells of the graft tissue.

FREE MUCOSAL AUTOGRAFT – differs from a FGG in that the **transplant is C.T. without an epithelial covering**.

- Epithelial differentiation is induced by the underlying C.T. so that free grafts of dense C.T. taken from keratinized areas result in formation of keratinized tissue even when transplanted to non-keratinized zones. FMA is more difficult than FGG, and is **often used on CANINES** where little keratinized gingiva exists to **create a band of gingiva-like tissue**.

PERIODONTAL FLAP – a segment of marginal periodontal tissue that is surgically separated coronally from its underlying support and blood supply, and attached apically by a pedicle of supporting vascular **C.T. FLAPS ARE MOST COMMON** of all periodontal surgical techniques. Flaps should be uniformly thin and pliable, the flap base must be uniformly thin (2mm thick), and all flap corners are ROUNDED.

- **PRIMARY OBJECTIVE of FLAP SURGERY** in treating periodontal disease is to provide access to root surfaces for debridement. Common goal of all flap procedures is to **PROVIDE ACCESS** for instrumentation and allow the clinician to visualize the roots so calculus can be removed more completely.
- Surgical Flap Goals to treat Periodontal disease: reduce or eliminate periodontal pockets, regrow alveolar bone, maintain biological width, and establish adequate soft tissue contours.

4 Rules of Flap Design:
1. Flap base is WIDER than the free margin to allow sufficient blood circulation to the flap's free margin.
2. Incision must not be placed over any defect in bone to prevent delayed healing.
3. Incisions that traverse a bony eminence (canine) are avoided because mucosa covering bony eminences is thin and healing is slow, and may result in scar formation. **Incisions made in tissues that harbor uncontrolled infection may cause rapid infection spread**. Most periodontal surgical procedures are performed only after anti-infective therapy is complete.
4. Flap corners are rounded, as sharp points delay healing.

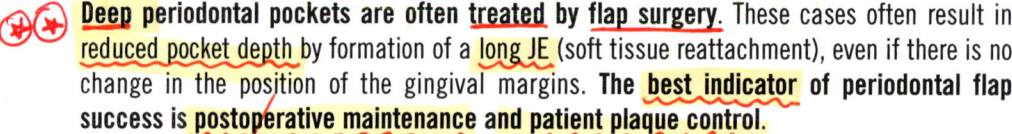
Deep periodontal pockets are often treated by flap surgery. These cases often result in reduced pocket depth by formation of a long JE (soft tissue reattachment), even if there is no change in the position of the gingival margins. **The best indicator** of periodontal flap success is postoperative maintenance and patient plaque control.

FULL-THICKNESS MUCOPERIOSTEAL FLAPS – reflects ALL of soft tissue and periosteum to expose underlying bone. Used where attached gingiva is THIN (< 2mm wide). Apically & Coronally positioned flaps are full thickness flaps.

- **Modified Widman Flap (MWF)**-a full-thickness flap used in open flap debridement and regenerative periodontal procedures, and is a mainstay of periodontal surgery on single-rooted teeth and on flap surfaces of molars affected by moderate pockets and infrabony defects. Objective is to gain access to underlying bone & root surfaces, reduced pocket depth by establishing a new attachment at a more coronal level, preserve an adequate zone of attached gingiva, and to provide an environment for healing by primary closure.
  - **Indications**: pocket bases located coronal to the MGJ, areas of little or no thickening of marginal bone, reduce shallow to moderate pocket depths, and when esthetics is important (anterior region).
  - **Repositioned Flaps**: include replaced flaps, MWF, and excisional new attachment procedures. These heal by repair (by a long JE and C.T. adhesion or attachment), and are pocket reduction procedures. Pocket reduction is achieved mainly by gains in clinical attachment mediated by repair.

POSITIONED FLAPS:

1. **Pedical Flap (Laterally Positioned Flap)**-a positioned full-thickness flap to correct defects in morphology, position, or amount of attached gingiva. Usually a full-thickness flap attached at its base with its free end adjacent to the defect (recipient site). The defect is covered by stretching the flap laterally until the free-end covers it.
   - **Indications**: areas where narrow gingival recession is adjacent to a wide band of attached gingiva that can be used as the donor site. Corrects or prevents recession by providing root coverage, creating a wider band of gingiva, and in the absence of recession to widen the zone of gingiva.
   - Positioned & Repositioned flaps are really pedicle flaps physically attached at their apical base by a pedicle of lining mucosa and an intact blood supply.
   - Important factors to evaluate before performing a laterally positioned flap: presence of bone on the facial surface of the donor tooth, gingiva thickness, and width of attached gingiva at the donor site.

2. **Apically Positioned Flap**-a full-thickness, mucoperiosteal flap with a high degree of predictability that is the "work horse" of periodontal surgery/therapy. Objective is to surgically ELIMINATE deep pockets by positioning the flap apically while retaining attached gingiva. Most commonly used in conjunction with osseous surgery as surgical access is obtained for osseous surgery, treatment of infrabony (intrabony) pockets, and root planing.
   - **Indications**: moderate or deep pockets, furcation-involved teeth, and crown lengthening.
   - **Contraindications**: patients at risk for root caries, as excessive root surfaces are often exposed AFTER performing an apically positioned flap, and where tooth exposure would be unesthetic.
   - In the course of flap surgery, after gaining access to underlying osseous tissue and performing the required therapy, the apically positioned flap is sutured to a place at a more apical level, exposing the alveolar margin. When this is done, additional attached gingiva granulates from the PDL and covers the barely exposed bone. This additional tissue joins the apically positioned attached gingiva to form a broader zone of gingiva.

3. **Coronally Positioned Flap**-a full-thickness mucoperiosteal flap almost exclusively used to restore gingival height and zone of attached gingiva over ISOLATED AREAS of gingival recession.

NOTES

There is no necrotic slough of positioned flaps because positioned flaps carry their vascular supply with them. In a FGG, healing involves revascularization of the graft. The graft's top layers are revascularized last. Thus, the epithelium dies off (degenerates), producing the necrotic slough.

PARTIAL-THICKNESS PERIODONTAL FLAP – incises ONLY the mucosa epithelium and layer of underlying C.T. Mucosa is separated from the periosteum by sharp dissection. Alveolar bone is not exposed. *Used to prepare recipient sites for free gingival grafts*, or when a dehiscence or fenestration is present on a prominent root. Used when attached gingiva is THICK (> 2mm).

Root Amputation & Hemisection MUST be done in conjunction with RCT of a particular tooth. Endodontic therapy is performed first, then periodontal therapy:

ROOT AMPUTATIONS – separation of an individual root from the crown. Most root amputations involve MAXILLARY 1st & 2nd MOLARS. Burs and diamond stones sever the crown and root before extracting by root tip forceps. After the root amputation is complete, the remaining apical area of the crown and furcation region are re-contoured to the shape of a pontic so maximal access for oral hygiene is provided.

HEMISECTION – vertical sectioning of the tooth through the crown & root. Used in a mandibular molar region were the crown is divided through the bifurcation region. 50% of the tooth is extracted if one specific root has excessive loss in osseous support, and the remaining half of the molar tooth is now treated as a PREMOLAR.

DISTAL WEDGE FLAP (PROXIMAL WEDGE) – the simplest distal flap procedure used for RETROMOLAR reduction. Often performed after 3rd molar extractions because the bone fill is usually poor, leaving a periodontal defect. This region is occupied by glandular and adipose tissue covered by unattached, non-keratinized mucosa. Only if sufficient space exists distal to the last molar, a band of attached gingiva may be present (in this case, as distal wedge operation can be performed).
- Distal Wedge flaps are performed in these areas: maxillary tuberosity region, mandibular retromolar triangle area, & distal to the last tooth in the arch, or mesial to a tooth that approximates an edentulous area.
- Make at least 2 incisions distal or mesial to the tooth, and carry these incisions parallel to the outer gingival wall to form a wedge (the wedge base is the periosteum overlying the bone, and apex is the coronal gingival surface). Detaching the wedge from the periosteal base and eliminating involved tissues in the distal pocket region reduces tissue bulk, and allows access to underlying bone.

OSSEOUS RECONTOURING SURGERY – main goal is to ELIMINATE PERIODONTAL POCKETS. Existing bony topography is changed to eliminate periodontal pockets. This surgery does not cure periodontal disease, but gives the patient access to maintain their own periodontium and dentition with routine oral hygiene procedures.
- Before using osseous resection or recontouring to treat an infrabony defect, consider these treatment alternatives: maintenance with periodic SRP, bone grafts, reattachment-fill procedures, hemisection or root amputation.
- Osseous resection surgery should NOT be done until etiologic factors that caused the osseous defects are arrested. Clinically detectable inflammation must be eliminated by SRP and by the patient's ability to maintain optimal plaque control.

OCCLUSAL TRAUMA

OCCLUSAL TRAUMA – injury from occlusal force (functional or parafunctional forces) causing tissue changes (trauma) within the attachment apparatus. There is trauma because the occlual force exerted exceeds the periodontium's adaptive and reparative capabilities. *Can occur in an intact periodontium or periodontium reduced by inflammatory disease.*

1. **Primary Occlusal Trauma**-excessive occlusal forces are applied to teeth with normal supporting structures (no periodontal disease). **Pathologic occlusal forces** are the primary etiology for periodontium changes. Usually reversible when the excessive forces are controlled. An early effect of primary occlusal trauma is **HEMORRHAGE & THROMBOSIS OF PDL BLOOD VESSELS**.
2. **Secondary Occlusal Trauma**-occurs when the periodontium is already compromised by inflammation and bone loss. Injury resulting in tissue changes from normal or excessive occlusal forces applied to tooth/teeth with reduced support. Occurs in the presence of bone loss, attachment loss, and normal or excessive occlusal forces. Consequently, occlusal forces that may otherwise be well tolerated in a healthy periodontium have deleterious effects due to pre-existing periodontal disease. Teeth with a reduced adaptive capacity and compromised periodontium may then migrate when subjected to certain occlusal forces. Factors like frequency, duration, and velocity of occlusal forces, may be more important factors in causing **tooth hyper-mobility** (common clinical sign of occlusal trauma).

Most common sign of occlusal trauma is **TOOTH MOBILITY**. Other signs: migration of teeth & tenderness to percussion.

RADIOGRAPHIC SIGNS OF OCCLUSAL TRAUMA – widened PDL space, lamina dura thickening/disruption, angular (vertical) bone loss, infra-bony pocket formation, root resorption, & hypercementosis, radiolucencies in the furcation or apex of a vital tooth,

CLINICAL SIGNS OF OCCLUSAL TRAUMA – mobility, fremitus, occlusal prematurities, wear facets, tooth migration, fractured tooth/teeth, thermal sensitivity. These features may be found in other conditions, so always use other diagnostic criteria like EPT or evaluate parafunctional habits to attain a definitive diagnosis.
- Tooth mobility, tooth migration, tooth pain on chewing or percussion.
- Tenderness of mucles of mastication and/or TMJ dysfunction.
- Wear facets beyond the normal level relative to the patient's age and diet. Chipped enamel or crown/root fractures.
- Fremitus.

Occlusal trauma is reversible, as body can repair the damage if excessive occlusal forces are eliminated. **Occlusal trauma does not cause periodontal pockets**. A local irritant and inflammation are necessary to cause an apical shift of the JE (attachment loss).

Other findings associated with Occlusal Tramua: alternating areas of resorption and repair of alveolar bone, fibrosis of alveolar bone marrow spaces, cemental resorption leading to dentinal resorption, cemental tears, ankylosis, occasional pulpal necrosis and calcification.

OCCLUSAL TRAUMA TREATMENT – usually addressed during initial therapy (except acute conditions) to eliminate or minimize excessive force or stress on the tooth (teeth). Treatment for a patient with Chronic Periodontitis with occlusal traumatism may include:
- Occlusal adjustment and/or management of parfunctional habits.
- Temporary or long-term stabilization of mobile teeth with a RPD or FPD.
- Orthodontic movement, occlusal reconstruction, or extraction.

If there are no clinical signs or symptoms, **prophylactic occlusal adjustment to obtain and "ideal" occlusion provides no benefit, thus is contraindicated**. Occlusal relationships may be evaluated as part of periodontal maintenance.

SPLINTING – the **primary reason for splinting teeth is to IMMOBILIZE excessively mobile teeth for patient comfort**. Temporary stabilization is achieved by splinting one or more mobile teeth to each other and to more stable teeth in a position that facilitates **a more AXIAL and EVEN distribution of occlusal forces** (*generally performed on teeth with reduced periodontal support*). Rational for splinting is improved patient comfort, function and plaque control, better distribution of occlusal forces, and improved tooth stability during clinical procedures.
- **There is no reason to splint non-mobile teeth as a preventive measure**. Splinting is only one type of measure used to treat periodontal disease, and should be used with other needed measures like root planning, OHI, pocket elimination, and occlusal adjustment.
- **Loose teeth splinted to adjacent teeth may become stabilized**. When many teeth are loose, adjacent sextants should be included in the splint. **Teeth tend to loosen B-L**, yet may remain firm M-D. Even when teeth do not tighten, the splint serves as an orthopedic brace that permits useful function to loose teeth.

Reasons to Perform Selective Grinding in the Natural Dentition:
1. Achieve a more favorable direction and distribution of forces.
2. Coordinate the median occlusal position with the terminal hinge position of the mandible.
3. Eliminate pre-maturities in excursive movements to gain group function or canine protected occlusion.
4. Direct occlusal forces centrally along the long axis of the tooth.
5. Improve or maintain masticatory performance.
6. Accomplish occlusal adjustment without reducing VDO and by retaining an acceptable inter-occlusal distance.
7. Reduce or eliminate fremitus.

Contraindications to Selective Grinding the Natural Dentition:
- Large pulp chambers or tooth sensitivity.
- Major occlusal discrepancies that may require orthodontics or reconstruction.
- Poor candidates for full-mouth reconstruction due to psychologic factors.

STEPS TO ADJUST OCCLUSION – eliminate prematurities in centric relation (CR), in protrusive movements, and lateral excursive movements. Then re-establish the physiologic occlusal anatomy and carefully polish all ground surfaces.

BRUXISM – an aggressive, repetitive, or **continuous grinding**, gritting, or **clenching of the teeth (cupping/hollowed out areas on the occlusal table of the most terminal tooth)** during the day and/or night in other than functional activities (chewing or swallowing). **Occlusal prematurities, muscle tension, and emotional factors** are causes.
- Signs & symptoms: PDL widening & thickening of lamina dura, sore muscles and jaw pain, TMJ dysfunction and difficulty opening the mouth, increased tooth mobility (especially in the morning), occlusal wear facets.
- Excessive forces produced by **bruxism can cause increased tooth mobility**.
- Treatment: behavioral, emotional, & interceptive modalities.

PERIODONTAL TREATMENT PLANNING

PRELIMINARY PHASE – treats EMERGENCIES ONLY (pulpal, periodontal, or other emergency).
1. **Phase I (Initial Therapy)**-plaque control, **extract hopeless teeth, mouth preparation** (initial full-mouth scaling, & definitive root-planing). Also includes:
   - OHI is the **most important part of initial therapy**. Hygienist or dentist teaches, motivates, and guides the patient in the performance of measures for disease control. Patient is shown proper brushing/flossing techniques, and these techniques are repeated to see if they understand what you are showing them. **If oral hygiene is poor, surgery is CONTRAINDICATED**.
   - Occlusal adjustments, night guards (if bruxism exists), **splinting** (stabilizing loose teeth).
   - **Re-examination** that involves charting probing depths.
2. **Phase II (Periodontal Surgery)**
3. **Phase III (Restorative Phase)**
4. **Phase IV (Maintenance Phase)**-started **after completing active periodontal therapy and continues at varying intervals for the life of the dentition or implant**. An extension of active periodontal therapy supervised by the dentist. The phase where periodontal diseases and conditions are monitored and etiologic factors are reduced or eliminated. Most patients with a **history of periodontitis should have maintenance every 3 MONTHS** to maintain and establish gingival health. Based on the evaluation of the clinical finding during the maintenance, the frequency may be modified or the **patient may be returned to active treatment**.

MISCELLANEOUS

ALVEOLAR PROCESS – the part of the maxilla & mandible that **HOUSES TEETH**.

Periodontal Ligament (PDL) – a complex, specialized, **soft, fibrous C.T. containing cells, vessels, nerves, & extra-cellular substances. HIGHLY VASCULAR & CELLULAR C.T.** that **surrounds teeth roots, connecting root cementum with alveolar bone.** Most abundant PDL cells are **FIBROBLASTS**.

- **Orthodontic treatment is possible as the PDL continuously responds and changes** based on functional requirements imposed on it by externally applied forces. **PDL's average thickness in an adult is .25mm**
- **Age** (PDL gets thinner with age) due to increased deposit of cementum and bone. Composed primarily of Type I **COLLAGEN FIBERS**
- **Principal Fibers**-PDL collagen fibers include: alveolar crest fibers, horizontal, oblique, apical, & interradicular fibers. **CONNECT ROOT CEMENTUM TO ALVEOLAR BONE**. Distinguished by their location and direction. **Sharpey's Fibers**-terminal portions of the PDL principal collagen fibers embedded into cementum & alveolar bone. Diameter of Sharpey's fibers is **much greater on the BONE SIDE** than cementum side.

JE – specialized epithelium surrounding each tooth that begins at the sulcus base. A collar-like band of stratified squamous epithelium firmly attached to the tooth by **HEMIDESMOSOMES**. 10-20 cell layers thick. In **IDEAL GINGIVAL HEALTH**, the JE is located **ENTIRELY ON ENAMEL** above the **CEJ**.

ULTRASONIC SCALING DEVICES – based on **HIGH-FREQUENCY SOUND WAVES** & involves lavage, vibration, & cavitation. Removes supragingival and subginval calculus, initial debridement of an **ANUG** patient, gross scaling prior to extractions, and removes orthodontic cement, bonding material, and overhanging restorations. **Never touch the tip of the ultrasonic on the tooth, use only the sides**. Ultrasonic instruments **ARE USED** for scaling, curetting, and removing stains.

- **Contraindications**: cardiac pace makers unless the pacemaker is shielded (newer models). First consult with patient's cardiologist.

SCALING & ROOT PLANING – removes **calculus, bacteria, & endotoxins**. When extensive SRP must be performed, the best approach is to **schedule a SERIES of appointments to SRP a segment or quadrant of teeth at a time. DO NOT** do gross debridement (subgingival & supragingival) of the entire mouth, then schedule a series of appointments for fine scaling and polishing.

- Re-evaluation after SRP is **4-6 weeks** to allow time for **repair of the dentogingival junction**.
- **MAIN OBJECTIVE OF ROOT PLANING:** provide optimally **smooth root surfaces** to reduce bacterial accumulation to achieve soft-tissue reattachment.
- **BEST CLINICAL AID** to determine if **sub-gingival calculus is removed is an EXPLORER & BITE-WINGS** to show inter-proximal calculus.

AVERAGE TIME for this entire calculus formation process to occur is **12 days**.
- **Supragingival Calculus**-main source of its minerals is from **SALIVA**. Occurs **ABOVE** the **free gingival margin** and is **white** or **pale yellow**, and easily removed by prophylaxis. Occurs **most often on the lingual of mandibular incisors and buccal of maxillary molars** due to the salivary ducts that secrete saliva rich in minerals needed for its formation.
- **Subgingival Calculus**-darker due to **blood breakdown pigments**, **harder**, & **more dense** than supragingival calculus. Its source of minerals is from **CREVICULAR FLUID**. **BELOW the free gingival margin**. More difficult to remove than supragingival calculus, and is usually **evenly distributed throughout the mouth**.

HOMECARE AIDS – **NOTHING REPLACES BRUSHING & FLOSSING** to disrupt and remove plaque. Patient can also use a perio-aid (round polished toothpick, good for furcations and gingival margins), Stim-U-Dent (wood wedges) for gingival massage and inter-dental recession. Proxabrush for wide embrasure spaces. **Interdental stimulator**- rubber tip attached to a handle or end of a toothbrush that massages and stimulates circulation of the interdental gingiva

IRRIGATION BENEFITS – reduces gingivitis, reduces/alters microbial flora, subgingival access (penetrates below the gingival margin), and delivers antimicrobial agents. **Fluoride, antibiotics, & chlorhexidine effectively inhibit** microbial plaque.
- Irrigation does not remove acquired tooth pellicle and cannot remove adherent plaque better than toothbrushes. It removes non-adherent bacteria from subgingival & supragingival sites.
- Oral irrigation devices are CONTRAINDICATED IN PATIENTS WITH PERIODONTAL INFLAMMATION. Water irrigation devices may be contraindicated in patients requiring antibiotic premedication prior to dental treatment since these devices have the potential for causing a bacteremia.

TOOTHBRUSHING METHODS – the effectiveness of toothbrushing is BEST measured by the amount and location of plaque. The manual toothbrush should have SOFT, NYLON bristles and a small head.
- **Bass Method ("Sulcular Technique")**-toothbrush bristles are placed 45° to the tooth surface at the gingival margin to try and get the bristles into the gingival sulcus. The brush is then moved in a back-and-forth motion for ~20 strokes. This is currently the preferred method of manual toothbrushing. The most effective toothbrushing technique.

IMPLANTS

BIOINTEGRATION – direct biochemical bond of bone to the implant surface at the electron microscope level. Independent of any mechanical interlocking.

DENTAL IMPLANT SYSTEMS – subperiosteal, transosteal, & ENDOSSEOUS (the most common). Placing endosseous implants is a predictable procedure. Criteria for success:
- No persistent signs/symptoms of pain, infection, neuropathies, paresthesia.
- Implant immobility and no continuous peri-implant radiolucency.
- Negligible progressive bone loss (< 0.2mm annually) after physiologic remodeling during the first year of function.
- Patient/dentist satisfaction with the implant restoration.

Implants have > 90% success rate for both maxillary & mandibular implants. Implants with rough surfaces offer advantages than smooth surface implants, and implants placed in the mandible have higher success rates than in the maxilla.

THERE ARE NO ABSOLUTE MEDICAL CONTRAINDICATIONS FOR PLACING IMPLANTS. There are "relative" contraindications: uncontrolled diabetes, alcoholism, heavy smoking, post-irradiated jaws, poor oral hygiene. However, patients with a strong susceptibility to periodontitis CAN BE SUCCESSFULLY TREATED WITH IMPLANTS.

Age is NOT an important factor that affects implant survival, but implants placed after age 15yrs in girls and 18yrs in boys have a better prognosis than when placed in younger children.

NOTES

3-D computerized tomography (CT) scans can provide accurate information about regional anatomy (max sinuses, foramina, mandibular canal, adjacent teeth/roots).

 LOWER success rates are associated with CANCELLOUS BONE (20-25% bone density) than with cortical bone (80-90% volume density of bone). Thus, cortical bone provides greater implant-bone contact and fixation.

PRE-TREATMENT CONSIDERATIONS – oral health status, medical/psychological status, patient motivation and home care ability, patient expectations, and assessing habits & conditions that increase the risk of implant failure (alcoholism, smoking, high ASA score, bruxism, periodontal disease, and radiation therapy).

Surgical considerations require evaluating the anatomy and location of vital structures, bone quality, quantity, and contour, and soft tissues. Diagnostic aids used in pre-surgical considerations to determine the number, location, type, and angulation of the implants and abutments (mounted or unmounted diagnostic casts, CT imaging, surgical template).

Placing implants involves analyzing the number & location of missing teeth, inter-arch distance, number, type, & location of implants to be placed, existing/proposed occlusal scheme, design of the planned restoration.

A "staged" approach has been used to place ENDOSSEOUS IMPLANTS. Implants can also be placed at the time of extraction. Mechanical failures of the implant components and prosthetic superstructures have been associated with **OCCLUSAL OVERLOAD**. The desired outcome of implant therapy is maintenance of a stable, functional, esthetic tooth replacement.

IMPLANT COMPLICATIONS – prosthesis instability, fixture mobility, occlusal trauma, fractured/loose components, inflammation/infection, excessive progressive loss of hard/soft tissues, pain, neuropathy/paresthesia.

ADDITIONAL NEGATIVE OUTCOMES – implant mobility or loss, persistent pain/loss of function, progressive bone loss, persistent peri-implant radiolucency and uncontrolled inflammation/infection, implant fracture, increased probing depths.

CHAPTER 6

REMOVABLE PARTIAL DENTURES

KENNEDY CLASSIFICATIONS – based on the **MOST POSTERIOR EDENTULOUS AREA to be restored**. Although Class III & IV RPDs are entirely supported by abutment teeth, **Class I & II RPDs are supported by abutment teeth, the residual ridges, subjacent tissues, and fibrous C.T. overlying the alveolar process**. Alveolar ridge resorption under the distal extension RPD is a concern, but is reduced by maximizing coverage of these supporting areas. Periodontal damage to abutment teeth is avoided with firm tissue support (maintaining a stable base-tissue relationship).

1. **Class I**: bilateral edentulous areas posterior to the natural teeth. **BILATERAL DISTAL EXTENSION**.
2. **Class II**: unilateral edentulous area posterior to remaining natural teeth. **UNILATERAL DISTAL EXTENSION**.
   - Kennedy Class I & II: must have a **MESIAL REST** on the abutment next to the posterior edentulous space.
3. **Class III**: unilateral edentulous area with natural teeth both anterior and posterior to it. A **tooth-borne RPD** because it depends entirely on abutment teeth for support.
4. **Class IV**: a single, but bilateral (it must cross the midline), edentulous area anterior to the remaining natural teeth. Anterior teeth are missing and across the midline. **DOES NOT HAVE MODIFICATION SPACES**. A tooth-borne RPD type because it depends entirely on abutment teeth for support.
   - **OCCLUSAL RESTS ARE PLACED ON THE DISTAL OF THE FIRST PREMOLARS!**

Applegate's Rules for Applying the Kennedy Classification:
1. **Rule 1**: classification is done AFTER extractions are done.
2. **Rule 2**: if a 3rd molar is missing and will not be replaced, it's NOT part of the classification.
3. **Rule 3**: if a 3rd molar is present and not used as an abutment, it's NOT part of the classification.
4. **Rule 4**: if a 2nd molar is missing and will not be replaced, it's not considered in the classification.
5. **Rule 5**: Most posterior area always determines the classification.
6. **Rule 6**: edentulous areas other then those determining the classification are "modifications".
7. **Rule 7**: the extent of the modification is not considered, only the number of additional edentulous areas.
8. **Rule 8**: NO modification areas in a Kennedy Class IV.

MAJOR & MINOR connectors MUST BE RIGID to evenly distribute functional stresses applied to the RPD throughout the mouth.

MAJOR CONNECTORS – connects components between both sides of the arches. **Major connector must be RIGID** so stresses applied to any area of the denture are effectively distributed over the entire supporting area.
- Major connector is free of movable tissues and does not impinge on gingival tissues. Relief should be provided.
- Bony and soft tissue prominences are avoided during placement and removal.
- Major connectors most frequently encounter interferences from **lingually inclined mandibular premolars**.

MINOR CONNECTORS – a **RIGID** component that connects the major connector (RPD base) to the other components (direct retainers, indirect retainers). Also transfers functional stress to abutment teeth, and transfers the effects of the retainers, rests, and stabilizing components to the rest of the denture ("abutment-to-prosthesis" function).
- 1.5mm thick, preserves tissue (does not impinge marginal gingiva) and is highly polished.
- Maximum gingival exposure = joins at right angle.
- **Minimum of 5mm space between vertical components.**

MANDIBULAR RPD MAJOR CONNECTORS

Basic **cross-section form** is **HALF-PEAR SHAPED** located above moving tissues but as far below the gingival margins as possible. To determine which mandibular major connector to use, measure from the height of the floor to the lingual gingival margins.

1. **LINGUAL BAR**: superior border must be at least **4mm below the gingival margins** (tooth-tissue junction) to prevent plaque collection and margin inflammation. There must be at least **7mm of space/clearance** between the gingival margin and mouth floor. **HALF-PEAR SHAPED in cross-section**.
   - **Indication**: Used when sufficient space exists between the slightly elevated alveolar lingual sulcus and lingual gingival tissues. **Must be a minimum of 7mm vertical height between the gingival margin and mouth floor** (inferior border of the bar). **3mm space between superior border of the bar and gingival margin + the bar must be 4mm wide = 7mm**.
   - **Contraindication**: when severely tipped premolars and molars are present, an alternate framework or crowns are recommended.

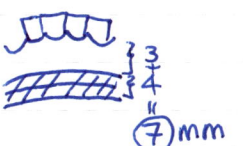

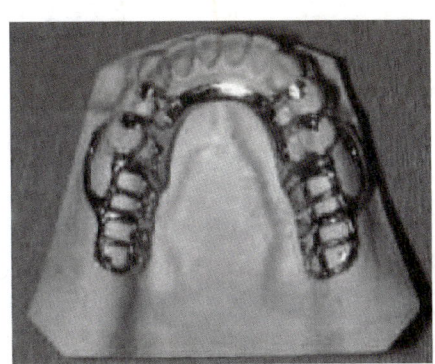

2. **SUBLINGUAL BAR**: used when there is INSUFFICIENT SPACE for a lingual bar. **HALF-PEAR SHAPED**.
   - Used when the **height of the mouth floor is ≤ 6mm from the free gingival margins** or when it is desirable to keep the free gingival margins of the remaining anterior teeth exposed, and there is inadequate depth of the mouth floor to place a lingual bar.
   - Its bulkiest portion is to the lingual and it's tapered is toward the labial.
   - Bar's **superior border MUST** be at least 3mm below the free gingival margin.
   - Bar's inferior border is at the height of alveolar lingual sulcus when the patient's tongue is slightly elevated.
   - Requires a **FUNCTIONAL IMPRESSION**.
   - **Contraindication**: remaining natural anterior teeth are severely lingually tilted.

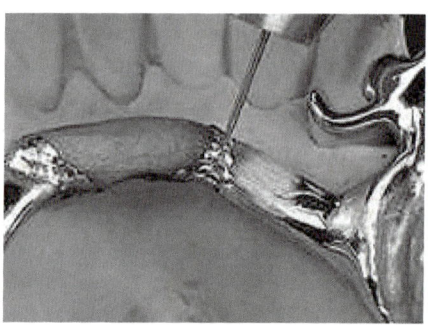

3. **CINGULUM BAR (CONTINUOUS BAR):**
   - Used when a lingual plate or sublingual bar is indicated, but the axial alignment of the anterior teeth is such that excessive blockout of inter-proximal undercuts is required.
   - **Contraindications**: anterior teeth severely tilted lingually, wide diastemas between anterior teeth causing the metal cingulum bar to be displayed.
   - It's a thin, narrow (3mm) strap located on the cingula of anterior teeth, scalloped to follow inter-proximal embrasures with its superior borders tapered to tooth surfaces. Originates bilaterally from rests of adjacent abutments.

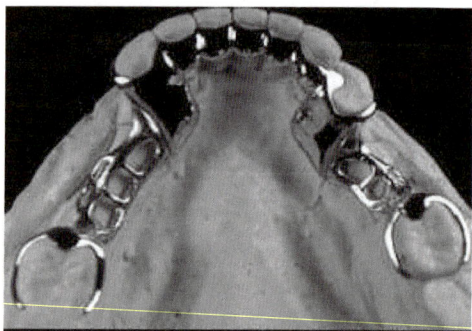

4. **LINGUOPLATE**: Indications:
   - High floor of the mouth (≤ 7mm vertical height) or high lingual frenum. **Preferred over a lingual bar when there is NO space in the floor of the mouth.**
   - INOPERABLE lingual mandibular tori that cannot be removed.
   - Anticipated loss of one or more of the remaining teeth.
   - Used in Class I designs where residual ridges have undergone **excessive vertical resorption**.
   - Used to stabilize periodontally weakened teeth (splinting) or lingually tilted mandibular incisors.

- Used when future replacement of 1 or more incisors is facilitated by adding retention loops to an existing linguoplate
- Used to avoid gingival irritation or food entrapment, or to cover generously relieved areas that would irritate the tongue.
- Extends to the rests on the terminal abutments, to the contacts inter-proximally, and covers anterior cinguli. Do not use if there are wide open anterior contacts because it is un-esthetic or if anterior overlapping exists.
- Superior border is at the middle 1/3 of the teeth's lingual surface and extends upward to cover inter-proximal spaces to the contact point.
- **Mandibular lingual tori require a linguoplate because there is often not 7mm of vertical space** for a lingual bar. Tissue covering the tori is thin and cannot tolerate vertical pressure from the major connector. **DO NOT USE IF SEVERE ANTERIOR CROWDING EXISTS.**

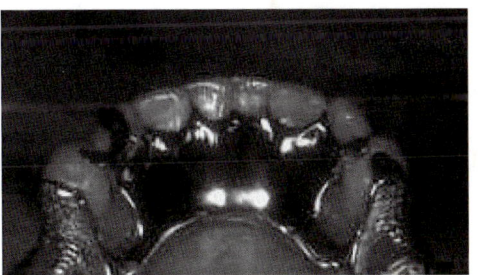

5. **LABIAL BAR**:
    - **Indications**: when severe lingual inclinations of remaining premolars & incisors cannot be corrected orthodontically, preventing placing a lingual bar. When severe lingual tori cannot be removed and prevent using a lingual bar or plate. Also used when severe and abrupt lingual tissue undercuts prevent using a lingual bar or plate.
    - Superior border is at least 4mm below the labial and buccal gingival margins.
    - Inferior border is in the labial-buccal vestibule at junction of attached (immobile) & unattached (mobile) mucosa.
    - **UNLESS TORI SURGERY IS ABSOLUTELY CONTRAINDICATED**, interfering tori are removed to avoid using a labial bar.
    - Trauma and congenital deficiencies occasionally produce dental arrangements where only a labial connector is feasible.

6. **DOUBLE LINGUAL BAR (WITH CONTINUOUS BAR)**:
    - Placed above the cingula and below inter-proximal contacts.
    - NEED 7-8mm above the mouth floor or cannot use.
    - Best indicated for **PERIOSURGERY CASES FOR WIDE EMBRASURES**.
    - Must have rests on the superior bar on at least the canines.

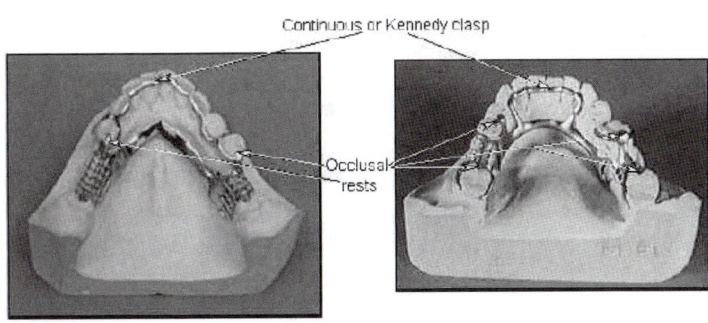

MAXILLARY MAJOR CONNECTORS

1. **MUST BE RIGID.** Superior border MUST be at least **6mm below the free gingival margins** and parallel to the mean curve of the free gingival margin.
2. Use metal plating if < 6mm exists from the gingival margins.
3. Posterior border of the major connector must **cross the palate at RIGHT ANGLES (90°) to the palate midline** and extend backward PARALLEL to the residual ridges to prevent tongue sensitivity.
4. **Anterior border of the major connector is perpendicular to the midline and buried in the VALLEY OF RUGAE.**
5. **NEVER PLACED ANTERIOR** to indirect retainers (anterior palatal coverage is avoided).
6. Exposed borders are **beaded** to produce a positive contact with the tissue.
7. Metal is in intimate tissue contact.

BEAD LINE (BEADED BORDERS) – USED **ONLY ON MAXILLARY MAJOR CONNECTORS** to SEAL the interface of the maxillary major connector to the tissues. It tapers off as it approaches the marginal gingiva around the abutment teeth.

- **Beading is done along the border of the major connector to seal it to the soft tissue.** Bead is made by scoring the cast .75-1mm wide and deep. The groove fades as it approaches within 6mm of the gingival margins and fades over a hard midline suture.
- Seal is 1mm thick (deep) to provide **POSITIVE DENTURE CONTACT WITH TISSUE** to prevent food entrapment under the maxillary major connector and retention when placed at the posterior border of a palatal plate major connector.

ANTERIOR-POSTERIOR PALATAL STRAP:

- MAXILLARY MAJOR CONNECTOR TO **ALMOST ALWAYS USE FOR ALL KENNEDY CLASSES**.
- Major connector of choice for inoperable tori cases where there is 6-8mm room to the vibrating line.
- **GREATEST STRENGTH & RIGIDITY** b/c of its circular shape and b/c its metal straps lie in different planes.
- Primarily used for a **LARGE EDENTULOUS SPAN** Kennedy Class **III mod I RPDs** with good residual ridges and strong abutment teeth (not good to use when edentulous spaces are small). A better choice than a single palatal strap because it covers less tissue (uses minimal palatal surface area).
- Must be at LEAST 15mm between the anterior and posterior straps!
- The anterior and posterior straps are 6-8mm wide, and must be 6mm below the free gingival margin to avoid rugae coverage and tongue interference. Anterior strap is just posterior to a rugae crest or in a valley between two crests.
- Posterior strap is thin, at least 8mm wide, and located entirely on the hard palate at right angles to the midline (not diagonally) to protect the TONGUE. It is NEVER placed on mobile tissue (soft palate).
- DO **NOT USE** when an inoperable palatal torus extends posteriorly onto the soft palate.

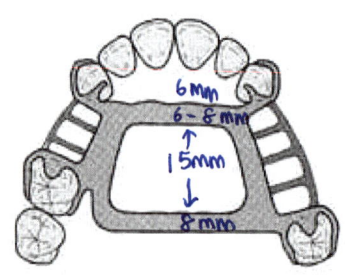

HORSESHOE (U-SHAPE PALATAL CONNECTOR):
- **LEAST DESIRABLE MAXILLARY MAJOR CONNECTOR** because has the LEAST strength & rigidity.
- Used **only** to go around **INOPERABLE PALATAL TORI** or with **MAJOR GAGGERS**. Used only when large inoperable palatal torus prevent using palatal coverage in the posterior area (interferences).
- LACKS RIGIDITY (unless it is bulky), can cause lateral flexure of abutments, and can impinge tissue during occlusion.
- Used in **Class III mod I designs** and/or when a palatal torus is within 6-8mm of the vibrating line.
- Requires good residual ridges and strong abutments.

SINGLE WIDE (MIDPALATAL) STRAP:
- Mainly used in **CLASS III designs**.
- Its width is kept within the borders of the rests (does extend posterior or anterior to rests).
- Used for a LARGE SPAN Class III mod I when residual ridges are good quality, but **molar abutment are weak**. Provides additional palatal support to the RPD when **abutments are weak**.
- With **weak abutments** in a Class III, more palatal support is desired and a wide palatal strap is preferred.

PALATAL PLATE (COMPLETE COVERAGE): AKA "METAL PLATE"
- Used mainly in Class I design. MAIN INDICATION: **when the last abutment tooth on either side of a bilateral distal extension is a CANINE or 1st PREMOLAR complete palatal coverage is advised**, especially when the residual ridges have undergone excessive vertical resorption.
- Used for long-span **Class I BILATERAL DISTAL EXTENSIONS** with poor residual ridges, and/or periodontally involved weak abutment teeth.
- Can be used in a Class II where there are missing anteriors with a posterior modification
- **Covers at least 50% of the hard palate and replicates the anatomy of the palate**.
- Posterior border is at the JUNCTION of the hard & soft palate, but does not extend to the soft palate.
- Should be anterior to the posterior palatal seal.
- Direct retention is a problem and can interfere with the patient's tongue and taste (some patients cannot tolerate). It **acts more in INDIRECT RETENTION**.

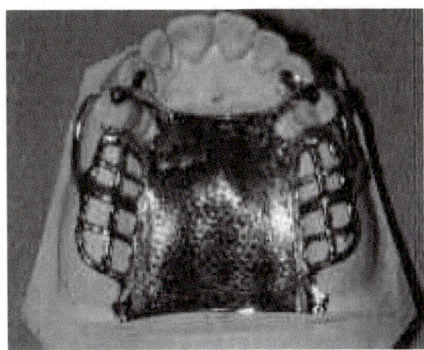

MODIFIED PALATAL PLATE: used for **maxillary Class II designs** and may or may not include lingual plating.

INDIRECT RETAINERS (Rests & Proximal Plates)

Indirect Retainers:
- Are placed as far away from the distal extension base as possible to **PREVENT VERTICAL DISLODGEMENT** of the base from the tissue (i.e. opening when eating sticky foods).
- Increases the effectiveness of direct retainers (clasps) when the RPD tries to dislodge, and **prevents the RPD from rotating around the fulcrum line** (axis of rotation).
- IR should be 90° (right angles) to the fulcrum line, and is placed in rest seats to **direct forces along the abutment's long axis.**
- **The greater the distance between the fulcrum line and IR, the more effective the IR.**
- IR may include: **RESTS, PROXIMAL PLATES, & MINOR CONNECTORS**.

Indirect Retainer Functions when the denture base tries to **MOVE AWAY** from the residual ridge:
1. **MAIN FUNCTION: Prevents VERTICAL DISLODGEMENT of the distal extension base away from tissues** (sticky food).
2. Protects soft tissues impingement by the major connector during downward movement (limits movement in a cervical/gingival direction).
3. Decreases antero-posterior tilting leverages when an isolated tooth is an abutment (but avoid this).
4. Helps stabilize against horizontal denture movement by contact of the minor connector with the axial tooth surfaces (guide planes).
5. Stabilizes against lingual movement of anterior teeth when used.
6. May act as an auxillary rest to support part of the major connector.
7. May provide the first visual indication for the need to reline a distal extension by acting as a reference for seating frameworks and making altered cast impressions (i.e. **can tell you if the rest is not fully seated in its rest seat**).

FULCRUM LINE (AXIS OF ROTATION) – the axis the RPD rotates around when the denture base moves AWAY from the residual ridge.
- Fulcrum line is mainly determined by the placement (location) of primary rests. The **fulcrum passes through the rigid metal above the tooth's height of contour and closest to the edentulous space**.
- Fulcrum line is the center of rotation as the distal extension base moves toward supporting tissues when an occlusal load is applied.
- **Class I & II always have a fulcrum line!**
  - **Class I**: fulcrum passes through the **most posterior abutment** next to the edentulous space.
  - **Class II**: fulcrum line is diagonal and passes through the most posterior abutment on the distal extension side, and most posterior tooth on the non-distal extension side.
  - **Class III & IV**: TOOTH-BORNE/SUPPORTED RPDs that **do not move toward tissue during function** thus (physiologic relief/adjustment is not required). In Class III & IV designs, **rests are placed immediately next to the edentulous space**.
- If the framework is properly designed, the fulcrum line will pass through **the most DISTAL REST on each side**.
- **CLASS III design does not have a fulcrum line (no axis of rotation).**

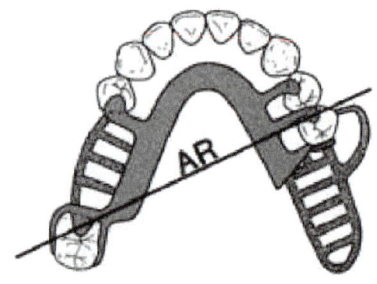

- **Class IV**: fulcrum line passes through the MESIAL rests next to the edentulous space.

RESTS – the indirect retainer united with the major connector by a minor connector. Rests augment mechanical retention. Rests should restore the original tooth topography that existed before the rest seat was prepared. Rests must be RIGID. **Rest Functions**:
- PRIMARY FUNCTION IS TO PROVIDE RPD VERTICAL SUPPORT! Prevents vertical dislodgement.
- Maintains components in position.
- Maintains established occlusal relationships by preventing settling of the denture.
- Prevents soft tissue impingement in a cervical direction.
- Directs and distributes occlusal loads (vertical forces) to the abutment tooth's long axis.
- Rests are prepared BEFORE the final impression is made and master cast is poured.
- NEED A MINIMUM OF 3 RESTS FOR ANY PARTIAL DENTURE.
- There MUST be a MESIAL rest on the most posterior abutment tooth with a distal extension.

1. **OCCLUSAL REST**: prepared only in enamel or any restorative material proven to resist fracture and distortion when a force is applied.
   - 2mm deep in the center (0.5mm deeper than the 1.5mm that the marginal ridge is lowered).
   - OUTLINE FORM: ROUNDED TRIANGLE with the apex toward the center of the occlusal surface.
   - CONCAVE (spoon-shaped) occlusal surface.
   - Occlusal rest is as long as it is wide, and the triangle base (marginal ridge) is at least 2.5mm wide for molars & premolars.
   - Marginal ridge is reduced/lowered 1.5mm to provide sufficient bulk of metal for strength and rigidity of the rest and minor connector.
   - Rest floor is slightly INCLINED APICALLY (deeper), than the 1.5mm depth of the marginal ridge.
   - Angle formed by the occlusal rest and vertical minor connector that is originates from must be LESS THAN 90° to direct occlusal forces along the abutment's long axis.
   - Occlusal rest is always be attached to a rigid minor connector.
   - Occlusal rest is ALWAYS PREPARED AFTER THE PROXIMAL GUIDE PLATES!

AUXILLARY OCCLUSAL REST – the most common indirect retainer placed on the occlusal surface as far away from the distal extension base as possible.
- **Class I design**: it is placed bilaterally on the M-marginal ridge of 1st premolars.
- **Class II design**: placed on M-marginal ridge of 1st premolar on the non-distal extension side.

EXTENDED OCCLUSAL REST – used in Class II (mod I) & III RPDs when the most posterior molar abutment is MESIALLY TIPPED. Minimizes further MESIAL tipping to help direct forces down the abutment's long axis.
- Extends more than ½ the tooth's M-D width and is 1/3 the B-L width.
- Allows minimum of 1mm metal thickness.
- Rounded rest seat preparation with no undercuts.

2. **EMBRASURE/INTERPROXIMAL REST**:
   - Used to prevent inter-proximal wedging of the framework and shunt food away from contact points.
   - Rest seat is preparation is extended LINGUALLY for bulk strength, but prepared just like an occlusal rest.
   - Marginal ridge is lowered 1.5mm on each abutment
   - Avoid creating a vertical groove to prevent the minor connector from torquing of the abutment tooth.

3. **CINGULUM REST (LINGUAL REST):**
   - The most satisfactory lingual rest for support is placed on a prepared rest seat in a cast restoration.
   - Canines are preferred over incisors.
   - Preferred to an incisal rest because it is more esthetic.
   - Limited to maxillary canines and centrals with exaggerated cingulums. Rarely satisfactory on mandibular anteriors due to lack of enamel thickness. **A risky preparation on lower incisors.**
   - Preparation is a slightly **rounded inverted V** (semi-lunar) placed at the **junction of GINGIVAL & MIDDLE 1/3 of the lingual surface** (just above the cingulum, but low enough to minimize abutment torquing forces).
   - 2mm wide F-L.
   - 2.5-3mm M-D length.
   - Minimum 1.5mm deep (incisal-apically)

4. **INCISAL REST:**
   - Used mainly as an auxillary rest or indirect retainer.
   - **Rounded notch is placed 3-4mm from either the MI or DI edge (canines or incisor).**
   - **LEAST ESTHETIC REST and most likely to cause orthodontic movement** due to unfavorable leverage.
   - Preparation is **2.5mm wide and 1.5mm deep** (deepest portion is apical to the incisal edge).
   - Not used on maxillary incisors unless it is the only option.
   - Beveled labially and lingually.

MAXILLARY RUGAE AS INDIRECT RETENTION WITH RPDs – Broad coverage over rugae can provide some support, but is **LESS EFFECTIVE** than tooth support, is undesirable, and avoided. Rugae can provide indirect retention with a **PALATAL HORSESHOE DESIGN** because the horseshoe's posterior retention is inadequate.

Guide Plate Functions:
- **Helps establish a definite path of insertion/dislodgement of the RPD.**
- Stabilizes the RPD by controlling its horizontal position.
- Provides contact with the adjacent tooth.
- Should extend just past the DL line angles to provide 180° encirclement, bracing, and reciprocation.
- Prepared in the occlusal 1/3 on the proximal surface.
- Guide plane is ~2-3mm in height occluso-gingivally, but its F-L width is determined by the tooth's contour.
- Guide plates for Class III & IV designs can extend above the abutment's height of contour because there is no functional movement.
- **Guide plates MUST be below the abutment's height of contour with Class I & II designs** to prevent abutment torquing during functional movements.
- When plates are used with I-bars and mesial rests on premolars to avoid lingual tori, the **plate must end EXACTLY at the height of contour.**
- Guiding planes ensure predictable clasp retention. Failure of partials due to poor clasp retention design can be avoided by altering tooth contours. Guiding planes serve to assure predictable clasp retention.

DIRECT RETAINERS (CLASPING)

ALL CAST CLASPS (DIRECT RETAINERS) both suprabulge & infrabulge are NEVER placed anterior to the fulcrum line (axis of rotation) because they would release during function and TORQUE the abutment. Only indirect retainers and stress breakers (Wrought Wires) are placed anterior to the fulcrum line.

To determine [number of clasps to use in an RPD = [Kennedy Class + 1]
- Does not apply to Class IV designs

PRIMARY RETENTION – provided by mechanically placing retaining elements on the abutment teeth.

SECONDARY RETENTION – provided by intimate relationship of minor connector contact with guiding planes, denture bases, and major connectors with underlying tissues.

Vertical Arm of Surveyor:
- Indicates areas of retention, areas of support on the abutment tooth, and tooth/tissue interferences to the path of insertion.
- A vertical arm represents the path of placement and removal of an RPD.
- Carbon marker is used to determine the tooth's height of contour (greatest convexity).
- Zinc Stearate Powder can identify the survey line (height of contour) for a crown wax-up abutment tooth. It is brushed on the wax-up and the analyzing rod is passed over wax surface and removes the powder.

DIRECT RETAINER – gives the RPD mechanical retention. Any RPD unit that engages an abutment to resist displacement AWAY from basal seat tissues using friction, engaging a depression, or undercut cervical (gingival) to the tooth's height of contour.

2 DIRECT RETAINERS: .01 = .25mm Cast Clasp
1. **Intra-Coronal Retainer ("Precision Attachment or "Internal Attachment"):**
   - **Advantages**: the most esthetic direct retainer. Provides the best vertical support through a rest seat located more favorably relative to the abutment's horizontal axis (does not allow horizontal movement).
   - It is cast or attached totally within the abutment's restored natural contours.
   - Has a prefabricated key & keyway with opposing vertical parallel walls to limit movement and resist removal by friction.
   - **Not used with extensive tissue-supported distal extensions unless a stress-breaker is used** between the movable RPD base and rigid attachment.

2. **Extra-Coronal Retainer (Clasps)**: placed on EXTERNAL surfaces of abutment teeth.
   - Has a **RETENTIVE clasp arm** that is **FLEXIBLE and placed in areas below (cervical) to the tooth's height of contour (tooth's gingival 1/3)**. Provides resistance to deformation from a vertical dislodging force. This generates the retentive action of the clasp. Which has a passive relationship with the abutment until a dislodging force is applied.
   - Lingual arms on molars are usually retentive b/c there are usually no usable facial undercuts on mandibular 2nd or 3rd molars.

NOTES

Clasp Arm Flexibility:
- Longer and thinner (smaller diameter) the clasp arm = **more flexible.**
- Most clasps are **½ round** in form. A round clasp form is the only circumferential clasp form that can be **safely used** to **engage an undercut** on the side of an abutment **away** from the distal extension base.
- Retentive arm must be **flexible** to provide **stress relief** for the abutment.
- **UNDERCUT LOCATION** is the **most important factor** when selecting a clasp for distal extensions. **DENTIST** decides which clasp design is best based on the diagnosis and treatment plan established.

- Has a **BRACING (stabilizing/reciprocating) clasp arm** placed **OCCLUSAL** to the tooth's height of contour (crown's middle 1/3). **MUST BE RIGID.**
- Composed of **chromium-cobalt alloys** to give **greater rigidity** with **less bulk.**
- RIGID because it is **greater in diameter (thicker)** than the retentive arm.
- **Tapered in** one dimension only.
- Horizontal force is transmitted by placing rigid portions of clasps in **NON-UNDERCUT areas** of abutment teeth.

RECIRPOCATION – occurs **only** when the **retentive arm and bracing arm CONTACT the tooth at the same time during seating and removing the RPD.** As the retentive arm tip **passes** over the height of contour and engages the undercut, the **rigid bracing arm must maintain contact** with the abutment. **TIMING IS CRITICAL IN RECIPROCATION.**

Clasp Assembly Components: Clasp assembly components provide **180° encirclement of the abutment** (clasp arms, minor connectors, guide plates all contribute to the 180° encirclement.
1. 1-2 rests & at least 1 minor connector.
2. Retentive clasp arm **(flexible)** to **engage** and **terminate in undercuts.**
3. Reciprocating (bracing) clasp arm **(rigid).**

When an RPD is **fully seated,** the clasp tips should **NOT EXERT ANY PRESSURE** against the abutment teeth. It must be **totally passive. The retentive arm is activated ONLY when vertical dislodging forces attempt to unseat the RPD away from the basal seat tissues.**

Fundamental Principles of a Clasp Assembly:
1. Clasp should be completely passive and its **retentive function** is activated **only** when **dislodging forces are applied.**
2. Each retentive clasp must be opposed by a **reciprocal (bracing)** clasp arm or another RPD element capable of **resisting horizontal forces** exerted on the tooth by the retentive arm.
3. Each clasp must be designed to **encircle more than 180°** (more then ½ the circumference) of the abutment tooth.
4. **Rest should only provide VERTICAL SUPPORT.**

EXTRA-CORONAL RETAINERS – suprabulge & infrabulge clasps **MUST** have **1 retentive arm** (flexible) and **1 rigid reciprocal bracing arm.**

SUPRABULGE RETAINERS – approach the retentive undercut from **ABOVE** the tooth's height of contour (usually from an occlusal rest).

1. **CIRCUMFERENTIAL CLASP (AKER'S CLASP):**
   - Engages > 180° of the abutment's circumference.
   - Terminal end of its retentive clasp arm provides retention (buccal) by engaging an undercut.
   - Has a non-flexible (rigid) lingual clasp arm for stabilization/reciprocation. Must always lie at or above the height of contour because it cannot flex to get in and out of undercuts.
   - Originates on or occlusal to the tooth's height of contour, then crosses in the terminal third, and engages an undercut as its taper decreases and flexibility increases.
   - Consists of 1 retentive clasp arm + 1 non-retentive reciprocal arm.
   - Clasp of choice in Class III & IV (tooth-borne designs) when the most posterior abutment undercut is AWAY from the edentulous space (i.e. MB) surface.
   - Undercut must be on the opposite side of the tooth/rest from where the clasp originates.
   - DO NOT USE when an undercut is adjacent to the edentulous space (DB or DL).
   - RPI Clasp Assembly: consists of mesial rest + distal guide plate + circumferential clasp.

2. **RING CLASP:**
   - Indicated to engage an undercut of a **MESIALLY-LINGUAL TILTED MOLAR** when a severe tissue undercut exists that prevents using an I-bar.
   - Used almost exclusively on mandibular molars that drifted MESIALLY & LINGUALLY to engage a LINGUAL UNDRCUT.
   - Indicated in reverse on an abutment anterior to a "tooth-bound" edentulous space.
   - Encircles nearly all of a tooth from its point of origin.
   - Used to engage a proximal undercut (i.e. ML undercut on mandibular molar cannot be directly engaged b/c of its proximity to the occlusal rest and cannot be approached with a bar clasp (infra-bulge) due to the molar's lingual inclination.
   - Allows the undercut to be approached from the tooth's distal.
   - Has a mesial primary rest & distal auxillary rest. Used almost exclusively on ML tilted molar abutments. Always used with a supporting strut on the non-retentive side with or without an auxillary rest on the opposite marginal ridge.
   - Used on protected abutments because it covers lots of tooth surface.
   - Used when caries risk is LOW and in NON-ESTHETIC areas.
   - Used when a DB or DL undercut on a molar cannot be approached directly from the occlusal rest and/or when tissue undercuts prevent engagement with a bar clasp (infrabulge).
   - Clasp can originate on the MB surface to engage a ML undercut, or ML to engage a MB undercut.

3. **REVERSE ACTION (HAIRPIN) CLASP:**
   - Used only on abutments of "tooth-borne" dentures (Class 3 & 4) where a proximal undercut is BELOW the point of origin only when a bar clasp (infra-bulge) is contraindicated due to a tissue undercut, tilted tooth, shallow vestibule, or high tissue attachment.
   - Used when lingual undercuts prevent placing a supporting strut without tongue interference.
   - Only the lower part of the clasp arm (after the curve) is flexible to engage the undercut.

4. **EMBRASURE CLASP:**
   - Used on sound teeth with retentive areas or when multiple restorations are justified.
   - Used when no edentulous space exists on the opposite side of an edentulous Class II or III with no modifications.
   - **Requires at least 1.5mm marginal ridge reduction to prevent fracture of the clasp assembly.**
   - ALWAYS USED WITH DOUBLE OCCLUSAL RESTS to prevent inter-proximal wedging of the framework.
   - A retentive arm and rigid reciprocating arm must be present for each abutment, but do not have to be on the same side.
   - Wrought wires are NEVER used with embrasure clasps.

5. **HALF-&-HALF CLASP:**
   - INDICATED FOR LINGUALLY INCLINED PREMOLARS (LINGUAL UNDERCUTS)
   - Consists of 1 circumferential retentive arm from one direction, and reciprocating arm that arises from the minor connector.

6. **BACK-ACTION CLASP:**
   - A ring clasp modification. **Its use is difficult to justify** because you could easily use a conventional circumferential clasp.
   - Can be used on a premolar abutment anterior to an edentulous space.

7. **MULTIPLE CLASP:**
   - **Two opposing circumferential clasps joined at the terminal end of the two reciprocal arms.**
   - Used when additional retention and stabilization is needed (tooth-supported RPDs).
   - **Disadvantage:** two embrasure approaches are necessary rather than a single embrasure for both clasps.

8. **COMBINATION CLASP:**
   - **Most commonly used when an abutment next to a distal extension (Class II, mod I) where only a MB undercut exists or if large tissue undercuts prevent a bar clasp from being used.**
   - Used when maximum flexibility is required (i.e. an abutment next to a distal extension, on a weak abutment when a bar direct retainer is contraindicated, or when esthetics is a concern).
   - Consists of a bracing arm, wrought wire retentive circumferential arm, and distal rest.
   - Use when the undercut is on the side of the abutment away from the edentulous space because it is more flexible than a cast clasp arm thus can dissipate functional stresses.

9. **EXTENDED ARM CLASP:**
   - NEVER used with Class I & II (distal extensions) b/c functional forces cause rotation around the rest and upward movement of the clasp tip. Used for abutment tooth-borne dentures next to an edentulous space.

INFRABULGE RETAINERS (BAR CLASPS = ROACH CLASP):
- Arises from the framework or metal base and approach the abutment's retentive undercut from a **GINGIVAL DIRECTION (BELOW THE HEIGHT OF CONTOUR)**.
- Indications: when a small undercut (0.01 inch) exists in the cervical third of the abutment, on abutment teeth for Class III & IV designs (tooth-supported), in distal extension base situations, and when esthetics is a concern.
- **Contraindications**: when a DEEP cervical undercut exists or when a severe tooth or tissue undercut exists. Not used if a tissue undercut exists (because is bothers the tongue and cheek and traps food debris) or with high frenum attachments (shallow vestibule) or excessive buccal or lingual tilt of the abutment tooth.
- **Advantages**: inter-proximal location for ESTHETICS, increased retention without abutment tipping, less chance of accidental distortion due to its proximity to the denture border.
- They type of bar clasp is insignificant as long as it is mechanically and functionally effective, covers as little tooth surface as possible, and displays as little metal possible.
- Vertical portion of the approach arm crosses the gingival margin at 90°.
- Infrabulge Clasps: T bar, Modified T bar, I bar, Y bar, Roach Clasp.

I BAR:
- Always place the tip of I bar's retentive arm **MESIAL to the greatest M-D curvature** on the abutment's facial surface to ensure retention in the undercut. The undercut must be MESIAL (in front of) the greatest M-D curvature on the abutment's facial surface.
- I-bar retentive arm with a MESIAL rest and distal guide plate (RPI SYSTEM) is the BEST clasp assembly to be placed on the terminal abutment for distal extensions.
- Indicated for a **Class I or II RPDs** using a MESIAL REST when there is no tissue undercut.
- Used to engage a ML undercut when there is no tissue undercut below the abutment.
- I-bar's superior border is located more than 3mm from the free gingival margin.
- Indicated for Class II mod I on a ML tilted molar with little tissue undercut.
- The foot of the I-bar is completely below the height of contour (survey line) in distal extension designs so it can release during functional movements of the extension base.
- When a patient bites down, the I-bar should release from the undercut. The retentive arm should only function when there is an attempt to dislodge the RPD (opening the mouth when chewing sticky food).

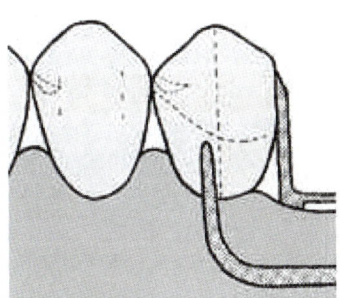

MODIFIED T BAR:
- Bar of choice for **DB undercuts** below the height of countour immediately next to an edentulous space.
- Primary indication is when abutment undercuts are immediately next to an edentulous area and no tissue undercuts. Can be used with a mesial or distal occlusal rest in tooth-supported designs since no functional movement occurs.
- When used on a terminal abutment for a Class I design, it is used with a mesial rest and the arm tip is placed into a **DB undercut**.
- Its vertical arm **must approach and engage MESIAL to the greatest M-D curvature on the abutment's facial surface** to prevent the RPD from being dislodged up and back.

"RPI" SYSTEM (REST, PROXIMAL PLATE, I-BAR) – an I-bar clasp that consists of a MO rest, and distal guide plate with the minor connector placed into the ML embrasure, but not contacting the adjacent tooth.
- **Used only with Kennedy Class I or II (DISTAL EXTENSIONS).**
- Must be 180 degrees around the tooth
- Distal guiding plane extending from the marginal ridge to the **junction of middle & gingival 1/3** of the abutment is prepared to receive a proximal plate.
- **MESIAL RESTS ARE PLACED ON THE TERMINAL ABUTMENT TOOTH FOR ALL DISTAL EXTENSIONS.**

RPI system is designed to allow vertical rotation of a distal extension saddle into the denture-bearing mucosa under occlusal loading without damaging the supporting structures of the abutment tooth. As the saddle is pressed into the denture-bearing mucosa, the denture rotates about a point close to the mesial rest. Both the distal guide plate and I- bar move in the directions indicated and disengage from the tooth surface. Potentially harmful torque is thus avoided.

RPD STRESS BREAKERS

STRESS-BREAKER – a device that relieves the abutment teeth to which an FPD or RPD is attached, of all or part of the forces generated by occlusal function. When a stress-breaker is incorporated next to a free-end distal extension RPD, the functional stress is directed onto the residual ridge and only minimal transfer of functional stress to abutment teeth occurs. Since vertical and horizontal forces are concentrated on the residual ridge, increased ridge resorption frequently occurs.

WROUGHT WIRE RETENTIVE CLASP (STRESS-BREAKER) – a stress breaker used because of its increased flexibility (it minimizing abutment torquing). **The simplest form of stress relief.** Has a flexible connection between the direct retainer and denture base. **Advantages:** higher yield strength, greater flexibility, more ductile and resilient.
- Often used with a **MESIAL rest in Class I & II** designs on the most posterior abutment tooth **(terminal abutment)** when there is a tissue undercut, or high frenum attachment that prevents using an I-bar.
- If occlusion prevents using a mesial rest on the most posterior abutment in a distal extension, only a WW can be used with a distal rest because it is OK for its retentive tip to be in front of the axis of rotation (fulcrum).
- Used on teeth with indirect retainers on them (both are anterior to the fulcrum line). Provides stress relief to the abutment tooth due to its flexibility when the distal extension moves toward the residual ridge.
- Tip of its retentive arm should engage the undercut ANTERIOR to the fulcrum line (axis of rotation). Terminal end of its retentive arm is optimally placed in the middle of the gingival 1/3 of the clinical crown. However, it is acceptable to place it at the junction of the gingival and middle 1/3 of the clinical crown. When the partial is completely seated, the retentive arm should be passive and applying no pressure on the teeth.
- NOT USED in Class III & IV (tooth-borne) designs because there is no functional movement of the RPD.
- DO NOT USE wrought wires through embrasures or with embrasure clasps.
- Has a tensile strength at least 25% greater than the cast alloy from which it was made. Wrought-wire clasps have greater flexibility and adjustability than the cast clasps, are tougher and more ductile than cast clasps, and have greater tensile strength. Thus can

be used in smaller diameters to provide greater flexibility without fatigue and fracture.
- Wrought wire is incorporated into the RPD by soldering it to the minor connector, meshwork, incorporating it into the wax pattern, or is embedded into the acrylic resin (makes it the most flexible). 20-gauge wrought-wire is 2x more flexible than an 18-gauge wire.
- .02 = .5mm wrought wire. Must be at least 8mm long and tapered round 18 gauge wire.
- .03 = .75mm and IS NOT JUSTIFIED.

FINISH LINES:
1. **External Finish Line**-the external junction (butt joint) of the metal framework and denture base plastic (acrylic).
   - The external finish line on a maxillary Class I RPD originates from the lingual of the guide plate of the terminal abutment and ends at the HAMULAR NOTCH.

2. **Internal Finish Line**-the butt joint between the metal and acrylic on the TISSUE SIDE of the edentulous area.
   - Junction of the major and minor connector at palatal finishing lines are 2mm medial from the imaginary line that would connect lingual surfaces of missing posterior denture teeth.
   - Internal and External finish lines are normally OFFSET from each other to avoid framework weakness/fracture.
   - Location of the finishing line at the junction of the major and minor connector is based on restoring the natural palatal shape while considering the location of replacement teeth.
   - Finishing line junction with the major connector should be no greater than 90°, thus being somewhat undercut.
   - Junction of minor connectors and bar clasps are 90° butt-joints that follow the guidelines for base contour and clasp length.

SURVEYING RPD ABUTMENTS

Surveying casts allows the dentist to record the dentures path of insertion, position of the survey line, and location of undercut and non-undercut areas. To do this, **TRIPOD MARKS are placed on the cast to record the cast's orientation to the surveyor**.
- **Tripod marks**-3 spots placed at 3 different locations around abutment teeth from a single point of view to ensure a reproducible orientation of the cast to the surveyor. Records the cast's position.
- **Dental Surveyor**-used to determine the relative parallelism of oral anatomy. **Areas used for support CANNOT be determined by surveying**. When surveying casts, the correct procedure is to first adjust the tilt to permit the establishment of guiding planes. The anterior edentulous space will frequently dictate the angulation needed. Normally, some re-contouring of the proximal walls of abutment teeth is needed to improve guideplane alignment by **disking the proximal surface** parallel to the path of insertion.
- **Tilting the cast during surveying** changes the **path of insertion, survey line position, and location of the undercut and non-undercut areas of each tooth**.

NOTES

PURPOSE OF SURVEYING (Using Diagnostic Casts):
- Determine the most desirable path of placement that will eliminate or minimize interference to removal and placement the RPD.
- Identify surfaces for guiding planes for the prosthesis.
- Locate and measure areas of teeth for retention.
- Determine if a tooth and/or bony areas require surgical removal or if another path of insertion will suffice.
- Determine the most suitable path of placement that will design of retainers and teeth to be most esthetic.
- Prepare an accurate charting for any mouth preparation to be made.
- Determine and delineate the tooth's height of contour.

FACE BOW – caliper-like device to record the patient's maxilla/hinge axis relationship (opening and closing axis) and to transfer this relationship to the articulator during mounting of the maxillary cast. If the transfer is done properly, the arc of closure on the articulator should duplicate the patient's true arc of closure.
- Before an accurate face-bow transfer record can be made, the **location of the hinge axis point (axial center of opening-closing)**, must first be determined.
- Facebow transfer is **NOT a maxillo-mandibular record, but a record to orient the maxillary cast to the hinge axis on the articulator**. The facebow transfers the maxilla/hinge axis relationship to the articulator during mounting of the maxillary cast.
- A face-bow transfer record **DOES NOT**: allow the dentist to locate the hinge axis, nor record CR more reliably, nor position the maxillary cast properly in relation to the mandibular cast, nor transfer the cast to the articulator maintaining the proper inter-occlusal relationships present in the mouth.
- **Hinge-axis face bow transfer enables the dentist to alter VDO on the articulator.** When altering VDO (either via restorations or with dentures), casts should be mounted on the hinge axis. **Hinge Axis Face Bow-used to record opening and closing of the mandible.**

FRAMEWORK TRY-IN:
- Before trying in a framework, inspect the master cast for damage and inspect the framework for sharp metal fins.
- When making maxillary & mandibular RPDs on the same patient, the dentist should first try each framework one at a time for fit, then adjust occlusion for each if needed, then adjust occlusion with both frameworks in place.
- **Damaged areas on the cast are the first areas adjusted if the framework does not fit.**
- If the framework fits the cast but not in the mouth, all other possible causes should be eliminated before making a new impression.
- If attempts to fit the framework to the mouth are unsuccessful after adjusting, then assume the impression or cast is inaccurate and the impression will need to be remade.
- **A MASTER CAST for a RPD should be blocked out and duplicated BEFORE the framework is waxed up.**

ADVANTAGES OF RPD CHROMIUM-COBALT ALLOYS – corrosion resistance, high strength, low specific gravity & VERY RIGID (inflexible). No ductility or malleability after they are cast.

Composition of Chromium Base Metal Alloys for RPDs:
1. **Chromium**-responsible for **CORROSION RESISTANCE** in cobalt-chromium alloys. Ensures the alloy will resist tarnish and corrosion by forming a complex chromium oxide film. An RPD made of a base metal alloy is resistant to tarnish and corrosion because of its surface oxide layer.
2. **Cobalt**-increases the framework's **RIGIDITY**, strength, and hardness.
3. **Nickel**-increases DUCTILITY. Measured as a percentage of elongation and determines how much margins can be closed via burnishing. **Nickel is the metallic component of a RPD with the greatest potential for ALLERGIC REACTIONS in the mouth.**

ADA ALLOY CLASSIFICATION:
- **Type I**: used for small inlays.
- **Type II**: larger inlays & onlays.
- **Type III**: onlays, crowns, and short-span FPDs.
- **Type IV**: thin veneer crowns, long-span FPDs & **RPDs**.

ALTERED CAST IMPRESSION:
- Purpose is to **obtain the maximum support possible from the edentulous ridges in Class I & II designs**.
- Captures edentulous ridge tissues in relation to the way the framework fits IN THE MOUTH (not cast).
- Helps avoid overextension that is common when a stock-tray alginate impression is used.
- A stock tray will perform adequately in areas where teeth remain but relatively poorer in edentulous areas. This is one of the major reasons an altered cast impression is done.

ALTERED CAST TECHNIQUE – the purpose is **to record the form of the edentulous segment without tissue displacement and to accurately relate the edentulous segment of the teeth via the metal framework**. The goal is to provide maximum support for the RPD denture base, thus maintaining occlusal contact to distribute occlusal load over both natural and artificial dentitions, while minimizing movement of the base that would create leverage on the abutment teeth.
- Altered cast technique **helps obtain soft tissue support** to aid abutments in resisting functional stresses. It is a **secondary impression system** that uses the metal framework to hold customized impression trays for the edentulous areas.

IMPRESSIONS:
- If a mandibular RPD abutment must be crowned, the FPD impression should include a full arch impression is required to capture all abutment teeth and the retromolar pads.
- When crowing an abutment tooth for an RPD, you must reduce more than the normal occlusal reduction for the rest seat.

COMPLETE DENTURES

Complete Denture Design Characteristics:
1. **Stability**-the quality of a denture or prosthesis to be firm, steady, constant, and **not subject to change position when forces are applied**. In dentures, stability is the relationship of the denture base to bone that **resists dislodgement of the denture in a HORIZONTAL direction**.
   - Stability involves **resistance to horizontal, lateral, & torsional forces (most important)**.
   - All RPD components, **except the retentive clasp tip**, contribute to denture stability.
2. **Support**-resists **VERTICAL** seating forces **provided by rests and denture bases**. For RPDs, support is provided by **occlusal rests and edentulous ridge areas**. Support is the MOST important design characteristic for oral health.
3. **Retention**-resists the force of gravity, sticky foods, and forces associated with mandibular movement. **Direct & indirect retainers provide retention**. **CLASPS in undercut areas of abutment teeth provide retention**.

Factors that impact retention, stability, & support: quality of oral mucosa, alveolar ridge contour, muscle attachments, saliva, and **neuromuscular control** (the most important because patient's muscles learn to hold their denture in place and chew efficiently).

BORDER MOLDING:
- **Masseter Muscle**: powerful muscle whose fiber run superior-inferior that pushes the buccinator into the DB corner of the denture base during contraction. **SHAPES DISTOBUCCAL AREA** during an altered cast impression. **Overextension** of a mandibular denture base in the **distofacial area** causes **dislodgement** of the denture during function as the result of the action of the **MASSETER**. An **overextended DB** corner of a **mandibular denture pushes against the MASSETER** during function.

- **Superior Constrictor Muscle**: shapes the **DISTOLINGUAL BORDER MOLDING**. Affects the most distal portion of the lingual flange. An overextended lingual flange can cause a sore throat.

- **MOST critical area in border molding a MAXILLARY DENTURE is the MUCOGINGIVAL FOLD above the maxillary tuberosity area** as this area is extremely important for maximal retention. Other critical areas are the labial frenum in the midline, and frena in the bicuspid area. Overextension in these areas often leads to decreased retention and tissue irritation.

- When border molding a **MANDIBULAR DENTURE** for a final impression, **the DB extension is determined by the position and action of the MASSETER MUSCLE**. The DL extension of the mandibular impression for a complete denture is limited by the action of the **SUPERIOR CONSTRICTOR MUSCLE**.

FRENUM – folds of mucus membrane containing fibrous C.T. Must provide denture relief/space in this area because it can limit the denture's extension.

Custom Tray & Border Molding:
- A **custom tray** fabricated on a preliminary cast is **trimmed ~2mm short of the mucosal reflection and frenae**. This is done by first checking the borders in the mouth and then trimmed down to allow uniform thickness of 2mm of modeling compound when the borders are molded. However, **the primary indicator of border molding accuracy is STABILITY and lack of displacement of the custom tray in the mouth**.
- Custom tray for a final mandibular or maxillary complete denture impression should have a spacer with tissue stops to ensure the tray seats in proper relationship to the arch, and to ensure adequate room for the impression material. **The space is created with wax covered by aluminum foil** over the master cast prior to forming the tray.
- **Border molding is completed in two stages**. The molding should approximate the tray borders and should be slightly overextended. Excess compound is trimmed from inside and outside the custom tray. The remaining modeling compound is then refined by repeating the process. **The final form of the border molding should represent an accurate impression of the peripheral tissues**. The border modeling compound should have a smooth, polished appearance.
- Palatoglossus, superior pharyngeal constrictor, mylohyoid, and genioglossus muscles are influential in border molding the **LINGUAL border of the mandibular impression** for an edentulous patient.

After extraction, alveolar ridge resorption occurs because there is no longer bone stimulation. Atrophy of supporting structures occurs (residual ridge resorption).
- **Maxillary arch**: bone loss/resorption occurs in a **VERTICAL & PALATAL direction (UPWARD & INWARD)**. (0.1mm/year is sustained). Initial loss in first year is greater, but varies.
- **Mandibular arch**: bone loss occurs in **VERTICAL direction (DOWNWARD & FORWARD/OUTWARD)**. Bone loss is **oriented along the cross-sectional shape** of the mandible. Mandibular bone resorption is 4x faster than in the maxilla, but varies. Severe bone resorption can cause a **Pseudo Class III malocclusion** appearance.

OCCLUSION RIMS – the resultant product after adding base-plate wax to a record base to approximate the tooth position and arch form expected in the completed denture. **Functions**:
- Determine and establish the patient's VDO (vertical dimension of occlusion) and **level of occlusal plane**.
- Make maxillo-mandibular **preliminary jaw relation** records.
- Establish and locate the future position of denture teeth (**arch for the lips, cheeks, tongue**).
- Maxillary rim is 22mm and mandibular rim 18mm.

When recording CR for an RPD, the **occlusion rim is attached to the completed partial denture metal framework** instead of to a record base as used with a complete denture.

Inferior surface of the **maxillary occlusion rim should be PARALLEL to CAMPER'S LINE** (the line/plane running from the inferior border of the nose ala to the superior border of the ear tragus). Significance of **Camper's Line**: the occlusal plane, established by the wax occlusion rims surfaces is parallel to Camper's line & inter-pupillary line.

Impression making of Complete Dentures Recommend using a technique that:
- Affords placement and control of the impression material in recording border tissues (border molding).
- Results in minimal tissue displacement under the denture (registers tissues in their passive position).
- Is dependent on the oral conditions present.
- Best impression technique for a patient with **loose hyperplastic tissue** is to **register the tissue in its PASSIVE position**. There must be **intimate contact of the impression material with the tissue**.

MANDIBULAR COMPLETE DENTURES

MANDIBULAR COMPLETE DENTURES – a primary support (stress-bearing) area is the **BUCCAL SHELF** because of its bone structure (resists resorption because it is dense cortical bone and does not change) and its trabeculation right angle (parallel) relationship to the occlusal plane.

- A **SECONDARY** peripheral seal area for a mandibular complete denture is the **anterior lingual border**.
- A SECONDARY relief area is the CREST OF RESIDUAL RIDGE WHEN IT IS SHARP.

Mandibular Support Areas:

1. **Buccal shelf**-the primary support area for a mandibular denture. **Buccinator muscle** limits a denture's extension in this area. The bigger the buccal shelf, the more denture support.
   - **Masseter** muscle affects the mandibular denture.
   - The boundaries of the buccal shelf are the buccal frenum to the retromolar pad crest of the residual ridges to the external oblique line (

2. **Alveolar ridge**- SECONDARY area of mandibular denture support.
   - RESIDUAL RIDGES if large and broad, may be primary support areas, but are usually SECONDARY STRESS-BEARING AREA because it is cancellous bone.

3. **Retromolar pad**-does not change or resorb. A primary support area, but must be captured in the impression. Lies at the crest of the mandibular residual ridge.

4. **Keratinized tissue**- the more keratinized tissue, the better denture support and comfort.

- When fabricating a mandibular complete denture for a patient with a "knife-edged ridge" you need maximum extension of the denture to help distribute occlusal forces over a larger area.

- Marked RESORPTION of the alveolar ridge will occur if a mandibular complete denture base terminates short of the retromolar pad. Underextension of the peripheral border of a complete mandibular denture decreases tissue-bearing surfaces, thus affecting denture STABILITY.

- Underlying basal bone (under the retromolar pad) resists bone resorption (does not resorb). Covering this area also provides some border seal. An overload of the mucosa occurs if the bases covering the area are too small in outline.

- Mandibular dentures do not rely on suction from a peripheral seal for retention like maxillary dentures, but rely on denture stability in covering as much basal bone possible without impinging on muscle attachments. The active border molding performed by the lips, cheeks, and tongue determines the peripheral areas of a mandibular arch, thus establishing maximal basal bone coverage.

- DO NOT PLACE mandibular molars over the ascending area of the mandible because occlusal forces over the inclined ramus DISLODGE the mandibular denture.

Thin mucosa is found in **mylohyoid area & over mandibular tori** (mandibular dentures) and on the midline of the palatal vault and over a torus palatinus (maxillary dentures).

Mandibular tori, sharp prominent mylohyoid ridges, and Epulis Fissuratum are evaluated for surgical removal before the fabrication of new dentures begins.

Tongue position affects denture stability & retention in the mouth. **A patient with a RETRACTED/RETRUDED tongue is a poor denture candidate.**

MYLOHYOID MUSCLE – affects the slope of the **lingual flange of the impression in the molar region** (at its most POSTERIOR (distal) aspect) causing the **flange to slope toward the tongue. FORMS THE MUSCULAR FLOOR OF THE MOUTH.** Arises from the mylohyoid ridge of the mandible near the mandible's inferior border in the INCISOR REGION and becomes higher on the mandible's posterior body until it terminates just distal to the lingual tuberosity.
- Connects at the midline and can **LIFT THE MANDIBULAR DENTURE** when the **TONGUE IS PROTRUDED**. It influences the molar region and slopes toward the tongue.
- Sublingual gland and anterior portion of the mylohyoid muscle cause the **LINGUAL FLANGE** to be lower in height in the anterior region.
- **RETROMYLOHYOID CURTAIN**-composed of the superior pharyngeal constrictor & palatoglossus. Determines how far posteriorly the lingual flange can go.
- **RETROMYLOHYOID FOSSA**-located at the **distal end of the alveolar LINGUAL SULCUS**. This is where the lingual flange turns toward the ramus making the famous **"S-CURVE"** with the flange sloping toward the tongue in the molar region of the mylohyoid muscle. **Bordered medially by the anterior tonsillar pillar and posteriorly by the retromylohyoid curtain.**
  - **S-CURVE** is seen in a mandibular impression due to the **MYLOHYOID MUSCLE** (slopes toward the tongue) and **RETROMYLOHYOID FOSSA** which slopes toward the buccal.

PTERYGOMANDIBULAR RAPHE – a **TENDON** lying between the **buccinator & superior constrictor muscles**.

Lingual Tubercle = Lingual Tuberosity

ALVEOLINGUAL SULCUS – the space between the ridge and tongue.

SUBMAXILLARY SALIVARY CARUNCLE – eminence on either side of the frenum on which the major sublingual ducts and submandibular ducts open.

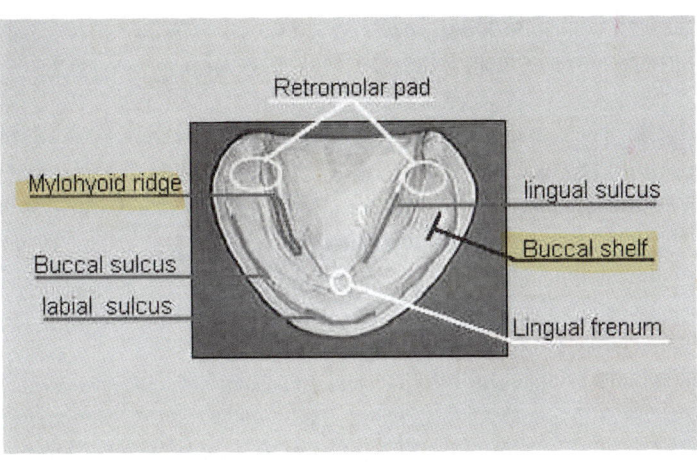

MAXILLARY COMPLETE DENTURES

PRIMARY support denture bearing areas (stress-bearing area) is the **POSTERIOR RESIDUAL RIDGES & PALATE.**

SECONDARY support areas are the **PALATAL RUGAE & ANTERIOR RESIDUAL RIDGE.** Secondary **RETENTIVE** area is the glandular region on each side of the palatal midline.

POSTERIOR PALATAL SEAL – extends through the **HAMULAR NOTCHES** in the maxilla, and passes **2mm** in front of the **FOVEA PALATINAE**. It is in an area of immovable tissue and compensates for denture processing errors. **Posterior palatine salivary glands help maintain peripheral seal.**

- Mark it in the mouth with a Thompson stick and carve/scribe this area into the cast.
- Compensates for acrylic shrinkage and is **in IMMOVABLE TISSUE**.
- Butterfly shape and in shallower in the center and hamular notch areas.
- Carried ~5mm **ANTERIOR TO THE VIBRATING LINE**.
- Posterior palatal seal outline and depth differs for every patient according to the palatal form of the patient.
- A posterior palatal seal is necessary when fabricating a complete denture on a patient with a flat palate. **THE FLATTER THE PALATE, THE WIDER THE POSTERIOR PALATAL SEAL.**
- Posterior palatal seal should never be removed.
- Middle of the posterior palatal seal is 0.5mm deep extending 3mm on both sides of the midline.
- Seal is 1.5mm deep lateral to the middle of the seal and should extend up to the medial boundary of the pterygomaxillary (hamular) notches. Width is 1-1.5mm high and 1.5mm broad at its base.
- **Excessive depth of the posterior palatal seal usually results in unseating of the denture.**
- WIDTH of the seal anterior to posterior is characterized by a concave surface, 3mm wide in the midline, and **6mm wide in the mid-lateral areas**.
- Placement of the posterior palatal seal is **always done by the DENTIST**.

Posterior Palatal Seal Functions:
1. Completes the border seal of the maxillary denture.
2. Prevents food impaction beneath the denture's tissue surface.
3. Improves the denture's physiologic retention.
4. **Compensates for polymerization and cooling shrinkage of the denture resin during processing.**

HAMULAR NOTCH (PTERYGOMAXILLARY) – a cleft of loose C.T. that extends from the maxillary tuberosity to the hamulus of the medial pterygoid plate.

FOVEA PALATINI – a group of **mucous gland ducts** whose location varies, but is usually slightly posterior to the junction of the hard & soft palates near the midline.
- **VIBRATING LINE**: ~2mm anterior to the fovea palatinae and **ALWAYS ON THE SOFT PALATE**. The imaginary line across the posterior palate that marks the division between the movable & immovable tissues.

Posterior Palatal Seal Landmarks:
- **Posterior outline** is formed by the "ah" line (vibrating line) and passes through the two pterygomaxillary (hamular) notches and is **2mm anterior to the fovea palatini**. Vibrating line IS AN AREA (imaginary line) that **dictates the distal palatal termination of the maxillary complete denture record base**. In determining the posterior limit of a maxillary denture base the **hamular notch is ON the posterior border**.

- **Anterior outline**-formed by the "**blow**" **line (valsalva line)**, located at the **distal extent of the hard palate**. The blow line is anterior to the vibrating line which freely moves when the patient attempts to blow through the nose when it is squeezed tightly. Blow line is a close approximation to the junction of the hard and soft palate.

PALATAL TORI – bony enlargements at the hard palate midline, **occurring in 20-25% of the population, more prevalent in women**. Usually covered by thinner and less resilient mucosa than the residual ridge, so it **may act as a fulcrum and cause rocking of the maxillary denture**.

- Because the soft tissues over the torus are generally thin with a **poor blood supply, post-operative healing is slow**. It is best to cover the operated site with a surgical stent lined with a sedative dressing. If a patient is having all maxillary teeth extracted at once, it is best to also remove the tori at that time.
- **NOT usually removed for denture fabrication**. However, **mandibular tori ARE usually removed prior to denture fabrication**.

Indications for Removing Palatal Tori.
1. Impinges on the soft tissue or the tori is undercut.
2. So large it fills the vault and prevents formation of an adequate denture base.
3. Extends too far posteriorly thus interferes with the posterior palatal seal.
4. Psychologically disturbing to the patient (cancerphobia).
5. Large palatal tori can cause problems with posterior palatal seal. Use a **Y-incision to remove palatal tori directly over the tori**.

If a patient complains "when I smile, my upper denture doesn't hold", the area of the denture base needs to be adjusted is the buccal notch & buccal flange due to **EXCESSIVE THICKNESS of the area**. As the buccal frenum moves posteriorly during smiling or other facial expressions, it encroaches on the denture border that is too thick, causing the denture to become loose.

MEDIAN PALATAL RAPHE (SUTURE) – area of very thin and tight attached tissue extending from the incisive papilla to the end of the hard palate. This is where the palatine processes of the maxilla join together. **MAXILLARY DENTURE SHOULD BE RELIEVED IN THIS AREA**.

Problems Due to ill Fitting Complete Dentures:
1. **Angular Chelitis**-cracking in the corner of the lips secondary to chronic candidiasis, or caused by a **LOSS of VERTICAL DIMENSION, or vitamin B deficiency**.

    - **Treat with anti-fungal therapy**: Nystatin powder applied to denture undersurface 3x/day for 3-4 weeks, or reline or remake the denture. **Nystatin rinse in ineffective**!

    - **Closed vertical dimension** is the most likely **cause of cheilosis** in patient who wears a complete denture and whose medical history is non-contributory.

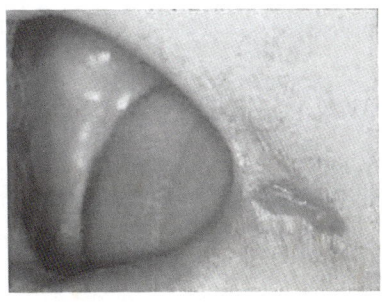

NOTES

2. **Inflammatory Fibrous Hyperplasia (Epulis Fissuratum)**-begins as a traumatic ulcer secondary to an ill-fitting denture flange. Can be caused by continued denture wear and irritation. **Treat**: with **SURGICAL EXCISION**. First thing you must do is **CUT THE DENTURE FLANGE BACK** because the denture is **OVEREXTENDED**. Then consider tissue conditioning.

   - **Denture-induced fibrous hyperplasia (Epulis Fissuratum),** due to clefts found in the hyperplastic tissue, is also related to chronic trauma produced by an ill-fitting denture. It occurs in the vestibular mucosa where the denture flange contacts tissue. Appears as **PAINLESS FOLDS** of fibrous tissue surrounding the overextended denture flange. If the amount of hyperplasia is minimal, tissue conditioning, fabrication of new dentures, and a change in denture habits may be sufficient to arrest tissue changes. However, **surgical excision is usually required**. The patient can also leave the denture out of the mouth.

   - The most likely tissue reaction to gross **OVEREXTENSION** of a complete denture that has been worn for a long time is an **EPULIS FISSURATUM (caused by an ill-fitting denture flange)**. This cleft-like lesion are caused mainly by overextension of denture flanges. The overextension may result from long-term neglect or settling subsequent to residual ridge resorption. **Traumatic occlusion of natural teeth opposing an artificial denture may also cause an epulis fissuratum.**

3. **Inflammatory Papillary Hyperplasia**-secondary to ill-fitting **MAXILLARY DENTURES** and sometimes complicated by chronic candidiasis. Treatment: condition the tissues. **Therapy**: topical anti-fungal medication. In extreme cases, surgical excision. Frequently found under an ill-fitting denture, especially dentures with a relief chamber produced in response to irritation from denture movement and accumulating food debris. The masses present as **PAINLESS, FIRM, pink or red nodular proliferations of the mucosa**. Candida Albicans may contribute to the inflammation.

   - Most patients are unaware of its presence. It usually involves only the **HARD PALATE**, but may also involve the residual ridges. IPH treatment depends on the lesion size. Although the nodules are not completely reversible, smaller papilla usually regress with treatment (removing the denture, soft relines, good oral hygiene, and Nystatin therapy).

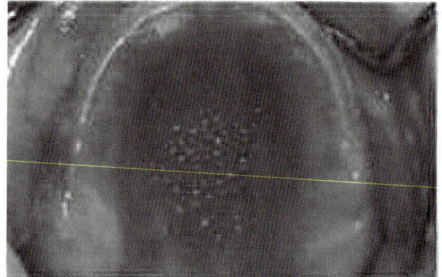

4. **Denture Stomatitis**-a localized or generalized **chronic inflammation (redness and burning) of the denture-bearing mucosa**. Discomfort may be or may not be present. **Caused by denture trauma and secondary fungal infections**. Treatment: improved oral hygiene, tissue rest, anti-fungal therapy (Nystatin), resilient tissue conditioners, and new, well-fitting dentures.

The most important reason to treat **hyperplastic tissue** before making a complete or RPD is **to provide a firm, stable base for the denture**. Treat **hyperplastic tissue**: tissue rest, soft reline of existing dentures, change denture habits (not wearing them 24hrs/day), or surgical removal of tissue (for extensive tissue changes).

COMBINATION SYNDROME – caused when an **edentulous maxilla is opposed by a partially dentate mandible (anterior teeth only)**, causing **SEVERE BONE RESORPTION OF ANTERIOR MAXILLA**. Thus,, **during chewing, the denture tips anteriorly compress the mucoperiostieum of the pre-maxilla**.
- **Characteristics**: maxillary tuberosity hypertrophy (fibrous hyperplasia), occlusal plane problems, & premaxilla resorption.

When a previously edentulous aged patient who now **wears a complete maxillary denture against the 6 mandibular anterior teeth for many years**, it is very common to have to do a reline due to **loss of bone in the ANTERIOR maxillary arch**. This is evident by a **FLABBY MAXILLARY ANTERIOR RIDGE** (loss of osseous structure in the anterior maxillary arch). A flabby, maxillary anterior ridge under a complete denture is frequently associated with **RETAINED NATURAL MANDIBULAR ANTERIORS**.
- Flabby ridges are due to unstable occlusion and or excessive loading of tissues. Causes replacement of bone by fibrous tissue. Use a VERY FLOWABLE IMPRESSION MATERIAL to record flabby ridges like ZINC OXIDE EUGENOL PASTE.
- **RESILIENT LINER is indicated** to improve/promote healing, where there is very little ridge left, or when a maxillary natural teeth oppose a mandibular full denture (decreases pressure on the ridge and causes less damage to vascularity which decreases bone resorption.

If you put pressure on incisive papillae, **the patient feels burning. To treat relieve the incisive papillae area**. A patient who wears a complete maxillary denture complains of a burning sensation in the palatal area of their mouth. This indicates too much pressure being exerted by the denture on the INCISIVE FORAMEN.

INCISIVE PAPILLA – soft fibrous C.T. elevation that covers the incisive foramen (opening). RELIEF areas are the **MEDIAL PALATAL SUTURE & INCISIVE PAPILLA** when burning occurs or to not compromise blood supply.

Burning sensation in the mandibular anterior area is caused by pressure on the **MENTAL FORAMEN**

Patient returns to your office a few days after delivery of new dentures and complains of generalized irritation of the basal seat. Potential Causes:
- **PREMATURE OCCLUSAL CONTACTS = MOST common cause of generalized irritation of the basal seat**.
- Lack of denture hygiene, nutritional and hormonal imbalance.
- Excessive VDO

METAL DENTURE BASE – metal is LESS irritating to tissue than acrylic, and more accurately fits the tissues.
- Has better thermal conductivity, so is better for tissues.
- Increased strength allows for less bulk to allow more tongue space and better phonetics.
- Increased weight which is better for mandibular denture stability.

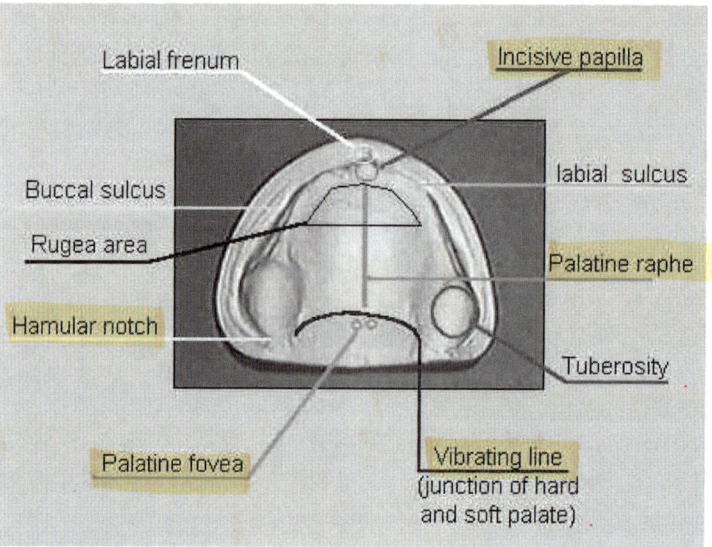

IMMEDIATE DENTURES

All new dentures should be evaluated 24hrs after delivery to correct any undetected errors. Tissue trauma attributed to denture function manifests as hyperemia, inflammation, ulceration, and pain. The basic sequence of the clinical procedure for a 24hr recall appointment is:
1. Remove the dentures from the mouth and thoroughly examine the mouth.
2. Ask the patient about the areas of tissue trauma observed. Permit the patient to describe additional complaints.
3. After collecting all diagnostic information, the dentist can determine the source of the problem and cure.

During the first few days after inserting complete dentures, the patient should expect some difficulty in masticating most foods and excessive saliva due to reflex parasympathetic stimulation of the salivary glands. Over time, this will subside and return to normal.

Ideal treatment is to fabricate the maxillary & mandibular immediate dentures simultaneously to avoid setting maxillary teeth to the likely malpositions of the remaining mandibular teeth.
- **If the master casts are altered in an immediate denture procedure** (e.g. elimination of gross undercuts), it is advisable to construct a second transparent denture base using a surgical stent or template. The stent is placed over the ridge after the teeth are extracted. Pressure points and undercuts are readily visible and surgical ridge correction can be performed.
- Duplicating a master cast to construct a surgical stent/template that is to be used at the time of immediate denture insertion is best made after wax elimination and after the cast is trimmed. Do **not make a 2ⁿᵈ denture set for at least 6 months**.

2-step schedule for tooth removal prior to delivery of immediate complete dentures:
1. **Step 1**: extract all posterior teeth EXCEPT a maxillary first premolar and its opposing tooth to provide a posterior "stop" to maintain the VDO.
2. **Step 2**: after the posterior residual ridges exhibit acceptable healing, the 2nd treatment phase (denture fabrication) can begin. **Anterior teeth are extracted at the time of denture insertion**.

To help the patient get through the first day of wearing immediate dentures, instruct them to **NOT REMOVE THE DENTURES**, eat soft foods, and return in 24hrs for the first adjustment/evaluation. **KEEP THEM IN THE MOUTH FOR 24hrs after delivery.**

Immediate Complete Denture Advantages:
- **MAIN INDICATION IS ESTHETICS**.
- Ability to duplicate the position of the natural teeth.
- **Continuously acceptable esthetics** as the patient is never without either natural or artificial teeth.
- **Improved speech adaptation**. Immediate dentures require only one period of speech adaptation, while conventional denture treatment requires two (one after extractions and another after the dentures are delivered).
- **Protects extraction sites from trauma by acting as a bandage** over the clot-filled sockets.
- **Continuously acceptable masticatory function**. Patient retains some perception of chewing during healing.
- **Prevents tongue enlargement**. When natural teeth are lost and not replaced, the tongue expands into the available space.

Immediate Complete Denture Disadvantages:
- **MAJOR disadvantage of immediate denture therapy is not being able to have an anterior tooth try-in to evaluate esthetics** (anterior tooth try-in is impossible).
- **Relining/rebasing the denture is required in 8-12 months**. Relining is simple, but must be carried out within 8-12 months depending on the rate of alveolar ridge resorption. Also, increased post-delivery soreness for a few days can be encountered.
- **Increased post-insertion care** (including relining or remaking the dentures). Contour changes occur in the residual ridge during the 8-12 month healing period.
- **Increased post-delivery soreness**. The combination of post-extraction pain and denture-related trauma often produces greater discomfort during the first few days after insertion.
- **Greater complexity of clinical procedures** (i.e. border molding & final impressions are more difficult when natural teeth remain).
- **Higher total cost of treatment due** to the need for relines and repeated equilibration of the occlusion.

Immediate dentures should be scheduled for **RELINES at 5 months and 10 months** post-extraction to **compensate for contour changes**. Re-contouring of the healing ridge progresses rapidly for 4-6 months and does not stabilize in form until 10-12 months post-extraction. Due to this, immediate dentures become progressively more ill-fitting. This is a general timeline, as each case must be evaluated monthly and if necessary, relines performed.

RELINE INDICATIONS – any denture when diagnostic information indicates a reline a will effectively solve the patient's chief complaint (when the denture record base adaptation is the major defect in the prosthesis.

RELINE CONTRAINDICATIONS – excessive over-closure of vertical dimension (**a large decrease in VDO**). In this case, new dentures are indicated at the proper vertical dimension.

NOTES

After relining dentures, if a patient constantly returns for adjustments due to sore spots on the ridge, check the occlusion because the relining may have changed the CR contacts.

INTERIM PARTIAL DENTURES CAN CAUSE TISSUE IRRITATION

 IMMEDIATE DENTURES – remove posterior teeth and allow tissue to heal to provide an area for support. Can keep the premolars to provide a VDO reference point.

OVERDENTURES

COMPLETE OVERDENTURE – a denture whose base is constructed to cover all of an existing residual ridge and selected roots. Retained roots help prevent resorption of the alveolar ridges, improve denture retention, and allow the patient some proprioceptive sense of "naturalness" in function of the dentures. **MOST important benefit of an overdenture (root-retained denture) is PRESERVATION OF THE ALVEOLAR RIDGE.**

- **It is not always necessary to cover a root beneath an overdenture.** However, if a root is not covered, the exposed surfaces are highly susceptible to decay. The patient's oral hygiene must be impeccable to prevent root decay.
- **Retained roots are the most common findings** when taking routine panoramic radiographs or patients who wear complete dentures (not necessarily over-dentures).
- For overdentures, retain **mandibular canines bilaterally because they provide SUPPORT, NOT retention** (a locator provides retention).

OCCLUSION

ARCON ARTICULATOR (ARTICULATED CONDYLE) – an articulator with its condylar elements on the LOWER member of the articulator and condylar path elements on the UPPER member. The angle between the condylar inclination and occlusal plane is FIXED on this articulator. **ANGLE BETWEEN CONDYLAR INCLINATION & OCCLUSAL PLANE REMAINS CONSTANT (MORE ACCURATE).**

- **Commonly used for diagnostic mounting of study casts** to allow examination of occlusal contacts in the retruded contact position and analysis of tooth contacts during excursive movements of the mounted models.
- Occlusal records in right and left lateral excursions are necessary for setting both the medial and superior condylar guides.
- Fabrication of cast and porcelain restorations to ensure correct tooth contacts in occlusion and mandibular movements.

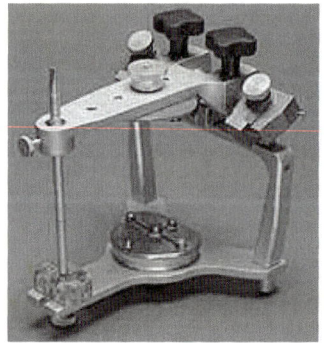

NON-ARCON ARTICULATOR (NON-ARTICULATED CONDYLE) – has condylar elements on the upper member and condylar path elements on the lower member.
- Angle between condylar inclination and occlusal plane is **NOT CONSTANT (NOT FIXED) WHEN OPEN vs. CLOSED (LESS ACCURATE)**. This design is more popular to fabricate dentures.
- **Non-adjustable**-has a SMALL AXIS OF ROTATION.
- **Semi-adjustable**-gives a closer approximation of the axis of rotation & teeth and does not allow intermediate tracking of condylar elements.
- **Fully adjustable**: reproduces ALL border movements including progressive side shift and immediate side shift (BENNET'S MOVEMENT).

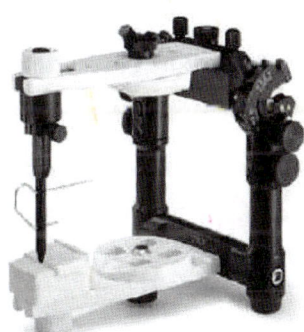

WORKING SIDE – teeth on the side the mandible is moving toward. When the mandible moves to the right and maxillary and mandibular teeth on the RIGHT side is the working side. For acceptable working contact, a denture must have the canine and at least 4 other cusps contacting the opposing teeth.

BALANCING SIDE – the side OPPOSITE to the side the mandible is moving toward. When the mandible moves to the right, the maxillary and mandibular teeth on the LEFT is the balancing side (with natural teeth, the balancing side = non-working side). For acceptable balancing side contact, at least 3 cusps must touch, but NOT THE CANINE.

PROTRUSIVE – forward movement of the mandible during which there must be at least 3 points of contact (the anterior incisor, and one tooth on EACH side of the arch as far posterior as possible).
- **Protrusive record**, records the relation of the maxilla & mandible, and is used to set the horizontal condylar guidance on the articulator. Made with mandibular anterior teeth 6mm forward of CR, or with mandibular & maxillary anterior teeth edge-to-edge).
- **Christensen's Phenomenon**-the space that opens b/t posterior teeth during anterior movement of the mandible. Amount of posterior separation is affected by both the incisal guidance and the horizontal condylar guidance.
- **Protrusive Movement**-accomplished when the mandible is moved straight forward until the maxillary and mandibular incisors contact "edge-to-edge". This movement is bilaterally symmetrical in that both sides of the mandible move in the same direction. **The mandible can protrude ~10mm.**

CURVE OF SPEE (MAXILLARY ARCH) – anterior-posterior curve from incisors to molars is **CONVEX** with respect to the maxillary arch and concave with respect to the mandibular arch.
- **Compensating Curve**-the **anteroposterior and lateral curvature** in the alignment of the occluding surfaces and incisal edges of artificial teeth which is used to develop a balanced occlusion. The form of the compensating curve is **entirely under the dentist's control** (i.e. if during a try-in evaluation a dentist notes that a protrusive excursion movement results in the separation of posterior teeth, the problem can be corrected by simply increasing the compensating curve).
- Compensating curve allows the dentist to **alter** the effective cusp angulation without changing the form of the manufactured denture teeth. The **function of this curve** is to **help provide a balanced occlusion**. A prominent compensating curve is required when there is a steep condylar path associated with a low degree of incisal guidance.

CURVE OF WILSON – mesio-distal concave curve across from one side of the mandibular arch to the other side.

BILATERAL BALANCED OCCLUSION – the stable **simultaneous contact of opposing upper & lower teeth** in CR position with a smooth bilateral gliding contact to any eccentric position within the normal range of mandibular function, developed to lessen or **limits tipping or rotation** of denture bases in relation to the supporting structures. **MAXIMUM NUMBER OF TEETH CONTACT IN ALL EXCURSIONS (CENTRIC & ECCENTRIC POSITIONS) for DENTURE STABILITY**. Posterior Teeth Contacts in a Balanced Occlusion:
- Cusp-to-fossa contact in centric occlusion (MICP) in an ideal Class I occlusion.
- During lateral excursions, opposing cusps contact on the **WORKING SIDE**.
- During lateral excursions, on the balancing side, maxillary lingual cusps (lingual inclines) contact mandibular facial cusps (lingual inclines).

Balanced occlusion occurs when a complete denture has balance on the working side, non-working side, and in protrusion. This assumes the denture has been constructed in proper CR and VDO. **BILATERAL BALANCED IS THE OCCLUSION FOR COMPLETE DENTURES**.

5 Factors Govern Establishing Balanced Articulation (some of these, if not all, are controlled by the dentist):
1. **Inclination of the condylar guidance** which is **completely dictated by the PATIENT**.
2. Inclination of the incisal guidance (horizontal and vertical overlap).
3. Inclination of the occlusal plane (plane of orientation).
4. Convexities of the **compensating curve**.
5. Angle and height of cusps.

GROUP FUNCTION ("UNILATERAL BALANCED OCCLUSION") – **ALL TEETH ON THE WORKING SIDE CONTACT DURING WORKING MOVEMENT**. ONLY working side contacts from anterior and posterior teeth and **no non-working side contacts**.
- **ALL** posterior teeth on a side contact evenly as the jaw moves toward that side (working side). All teeth on the non-working side **DO NOT** contact. Only teeth on the working side contact during a lateral excursion.
- Non-working (balancing) interferences: occur on **inner inclines of FACIAL** cusps of mandibular molars.
- Working side (non-balancing) interferences: occur inner aspects of **LINGUAL** cusps of maxillary molars.
- **Protrusive Interferences**-occur between **DISTAL inclines** of **FACIAL cusps** of maxillary posterior teeth and **MESIAL inclines** of **FACIAL cusps** of mandibular posterior teeth. Purpose of making a record of protrusive relation is to register the condylar path and adjust the condylar guides of the articulator so they equal the patient's condylar paths.

VERTICAL DIMENSION OF OCCLUSION

In a complete denture patient, when the **teeth, occlusal rims, and central bearing point are in contact**, and the mandible is in CR, the **LENGTH of the face** is the **occlusal vertical dimension**.

Correct VDO is evaluated using 4 methods:
1. evaluating overall appearance of facial support.
2. visual observation of space between the occlusal rims at rest.
3. measurment b/t dots on the face (**placed on the tip of nose and chin with a Thompson stick**) when the jaws are at rest and when the rims are in contact.
4. observation when "s" sound is enunciated accurately and repeatedly to ensure adequate speaking space between the occlusal rims/occlusal plane.

Excessive VDO may result in trauma to underlying supporting tissues. A **CLOSED vertical dimension** is the most likely **cause of CHEILOSIS** in patients who wear a complete denture with a non-contributory medical history.
- **Establish the VDO BEFORE making a CR record.**
- Teeth contact during swallowing, but NOT during speech. If teeth touch during speaking, VDO is too great.

When the mandible is in it's physiologic rest (postural position), TEETH DO NOT CONTACT. Physiologic rest position occurs when the mandible and all of its supporting muscles (8 muscles of mastication + suprahyoids & infrahyoids) are in their resting posture (there is muscular equilibrium). This **lack of tooth contact is the "freeway space" or "interocclusal distance" and averages 2-6mm**. This position is a "muscle-guided" position and is the beginning and end point of most mandibular movements.

INTEROCCLUSAL DISTANCE ("FREEWAY SPACE") – the **vertical distance** or space created when the mandible is in its physiologic rest position between incisal and occluding surfaces of maxillary and mandibular teeth or occlusion rims. **NEVER INCREASE the freeway space more than 1.5mm**.
- Rest position of the mandible (postural position) is determined mostly by musculature. The usual reflex cited as the basis for the mandible's postural position is the **tonic stretch reflex** of the elevator muscles. The rest position is a **"muscle-guided"** position.

VERTICAL DIMENSION OF OCCLUSION (VDO) – the vertical length of the face as measured between tow arbitrary selected points (one above and one below the mouth) when the teeth or any substitute material (occlusal rims) are in contact in CR. **Phonetics** and **esthetics** help verify a patient's **vertical dimension of occlusion**.

EXCESSIVE VERTICAL DIMENSION (VDO) – may result from trauma to underlying supporting tissues (denture patient), straining of the elevator/closing muscles, and adversely affects interocclusal clearance (decreased freeway space) causing loss of interocclusal distance in the rest position. Excessive vertical dimension is **the usual causes of CLICKING OF DENTURE TEETH** (to treat remount and fabricate a new complete denture).
- Clicking of dentures **can also be caused by lack of retention of the maxillary & mandibular dentures**. To treat, **if due to underextension**, border mold and reline. **If due to overextension**, reduce as indicated with PIP and disclosing wax.
- **Porcelain teeth can also cause denture clicking**. To treat, use acrylic resin teeth. **Increased VDO** is the usual cause of **contacting/clicking** of posterior teeth when a patient speaks.

DECREASED VERTICAL DIMENSION (VDO) – an occluding vertical dimension causing **EXCESSIVE INTER-OCCLUSAL DISTANCE (increased freeway space)** when the mandible is in the physiological rest position.

- **Example**: people with no teeth or who have worn dentures for a long time present with the lower portion of the face scrunched up, or do not show their lips anymore (poor facial profile). **To correct, make new dentures and increase VDO**. This decreases inter-occlusal distance (freeway space).
- **DECREASED VDO** often results in **CHEEK BITING**.

Factors to consider when verifying VDO:
- Pre-extraction records
- Amount of interocclusal distance (freeway space) to which the patient was previously accustomed.
- Esthetics (facial harmony and facial expression are considered).
- Phonetics (speech sounds).
- Length of the lip in relation to the teeth.
- Condition and amount of shrinkage of the ridges.

VERTICAL DIMENSION OF REST (VDR) – the vertical length of the face measured between two arbitrary points (1 point above & 1 below the mouth) when the mandible is in the rest position. In a physiologically healthy individual, there is always a vertical space between the teeth (freeway space) when the mandible is in the rest position. This position is important in complete denture fabrication because it provides a guide to the **VDO**.
VDR = Vertical Dimension of Occlusion (VDO) + Interocclusal Distance.

Balanced Centric Occlusion in partial dentures is necessary for appliance stability. The framework's design and relationship of the teeth to the ridges also influence RPD stability.

Bilateral Eccentric Occlusion is **NOT an objective in RPD construction**, UNLESS **the partial prosthesis is opposed by a complete denture**. The vertical relation for RPDs is usually determined by the remaining natural teeth (unlike complete dentures).

TEMPOROMANDIBULAR JOINT (TMJ) – **a combined hinge & gliding joint (ginglymoarthrodial joint)** that permits both hinge-like rotation and gliding (sliding) movements. Ginglymus means "rotation" and arthrodial means "freely movable".

- In the **lower (condyle-disc) compartment**, **only a hinge-type (rotary motion) can occur**. This rotational or terminal hinge-axis opening of the mandible is possible only when the mandible is retruded in CR with a conscious effort by the patient or by the dentist's control. A pure hinging movement is possible only in the terminal hinge position.
- In the **upper compartment (mandibular fossa-disc) only sliding movements (translation) can occur**. When the lateral pterygoid muscles contact simultaneously, the discs and condyles slide forward down over the articular eminence (protrusion), or can move backwards together (retrusion) during opening and closing of the mouth, respectively.

Muscles Acting on the TMJ:
- **Elevator Muscles (Close) mandible**: masseter, medial pterygoid, & temporalis (anterior fibers). Posterior fibers of temporalis **retract the mandible**. If the mandible fractures, UPWARD displacement of the fractured segment would be caused by the elevator muscles (masseter, medial pterygoid, & temporalis).
- **Depressor Muscles (Open) mandible/mouth**: lateral pterygoid, anterior belly of digastric, & omohyoid.
- **Protrusion Muscles**: lateral pterygoids together (individually, lateral pterygoids cause **lateral excursion**). Lateral pterygoids are mainly responsible for **positioning and translating the condyles**.

CENTRIC RELATION ("RETRUDED CONTACT POSITION") – a "ligament-guided" position that is the **supero-anterior position of the condyle** along the **articular eminence of the condyle with the articular disc interposed between the condyle and eminence**. This position is an optimum relative position between all anatomic components, and is a REPEATABLE reference position to mount casts on the articulator.

- CR is the **most unstrained, retruded anatomic and functional position of the mandibular condyle heads in the mandibular glenoid fossae of the TMJs**. **CR is a "bone-to-bone" relationship** (bones of the upper and lower jaws) **independent of tooth contact**. The presence or absence of teeth and type of occlusion are not factors.
- Malposed or super-erupted teeth can cause a discrepancy between CR & CO, so opposing teeth should not contact when making a CR record to mount diagnostic casts because the contact causes the mandible to deflect or move away from CR.
- Mandible cannot be forced into CR from the rest position because the patient's reflex neuromuscular defense would resist the applied force. Rather, the mandible should be relaxed and gently guided into CR.
- To place a patient in CR, have the patient swallow, turning the tongue upward towards the palate, relax the jaw muscles, or protruding and retruding the mandible can be effective ways to help record CR.
- In fixed and removable prosthodontics, CR should be established PRIOR to designing the frameworks.
- When a CR record is taken in the natural dentition, imprints of the teeth should be confined to CUPS TIPS and the registration material should not be perforated.
- CR is a "ligament-guided" position. CR is the closing end-point of the retruded border movement (terminal-hinge movement).
- Transverse Horizontal Axis (Terminal Hinge Position)-the one relation of the condyles to the fossae in which a pure hinging movement is possible.
- In complete denture prosthodontics, the position of the planned MIC of the teeth in centric occlusion is established to coincide with the patient's CR (CO = CR).

Primary Requirements for making a CENTRIC RELATION record when fabricating a RPD:
- Record the correct horizontal relation of the mandible to the maxilla.
- Stabilize the lower record base with equalized vertical pressure.
- Retain the record in an undistorted condition until the casts have been accurately mounted on the articulator or until a previous record can be verified.

Materials used to record jaw relationships have varied widely over the years. An ideal recording medium is easy to handle, uniformly soft while the record is being made, rapid setting, and totally rigid but not brittle when set. Rapid setting plaster **zinc oxide & eugenol pastes, and modeling plastic are ideal. Avoid** soft waxes as a recording material because they **never become rigid** and are likely to distort during the cast mounting procedure.

If sufficient natural posterior occlusion exists, the mandibular cast may be mounted in CO using a ZOE reinforced wax bite. **In the case of a distal extension RPD, base plates and occlusion rims should be placed on the framework, and the patient closed into softened recording wax or zinc oxide-eugenol paste (preferred).** Whether this record will be in CO or CR depends on the case, and is dictated by the presence or absence of any natural posterior occlusion in the patient.

CENTRIC OCCLUSION (MICP) – a "tooth-guided" position defined as the maximum intercuspation of the teeth. During typical "empty mouth swallowing" the mandible is braced in the inter-cuspal position.
- **Empty mouth swallowing** occurs frequently during the day and is an important to rid the mouth of saliva, and moisten the oral structures. The hourly rate of non-masticatory swallowing is related to the amount of salivary flow and is usually an involuntary reflex activity.
- **Masseter muscles contract** and the tongue tip touches the roof of the mouth during normal swallowing.
- **Tooth contacts are longer during swallowing than chewing**, but this varies among people.

ARTICULATION – relationship of teeth during movements into and away from the eccentric position, while the teeth contact.

CONDYLAR GUIDANCE – a factor **TOTALLY dictated by the patient**. It is the mechanical device on an articulator intended to produce similar guidances in articulator movement that are produced by the condyle paths during mandibular movements.
- **Condylar guidance is completely dictated by the patient and cannot be varied or "adjusted" by the dentist.**
- **The inclination of condylar guidance depends on**: shape & size of the bony contour of the TMJ (fossae and disc), action of the muscles attached to the mandible, limiting effects of the ligaments, and the method used for registration.
- The incline (angulation) of the condylar element on the articulator is anatomically related to the slope of the condylar articular eminences (condylar inclination).
- When adjusting the condylar guidance for protrusive relationship, the incisal guide pin on the articulator should be raised out of contact with the incisal guide table. **The protrusive record is probably the LEAST reproducible maxillomandibular record.**
- When restoring the entire mouth with crowns, the protrusive condylar path inclination influences the mesial inclines of the mandibular cusps.
- **RETRUSIVE MOVEMENT** requires the condyles to move **BACKWARD & UPWARD**.
- **LATERAL MOVEMENTS**, the working condyle moves **down, forward, and laterally**, and non-working condyles move **down, forward, and medially**.
- The inclination of the condylar path during protrusive movement forms an average angle of ~30° with the horizontal reference plane. If the protrusive inclination is steep, the cusp height may be obviously longer. If the inclination is shallow, the cusp will be shorter. **This factor is the MOST important aspect of condylar guidance that affects the selection of posterior teeth with appropriate cusp height.**
- In complete dentures, the condyle path during free mandibular movements is governed mainly by the **SHAPE of the fossa and meniscus (articular disc) and the muscular influence**.

Determinants of Occlusion:
- Right & left TMJs
- **Occlusal surfaces of teeth and the neuromuscular system**. The concepts of occlusal arrangement aim to place artificial teeth in harmony with the TMJ and neuromuscular system. If done properly, it results in minimum stress on the teeth and requires minimal effort by the neuromuscular system when performing mandibular movements. Optimal occlusion requires minimum adaptation by the patient.

4 Dentition Features that Directly Effect PDL Health & Hard Tissue Anchorage to Resist Occlusal Force:
1. anterior teeth have slight or no contact in MICP (intercuspal position).
2. occlusal table is < 60% of the overall F-L width of the tooth.
3. occlusal table is at right angles to the tooth's long axis.
4. mandibular molar crowns are inclined 15-20° toward the lingual.

4 Theoretical Determinants Required to Restore a Complete & Functional Occlusal Surface of a Tooth:
1. Amount of vertical overlap of **anterior teeth**. The anterior determinant of occlusion is the horizontal and vertical overlap relationship of the anterior teeth.
2. Contour of the **articular eminence**.
3. Amount and direction of lateral shift in the **working side condyle**.
4. **Tooth position** in the arch.

However, the jaw relationship most commonly used in the ACTUAL design of restorations is the ACQUIRED centric occlusion. The height of the pulp horn of a particular tooth is NOT a required determinant to restore a complete and functional occlusal surface.

OCCLUSAL PLANE – an imaginary surface related anatomically to the cranium and theoretically touches the incisal edges of the incisors and tips of the occluding surfaces of the posterior teeth. It is not really a plane, but represents the mean curvature of the surface.
- Anterior point of the occlusal plane is determined by the position of the anterior teeth.
- Posterior determinants are anatomical landmarks (2/3 the heights of the retromolar pads). Thus, it is debatable as to the extent of control the dentist may exercise over the orientation of the occlusal plane.

CUSP INCLINATION – angle made by the slopes of a cusp with a perpendicular line bisecting the cusp, measured mesiodistally or buccolingually. Cusp inclination is under the dentist's control (choosing 30° teeth, monoplane teeth, etc.).
- In a **protrusive** condylar movement (protrusion), interferences can occur between DISTAL inclines of maxillary posterior cusps and MESIAL inclines of mandibular posterior cusps.
- In a protrusive movement, the mandibular condyles move **DOWNWARD & FORWARD**.
- During protrusive movement, there are occlusal contacts occurring on the maxillary distal inclines and mandibular mesial inclines. Anteriorly, the facial surface of the mandibular incisors will contact the guiding inclines (lingual) of the maxillary incisors and canines.
- In any restorative case involving ALL teeth in the mouth, the protrusive condylar path inclination will have its primary influence on the same inclines (distal of maxillary & mesial of mandibular).
- The pathway followed by the anterior teeth during protrusion may not be smooth or straight because of contact between the anterior teeth and sometimes the posterior teeth.
- Centric Interference (Forward Slide)-corrected by grinding MESIAL INCLINES of maxillary teeth and DISTAL INCLINES of mandibular teeth.
- **This group function of teeth on the working side evenly distributes the occlusal load**. While, the lack of contact on the non-working side prevents those teeth from receiving destructive, obliquely directed forces found in non-working interferences, and saves the centric holding cusps (i.e. mandibular buccal cusps and maxillary cusps) from excessive wear. The advantage is the **maintenance of the occlusion**.

MUTUALLY PROTECTED OCCLUSION ("CANINE GUIDED" OR ORGANIC OCCLUSION) – anterior teeth protect the posterior teeth in all mandibular excursions. Canines DISCLUDE the posterior teeth during working and non-working movements.
- Canine Guidance is **an occlusal relationship exists where the vertical overlap of maxillary & mandibular canines causes disclusion (separation) of ALL posterior teeth when the mandible moves to either side**. All other teeth do not contact once they move from CR. If there is contact of other teeth, "working side" or "non-working side" interferences occur depending on which side the mandible moves towards.
- When placing a crown on a maxillary canine, if you change a canine protected occlusion to group function, you increase the chance for "non-working side" interferences.

ANTERIOR GUIDANCE (ANTERIOR COUPLING) – result of horizontal & vertical overlap of anterior teeth. A tightly overlapping relationship of opposing maxillary and mandibular incisors and canines that **DISCLUDE the posterior teeth** when the mandible protrudes and moves in lateral excursion. Anterior guidance also affects the surface morphology of posterior teeth. **The greater overlap, the longer the cusp height**.

INCISAL GUIDANCE – a measure of the amount of movement and the angle at which the lower incisors and mandible must move from the overlapping position of centric occlusion to an edge-to-edge relationship with the maxillary incisors. **Incisal guidance is the second end-controlling factor in articulator movement and is to some degree, under the dentist's control.** Influencing factors are esthetics, phonetics, ridge relations, arch space, and inter-ridge space.
- **Esthetics & phonetics** are the main factors the LIMIT a dentist's control of incisal guidance.
- Incisal guidance on the articulator is the mechanical equivalent of horizontal and vertical overlap.

SUPPORTING CUSPS ("STAMP CUSPS" OR "CENTRIC CUSPS") – these cusps contact the opposing teeth in their corresponding F-L center on a marginal ridge or fossa. These cusps are **more robust** and **better suited to CRUSH food**. When posterior teeth are in a normal ideal relationship, **maxillary lingual cusps** + **mandibular buccal cusps** are considered the **SUPPORTING CUSPS**.
- **Centric stops** - areas of contact that a supporting cusp makes with opposing teeth (i.e. the ML cups of the maxillary 1st molar (a supporting cusp) makes contact with the **central fossae (centric stop)** of the mandibular 1st molar.

5 Characteristics of Supporting Cusps:
1. **contact the opposing tooth** in the intercuspal position.
2. support the **vertical dimension** of the face.
3. are **closer to the F-L center of the tooth** than non-supporting cusps.
4. their outer incline has a potential for contact.
5. have **broader, more rounded cusp ridges** than non-supporting cusps.

NON-SUPPORTING CUSPS ("GUIDING" OR "SHEARING" CUSPS) – **maxillary buccal (facial) cusps + mandibular lingual cusps**. These cusps overlap the opposing tooth without contacting the tooth and have **narrower and sharper cusp ridges** that serve to **SHEAR** food as they pass close to the supporting cusp ridges during chewing strokes.
- The inner occlusal inclines leading to the guiding cusps are "**guiding inclines**" because in contact movements, they guide supporting cusps away from the midline. Thus, there are the bucco-occlusal inclines (lingual inclines of buccal cusps) of the maxillary posterior teeth, and the linguo-occlusal inclines (buccal inclines of lingual cusps) of the mandibular posterior teeth.

In a posterior **cross-bite situation, supporting and guiding cusps are opposite**. The maxillary buccal and mandibular lingual cusps are now the supporting cusps and the maxillary lingual and mandibular buccal are the guiding cusps.

SELECTIVE GRINDING – the reduction of occlusal interferences usually done **BEFORE** constructing a fixed bridge or denture for a patient to **PREVENT** duplicating the deflective occlusal contacts in the final restoration. The purpose of selective grinding is to remove all interferences without destroying cusp height. Thus, when interferences exist in centric, but not in lateral excursions, the fossa or marginal ridge opposing the premature cusp is deepened. It is important that whenever a prematurity is found, the occlusion be checked in all centric positions before any adjustment is made. If cusps interfere with each other in excursions, then only the non-holding cusps are ground to prevent a decrease in VDO.

- A common case where it is preferable to selectively grind **AFTER** a fixed bridge or RPD is in place is when a FPD or RPD is to be constructed for a space over which the opposing tooth has extruded slightly. The bridge or partial is frequently constructed to the ideal plane of occlusion and the opposing tooth is adjusted after insertion.
- The most common complaint after cementation of a fixed bridge is **sensitivity to hot & cold and indicates a deflective occlusal contact**. The involved teeth may be sensitive to touch and when brushing. In these cases, an immediate correction of occlusion must be made.
- **Important**: if you plan on changing a patient's vertical dimension using crowns, it is critical to mount the casts on the true hinge axis (face bow).

With Selective Grinding in Complete Denture Fabrication in Centric Relation (CR):
- Secondary centric holding cusps are the mandibular buccal cusps. Grind these cusps only if there is a balancing side interference. (non-working side)
- **Primary centric holding cusps are the maxillary lingual cusps. Never grind these cusps.**
- Ideally, selective grinding should result in harmonious cusp-fossa contacts of all upper and lower fossa (and marginal ridges of premolars). Do **NOT** grind the upper lingual or lower buccal cusps. A forward slide from CR can be corrected by grinding the mesial inclines of maxillary teeth and distal inclines of mandibular teeth.
- Selective grinding of inner inclines of secondary centric holding cusps is done if a **balancing (non-working) side** interference exists.
- **Only grind cusp tips on maxillary buccal & mandibular lingual (BULL) cusps if they are premature in centric, lateral, or protrusive movements.** Check before grinding.
- **Selective Grinding in Working Side (non-balancing side) Relation**: the rule for selective grinding interferences during working side movements follows the rule of **BULL** (buccal cusp inner inclines of **upper** teeth & **lingual** cusp inner inclines of **lower** teeth).
- **Selective Grinding in Non-Working Side (balancing side) Relation**: grind the inner inclines of mandibular buccal cusps, and **NEVER GRIND MAXILLARY LINGUAL CUSPS** (primary centric holding cusps).

Basic Principles of Occlusal Adjustment:
1. The **maximum distribution of occlusal stresses** in centric relation (CR).
2. **Forces of occlusion** should be borne as much as possible by the long axis of teeth.
3. When surface-to-surface contact of flat cusps occurs, it should be changed to a "point-to-surface" contact (the cusp tip of the tooth occludes with the flat surface of it's opposing tooth's cusp).
4. When centric occlusion is established, **NEVER take the teeth out of centric occlusion**.
5. **Never adjust cusp tips**. Only marginal ridges and fossa.

DENTURE TEETH SELECTION

SMILE LINE (INCISAL CURVE) – composed on the incisal edges of maxillary anteriors and parallels the inner curvature of the lower lip. **Parallel with the inter-pupillary axis and perpendicular to the midline (middle of the face).**

- **PHI (1.618:1)** EACH NUMBER IS THE SUM OF THE TWO NUMBERS PRECEEDING IT. The size of the front teeth should become progressively smaller as you proceed toward the back of the mouth in the ratio of 1.6 to 1.0 to 0.6 = **Golden Proportion**.

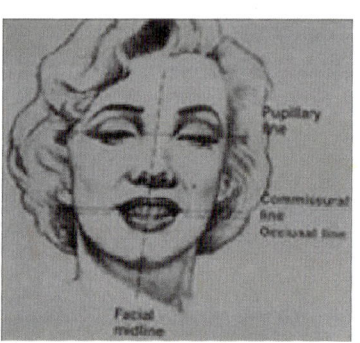 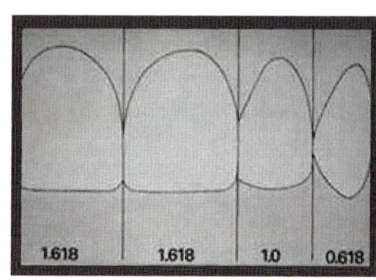

- Long axis of posterior teeth are inclined toward the LINGUAL.
- Long axis of maxillary incisor crowns CONVERGE slightly toward the midline.
- There should be slight irregularities on either side of the midline, even though the teeth are similar in size, shape, and alignment.
- In younger patients, maxillary incisors are more prominent, while mandibular incisors are more visible with age.

Guides for selecting artificial denture teeth for edentulous patients: pre-extraction records, teeth of close relatives, diagnostic casts, radiographs, photographs, extracted teeth, and following the lines placed on the occlusal rims.

Rules for Setting Teeth:
- Incisal edges of maxillary central incisors and cusp tips of canines lie on the SAME CURVED LINE with the incisal edges of lateral incisors 1mm above the same line.
- Interproximal contacts of the maxillary anterior teeth are situated progressively closer to the gingiva the more distal they are from the midline.
- Incisal embrasure become progressively LARGER from the central incisor, lateral, to canine (the more posterior you go). Incisal embrasures in younger patients become smaller, sometimes to the point of disappearing as the teeth wear.
- MANDIBULAR POSTERIOR teeth are placed over the crest of the residual ridge. MAXILLAR POSTERIOR functional cusps are placed in the fossae of mandibular teeth, and can be no farther than the facial vestibule.
- MAXILLARY ANTERIOR teeth are set FACIAL to the ridge for phonetics and esthetics. Canine cups tips should be parallel to the posterior border of the incisive papilla. MANDIBULAR ANTERIOR teeth are set base on the maxillary anterior teeth.

Primary role of ANTERIOR TEETH on a denture is ESTHETICS. Spaces, lapping, rotation, and color changes can be judiciously used to create a natural appearance.

Setting anterior teeth too far lingually or facially to satisfy esthetic concerns should NOT be done. When selecting teeth, pre-extraction records are extremely valuable. **Maxillary and mandibular anterior teeth should NOT contact in centric relation.** Setting maxillary and mandibular anterior teeth so they contact in CR produces an unsatisfactory arrangement of artificial teeth for complete dentures.

Error that most often contribute to poor denture esthetics is placing maxillary anterior teeth directly over the edentulous ridge. Maxillary anterior denture teeth should be placed slightly ANTERIOR to the ridge.

The outline of anterior teeth should harmonize with the face form. Convex profile faces should have a similar convex labial surface of anterior teeth. Broader contact areas of teeth look more natural on dentures as they are more compatible with aging.

For best esthetics, maxillary anterior teeth in a complete denture are arranged **FACIAL TO THE RIDGE**. Setting anterior teeth directly over the ridge causes poor esthetics. Also, it is important to have accurate adaptation of the border seal and adequate bulk of the maxillary facial flange for good esthetics. VDO also affects the lip support. **Maxillary central incisors are the MOST important teeth for esthetics.** Their placement controls the midline, speaking line, lip support, and smiling line composition.

For most patients, the labial surface of the central incisor should be ~8mm anterior to the center of the incisive papilla. The labioincisal 1/3 of maxillary central incisors should support the lower lip when the teeth are in occlusion.

FUNCTIONAL needs overshadow esthetic needs when selecting **POSTERIOR TEETH**. Do not set mandibular molars over the ascending area of the mandible as occlusal forces in the area dislodge the mandibular denture.

Size of POSTERIOR TEETH for a RPD is determined primarily by the amount of useful posterior tooth space and characteristics of the denture-supporting tissues. Other factors relevant to selecting posterior RPD teeth include:
1. **Occluso-gingival length:** MOST important factor to determine posterior tooth length is available inter-arch space.
2. **M-D width:** the total MD space available for posterior teeth is determined by measuring from the distal of the lower canine to the point where the mandibular residual ridge begins to slope upward.
3. **B-L width:** the BL width is narrowed in relation to the missing natural tooth. Reducing the area of the occlusal table decreases stress transferred to the denture support area during food bolus penetration. Also, reducing the B-L width increases tongue space.
4. **Shade:** posterior tooth shade of is usually selected to harmonize with the anterior teeth.
5. **Occlusal surface form:** no superior tooth form or arrangement is identified. Thus, it is logical to use the least complicated approach that fulfills the patient's needs.
6. **Materials:** plastic bonds well to acrylic resin. Thus, plastic teeth are retained better than porcelain teeth. **Primary reason for using PLASTIC teeth** in a denture is because **plastic teeth are retained well in acrylic resin.**

Common Errors Made When Arranging Denture Teeth:
- Setting mandibular anterior teeth too far forward to meet the maxillary teeth.
- Failure to make canines the turning point of the arch.
- Setting mandibular first premolars buccal to the canines.
- Establishing the occlusal plane by an arbitrary line on the face.
- Not rotating anterior teeth enough to give an adequately narrower effect.

Lower 1/3 of a patient's face appears too short and there is apparent loss of the vermilion border of the lips. The procedure indicated to correct this situation is **increasing occlusal vertical dimension (VDO)**.

Errors in occlusion are checked most accurately by **REMOUNTING** the dentures on the articulator using remount casts and new inter-occlusal records.

Potential Problems with New Dentures:
1. **Cheek Biting** is caused by:
   - **Posterior teeth set edge-to-edge**. Treat by reducing BUCCAL CUSPS of mandibular molars to create proper horizontal overlap.
   - **Inadequate VDO**. Treat by relining dentures at the corrected VDO, CR remount, and fabricate a new denture.
   - **Biting corners of the mouth**. Treat by RESET CANINES & PREMOLARS.
2. **Lip Biting** - caused by reduced muscle tone and/or a large anterior horizontal overlap (overbite).
3. **Tongue Biting** - caused by having posterior teeth **set too far lingually**.
4. **Generalized speech difficulty with complete dentures** is usually caused by faulty tooth position and/or faulty palatal contours.
   - Speech problems due to faulty tooth position are avoided by placing the denture teeth as close as possible to the position of the natural teeth. Note: the most effective time to test for phonetics is at the time of the wax try-in of the trial denture (usually the 4th appointment).
   - Faulty palatal contours are corrected by trial and error. Add wax to increase contours and remove wax to improve articulation of sounds.

PHOENETICS

Patients edentulous for many years often have more distorted speech than patients edentulous for a short time due to a loss of tonus of the tongue musculature.

"S" Sound: mandibular incisal edges should be even with or just lingual the maxillary teeth incisal edges. Formed when the **tip of their tongue** approaches the anterior palate and lingual surfaces of maxillary teeth. **These sounds bring the mandible and maxilla close together**. "S" sounds are the speech sounds that **bring the mandible closest to the maxilla**.
- If a patient complains when he/she tries to make an "s" sound, it sounds like "th", the two most probable causes is either the maxillary incisors are set too far palatally, or the palate is made too thick.
- Words with the sibilant sound (hissing sounds) are pronounced correctly with the incisal edges of maxillary and mandibular almost touching. These sounds are usually produced between rest and the occluding position.
- Incisal edges of mandibular incisors are established by occlusal contact with maxillary incisors and by their position 1mm behind (lingual) and 1mm below the maxillary incisal edges when saying "S". Incisal edges of mandibular incisors are 1mm anterior and lingual to maxillary incisal edges when making "S" sound.
- **SIBLANTS (CH, J, S)** - produced by maxillary and mandibular incisors approximating each other. Palate and tongue controlling valve.

"TH" LINGUODENTAL SOUND – tongue should protrude slightly (2-4mm) between maxillary & mandibular anterior teeth to form this sound. Made by putting tongue b/t max and mandibular teeth (1/8 inch (3mm) tip of tongue should be visible.

"F" & "V" LABIODENTAL SOUNDS – formed by incisal edges of the maxillary incisors and lower lip (incisal edges should just touch the wet/dry line of the lower lip).

"P" & "B" LABIAL SOUNDS – are formed totally by the lips. Made by pressure behind the lips. If teeth are not set correctly, it can affect this seal of lips to build-up pressure. P & B sounds are affected by: anterior-posterior position of teeth, incorrect VDO, and labial flange thickness.

"T" & "D" (ANTERIOR LINGUAL PALATAL SOUNDS) – If teeth are set too FAR LINGUAL, "t" sounds like "d". If the teeth are set too FAR LABIAL, then "d" sounds like "t". A patient who wears complete dentures is having difficulty trouble pronouncing the letter "t" due to incorrect positioning of the maxillary incisors. Made by tip of tongue touching the anterior palate.

"K" & "G" VELAR SOUNDS (POSTERIOR LINGUAL PALATAL) – produced when tongue touches posterior palate. Tooth set-up DOES NOT AFFECT VELAR SOUNDS.

A high palatal vault or a constricted palate can cause whistling sounds. Whistling during speech with dentures (complete or RPD that replaces the incisors) can be caused by either **insufficient vertical overlap (overjet), excessive horizontal overlap (overbite), or the area palatal to the incisors is improperly contoured**.

FIXED PARTIAL DENTURES

TEMPORARY (PROVISIONAL) RESTORATIONS MUST PROVIDE:
1. **Pulpal protection**: restoration must be fabricated from a material to prevent conducting temperature extremes. Margins should be adapted well enough to prevent saliva leakage.
2. **Positional stability**: the tooth should not extrude or drift so **INTERPROXIMAL CONTACTS PROVIDE THIS**.
3. **Occlusal function**: the temporary's ability to function occlusally aids in patient comfort & prevents tooth migration, and prevent joint/neuromuscular imbalance.
4. **Easily cleaned**: the temporary must be made of a material and contour that the patient can keep clean.
5. **Non-Impinging Margins**: it is VERY important that the temporary's gingival margins do not impinge on the gingival tissues to prevent inflammation that can cause hypertrophy, gingival recession, bone loss. Margins should be well polished. An OVERHANG can result from a preformed metal or resin provisional improperly contoured, while a CUSTOM PROVISIONAL can cause horizontal overhang if improperly trimmed.
6. **Strength & retention**: temporary must withstand the forces it is subjected to without breaking or coming off.
7. **Esthetics**: if the temporary is on an anterior tooth, it must provide a good cosmetic result.

CUSTOM INDIRECT TECHNIQUE (outside the mouth in the LAB) FOR MAKING TEMPORARY CROWNS IS PREFFERED BECAUSE IT IS MORE ACCURATE, BETTER FIT, & PROTECTS THE PULP because when poly(methyl-methacrylate), is placed on freshly cut dentin, (as in a direct technique), it can cause thermal irritation and acute pulpal inflammation. Can make custom provisionals using over-imperssions, templates, or a thin shell crown.

CROWNS

Principles of tooth preparation for a complete crown:
1. **Retention & Resistance form**:
    - **RETENTION**: prevents removal of the restoration along the path of insertion or long axis of the preparation.
        - Achieved by two opposing vertical surfaces (i.e. buccal & lingual walls).
        - Tooth preparation taper is kept to a minimum to enhance retention (as taper decreases, retention increases).
        - Greater surface area of a preparation, the greater retention (boxes and grooves increase surface area.
        - Maximum retention is achieved when there is only one path of draw.
        - PINS INCREASE RETENTION by increasing length internally and apically (not externally).
    - **RESISTANCE**: prevents DISLODGEMENT of the restoration by forces directed apical or oblique and prevents any movement of the restoration under occlusal (vertical) forces.
2. **Structural durability**
3. **Marginal integrity**
4. **Preservation of tooth structure**.

✈ IDEAL TAPER FOR A CROWN is 5-6° (2.5-3.0° inclination on each opposing axial wall). Axial walls in a crown preparation should taper no more than 3-6°.

GUIDING GROOVES PLACED IN THE CROWN PREPARATION PROVIDE – Resistance to rotation, Retention, & path for seating the crown. MAIN purpose of a buccal or lingual groove in a single crown preparation is IMPROVE CROWN RETENTION.

OCCLUSAL CLEARANCE is one of the most important features to provide adequate bulk of metal and strength.
- **GOLD Crown** = 1.5mm clearance functional cusps (lingual max, buccal mand). 1mm for non-functional.
- **PFM Crown** = 1.5-2mm functional cusps; 1-1.5mm non-functional cusps.
- **ALL-CERAMIC Crowns** = 2mm clearance on preprations.

A wide **FUNCTIONAL CUSP BEVEL** provides space for adequate bulk of metal and prevents perforation of the metal due to heavy occlusal contact.

PFM Coping Alloys:
1. **High Noble alloys**: used to fabricate metal-ceramic restorations (PFMs) consist of **98% gold, platinum, & palladium (with trace elements)**. These noble alloys (gold, platinum, palladium) do not oxidize on casting. This feature is important in a metal substrate so that oxidation at the metal-porcelain interface is controlled by adding trace elements to the metal (silicon, indium, iridium). This is the BEST TO USE.
    - Gold-Platinum-Palladium; Gold-Palladium-Silver, Gold-Palladium.
2. **Palladium-Silver alloys (Noble)**: 50-60% palladium + 30-40% silver (not a noble metal, thus oxidizes on casting).
3. **Nickel-Chromium alloys (Base metal alloys)**: 70-80% nickel + 15% chromium. These base metal alloys readily oxidize and can create porcelain-to-metal interface problems. Nickel-Chromium; Nickel-Chromium-Beryllium; Cobalt-Chromium.

4 Coping Features:
1. Thickness of metal and joining porcelain. Noble metal (0.3-0.5mm thickness). Base metal (can be as thin as 0.2mm, and must have a higher yield strength and melting temperature).
2. Placement of occlusal and proximal contacts.
3. Extension of the areas to be veneered for porcelain.
4. facial margin design

ABSOLUTE MIMIMUM PORCELAIN THICKNESS is 0.7mm (ideal is 1mm).

CROWN MARGINS:
1. **Bevel (Feather-Edge) Margin**-the best **finishing margin for CAST FULL GOLD restorations**, allowing burnishing and adaptation of the gold to the tooth. However, in practice it is **difficult to read on the impression and die**, and may lead to **inaccurate extension and distortion of the wax pattern**, and subsequent casting, as a result of the thin wax. It also has the **LEAST MARGINAL STRENGTH** to the casting. **An acute edge/angle** with a nearby bulk of metal is the optimum margin for a casting because it is easily burnished to improve crown fit.

2. **Chamfer Margin**-the **PREFERRED FINISHING LINE** for cast full gold restorations. The resultant casting has sufficient marginal strength while allowing the sliding joint at its periphery to minimize the gap between the tooth and preparation, thus reducing the cement thickness. **Combines the advantage of an easily definable margin on the impression and die, with minimal tooth preparation.** Preferred gingival finish line for veneer metal restorations.

3. **Shoulder Margin (Butt Joint)**-finishing line of choice for ALL CERAMIC crowns (porcelain jacket crown). Edge strength of porcelain is low, thus a **BUTT JOINT** is required. Shoulder provides resistance to occlusal forces and minimizes porcelain stresses. The margin is easily read on the impression and die. Main disadvantage is any inaccuracies in the crown fit are reproduced at the margin, causing increased thickness of cement. SHOULDER MARGIN (butt joint) is the **POOREST** finish line used with cast metal restorations.
   - Unlike the PFM restoration which accepts any marginal design (bevel, chamfer, shoulder), marginal tooth preparation for the **ALL-ceramic crown or porcelain jacket crown MUST BE A SHOULDER**.
   - **Radial Shoulder**-a modified form of a shoulder used on all-ceramic crowns that combines maximum support of the ceramic, with a stress-reducing rounded gingioaxial angle.
   - **Heavy Chamfer**-can be used on all-ceramic crowns (but not as good as a shoulder). A bevel can be added for metal restorations.
   - **All-Ceramic Crown** margin design is **INTERNALLY ROUNDED SHOULDER**.
   - Main reason to use porcelain jacket crowns and all-ceramic crowns is ESTHETICS. These crowns can mimic the optical properties of a natural tooth. However, the guidelines for usage, such as tooth preparation are more critical and more complicated than for PFM restorations. It is advisable to use all ceramic crowns only in the anterior region where esthetics is critical.
   - All-ceramic crowns are known for their **LOW FLEXURAL STRENGTH** (this inability to flex is the major weakness of all-ceramic crowns). Their relative tendency to fracture at a minimum deformation. Microscopic surface defects, under load lead to crack propagation and eventually to failure.

4. **Shoulder with a Bevel**-this margin **allows a sliding fit to occur at the margin**, thus may be used on the proximal box of inlays and occlusal shoulder of the mandibular ¾ crowns, or labial margins of PFM crowns (metal ceramic). If these margins are placed in the gingival crevice (subgingival), little display of metal is seen. Can be used for metal-ceramic (PFM) with metal collars. Used as the finish line on the proximal box of inlays and onlays, and occlusal shoulder of onlays and ¾ crowns. Also used for the facial finish line of PFM restorations where gingival esthetics is not critical.

Periodontium remains healthier when crown margins are **ABOVE THE GINGIVAL CREST (SUPRAGINGIVAL),** however, supragingival margins are often not possible due to esthetics or caries, so the margins must be placed subgingivally. **If a margin must be placed subgingivally, the major concern is NOT TO EXTEND the preparation into the tooth's attachment apparatus (invade biologic width).** If the margin extends into the biologic width, a constant gingival irritant occurs and ultimately the crown will fail. In this case, the tooth should have crown lengthening performed PRIOR to final crown preparation.

CROWN LENGTHENING may be done to surgically move the ALVEOLAR CREST **3mm apical to the proposed finish line (margin) to ensure biologic width and prevent periodontal pathology.**

EMERGENCE PROFILE – the axial contour that extends from the base of the sulcus, past the free gingival margin. It extends to the tooth's height of contour to produce a STRAIGHT LINE PROFILE in the gingival 1/3 of the axial surface. **A STRAIGHT LINE ACCESS (EMERGENCE PROFILE) IS THE TX GOAL WHEN RESTORING TEETH, because it facilitates ACCESS FOR GOOD ORAL HYGIENE** (toothbrush bristles can reach into the sulcus).
- The most common error is creating a bulge or excessive convexity.

FEATURES OF THE ANTERIOR PFM:
1. Radial shoulder: periodontal preservation and structural durability.
2. Chamfer: marginal integrity and periodontal preservation.
3. axial reduction: retention and resistance and structural durability.
4. Incisal notch: structural durability.
5. Wing: retention and resistance, & preservation of tooth structure.

PORCELAIN SHADE SELECTION

DENTAL PORCELAIN – a mixture of FELDSPAR (main constituent), QUARTZ, & metallic oxides used to impart proper shade to the porcelain. When feldspar undergoes fusion, it forms a glassy material, which gives porcelain its translucency. It acts as a matrix for the high-fusing quartz, which then forms a refractory skeleton for the other materials to fuse around. Porcelain's compressive strength is GREATER than it's tensile or shear strengths. Dental porcelain restorations are BRITTLE and are not capable of much plastic deformation.

METAMERISM – a phenomenon that causes teeth/porcelain to appear color matched under one light source, but appear very different under another light source (appears different under different lights). This property is important in matching the shade of a PFM crown to a natural tooth.

SHADE of a ceramic crown is matched first based on the color's **value, chroma, then hue**.
1. **Value**-a color's brightness. **The most critical characteristic that is matched first**. Value is the relative amount of lightness or darkness in a color (intensity of a color). In esthetics, the value of a denture tooth depends on the relative whiteness or blackness of its color. Staining a porcelain restoration or using a complementary color will reduce the value. **It is almost impossible to increase the value**. A 60-year old patient, compared to a 25-year old patient is most likely to have teeth with a color that is lower in value and higher in chroma.
2. **Chroma**-a color's strength or saturation. **Aspect of color that indicates the degree of SATURATION** of the hue. The single most important factor in shade matching that is successfully increased by using stains.
3. **Hue**-the basic colors (color families) like red, blue, yellow, green. Drastic changes of hue (color or shade) are often impossible. **Orange stain is most often used to change the hue**.

3 light sources used in the dental office:
1. Natural
2. Incandescent-lacks blue, but increase in RED & YELLOW.
3. Fluorescent-decrease in red, but increase in BLUE & GREEN.

DO NOT place the rubber dam on before selecting the shade. Teeth should be clean and make-up removed from the patient's face.

3 Types of Dental Porcelains:
1. **High-fusing porcelains**-used to manufacture DENTURE TEETH.
2. **Medium-fusing porcelains**-used for all-ceramic and porcelain jacket crowns. Medium fusing porcelains also contain oxides of lithium, magnesium, and phosphate (in addition to silicone dioxide, aluminum oxide, potassium oxide, and sodium oxide).
3. **Low-fusing porcelains**-used for metal-ceramic (PFM) crowns. Aluminum oxide-agent added to low-fusing porcelains during its manufacture to **increase its resistance to "slumping down" during firing**.

PONTIC DESIGN

PONTIC – the suspended member of a fixed bridge that replaces a missing tooth that MUST provide patient comfort, convenient contours for hygiene, and be esthetic.
- Proper design is more important to cleanability and good tissue health than is choice of materials.
- Excessive tissue contact is a major factor in the failure of FPDs.
- Area of contact between pontic & ridge should be small and the part touching the ridge should be CONVEX.
- Pontic tip should not extend past the mucogingival junction to prevent ulceration.
- **Pontic should only touch ATTACHED KERATINIZED GINGIVA to prevent ulcers**.
- Mesial, distal, and lingual gingival embrasure of the pontic should be open for easy cleaning access.
- Pontics placed in the non-appearance zone are there to restore function and prevent drifting.
- **Success or failure of a bridge depends mostly on the pontic design** which is dictated by function, esthetics, ease of cleaning, patient comfort, and the maintenance by the patient of healthy tissues on the edentulous ridge.

NOTES

1. **MODIFIED RIDGE LAP PONTIC:**
   - Pontic of choice in the "APPERANCE ZONE" for maxillary & mandibular FPDs.
   - Uses a ridge lap for minimal ridge contact, but **gives the illusion of being a tooth**.
   - **HAS ALL CONVEX SURFACES FOR EASY CLEANING & PREVENT FOOD IMPACTION.**
   - Ridge contact cannot extend farther lingually than the midline (CREST) of the edentulous ridge.
   - Contact with the tissue should not fall just along the gingivofacial line angle (there should be no space between it and the crest, a debris trap results.
   - Pontic contact with the ridge should be compact, facial to the ridge crest, slightly wider M-D at the facial, and narrower at the lingual aspect.

2. **SADDLE PONTIC (RIDGE LAP):**
   - Forms a large **CONCAVE CONTACT** with the **ridge**. Overlaps the facial and lingual aspects of the ridge.
   - **UNCLEAN & UNCLEANABLE & CAUSES TISSUE INFLAMMATION SO DO NOT USE!**

3. **HYGIENIC PONTIC (SANITARY PONTIC): "FISH BELLY"**
   - **DOES NOT CONTACT THE EDENTULOUS RIDGE.**
   - **PONTIC OF CHOICE IN A NON-APPERANCE ZONE** (replaces mandibular 1st molars).
   - Occlusogingival thickness **must be at LEAST 3mm with adequate space under it for cleaning.**
   - Restores occlusal function and stabilizes adjacent and opposing teeth (prevents drifting).
   - CONVEX in all areas (F-L & M-D) for easy cleaning.
   - Floss passes over smooth round surfaces more easily than it does flat surfaces with sharp angles.
   - **"Arc-Fixed Partial Denture" (Perel Pontic)** = an esthetic modification of the hygienic pontic that veneers visible parts of the pontic with porcelain (occlusal surface and occlusal half of the facial surface which is all of this pontic's facial surface).
     - Pontic has a concave archway M-D and convex underside F-L (HYPERBOLIC PARABOLOID).
     - Added bulk in the connectors decreases stress to the connectors with diminished deflection in the pontic's center with less gold used. Increased access for cleaning.

4. **CONICAL PONTIC:**
   - PONTIC OF CHOICE FOR A **THIN MANDIBULAR RIDGE** in a **non-appearance zone**.
   - **ROUNDED & CLEANABLE** but the tip is small relative to its overall size. When used on a broad, flat ridge it creates large triangular embrasure spaces that collect food.

5. **OVATE PONTIC:**
   - **PONTIC OF CHOICE** with a **BROAD, FLAT RIDGE** giving it the appearance that it is GROWING FROM THE RIDGE. Used where esthetics is a primary concern.
   - It is bluntly rounded (round-ended design that **fits into a ridge depression**) where it contacts the tissue and is set into a ridge concavity. Can extend ¼ into the socket after an extraction. **EXTRACTION SITE PONTIC**

CANTILEVER BRIDGES

CANTILEVER BRIDGE has abutments at ONLY ONE END and a pontic attached at the other end.

INDICATIONS:
- MUST HAVE A VERY STRONG ABUTMENT & MINIMAL OR NO OCCLUSAL CONTACT ON THE PONTIC.
- Pontic can replace a missing **MAXILLARY LATERAL**, but the CANINE MUST be the abutment.
- Pontic can replace a **FIRST PREMOLAR** if full crowns are used on the 2nd premolar and 1st molar abutments.
- Pontic can replace **1st MOLAR** to avoid UNILATERAL RPD OR PREVENT SUPRA-ERUPTION.

3 SITUATIONS TO USE CANTILEVER BRIDGE:
1. **MISSING MAXILLARY LATERAL**: CENTRAL INCISOR IS NEVER AN ABUTMENT IN A CANTILEVER BRIDGE UNLESS a rest seat is prepared on the DISTAL of the central (inlay or metallic rest) AND MESIAL OF THE PONTIC TO PREVENT ROTATION.
2. **MISSING MANDIBULAR 1st PREMOLAR:**
   - 2nd premolar and 1st molar are the abutments and must have full coverage crowns on them.
   - Occlusion must be in the MOST DISTAL FOSSA OF THE PONTIC (1st premolar) b/c shorter lever.
   - Ideal when the 1st molar needs full coverage and the canine is virgin and full coverage is not desirable (cosmetic concern).
3. **Pontic can replace MISSING 1st MOLAR to avoid UNILATERAL RPD OR PREVENT SUPRA-ERUPTION**.
   - BOTH PREMOLARS MUST BE ABUTMENTS & THE PONTIC MUST RESEMBLE A PREMOLAR (not a molar) to decrease the length of the lever arm and minimize stress on the premolar abutments.

In a posterior FPD, a pontic should be: in contact in centric occlusion, may or may not be in contact in working-side movements, and should NOT be in contact in non-working side movements.
- Be non-porous, smooth, with a polished surface.
- Make passive pinpoint contact with the gingival tissue.
- Not be concave in two directions.
- Be readily cleanable by the patient.
- Be narrower at the expense of the lingual aspect of the ridge.
- Be on as straight a line as possible between the retainers to prevent any torquing of retainers or abutments.

PIER ABUTMENTS

A traditional rigid SOLDERED 5-unit bridge is NOT desirable because of physiological tooth movement, arch position of abutments, and the retentive capacity of the retainers. So, you need a STRESS-BREAKER, NON-RIGID CONNECTOR to prevent the "PIER ABUTMENT" from acting as a FULCRUM or LEVER.

PIER ABUTMENT – freestanding abutment with edentulous spaces on each side that requires a NON-RIGID CONNECTOR. A pier abutment does not require a rigid connector (i.e. solder joint) which is the PREFERRED way to connect the abutments and pontic of a bridge.

NON-RIGID CONNECTOR-a broken stress mechanical union of a retainer (abutment) & pontic.
- **USED ONLY FOR A SHORT-SPAN BRIDGE REPLACING ONE TOOTH**.
- NON-RIGID CONNECTORS DECREASE OR NEUTRALIZE DISPLACING FORCES ON ABUTMENTS BY ELIMINATING A FULCRUM EFFECT ON THE PIER ABUTMENT.
- DO NOT USE IF ABUTMENTS HAVE SIGNIFICANT MOBILITY (PERIODONTALLY COMPROMISED).
- **TRANSFERS SHEAR STRESS TO SUPPORTING BONE, NOT TO THE CONNECTORS**.
- MINIMIZES M-D TORQUING OF ABUTMENTS, BUT ALLOWS THEM TO MOVE INDEPENDENTLY.
- Stress-breaking device in a five-unit FPD is **PLACED ON THE MIDDLE ABUTMENT (PIER)** to eliminate a lever and fulcrum by ISOLATING THE FORCE ONLY TO THE FPD SEGMENT WHERE IT IS PLACED.
- **DOVETAIL KEYWAY** of the connector is placed on the **DISTAL SIDE of the pier abutment** (middle abutment tooth) because 98% of posterior teeth TILT MESIALLY when subjected to vertical occlusal forces. Thus, mesial tooth movement **seats the key into the keyway** more solidly. If the keyway were placed on the mesial side, the key would unseat during mesial movements.
- **KEY** is placed on the **MESIAL OF THE DISTAL PONTIC**. The most common key design is a T-SHAPED KEY. The path of insertion of the key into the keyway is parallel to the pathway of the retainer that is not involved with the keyway.

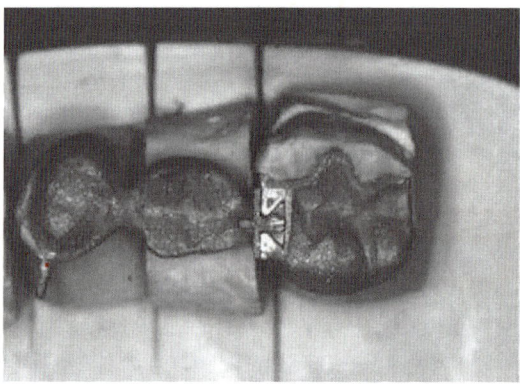

MARYLAND BRIDGE (RESIN-BONDED FPD)

A conservative restoration (etched-material prosthesis) with solid metal retainers that relies on the etched inner surface in the enamel of the retainers for its **RETENTION**. The **grooves give increase RESISTANCE FORM**.
- Requires an abutment MESIAL & DISTAL to the edentulous space.
- Requires a shallow preparation in enamel (**useful in children with large pulps** who are at risk for exposure).
- Both abutments inclination M-D difference cannot be ≥ 15° with no difference in the abutment's inclination F-L.
- Preparations demand additional RESISTANCE via long, well-defined grooves.
- Can be moderate resorption with no gross soft tissue defects.
- Abutment teeth are basically left intact
- ⍟ **Grooves** for a resin-bonded FPD (Maryland Bridge) provide mainly **RESISTANCE FORM** by preventing B-L rotation. The grooves can also provide RETENTION on crowns.

INDICATIONS:
- RESTORATION OF CHOICE to replace **1-2 missing MANDIBULAR INCISORS** when abutments are unblemished (caries-free).
- Replace **MAXILLARY INCISORS** if patient has an open-bite, end-to-end, or moderate overbite.
- Used as a **PERIODONTAL SPLINT** (but abutment mobility can cause failure).
- Can replace molars if child's masticatory muscles are not well developed.
- Replace **SINGLE POSTERIOR TOOTH** (10% higher risk of failure if more than 1 pontic).
- Not used for FPDs > 3 units unless a mitigating tx-plan consideration exists (i.e. opposing RPD which results in less occlusal stress.

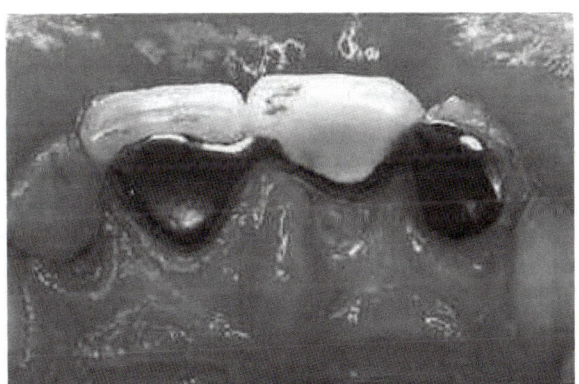

Preparation Features:
- Should encompass at least 180° (guide surfaces/planes interproximal and extend onto the facial to achieve a facial-lingual lock). Want to extend as far as possible to provide maximum surface area for bonding.
- **Vertical stops are placed on all preparations for RESISTANCE & RIGIDITY.**
- **Grooves increase RESISTANCE TO DISPLACEMENT ON ANTERIOR PREPARATIONS.**
- Occlusal clearance is needed on very few teeth prepared for abutments (.5mm is needed for maxillary incisors).
- **Light chamfer (1mm) finish line** is placed **SUPRAGINGIVAL** throughout the length to minimize deleterious effects to the periodontium.

CONTRAINDICATIONS – patients with **DEEP VERTICAL OVERBITE (VERTICAL OVERLAP)**, **EXTENSIVE CARIES, & NICKEL SENSITIVITY, MOBILITY.**

ADVANTAGES OF MARYLAND BRIDGES – reduced cost, no anesthesia required, supragingival margins (mandatory), minimal tooth preparation, and rebonding is possible if the wings are not bent or sprung.

Disadvantages of Maryland Bridges:
- IRREVERSIBLE and uncertain longevity
- No space correction (if M-D width is very wide, only so much porcelain can be added to fill the embrasure space)
- No alignment correction (cannot correct alignment of teeth due to not restoring facial, proximal, & incisal areas).
- Difficult to temporize (cannot make a provision FPD).

BRIDGE ABUTMENTS

IDEAL ABUTMENT is **VITAL TEETH** with **NO MOBILITY**. Abutment is evaluated for 3 factors: crown:root ratio, root configuration, and periodontal surface area.

- OPTIMUM CROWN-ROOT RATIO FOR A TOOTH TO BE USED AS A FPD ABUTMENT IS 2:3.
- 1:1 is the MINIMUM acceptable abutment under normal circumstances.
- Crown-to-root ratio: 1:2 is the **IDEAL crown-to-root ratio** of an abutment tooth for a bridge ABUTMENT. This high a ratio is rarely achieved, thus a ratio of 2:3 is more realistic. A 1:1 ratio is the minimum acceptable ratio for a prospective abutment under normal circumstances. Crown-to-root ratio alone is NOT adequate criteria for evaluating a prospective abutment tooth.
- **Secondary Retention**-double abutments (secondary abutment) to overcome unfavorable crown:root ratios and long spans. The secondary abutment MUST have at least as much root surface area and as favorable a crown:root ratio as the **primary abutment** (abutment next to the edentulous space). A canine is a good secondary abutment vs. a first premolar, while a lateral is NOT a good choice as a secondary abutment to a canine.
- ROOT CONFIGURATION WITH THE WIDEST F-L DIMENSION IS THE BEST ABUTMENT.
- 1ST MOLAR IS THE BEST ABUTMENT & CANINE IS THE 2ND BEST ABUTMENT BECAUSE THEY HAVE THE LARGEST ROOT SURFACE AREA.
- SINGLE-ROOT TOOTH WITH AN IRREGULAR CONFIGURATION OR CURVATURE IN ITS APICAL THIRD IS PREFFERED TO A ROOT WITH A PERFECT TAPER.
- ROOTS THAT ARE BROADER F-L THAN M-D ARE PREFERRED TO ROOTS THAT ARE ROUND.
- DIVERGENT ROOTS ARE BETTER ABUTMENTS THAN FUSED/CONCIAL ROOTS.

ANTE'S LAW – the combined abutment teeth root surface area must be **equal or greater** than the edentulous space (pontic space). Any FPD replacing more than two teeth is high risk.

TILTED MOLAR ABUTMENTS – A 3-unit bridge will not seat if the distal abutment intrudes (tilts mesially) on the line of draw. 98% of posterior teeth TILT MESIALLY when subjected to occlusal forces. The long axis of FPD abutments must converge **no more than 25-30°**. Any greater mesial tilt requires either:

1. **orthodontics (uprighting) is the TREATMENT OF CHOICE to better position a mesially tilted FPD abutment**, distribute forces, and helps eliminate bony defects along the root's mesial surface. Takes around 3 months.
2. **PROXIMAL ½ crown**: used if orthodontics is impossible, (a ¾ rotated 90° so the distal surface is uncovered). Only used if the distal is caries-free. Contraindicated if there is a severe marginal ridge height discrepancy between the distal of the 2nd molar and mesial of 3rd molar due to the tiping.
3. **Telescoping crown and coping**. A full crown preparation follows the tipped molars long axis and an inner coping fits the prep, and a proximal ½ crown fits over the coping. Allows full coverage while compensating for the discrepancy between the paths of insertion of the abutments. The coping provides the marginal adaptation. Indicated if extensive facial/lingual restorations on the tilted molar exists.
4. **Non-Rigid Connector**. Full crown preparation with a box placed in the distal of the premolar (keyway) Most useful when the molar has marked lingual and mesial inclination. Used if a post-core or DO amalgam exists on the premolar abutment.

BRIDGES

RIGID CONNECTOR – (solder joints) the PREFERRED way to connect the abutments and pontic of a bridge (FPD). A rigid connector distributes occlusal load more evenly than a pier abutment (non-rigid connector), thus is **PREFFERED FOR TEETH WITH DECREASED PERIODONTAL ATTACHMENT (PERIODONTALLY INVOLVED CASES)**.

Factors that Determine a Fixed Bridgework Design:
1. **Root configuration:** important when assessing an abutment's periodontal suitability. Roots broader F-L than M-D are preferred to roots round in cross-section.
   - Multi-rooted posterior teeth with wide separated roots provide better periodontal support than roots that converge, fuse, or are conical.
   - Single-rooted teeth with an irregular configuration or some curvature in the root's apical 1/3 are better abutments than teeth with a nearly perfect taper.
   - Root surface area on a prospective abutment should also be evaluated.
2. **Crown-to-root ratio:** 1:2 is the **ideal crown-to-root ratio** of a tooth to be used as a bridge ABUTMENT. This high a ratio is rarely achieved, but a ratio of **2:3 is more realistic**. A 1:1 ratio is the minimum acceptable ratio for a prospective abutment. Crown-to-root ratio alone is NOT adequate to evaluate a prospective abutment tooth.
3. **Axial alignment of teeth:** parallelism of abutment prep is BEST determined by the LONG AXIS of the preparations.
4. **Length of Lever Arm (Span).** REPLACING **3 TEETH IS THE MAXIMUM!** The absolute MAXIMUM number of posterior teeth that can be safely replaced with a fixed bridge is THREE, and only under ideal conditions. Any bridge replacing more than two teeth is high risk.
   - An edentulous space involving **4 adjacent teeth** other than **four incisors** is usually **best treated with a RPD**. If more than one edentulous space exists in the same arch, even though each of them could be individually restored with a bridge, it may be desirable to restore them with a RPD, especially if the spaces are bilateral and each space involves two or more missing teeth.
   - 3rd molars can rarely be used as abutments since they often display incomplete eruption, short-fused roots, and a marked mesial inclination in the absence of a 2nd molar. To use a 3rd molar, it must be completely erupted, periodontally sound, long-separated roots (multirooted), and must display little or no mesial inclination.
   - A simple bridge replaces 1-2 teeth, while a complex bridge replaces 2 or more teeth.
   - Edentulous areas involving 4 or more missing teeth (except 4 incisors), should be restored with an RPD.

Fixed Bridge Contraindications:
- Poor oral hygiene, high caries rate, or multiple spaces in the arch or teeth likely to be lost in the near future.
- Space not detrimental to the maintenance of arch stability or dental health.
- Unacceptable occlusion or bruxism.
- Anterior fixed bridge is contraindicated when considerable residual ridge resorption exists. Use an RPD.

ELECTROSURGERY – an acceptable method of **gingival tissue retraction** that passes small currents of electricity through the gingival tissues, causing cells to desiccate (scorch). Usually results in some delayed healing because of the lack of proper clot formation, but is very good at stopping hemorrhage. Too low of an electrical current in an electrosurgical electrode is detected by tissue drag.

- **Electrosurgery Objectives**: coagulation, hemostasis, access to cavosurface margins, and reduce the inner wall of the gingival sulcus (removing a thin layer of crevicular gingival tissue).
- **Indications**:
  - Remove hyperplastic gingival tissue where it has proliferated into preparations or over crown margins.
  - In place of gingival retraction cord where substantial attached gingiva is present.
  - Crown-lengthening procedures prior to fabricating a provisional crown.
- **Contraindications**: areas of thin attached gingiva, or underlying dehiscence because gingival recession occur in these areas after electrosurgery. **CARDIAC PACEMAKERS, METAL INSTRUMENTS, FLAMMABLE AGENTS (N2O), KEEP THE ELECTRODE MOVING**, and do not touch a metal rest, tooth, or bone.
- Great care is used during electrosurgery due to **potential serious damage to the PDL and surrounding bone, resulting in loss of attachment**.

ELECTROSURGERY WAVEFORMS:
1. **Unrectified, Dampened**: recurring peaks of power that diminishes rapidly. Causes dehydration and necrosis, slow, painful healing, but good hemostasis.
2. **Partially Rectified, Dampened**: damping occurs in the 2nd half of the cycle. Good lateral heat penetration, greater tissue destruction with slow healing in deeper tissues. Good coagulation.
3. **Fully Rectified**: continuous flow of energy. Good cutting and some hemostasis.
4. **Fully Rectified Filtered**: continuous flow of energy. Excellent cutting with less tissue injury and greater healing.

POSTS (DOWELS) & CORES

Posts & Cores:
- If 50% of the clinical crown is destroyed, an amalgam or composite core-build up is indicated.
- Composite cores have greater microleakage than amalgam cores, and they are not as dimensionally stable.
- A core must be anchored to the tooth (with pins or another retentive feature) and not just placed to fill the void.
- Not all endodontically treated anterior teeth require posts and a full crown. Placing a post in a conservatively treated tooth weakens it.
- Posterior teeth must have a CAST RESTROATION with occlusal coverage (at least an onlay).
- **Endodontically treated teeth should NOT serve as abutments for distal extension RPDs (4x greater failure rate than non-abutment RCT teeth).**
- Pulpless FPD abutments fail 2x more than vital abutments. They should not be abutments with a span longer than 1 pontic.
- For a **custom cast-post-core, place a KEYWAY or GROOVE to prevent rotation (anti-rotational device)**. Anti-rotational features (pot holes, slots, channels), but NOT PINS.
- Post's diameter must not be > 1/3 the root's diameter at the CEJ. Must be a minimum thickness of 1mm tooth structure at the mid-root and beyond.
- All cusps thinner than ½ must be shortened or removed.
- Posts do not strengthen roots – it's a myth! They simply provide retention for a core. A poorly designed or fitted post will cause premature failure of the root.

Primary Function of Post is to PROVIDE A PLATFORM FOR THE CROWN (retain the core).

Post material can be metal or fiber (esthetic and bondable). Cast post is becoming passé.
- **Carbon & Glass Fiber Posts**: flexible, absorbs and dissipates forces acting against the tooth.
- **Ceramic Posts**: are more rigid, so provide more flexure. Resistance to remaining radicular tooth structure.
- **Post Shapes**:
  - **Tapered**: usually requires the LEAST internal dentinal structure and corresponds to the shape of the remaining root.
  - **Parallel**: can be just as conservative if selected within the minimum canal diameter.
  - **2nd Stage**: have both parallel and tapered sections.

POST WIDTH – should involve the minimum amount of dentin removal, but provide some passive engagement (non-contact) of the outer periphery of the post and inner canal space.

POST LENGTH – no clear formula exists for determining the ideal depth of the post preparation. Post LENGTH must be 4-5mm from the apex. The post must be AT LEAST as long as the clinical crown. **The post should equal the crown length or 2/3 the root length (whichever is greater).** There must be at least 4mm of gutta-percha at the apical end of the canal.

POST DESIGN – active vs. passive. Just because a post has threading, does not mean it is active. **The diameter of the preparation drill and post diameter determine if the post is active.**

Post Color:
- Ideal color is that of DENTIN (ceramic restorations).
- Translucent, may need to be masked with dentin-colored core material.
- Carbon-fiber posts are black and used with a PFM or crown with a completely opaque substructure.

FERRULE EFFECT – the preparation margin (finish line) MUST extend at beyond (apical) to the core and into SOUND TOOTH STRUCTURE. Ferrule is the 1.5- 2mm or so of sound root structure apical to the core that the margins of the crown should engage to **PROTECT AGAINST ROOT FRACTURE**. A ferrule makes post-retained full-coverage restorations significantly more retentive and dramatically strengthens the tooth to resist fracture. It surrounds the circumference of the tooth, holding it together like the metal bands around the head of a wooden mallet.
- Preparation for a post-core should preserve solid tooth structure. **The margin should be APICAL to the dowel-core margin to enable the crown to girdle the tooth and brace it externally.**
- If the tooth is flush with the gingiva, fabricating a post-core and crown without encircling the tooth structure by the crown walls can cause ROOT FRACTURE.

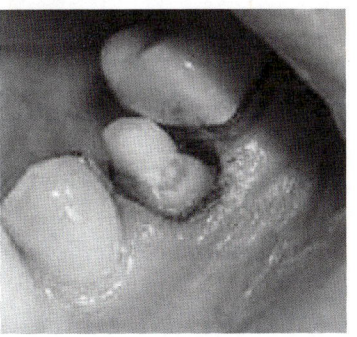

NOTES

Advantages of using a post & core, rather than a post crown when restoring RCT treated teeth:
- Marginal adaptation and fit of the restoration is independent on the fit of the post.
- Restoration can be replaced in the future if needed, without disturbing the post and core.
- If the endodontically treated tooth is to serve as a bridge abutment, it is not necessary to make the root canal preparation parallel with the line of draw of other preparations (it can be treated as an independent abutment).

- Post and core is made separate from the final restoration. The crown is fabricated and cemented over the core just as a restoration is placed over a preparation done on tooth structure.

- **Post & core can be used for teeth with little or no clinical crown, but with roots with adequate length, bulk, and straightness.** For posterior teeth with less extensive destruction of coronal tooth structure, or teeth with less favorable root configurations, a pin-retained amalgam or composite core can be used.

PORCELAIN VENEERS

Porcelain Veneer Indications:
1. Covering labial surface defects like enamel hypoplasia.
2. Masking discolored teeth like tetracycline staining, discoloration after loss of tooth vitality.
3. Repair structural damage like fractured incisal edges.
4. Improve tooth contour (i.e. peg-shaped lateral incisors).
5. Reducing spaces in cases when orthodontics are inappropriate.

PORCELAIN VENEER CONTRAINDICATIONS – severe imbrication of teeth, traumatic occlusal contacts, unfavorable morphology, insufficient tooth structure and enamel. A patient with a high caries index, short clinical crown, and minimal horizontal overlap are not candidates for partial veneer crowns. Rather, the restoration of choice is a full PFM crown.

Advantages of Partial Veneer Restorations (3/4 & 7/8 crowns):
1. Primary reason for choosing a ¾ crown over a full cast crown is **TOOTH STRUCTURE IS SPARED**.
2. A great deal of the margin is in an area accessible to the dentist for finishing and to the patient for cleaning.
3. **Less of the restoration margin** is in close proximity to the gingival crevice, thus decreasing the chance of periodontal irritation.
4. Can be **more easily seated completely** during cementation. With at least part of the margin visible, complete seating of a partial veneer crown is more easily verified by direct vision.
5. If it is ever necessary to do an electric pulp test (EPT) on the tooth, **a portion of the enamel is un-veneered & accessible**.

IMPRESSION MATERIALS

HYDROCOLLOIDS – have the advantage of **WETTING INTRAORAL SURFACES** well, but have very limited dimensional stability **because they are composed of 85% water**.

1. **Reversible Hydrocolloid (Agar-Agar)**-an impression material whose **physical state is changed from a GEL SOL** by applying **HEAT** and is **reversed back by removing heat**. Reversible hydrocolloids are **composed of 85% water, 12-15% agar**, traces of borax, potassium sulfate, & sodium tetraborate. Agar impression materials and dental compounds do not involve a chemical reaction to set.
   - **Advantages**: Easy to pour, no mixing is required (but a hydrocolloid-conditioning unit is required). No custom tray is required. Moisture tolerant, clean & pleasant with acceptable odor, excellent shelf-life, inexpensive.
   - **Disadvantages**: must be poured immediately, finish line is difficult to read, weak in a deep sulcus, and potentially injurious to the patient if not handled properly. **Very limited dimensional stability**.
2. **Irreversible Hydrocolloids (ALGINATE)**-an elastic impression material with **very limited dimensional stability**.
   - **Advantages**: inexpensive, can use stock tray, easily mixed, and easy to pour.
   - **Disadvantages**: unstable, fragile, may affect the cast surface, and must be poured immediately.

SODIUM PHOSPHATE – a component found in alginate powder that **controls the SETTING TIME of alginate**.

After taking alginate impressions, if you place the impressions in a bowl of water for a few hours to try and prevent them from drying up before pouring the casts, **IMBIBITION** can occur (the impressions absorb water and expands). When imbibition occurs, the impression is no longer accurate.

Shrinkage occurs in alginate impressions even when placed under 100% relative humidity = **SYNERESIS** (occurs when exudate like droplets of the liquid medium forms on the impression surface). Since shrinkage is undesirable (causes distortion of impressions), alginate impressions should not be left in water (causes expansion) or exposed to air (causes shrinkage). Impressions should be poured immediately to ensure accuracy. When immediate pouring is not possible, alginate impressions can be stored only briefly in a moist paper towel.

Techniques to help prevent **GAGGING** while taking alginate impressions:
- Decrease the time to take an impression and have the patient breathe through their nose.
- Seat the patient in an upright position.
- Seat the posterior part of the tray first. Mixing the alginate rapidly causes it to set more rapidly.
- Decreasing water-to-powder ratio causes alginate to set faster (affects mix consistency as the mix is much thicker when less water is used).
- DO NOT use cold water to mix the alginate because it retards alginate's setting time.

Mandibular alginate impression is taken **FIRST** since gagging is more likely to occur while taking the maxillary impression. For the maxillary impression, **seat the posterior portion of the tray first**, then the anterior portion to help prevent alginate from being squeezed out of the tray back toward the patient's throat. Always remove alginate impressions in one quick movement with a snap to help decrease permanent deformation. Do not over-seat the tray (0.25 inch) minimum of alginate should remain over all critical structures (especially occlusal surfaces).

NOTES

When taking an alginate impression, it is advised that the tray be placed in the mouth after all critical areas are wiped with alginate. Critical areas are buccal to the maxillary tuberosities and retromylohyoid space. Rest seats and guide planes should be covered with alginate and any other soft tissue undercuts.

When taking alginate impression for a RPD, it is best to apply some alginate directly on the teeth to eliminate bubbles and saliva from the rest seat preparations.

ELASTOMERS – impression materials with **elastic or rubber-like qualities** used for crown & bridge, secondary impressions for dentures, and inlays/onlays. When removing elastomeric impressions, use steady force (a snap is not required) to minimize permanent deformation. Elastomers set via a chemical reaction. **Elastomers are NON-AQEOUS polymer-based rubber impression materials with good elasticity.**

1. **Polysulfides (Rubber Base, Mercaptan, Thiokol)**-the base contains a liquid polysulfide polymer (mercaptan polymer) mixed with an inert filler. The accelerator is usually lead dioxide. When these two pastes are mixed, the polymer chains are lengthened and cross-linked through oxidized thiol groups to form a rubber-like material.

   - A tray for a polysulfide rubber impression that lacks occlusal stops may result in an inaccurate final impression because of permanent distortion during polymerization.

   - Sets in 12-14 minutes (the longest setting time).

   - Moisture tolerance in the mouth is acceptable.

   - Wettability with gypsum is poor, and it has poor taste and odor. Has an 18-month shelf-life.

   - Polysulfide polymerization of is exothermic and accelerated by an increase in temperature or humidity.

   - Polysulfides have **good flow properties, high flexibility, and high tear strength.** Polysulfides have the strongest resistance to tearing, but impressions can distort when removed from areas where deep undercuts exist. Polysulfides have a long working time and relatively long polymerization time, which may add to patient discomfort. They have a low resistance to deformation.

2. **Polyvinyl Siloxanes (Additional Silicones or Vinyl Polysiloxanes)**-one tube contains silicone with terminal silane H+ groups and an inert filler. The other tube is a vinyl silicone with terminal vinyl groups, chloroplatinic acid catalyst, and filler. Upon mixing, there is **an addition of silane hydrogen groups** across vinyl double bonds and does not form by-products, resulting in a very dimensionally stable material. **PVS can be poured up to 1 week.**

   - Latex gloves should not be worn when mixing polyvinyl siloxanes because **sulfur in the latex retards the setting of addition silicone materials.** Sulfur in ferric and aluminum sulfate reaction solution may also inhibit polymerization of PVS. **Some latex gloves might inhibit the setting of polyvinyl siloxane.**

   - Mixing time (30-45 sec), Moderate working time (2-4 min); moderate setting time (6-8 min).

   - Excellent dimensional stability and very low permanent deformation.

   - Poor tear strength, lowest temperature rise, very high stiffness, very poor wettability by gypsum. Addition silicones are **temperature sensitive** (increases in temperature shorten working & setting times). Easy to mix, easy to clean-up, and acceptable odor and taste.

- **Polyvinyl siloxanes (PVS)** are the **MOST WIDELY USED & MOST ACCURATE elastic impression materials**. They have less polymerization shrinkage, low distortion, fast recovery from deformation, and moderately high tear strength. Most PVS **can be poured up to 1 week after impression** making and are stable in most sterilizing solutions.

3. **Polyethers** (Impregnum/Premier & Polygel (Caulk)-are two component materials. The rubber **base** includes a polyether polymer with ethylene imine groups, silica filler, and plasticizer. The **accelerator** contains a cross-linking agent (**aromatic sulfonic acid ester**) which produces cross-linking by cationic polymerization. When mixed, a rubber forms by a cationic polymerization process.

   - **Advantages**: excellent dimensional stability (when dry), clean, pleasant taste & odor, **FAST SETTING**, dimensionally stable if more than one cast is poured, stable even if poured 24hrs after taking an impression (very low permanent deformation) as it can be poured up to 1 week, and are truly hydrophilic which results in superior wettability by gypsum. Polyether impression material tolerates moisture better than any other elastomer.

   - **Disadvantages**: the most difficult material to remove from the mouth (**the most rigid/stiff material**), tears easily (poor tear strength), may adhere to teeth, high water absorption (dimensionally unstable in the presence of moisture), and fine margins may break. Compared to other materials, the main disadvantage of using **polyether elastomeric impression materials** is they are much stiffer. Has the highest temperature rise and highest stiffness.

   - Polyethers have the **SHORTEST WORKING & SETTING TIMES** of the elastomeric impression materials. Mixing time is 30-45 seconds (mixes easily); Working time is 2-3 minutes; Setting time 6-7 minutes.
     - All elastomeric impression materials **CONTRACT SLIGHTLY** during setting (they do not expand).

   - For best results with elastomeric impression material, the prepared tooth should be free of surface moisture. Compared to hydrocolloids, elastomeric impression materials are easier to prepare, more resistant to tearing upon removal, and have a superior dimensional stability.

   - **Custom Trays** are an important part of rubber base impression techniques since elastomers are more accurate in uniform thin layers that are 2-4mm thick. With all elastomers, a custom tray should be fabricated with a plastic material, should be rigid, have occlusal stops to avoid permanent distortion during polymerization, and be coated with an adhesive that should dry completely before taking the impression to prevent the impression material from pulling away.

ZINC OXIDE-EUGENOL – an **impression paste** whose setting time is **accelerated by ADDING a drop of water to the mix**. To retard the setting of ZOE, add inert oils (olive or mineral oil) during mixing. ZOE sets via a **chemical reaction**.
- **Advantages**: can record soft tissue at rest, sets hard in 5 minutes, stable, & less expensive than polysulfides.
- **Disadvantages**: messy to mix, very sticky, tissue irritant, not elastic, difficult to manipulate, not recommended for gagging patients.

Impression Problems:
1. **Grainy Material**: caused by improper or prolonged mixing, undue gelation, or too low a water-powder ratio.
2. **Tearing of Material**: caused by inadequate bulk, moisture contamination, premature removal from the mouth, or prolonged mixing.
3. **Irregularly Shaped Voids**: due to moisture or debris on tissue.
4. **Rough or Chalky Stone Cast**: caused by inadequate cleaning of the impression, excess water left in the impression, premature removal of the cast, leaving the cast in the impression too long, or improper manipulation of stone.
5. **Distortion**: impression not poured immediately, movement of tray during gelation, premature or improper removal from the mouth, or tray was held in the mouth too long (only with certain brands).

Bite Registration Material used to make an accurate interocclusal record **should offer a MINIMUM RESISTANCE to the patient's jaw closure and have LOW FLOW at mixing**. Recently, **addition-reaction silicone impression materials have dominated the interocclusal record (IOR) market** since these materials have **VERY LOW FLOW when mixed and become rigid after setting**.

GYPSUM

Main constituent of dental plasters and stones is **Calcium Sulfate Hemihydrate**.
Type I: rarely used today.

Type II: used to make casts when strength is not important (orthodontics). **Dental Model Plaster (Type II)**-heating gypsum in an open kettle. This process produces porous and irregularly-shaped particles. Dental plaster is **the WEAKEST GYPSUM PRODUCT**.

Type III: used for preparing casts of an alginate impression upon which dentures are processed.
- **Dental Stone (Type III)**-produced by HEATING GYPSUM under pressure with water vapor in an autoclave. This process produces uniform-shaped and less porous particles. **Heating gypsum in a 30% solution of calcium chloride** produces **high strength** (improved) die stone. Produces the least porous and strongest particles.

Type IV: used when making stone "**dies**" (reproductions of teeth with prepared cavities) used for crown & bridge, and operative (inlays and onlays).

CEMENTS – cements do NOT increase crown retention. A tooth must be **WIPED DRY** before crown cementation, as opposed to drying the tooth with alcohol and warm air to decrease the possibility of pulp damage. Also, ALWAYS apply cement to both the restoration and the tooth.

1. **Composite Resin**-the luting material of choice to cement a ceramic crown and can provide the **STRONGEST BOND**. **Ceramic crowns** are bonded with composite resin after etching the internal surface of the crown, and are shown to be better in bonding strength than other materials.

2. **Zinc-Phosphate Cement**-may also be used to cement porcelain crowns. It has good compressive strength (14,000-16,000 psi), but **its high pH is a problem because two layers of varnish must be applied to protect the pulp**. ZPC is one of the oldest and widely used cements for luting permanent metal restorations and as a used as a base. It is a high-strength cement base, **mixed from zinc oxide powder and phosphoric acid liquid**. Due to its **low initial pH, it may cause pulpal irritation**, especially where only a thin layer of dentin exists between the cement and the pulp.

    Notes: - low PH - 2 layers of varnish → protect the pulp.

3. **Zinc polycarboxylate or ZOE**-these **biologically compatible cements** are used on teeth with preparations with adequate length and retentive features, or when the preparation depth raises some concern regarding pulp vitality. Also, these cements exhibit better resistance to solubility than zinc phosphate cement. Zinc polycarboxylate and GIC adhere to calcified dental tissue, and have superior biologic compatibility than zinc phosphate cements.

4. **Glass Ionomer Cement (GIC)**-a dental restorative material used in dentistry for restoring teeth and luting cements. These materials are **based on the reaction of silicate glass powder and polyalkenoic acid**. These tooth-colored materials were introduced in 1972 for use as restorative materials for anterior teeth (particularly for eroded areas, Class III and V carious lesions). As they bond chemically to dental hard tissues and release fluoride for a relatively long period modern day applications of GICs have expanded. The desirable properties of glass ionomer cements make them **useful materials in the restoration of carious lesions in low-stress areas** such as **smooth-surface** and **small anterior proximal cavities in primary teeth**.
   - **GC Fuji PLUS** is a resin reinforced glass ionomer luting cement designed for final cementation of metal, porcelain-fused-to-metal and metal free crowns, bridges, inlays and onlays. It bonds chemically and mechanically to tooth structure and to all types of core material. Its simple placement technique produces significantly higher bond strengths than conventional glass ionomer cements while maintaining the favorable characteristics of glass ionomers-fluoride release, low coefficient of thermal expansion, and biocompatibility to tooth structure and soft tissues. For indirect metal-free restoration that recommend a resin-reinforced / resin-modified glass ionomer for final cementation – cementable reinforced all ceramic crowns like PROCERA or cementable composite resin restoration like GRADIA.

Prolonged sensitivity to heat, cold, and pressure after cementing a crown or fixed bridge is usually related to **OCCLUSAL TRAUMA**. If CR occlusion is high, patient complain of cold sensitivity and pain on biting down hard. All patients should have an appointment specifically to check the occlusion on all crowns and bridges. Excursive movements should also be evaluated, since often patients complain of pain on chewing soft foods (this indicates improper balancing or working contacts). **The occlusion of gold restorations is best checked with SILVER PLASTIC SHIM STOCK**.

CHAPTER 7

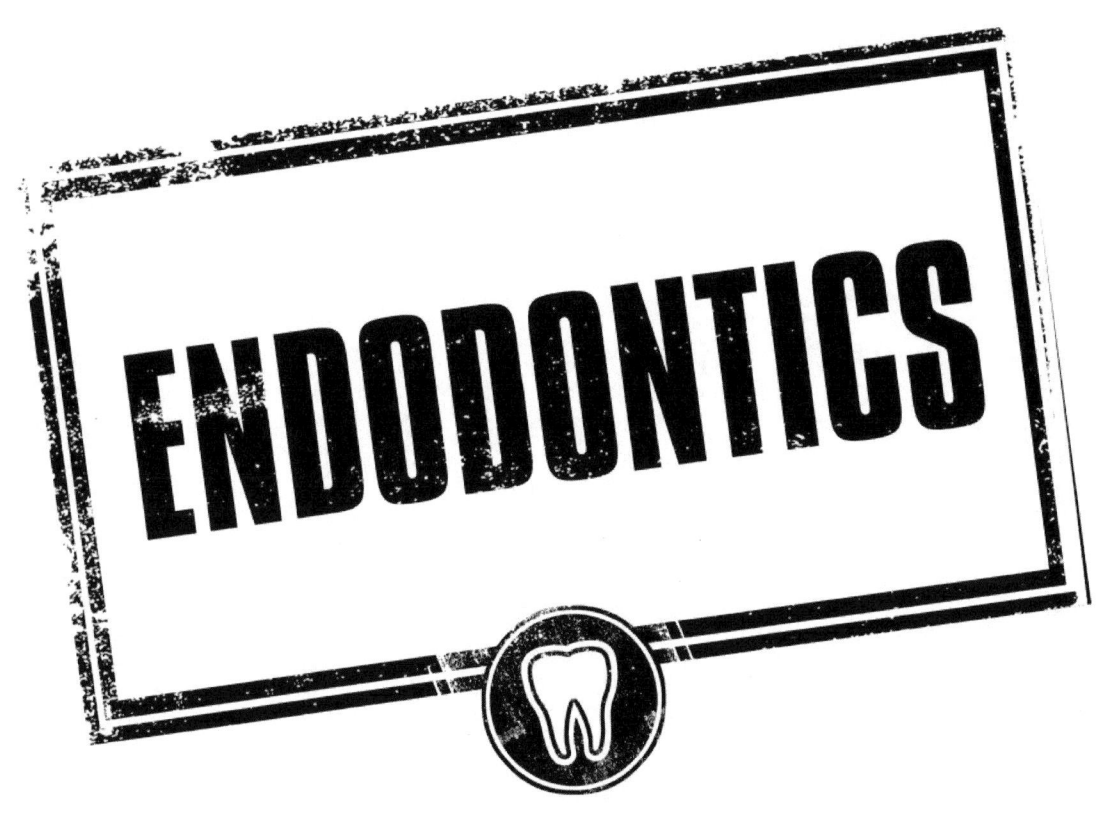

Diagnostic Aids to identify a Vertical Root Fracture:
1. **Fiberoptic light** for transillumination.
2. **Wedging** the tooth in question and take an x-ray.
3. **Persistent periodontal defects** in an otherwise healthy tooth.
4. Have patient **bite forcefully on a bite stick (tooth slooth).**

Root fractures are **only visualized** on a radiograph if the x-ray beam **passes THROUGH THE FRACTURE LINE.** Since the fracture line can **extend diagonally**, an additional radiograph is taken with a **steep (45°) vertical angulation in** addition to the **conventional 90° degree.**

Inlays can cause fractures. If a patient complains of **pain during mastication since inlay placement**, suspect a fractured cusp (using a **bite stick or tooth slooth** helps determine which cusp is fractured).

VERTICAL TOOTH FRACTURE – symptoms and clinical tests show **pulpal pathosis** in a **posterior tooth**, but **no decay or restoration** in any proximity to the pulp on the radiograph is pathognomonic of a vertical tooth fracture.

- Radiographic exam **rarely reveals** the fracture because the crack is usually **parallel** to the x-ray film. Radiographs (without first wedging the tooth) **RARELY** show vertical tooth fractures.

- Vertical fractures through root structures have an **almost HOPELESS prognosis**, unless the fractured segment can be **removed**, and **gingivoplasty** & **alveoplasty** are performed. However, unrealistic or overambitious case selection leads to failure.

- A tooth with a **vertical root fracture** has a **POOR** prognosis. Studies show **most vertical root fractures** are caused by using **too much condensation force** during **obturation** with **gutta-percha**.

Anterior tooth root fractures, usually occur in a **more HORIZONTAL PLANE** and may be **visible** on the radiograph. Anterior tooth fractures are **usually due to accidental trauma** (i.e. blow to the jaw/teeth). If the fracture line is **not too far down the root**, it may be **saved** with **RCT** and a **crown**.

Therapy for **horizontal root fractures** is always difficult. **Root canal treatment (RCT)** is **NOT** indicated if the fracture site remains in **close proximity** and if **pulp retains** its **vitality**. However, if clinical symptoms develop, or the segments appear to be separating on the x-ray, some treatment is necessary.

CRACKED-TOOTH SYNDROME – one of the **most frustrating dental conditions** involving the possible need for **endodontic treatment**, because its symptoms are usually characterized by a **SHARP**, but **BRIEF PAIN** occurring **unexpectedly** only when the patient is **chewing**. Having a patient **bite forcefully** on a bite stick (tooth slooth) and noticing the cusps that occlude when the pain occurs helps **locate** the cracked tooth.

SUBMARGINAL CURVED FLAP (SEMILUNAR FLAP) – a half-moon shaped flap raised with a curved horizontal incision in the mucosa or attached gingiva with the concavity towards the apex. While it is simple and does not impinge on surrounding tissue, its **disadvantages** outweigh its advantages, thus **it is NOT used for anterior tooth root-end surgery**.
1. limited access and visibility.
2. tearing of incision corners when trying to improve accessibility by stretching the flap.
3. if a lesion is larger than expected, the incision lies over the bony defect, and healing occurs by scarring.
4. incision extent is limited by attachments (i.e. frenum, muscles).

SUBMARGINAL TRIANGULAR & RECTANGULAR FLAP (OCHSENBEIN-LEUBKE) – requires **at least 4mm of attached gingiva and a healthy periodontium**. This flap is raised by a SCALLOPED INCISION in attached gingiva with 1 or 2 vertical incisions. Less risk of incising over bony defects, with no post-surgical gingival recession. May be indicated for root-end surgery on an anterior tooth.
- **Disadvantages**: hemorrhage from the cut margins & scarring.
- **Advantages**: better access & visibility than a semilunar flap, but **NOT better than a full mucoperiosteal flap**.

FULL MUCOPERIOSTEAL FLAP (FULL-THICKNESS) – allows MAXIMUM access & visibility. This wide flap is **raised from the gingival sulcus** (elevating gingival crest & interdental gingival), and its outline precludes any incisions over bony defects, and allows various periodontal procedures (i.e. curettage, SRP, bone re-shaping). Can be indicated for root-end surgery on an anterior tooth. **Disadvantages**: it's a large flap that may be difficult to reposition, suture, make alterations, and post-surgical gingival recession is possible.

ELECTRIC PULP TESTER (EPT = VITALOMETER) – usually elicits a response at a HIGHER current than normal if the tooth being tested has CHRONIC PULPITIS. EPT checks **tooth sensibility/vitality** by stimulating nerve endings with a **low current and high potential difference** in voltage. While EPT manufacturers give normal reference values of current the BEST way to check "normal/baseline" values is to use it on adjacent (non-pathological) teeth, then compare the normal values with the values obtained on the tooth in question. EPT Responses:

1. **Acute** pulpitis-indicated by a **lower** than normal current, as acute inflammation mediators lower the pain threshold.
2. **Chronic pulpitis**-indicated by a response at a HIGHER current than normal.
3. **Hyperemia**-indicated by a LOWER than normal current, but a higher current than with an acute pulpitis.
4. **Pulp necrosis/Abscess**-indicated by no response at any current level.

EPT is **NOT r**eliable in these circumstances:
1. Pus-filled canal or a nervous patient (gives a false +).
2. Recent dental trauma, an insulating restoration, or wearing gloves (gives a false (-) response). Do not wear gloves when using the EPT.
3. Secondary dentin deposits, moisture contamination, immature tooth (open apex), patient taking analgesics, improper application, or weak EPT batteries.

Buccal Object Rule (SLOB Rule = Same Lingual, Opposite Buccal) – a shift-cone technique/rule that **allows the dentist to determine on** the radiograph which canal is the buccal and which is lingual. Buccal object rule also allows one to determine *working length of superimposed canals, root/canal curvatures, and the facial-lingual orientation of instruments or other anatomical objects*.

- The lingual surface is always CLOSEST to the cone, while the buccal surface is always FARTHER away from the cone. To apply SLOB rule, you **MUST have a reference object**.

- If taken from the mesial, the lingual surface (ML canal) will appear more mesial (closer to the cone) than buccal surface (MB canal) which appears farther distally.

- If taken from the distal, the lingual surface appears more distal (closer to the cone) than the buccal surface which appears father mesially.

- According to **buccal object rule**, when the x-ray tube is repositioned either at a more mesial or more distal angulation and a film is exposed, **the root/canal farther from the film (the buccal) moves in the SAME direction that the cone is directed. Thus, when the cone is aimed to the distal** (angled from the mesial direction), the buccal root/canal moves to the distal and appears distal to the lingual/palatal root/canal.

- The **object toward the lingual side (closer to the film) appears to shift on the film to the same direction as the repositioned x-ray cone**. If the x-ray cone is angulated mesially, the lingual/palatal root shifts toward the same (mesial) side in the resultant radiograph, and is easily visualized.

- When treating multi-canaled bicuspids & molars, it is often difficult to determine radiographically which canal is more toward the buccal. When a straight-on exposure is taken of a bicanaled tooth, the canals become superimposed on the film, and visualization of each canal is impossible. If the x-ray cone is moved to give an angled exposure, the roots will be separate on the film.

Diagnostic tests indicated for recently traumatized teeth:
1. **Soft tissue exam** to observe lips, face, tongue, etc.
2. **Hard tissue exam** to visually look and then palpate the injured tooth and alveolus to reveal the extent of tooth mobility, any alveolar fractures, and areas of inflammation. Check for occlusal disharmonies to help detect tooth displacements and jaw fractures.
3. **Radiographic examination** to reveal tooth displacement, root fractures, previous RCT, periapical radiolucencies.
4. **Other diagnostic tests.** EPT (pulp vitality testing) is **CONTRAINDICATED** since the traumatized pulp undergoes temporary paresthesia thus giving a false reading. A percussion test is **NOT** usually performed since it is painful.
5. Observe adjacent and opposing teeth for injury.

Traumatized teeth may be fine for a long time, but many develop **radiolucencies**. Thus, do not indiscriminately do root canals before checking pulp vitality. Perform RCT only in teeth that do not respond to pulp testing (i.e. trauma to maxillary anterior teeth. A few years later x-rays reveal radiolucencies around incisor apices). Check pulp vitality of all anterior teeth before performing root canals.

Trauma causing **deep intrusion** to a permanent tooth causes **PULP NECROSIS** and conventional RCT is necessary.

Radiation Safety: Endodontic procedures involve taking multiple radiographs.
1. To protect the dentist and staff if there is no barrier available to stand behind, the **stand at least 6 feet away** in the area that lies between 90-135° to the x-ray beam (an area of minimal scatter radiation).
2. A fast (sensitive) film like "E-speed" film is preferred over slower films, since faster films require less radiation exposure while providing a quality image.
3. Dental units should operate at 70kVp or higher. The **higher kVp = lower patient skin doses or radiation**.
4. Collimation (i.e. restricting x-ray beam size so it does not exceed 2.5inch at the patient's skin) decreases exposure.
5. Patients must be protected with a lead apron and thyroid collar for each exposure.
6. Dental personnel who may get exposed to occupational x-radiation MUST wear film badges to record exposure, and must **never exceed the max permissible dose (MPD) of 50mSv per year per person**.

Pulpotomy-removal of a **portion of the pulp** that is indicated for:
1. cariously exposed deciduous (primary) teeth with healthy radicular pulps.
2. traumatic or carious exposure of permanent teeth with undeveloped roots.
3. an alternative to extraction when endodontic treatment is not available.
4. emergency treatment in permanent teeth with acute pulpitis.

Pulpotomy procedures performed on fully developed permanent teeth are **NOT** successful. Thus, it is only a temporary procedure for fully developed permanent teeth.

While doing a vital pulpotomy on a young, immature permanent tooth, if hemorrhage after pulpal amputation cannot be controlled with cotton pellets even after several minutes, the **next step is to perform the amputation at a more apical level**.

- Uncontrolled bleeding is a sign of inflamed pulp tissue. Radicular pulp must be uninflamed for a successful pulpotomy. It is not uncommon to find uninflamed pulp at a more apical level, especially in cariously exposed teeth.

- If bleeding does not stop even after more apical amputation, then hemostatic agents are used as a compromise treatment. These are closely monitored, and if pulp vitality is lost, then **apexification (pulpectomy)** procedures are performed.

- Pulpotomy is the removal of the pulp chamber contents only.

NOTES

APEXIFICATION – goal is to **INDUCE FURTHER ROOT DEVELOPMENT** in a pulpless tooth (dead tooth) by stimulating the formation of a hard substance at the root apex to allow obturation of the root canal space. Apexification may be required after pulpectomy (as at age 7, the root apex must be open). The apex closes 2-3 years after eruption.

1. Isolate the field with a rubber dam, make an access cavity, and remove all pulp using reamers and files.
2. Premixed syringe of **calcium hydroxide-methylcellulose paste** (i.e. Pulpdent syringe) is injected into the canal and filled to the cervical level. The paste must reach the apical portion of the canal to stimulate tissues to form a calcific barrier. A double cement seal is made to close off the access cavity.
3. Patient is recalled after 3 months to see if apexification occurred. If not, a fresh supply of paste is placed. Once apexification occurs, only then is conventional RCT performed.

CALCIUM HYDROXIDE (CaOH) – its action promotes formation of a hard substance at the root apex by creating an ALKALINE environment that promotes hard tissue deposition.

If a permanent tooth fractures, but has a fully formed root and the pulp is exposed (large exposure), **complete RCT is the treatment of choice**. Apexification is **NOT** needed because the root is fully formed. If the pulp exposure is small and the length of time is short (30min-1hr), then direct pulp capping with CaOH followed by a restoration is the treatment of choice.

PULP CAPPING – placing a sedative and antiseptic dressing on an exposed healthy pulp to allow it to recover and maintain normal function and vitality. **Dycal** (CaOH2 = calcium hydroxide) is the most commonly used dressing.

- Pulp capping is overused in dentistry today, with very few indications for its use. Young pulps are more vascularized, thus more amenable to repair. **Accidental exposure of the pulp and the pulp of a young child are two situations where pulp capping offers better success**. Carious exposure of the pulp or the pulp of a middle-aged person are not indications for pulp capping.

- Pulp cappings are more successful if the exposure was accidental (*trauma or with a dental bur = mechanical*) rather than carious. Also, the pulp exposure should only be pinpoint in size to expect success. **Repair occurs when a dentin bridge forms at the pulp exposure site**. Even a small carious exposure should have RCT for the best long-term prognosis.

- Pulp capping-not recommended in primary teeth with carious pulp exposures due to its high failure rate and because pulpotomy (having similar time requirements) is very successful. Pulp capping can be done if a mechanical pulp exposure occurs.

- A tooth can stay asymptomatic for several weeks after pulp capping is performed, but this may only be temporary. If pulp capping fails and the tooth becomes symptomatic, it may be nearly impossible to treat with routine endodontics due to the severe calcifications in the root canal. Perforations may occur when attempting to follow the obliterated canal to gain apical patency (**perforations into furcations of multi-rooted teeth have the poorest prognosis**).

- Traumatic blows to teeth also cause pulp space calcification sometimes to a point where locating the canal is very difficult. With primary teeth, trauma may cause calcifications in the pulp chamber, which can cause a yellowish discoloration of the tooth.

- The success of pulp capping is recognized by the formation of a complete barrier of dentin at the site of pulpal exposure.

Two Pulp Capping Procedures:
1. **Indirect Pulp Capping**-a calcium hydroxide base is placed on a thin layer of questionable dentin remaining over the pulp. It is performed when a carious exposure is anticipated. After a 3-4 month waiting period, the tooth is re-opened and remaining decay is removed. During the waiting period, hopefully secondary dentin formation occurred, allowing complete removal of the decay without pulp exposure.
   - Ex: a radiograph of a 1st molar shows gross decay that may involve a dental pulp horn. The ideal treatment is to do an indirect pulp cap and place a sedative filling (IRM). If the tooth remains asymptomatic, in 3-4 months you can re-enter the tooth and remove all decay with subsequent placement of a permanent filling. *If this patient had tooth pain (aggravated by heat and tender to percussion), and excavation of the caries revealed pulp horn exposure without evidence of vital tissue, the emergency treatment pending eventual RCT is to place a small cotton pellet dampened with eugenol over the exposure and seal the cavity with a temporary material (IRM).

1. **Direct Pulp Capping**-placed a calcium hydroxide base directly on a pulpal exposure. **Favorable factors for direct pulp capping**:
   - Visual evidence of un-inflamed (pink) pulp tissue.
   - Absence of copious hemorrhage through the exposure.
   - No previous symptoms of pulpitis.
   - Small non-carious exposure (mechanical pulp exposure)
   - Clean cavity uncontaminated with saliva.
   - Direct pulp capping is very successful in immature teeth.
   - Direct pulp capping involves prompt application of a setting calcium hydroxide cement to a small (< 1mm in diameter), well isolated traumatic pulp exposure. **Direct pulp capping is expected in most instances, to stimulate formation of a reparative "dentin bridge" over the exposure site and preserve underlying pulpal tissue in a healthy condition.**
   - Direct pulp capping should **NOT** be attempted on teeth with a history of pain, sensitivity to percussion, or periapical radiolucencies. Instead, RCT may be indicated.
   - Failure of a direct pulp capping procedure is indicated by symptoms of pulpitis at any time, or the lack of vital response after several weeks or months.
   - **Adverse responses that can occur after a direct pulp capping procedure**:
     - Physical or microbial insult to the pulp may cause persistent inflammatory changes that can culminate in partial or complete pulpal necrosis.
     - Regulation of the mineralization process involved in dentin bridge formation may become deranged, causing extensive calcification and obliteration of the pulp canal space by mineralized tissue.
     - Very rarely, the differentiation of odontoclasts may be induced with the development of internal resorptive lesions.

Criteria that must be met BEFORE a canal is obturated with gutta-percha:
- Canal must be prepared in a manner that ensures optimum canal debridement and access to the apical area so the filling material can be condensed to obliterate the entire preparation.
- Tooth must be asymptomatic, and canal must be dry at the time of fill.
- If a bacteriologic culture test is being used, a negative culture must be obtained.

A tooth prepared for RCT that responds to thermal tests, indicates inadequate debridement (cleaning), since a pulpless tooth should **NOT** respond to any stimuli. Thus, all nerve must be removed before the canal is obturated.

Access Preparation Objectives: straight-line access, conservation of tooth structure, pulp chamber un-roofing, and remove pulp horns.
- Root canal access is the **INITIAL STEP** in canal preparation. Straight-line access to the apical foramen must be established to ensure free movement of the instrument during debridement and canal preparation. All subsequent treatment hinges on the correctness of the access preparation.
- All access cavities are made through the **LINGUAL** on anterior teeth & **OCCLUSAL** on posterior teeth.
- A facial access is recommended for maxillary primary incisors.

Access Preparation:
- **Mistakes L:** During **mandibular molar access preparation**, two regions tend to be "overcut" resulting in undesirable over preparation of the canal access (**mesial aspect under marginal ridge & lingual surface under lingual cusps**). Mandibular molars tip mesially and lingually, thus if a bur is directed straight inferior, it may cause unnecessary loss of tooth structure in the mesial and lingual areas.
- **Mistakes L:** mandibular incisors & maxillary 1st premolars are the **EASIEST teeth to perforate** during access preparation due the limited access mesiodistally. Thus, care must be taken when initiating treatment on these teeth.

DEBRIDEMENT – the removal of foreign material & contaminated or devitalized tissue from or adjacent to a traumatic infected lesion until surrounding healthy tissue is exposed. **Chemomechanical debridement** of the root canal system is the **MOST crucial aspect** of root canal treatment.

- Achieving **GLASSY, SMOOTH CANAL WALLS** is the **BEST** and most reliable indicator of adequacy of root canal debridement.

- Obtaining clean canal shavings on a file or clean irrigating solution are **INACCURATE** measures to determine the end point of debridement.

- **MOST** important consideration **BEFORE filling a root canal is PROPER CLEANING** (debridement) and **SHAPING** (instrumentation) of the canal. Once the canal is obturated, any organisms that enter periapical tissues from the canal are eliminated by the body's natural defenses. **The MOST common cause of root canal failure is incompletely and inadequately disinfecting the root canal system.**

- **SECOND** most common cause of root canal failure is **LEAKAGE** from a **poorly filled canal**. This is common even after apical curettage (i.e. RCT performed on a tooth with apical curettage of a lesion that was found to be a cyst. 3 years later the lesion was even bigger than before). Thus, the failure was due to **LEAKAGE from a poorly filled canal**. When a canal is prepared properly, any of the acceptable filling methods will produce a successful result as long as the canal is **COMPLETELY** filled.

- Complete canal debridement is the **MOST EFFECTIVE way** to **reduce** canal microorganisms. Debridement is done using various ways depending on the case, and may involve canal instrumentation, placement of medicaments/irrigants, and/or surgery.

Objectives of Root Canal Obturation (Filling with Gutta-Percha):
1. Develop a fluid-tight seal at the apical foramen.
2. Complete filling of the root canal space.
3. Create a favorable biologic environment for the process of tissue healing.

The importance of canal obturation (filling) is **SECOND only to canal debridement**. ~40% failures are caused by incomplete obturation of the canal (**most failures are due to incomplete debridement**). If the canal is not filled, tissue fluid and microorganisms from periapical tissues can enter the voids, causing endodontic failure. However, **if an accessory (lateral) canal is not totally filled during obturation, the appropriate treatment is to observe the tooth and evaluate every 3 months.**

After RCT is completed on a tooth with a periapcial radiolucency, it takes 6-12 months before a marked reduction in the size of the radiolucency is evident on a radiograph. Desired periapcial tissue changes are regeneration of alveolar bone, deposition of apical cementum, and PDL re-establishment.

Indications for using solvent-softened custom gutta-percha cones: lack of an apical stop, abnormally large apical portion of the canal, or an irregular apical portion of the canal. Tugback within 1mm of working length is NOT an indication.
- Studies show **solvent softening DOES NOT** ultimately result in a better apical seal. Thus, this **time consuming procedure is not used if tugback** (slight resistance to dislodgement) is achieved. The gutta-percha cone should also have a definite **apical seat** (should not be able to be pushed further apically).
- If the canal preparation is properly flared, fitting the master cone is not a time-consuming procedure. A gutta-percha cone the same size as **the last file used during preparation (MAF)** is selected and placed as far as possible into the canal, but NOT past the working length.

- Once tugback and apical positioning are obtained, a radiograph is taken to verify cone positioning. If an accurate determination and careful enlargement are performed, the x-ray will show the **master cone reaching the most apical position of the preparation or extending just 1mm short of the apical foramen**. When the cone is slightly short, the **pressure of condensation & the sealer's lubrication action** are sufficient to produce complete seating of the cone. If the cone is > 1mm from the radiographic apex, remove the cone and fit a smaller one, or instrument more in the apical third.

- **MAIN reason for recapitulation** (using your MAF after each increase in file size) during canal instrumentation is **to clean the canal's apical segment of any dentin filings not removed by irrigation**.

When regaining CANAL PATENCY:
- A "crown-down" sequence (larger to smaller) of instruments is used from coronal to apical.
- Rotary instruments work faster and improve the access early in the treatment compared to heated instruments.
- Very light apical pressure is applied when using Nickel Titanium (NiTi) rotary files.
- Over-extended gutta-percha cones had to be removed by extending the file periapically.
- **Glass Bead Sterilizer**-sterilizes endodontic files in **15 sec at 220° C (428°F)**.

If a gutta-percha cone passes past the apex, a file must then be used beyond the apex to avoid breaking the cone. A broken cone in the periapical area can cause orthograde re-treatment failure.
- **Techniques to remove gutta-percha**: rotary instruments, ultrasonic, heat, heat & instrument, and file & chemical.

CHLOROFORM – reagent of choice to **DISSOLVE** gutta-percha. Highly concentrated chloroform is very effective, but use with caution because its **vapor is potentially hazardous**, so it is **dripped directly** in the canal to **avoid excessive flooding**.
- **Other chemicals that dissolve gutta-percha**: xylol, halothane, benzene, carbon disulfide, essential oils, methyl chloroform, and white rectified turpentine.

IRRIGANTS – destroy bacteria during endodontic therapy. **Irrigant's bactericidal action is much greater than the action supplied by intracanal medicaments,** thus are used COPIOUSLY throughout the instrumentation phase of root canal procedures.
1. **Sodium Hypochlorite (NaOCl)**-the **most commonly used IRRIGANT** in endodontics to aid in canal preparation used in concentrations of **1%, 2.6%, or 5.25%**. There is **no** agreed single-concentration value of NaOCl that is **most effective** while being the safest, thus these percentages are all acceptable.
    - 5.25% solution provides **excellent** germicidal solvent action, but is dilute enough to cause only mild irritation when contacting periapical tissue. Thus, gutta-percha points can be disinfected by placing them in **5.25% NaOCl solution for 1 minute**.
    - NaOCl is **a good tissue solvent,** has some **antimicrobial effects,** and acts as a **lubricant** for **root canal instrumentation. NaOCl is toxic to vital tissue so ALWAYS use a rubber dam**.

2. **Hydrogen Peroxide (3% solution)**-**much less solvent action than NaOCl**, but a widely used irrigant in endodontics as many clinicians use H2O2 & NaOCl alternately during treatment. **H2O2 has two modes of action**:
    - **Bubbling action** occurs when it contacts tissue, and certain chemicals physically **foams debris from the canal (*effervescent effect*)**.
    - **Liberation of oxygen** strictly destroys anaerobic microorganisms.

3. **Urea Peroxide (Gly-Oxide)**-useful **irrigant** available in an **anhydrous glycerol base (Gly-Oxide) to prevent decomposition**. Better tolerated by periapical tissue than NaOCl, yet has greater solvent action and is more germicidal than H2O2, thus is **an EXCELLENT IRRIGANT for treating canals with normal periapical tissue and wide apices**.
    - Best use for Gly-Oxide is in **NARROW and/or CURVED canals**, utilizing glycerol's slippery effect.

CHELATING AGENTS – aid and simplify preparation of highly sclerotic canals after the apex is reached with a fine instrument. Chelating agents **act on calcified tissues only with little effect on periapical tissue**. Chelating agents **act by substituting Na+ ions that combine with dentin to form soluble salts for Ca+ ions that are bound in a less soluble combination**. Thus, canal edges become softer, to facilitate canal enlargement.

1. **Ethylene Diamine Tetra-Acetic Acid (EDTA)**-a chelating agent that removes the mineralized portion (decalcify) of the smear layer. EDTA's decalcifying process is self-limiting, and can decalcify up to a 50mm thin layer of root canal wall.
   - EDTA is normally used in 17% concentration.
   - RC-Prep & EDTAC are types of EDTA preparations.
   - EDTA has a limited value as an irrigation solution, since the decalcifying process induced by EDTA is self-limiting and stops as soon as the chelator is used up.
   - EDTA remains active in the canal for 5 days if not inactivated. Thus, upon appointment completion, the canal MUST be irrigated/inactivated with sodium hypochlorite (NaOCl) containing solution.
2. **EDTAC**-is **EDTA + Cetavlon** (a quaternary ammonium compound) with a greater antimicrobial action than EDTA, but has more inflammatory potential to tissues. NaOCl inactivates EDTAC.
3. **RC-Prep**-a **foamy solution** that combines functions of **EDTA + urea peroxide** to provide chelation & irrigation. RC-prep **has a natural effervescence** that is increased by irrigation with NaOCl to help remove canal debris.

ZINC OXIDE-EUGENOL – a **cement** with a long history of successful use as a **based root canal sealer**. The **MAIN** function of a root canal sealer is **to FILL DISCREPANCIES** between the **core-filling material and the dentin walls**. This function makes it even more important than the core filling material. **ZOE (root canal sealer) functions**:

- Acts as a **lubricant** to facilitate gutta-percha cone placement.

- Forms a **bond between the gutta-percha and dentin walls**.

- Exerts **antibacterial activity** (some exert more than others) which is highest in the period of time immediately after its placement.

- **ZOE Disadvantages**: staining, slow setting time, non-adhesion, and solubility.

Most root canal sealers are **some type of ZOE cement** capable of producing a seal while being **well-tolerated by periapical tissues**. All sealers have some **radiopacity** (caused by metallic salts in the sealer), thus are visible on a radiograph. This radiopacity helps disclose any accessory canals, resorptive areas, root fractures, and the shape of the apical foramen.
- **Note**: after filling a canal with gutta-percha, if there is a **horizontal line of material (gutta-percha or sealer) extending both mesially & distally from the canal to the PDL space**, this indicates a **ROOT FRACTURE**.

Mineral Trioxide Aggregate (MTA) – MOST superior **retro-filling** (reverse filling = retrograde amalgam filling) material and material of choice today. MTA seals the **APICAL portion of the root canal**, and is ALWAYS after an apicoectomy alone will not yield a good result. **A reverse filling (MTA) MUST always be placed when an apical seal may be faulty** (i.e. with a calcified root canal, it is impossible to obdurate most of the canal and get an apical seal. If just the root apex where cut off (apicoectomy), the incompletely filled canal might act as a source of reinfection. To prevent this, after the root tip is resected, the apical foramen is found, enlarged, and filled with zinc-free amalgam to create a seal.

- **Advantages**: radiopaque, hydrophilic, biocompatible, non-toxic, induces hard tissue formation.

- **Disadvantages**: difficult to manipulate & long-setting time.

APICOECTOMY (ROOT RESECTION = ROOT AMPUTATION) – a procedure where the buccal tissue is flapped back, the buccal bone around the root apex and the root apex itself are removed, and the area is curetted out. Apicoectomy is a resection of the most apical portion of the root. It is best accomplished by obliquely RESECTING the most apical portion of the involved root.

- **Indications**: if a reverse filling (MTA) must be placed, it is necessary to gain access to an area of pathosis, the poorly filled apical portion of the root is to be removed to the level of canal obturation. Retreating teeth with posts are the MOST common reason for an apicoectomy and retrograde filling.

- If a tooth with previous endodontic treatment becomes reinfected, it is best to retreat it conventionally by removing the filling material, debride the canals, and refill. However, if the tooth has been restored with a post, core, and crown, then apical curettage, then an apicoectomy and retrofill should be performed.

Periradicular Surgery Indications:
1. non-negotiable canal, blockage or severe root curvature in which non-surgical treatment is impossible.
2. complications arising from procedural accidents (i.e. instrument separation, ledging, or perforations) that cannot be handled without surgical exposure of the site.
3. failed treatment due to irretrievable posts or root fillings.
4. horizontal apical fractures where the apical end of the pulp becomes necrotic.
5. biopsy to diagnose non-odontogenic causes of symptoms (i.e. patient with a history of previous malignancy, lip paresthesia, or anesthesia).

PERIAPICAL CURETTAGE – the same procedure as an Apicoectomy that flaps back the buccal tissue and buccal bone removal, but DOES NOT remove the root apex. Removal and examination of the diseased tissue and determining the extent of the lesion are the objectives of apical curettage.

SUPEROXOL – the MOST COMMON bleaching agent for endodontically treated teeth that is a 30% aqueous solution by weight of H_2O_2 in distilled water. It is a potent oxidizing agent whose bleaching effect is due to direct oxidation of stain-producing substances. Tooth bleaching causes color change in enamel and dentin.

- **Chairside Technique**: apply heat to Superoxol-saturated cotton pellets in the tooth chamber, and repeat until the tooth is lighter. This heat liberates the oxygen in the bleaching agent.

- The most probable post-operative complication of tooth bleaching that has not been properly obturated is **acute apical periodontitis**.

- **Acute Apical Periodontitis (AAP)**-characterized by pain commonly triggered by chewing or percussion. AAP alone does not indicate irreversible pulpitis. **AAP indicates irritated apical tissues possibly associated with a vital pulp with a potential reversible pulpitis**. In the absence of acute pain, a negative EPT or frank apical radiolucency, a carious tooth with sensitivity to percussion may respond to caries control (temporary filling). If it does not respond to a sedative filling, RCT is indicated.

- **Walking Bleach Technique**: place a thick paste consisting of sodium perborate and 2-3 drops of Superoxol in the tooth chamber with a temporary restoration. Several repetitions of this technique works well.

ENDODONTIC INSTRUMENTS

Broken Instruments: When a broken instrument (file) protrudes past the apex, surgery should be performed to remove it because it is a constant irritant (i.e. during cleaning & shaping of a canal, your K-file (#25) separates in the canal. Your first attempt to retrieve it results in a broken instrument through the apex). To manage this case, raise a flap and remove the instrument surgically, then fill the canal with gutta-percha.

- It is easier to retrieve an instrument if it is wedged coronal or at the curvature of the canal, but very difficult if the instrument has passed the canal curvature.
- When an instrument breaks off anywhere in the canal and a periapical radiolucency is present and minimal canal enlargement has been performed before the accident, surgery is indicated since the periapical tissues have had little opportunity for healing to be stimulated. You would prepare and obturate to the point of blockage, and then perform an apicoectomy and retrofilling.
- When an instrument breaks off in the canal's apical third and is lodged tightly with no evident periapcial radiolucency, the remaining root canal space can be filled with gutta-percha, the patient is informed, and placed on a 3-6 month recall.
- Prognosis of a tooth with a broken instrument is best if the tooth had a vital pulp and no periapical lesion.

NICKEL TITANIUM INSTRUMENTS (NITI) — hand-operated or engine-driven instruments to CLEAN & SHAPE. NiTi methods:

- Push & pull stroke, reaming motion, or engine-driven rotary motion (uses only a reaming motion).
- Hand instrumentation is done by either filing (push & pull) or reaming (repeated rotations).
- The instrument's action, **NOT** type of instrument used, determines the canal preparation's general shape:
    - **Filing**-a push-pull action with emphasis on the withdrawal stroke. Its efficiency is greater with files than with reamers to remove dentin due to the greater number of flutes in contact with canal walls during the rasping motion of removing the file. Filing action produces a canal that is **irregular in shape**, thus a canal prepared with this push-pull filing action MUST be filled with gutta-percha in a condensation procedure.
    - **Reaming**-repeated clockwise instrument rotation especially during insertion. A reaming action produces a canal that is relatively **ROUND in shape**. A reaming method is usually most efficient if using a silver cone to fill a canal.
    - **Circumferential filing**-a push-pull filing action that SCRAPES canal walls to create a smooth, tapered preparation. The file is moved first towards the canal's buccal side, reinserted, then removed slightly mesially. This is done all the way around the canal until all dentin walls are planed. Circumferential filing technique **enhances preparation when a flaring method is used**.

Important: A canal is instrumented and shaped so it has a continuously TAPERING FUNNEL SHAPE. The canal's widest diameter should be at the orifice (opening), while its narrowest diameter is at the dentinocemental junction (DCJ or .5-1.0mm from the radiographic apex). Ideally, .5-1.0mm from the canal apex is where all teeth should be filed to and filled.

BARBED BROACHES — intracanal stainless steel instruments designed to remove pulp tissue, cotton pellet absorbent points, and other soft materials. It is NOT used for canal enlargement. The barbs are notched out of the instrument shaft and represent a weakened point. If the broach is not used with utmost care or is forced apically, the barbs will bend and engage the canal walls, making removal difficult.

HEDSTROM FILES — an effective "H-Type" stainless steel CUTTING instrument made using a sharp, rotating cutter to gauge triangular segments out of a round blank shaft to produce a very sharp edge. Used carefully with ONLY a filing action, this file successfully **planes dentin walls much faster than K-type files or reamers**. **S-file**-a modified Hedstrom file.

K-Type Instruments:
1. **K-Files**-the most useful instruments for removing hard tissue to enlarge canals. Files are made by twisting a blank (a square stainless steel rod producing a series of cutting flutes). The K-type file's action in the canal is a clockwise-counterclockwise motion while directing pressure apically (can be a filing or reaming action). **K-type files are the STRONGEST and cut the LEAST aggressively.** K-flex file-a modified K-type file.
2. **Reamers**-manufactured similar to files, but with fewer flutes. Reamers are used in canal preparations to **SHAVE DENTIN** using **ONLY** a reaming action to enlarge canals. Reamers remove intracanal debris with a **CLOCKWISE** reaming action, and **place materials into the apical portion of the canal using a COUNTERCLOCKWISE rotation.**

5 Critical Factors to Manage Traumatic Avulsion Injuries:
1. **Time**: the time interval from injury until tooth replacement is a MAJOR factor in maintenance of PDL viability & subsequent root resorption. Teeth replanted within 30min exhibit very little resorption, while most teeth replanted after 2hrs have extensive external root resorption (MAIN cause of failure of replanted teeth is external root resorption).
2. **Storage Media**: if the tooth cannot be replanted immediately, proper storage can favorably influence PDL cell viability. MILK is the BEST storage media due to its near neutral pH (6.5-6.8) and osmolality which is conducive for cell survival. Physiologic saline and saliva are other tooth storage media.
3. **Tooth Socket**: should not be damaged by curettage or forceful replantation.
4. **Root Surface**: should not be scraped, dried, or manipulated with caustic chemicals.
5. **Splint Stabilization**: a splint that allows physiologic movement is placed for a maximum of 2 weeks to allow the initial reattachment of the PDL fibers.

*When a tooth has been avulsed (out) of the mouth for > 2hrs, the treatment of the tooth socket, root surfaces, and time required for splint stabilization changes.

Proper management of an avulsed PERMANANT tooth replanted by the dentist within 2hrs of the accident:
- 10-14 days after replantation, clean and shape (prepare) the root canal, and place calcium hydroxide paste into the canals. Replace this paste every 3 months for on year. After 1 year, if the root resorption has reversed or stopped, a permanent gutta-percha filling can be placed.

Proper management of an avulsed PERMANANT tooth out for > than 2hrs of the accident:
- Ankylosis & external root resorption will probably occur within 2 years. Ankylosis caused by the replacement gives a better prognosis than external root resorption which leads to failure.
- RCT is performed in its entirety PRIOR to replantation.
- Soak the tooth in 2.4% fluoride solution acidulated at 5.5pH for at least 20min. Fluoride slows the resorptive process.
- Gently curette the blood clot out of the alveolar socket and irrigate with saline.
- Rinse the tooth with saline, replant it into the socket, and splint for 4-6 weeks.

Avulsed Tooth Management:
- After 60 min of dry storage of an avulsed tooth, few periodontal ligament cells survive.
- Storage of an avulsed tooth in tap water is as bad as dry storage.
- Saliva is hypotonic, thus allows storage for up to 2hrs, but **MILK has a maximum storage time of 6hrs.**
- Teeth with complete root development should be treated endodontically ASAP even if replanted within 30 min.
- Teeth with incomplete root development that are replanted within 30 min may not require endodontic treatment.

ROOT RESORPTION – the MOST frequent sequela to avulsed tooth replantation.

EXTERNAL ROOT RESORPTION
caused by periradicular inflammation, dental trauma (resulting in damage to attachment apparatus), excessive orthodontic forces, impacted teeth, bleaching of non-vital teeth. External resorption is **ALWAYS** accompanied by bone resorption and is the chief cause of failure of replantation of permanent teeth (it is the main cause of failure of replanted teeth). 3 Types of External Root Resorption:

1. **Surface resorption**-caused by acute injury to the PDL & root surface. If injury is not repeated, healing occurs forming new cementum and PDL. Root surface resorption is limited to cementum, may heal itself, and is not visible on a radiograph.
2. **External Inflammatory resorption**-external resorption in which an infected pulp may further complicate the resorptive process. Characterized by bowl-shaped resorption areas involving cementum and dentin that rapidly progresses and continues if treatment is ignored.
   - Necrotic pulp and bacteria are necessary components of inflammatory resorption. Thus, this process is arrested with immediate RCT (open the tooth, clean & shape the canal, and place calcium hydroxide paste in the canal every 3 months for 1 year). If resorption stops after 1 year of treatment, then place a permanent root canal filling (gutta-percha). A calcium hydroxide-based root canal sealer is strongly recommended.
   - cervical root resorption does not occur exclusively at the cervical area of the root. Pulp does NOT play a role in cervical root resorption.
3. **Replacement resorption (ankylotic resorption)**-external root surface resorption that becomes substituted by bone, causing ankylosis (common in unsuccessful avulsed tooth replant cases). Replacement resorption accompanies dento-alveolar ankylosis due to extensive trauma to the tooth's attachment apparatus. It is characterized by progressive replacement of the root by bone. Histologically, it shows direct contact between dentin and bone, with no intervening PDL or cemental layer.
   - **Pathognomonic signs of external resorption**: lack of mobility, metallic sound to percussion, and infra-occlusion of the involved tooth in the developing dentition.

INTERNAL (INFLAMMATORY) ROOT RESORPTION
caused by dental trauma, partial removal of pulp (pulpotomy), caries, pulp capping with calcium hydroxide, or a cracked tooth. Internal resorption causes loss of pulp vitality & subsequent infection of coronal pulp causing inflammation. Inflammation due to an infected coronal pulp is generally the cause of internal resorption. Teeth with internal resorption have a history of trauma, crown preparation, or pulpotomy.

- Internal resorption is **often precipitated** by traumatic injury to the tooth. Undifferentiated reserve C.T. pulp cells are activated to form dentinoclasts that resorb the tooth structure in contact with the pulp.

- Internal resorption is usually asymptomatic, and discovered on routine radiographic evaluation. The root canal's anatomic configuration is altered and increases in size, appearing as an irregular radiolucency anywhere along the canal space. Radiographic presentation of internal resorption is a fairly uniform enlargement of the root canal space. **The root canal "disappears" into the lesion.**

- Sometimes on a radiograph, an external resorptive lesion can superimpose the canal space to mimic internal resorption. In such cases, another radiograph is taken at a different angle since the radiolucent lesion inside the canal space will not shift.

- A tooth with internal resorption may respond to pulp vitality tests, but when detected, **a pulpectomy should be performed**. Once the pulp tissue responsible is removed, all resorption stops. To "wait and see" may cause sufficient destruction to perforate the root.

- While internal resorption can occur ONLY when some pulp tissue is still vital, a NEGATIVE sensibility test does NOT rule out this etiology.

- **Pink Tooth**-a pathognomonic sign of internal resorption (not replacement resorption), and sometimes a sign of cervical root resorption, characterized by a pinkish appearance of the tooth due to granulation growth undermining the coronal dentin.

INTENTIONAL REPLANTATION (REPLANT SURGERY) – a tooth that requires endodontic therapy is purposely REMOVED from its socket, some type of canal or apical preparation and/or filling is performed, and the tooth is RETURNED to its original socket. **Replant Surgery Indications**:
1. When routine endodontic therapy is impractical or impossible.
2. When a canal is obstructed via a broken instrument or calcification, and periapical surgery is impractical (a lower molar with the mandibular canal is close proximity).
3. When perforating internal or external is present, yet surgery is impractical.
4. When previous treatment has failed, but non-surgical treatment or surgery is impractical.

Intentional replantation is considered ONLY when there is no other alternative treatment to maintain a "strategic" tooth. Long-term follow-up is required to monitor for complications, periodontal defects, and ankylosis with replacement resorption.

Procedures essential for successful intentional replantation of an avulsed tooth include: skillful extraction, minimum out-of-socket time, minimum root damage while the tooth is held during apical root end preparation, and repair of any perforation or resorptive defect before replantation.
- Curettage of the socket to remove periapical pathosis is unnecessary because the socket wall should be MINIMALLY manipulated during replantation.

Replantation of a **PRIMARY TOOTH is NOT** recommended due to potential danger to the permanent successor tooth from sequels of trauma (i.e. infection, ankylosis, or damage due to manipulation during the procedure). Thus, if a mother of a 4 year old child calls your office reporting that her child has suffered a trauma to one of his front teeth that has avulsed out of the socket, advise the mother to leave the tooth and come to the office immediately.

PULP – primary function of pulp is DENTIN FORMATION. Other pulp functions:
1. **induction**-forms dentin which then induces enamel formation.
2. **nutrition**-dentinal tubules are linked to the pulp to maintain pulp hydration and formation of peritubular dentin.

MANTLE DENTIN – the first formed dentin that is laid before the odontoblast layer is organized. Thus, the pattern of deposition and size of collagen fibers differs from circumpulpal dentin.

CIRCUMPULPAL DENTIN – represents most of the dentin formed.

SECONDARY DENTIN – forms after tooth eruption & throughout life, resulting in a gradual, but asymmetric reduction in pulp size.

TERTIARY DENTIN (REPARATIVE DENTIN) – an irregular and disorganized dentin layer laid down in response to any injurious or irritant stimuli.

As dental pulp ages the number of reticulin fibers decreases (pulp becomes less cellular and more fibrous), and the size of the pulp decreases due to the continued deposition of dentin. However, as pulp ages, **collagen fibers & calcifications within the pulp (denticles or pulp stones) both increase**.
- **Pulp stones**-calcifications associated with chronic pulpal disease from advanced carious lesions or large restorations.

Pulp contains **myelinated (sensory) & unmyelinated (motor) nerve fibers** that are afferent & sympathetic. Unmyelinated fibers regulate the lumen size of the blood vessels. However, **proprioceptors** (respond to stimuli regarding movement) are NOT found in dental pulp.
- **Free nerve endings**-the only nerve ending found in pulp. Free nerve ending is a specific pain receptor. Regardless of the source of stimulation (heat, cold, pressure), **the ONLY response will be PAIN**.
- **Cells Found in Dental Pulp**: fibroblasts (the main cell), odontoblasts, histiocytes (macrophages), & lymphocytes.
- **Cells Found in Diseased Pulp**: PMN's, plasma cells, basophils, eosinophils, lymphocytes, & mast cells (contain histamine & heparin).

NOTES

At the **ONSET of pulpal inflammation**, these **cells are involved in the cellular response**: **plasma cells, macrophages, & lymphocytes**, but **NOT Polymorphonuclear (PMN) Leucocytes**.
- **The onset of pulpal inflammation is** an insidious process characterized by a **chronic cellular response** of plasma cells, macrophages, and lymphocytes. There is no direct pulp exposure to caries, thus the cellular response is not acute.
- **After pulp exposure, acute inflammatory cells (mainly PMNs) are chemotactically attracted to the area**. Histologically, the tissue is likely to show signs of acute inflammation near the exposure site, and a band of chronic inflammatory cells b/t the acute inflammation and the underlying normal pulp.

- **The response of vital pulp to microbial invasion is very resistant** based on observation that even **after 2 weeks of traumatic pulp exposure, only 2mm of coronal pulp may "give in" to microorganisms**. However, non-vital pulp is a "fertile ground" for microbial growth.
- Carious exposures in permanent teeth pulp usually require RCT. Immature (open apex) permanent teeth with carious exposures can be treated with pulp capping or a pulpotomy.
  - **Pulp capping-not recommended in primary teeth with carious pulp exposures** due to its high failure rate and because pulpotomy (having similar time requirements) is very successful. Pulp capping can be done if a mechanical pulp exposure occurs.

APICAL portion of pulp contains more collagen than the coronal portion. This facilitates a pulpectomy using barbed broaches or endodontic files.
- **Type 1 & 3** collagen is mainly found in pulp in a 55%:45% ratio. Type 5 collagen is found in only small amounts.
- **Type 1 collagen** predominates in **DENTIN**.
- Odontoblasts synthesize **Type 1 collagen**.
- Fibroblasts in pulp synthesize **Type 1 & 2 collagen**.

Central Zone (Pulp Proper)-area that **contains large nerves & blood vessels**, and is lined peripherally by a specialized odontogenic area that has **3 layers**:
1. **Cell-rich zone**-**INNERMOST pulp layer** that contains fibroblasts.
2. **Cell-free zone** (zone of Weil)-pulp layer rich in capillaries, nerve networks, and contains the **Nerve Plexus of Rashkow**.
3. **Odontoblastic layer**-**OUTERMOST pulp layer** that contains odontoblasts, and lies next to predentin & mature dentin.
   - The **absence** of the **predentin layer predisposes dentin to internal resorption by pulp cells**. Immediately adjacent to the odontoblastic layer in the pulp, 10-47mm of the dentin matrix remains unmineralized. If this unmineralized dentin layer is lost due to trauma or an infectious process, it predisposes the dentin to internal resorption by odontoclasts.

MANDIBULAR TEETH ROOT ANATOMY – the lingual wall of mandibular teeth is most easily perforated when preparing an access opening due to the lingual inclination of these teeth.

- Mandibular 1st Premolar: **25% MAY have 2 canals with 2 apical foramina**. Thus, treatment can be tricky. At least 23% can have 2 or 3 canals starting anywhere down the root. **If a straight-on preoperative radiograph of a mandibular 1st premolar shows the pulp canal disappearing in midroot, this is an important indication that 2 canals are present. Pulpitis can cause referred pain to the MENTAL REGION OF THE MANDIBLE**.

- Mandibular 2nd Premolar: **97% have 1 canal at the apex**. It has less variation than the mandibular 1st premolar. It usually has 1 root and 1 well-centered canal, with an oval access opening. The **mental foramen lies in close proximity to the root apex, so avoid overinstrumentation and overfill, and do not misdiagnose the foramen as a premolar abscess on a radiograph**. Thus, before performing root canal therapy, ensure that all diagnostic test confirm your finding. **Pulpitis can cause referred pain to the MENTAL REGION OF THE MANDIBLE**.

- Mandibular Molars: usually have a **TRAPEZOIDAL outline of the pulp chamber** formed by two canals in the mesial root, and one oval canal in the distal root. ~40% of cases, the distal root may have a 2nd canal (4th canal overall). The pulp chamber is located in the mesial 2/3 of the crown. Look for a 4th canal if the first canal found in the distal root lies more toward the buccal, rather than in the center.
  - **Mandibular 1st molar** requires endodontic treatment more than any other tooth in the oral cavity. Pulpitis can cause referred pain to the **EAR**.

- **Mandibular Canine**: the **root canal is THIN mesiodistally, but WIDE labiolingually.** They usually have **1 root**, but in rare cases may have 2 separate roots. The **access opening is a large OVAL** with the greatest width placed incisogingivally. This tooth usually has a slightly labial axial inclination of the crown. Thus, the access opening must be directed towards the lingual surface. **Pulpitis can cause referred pain to the MENTAL REGION OF THE MANDIBLE.**

- **Mandibular Central Incisor**: has **ONLY 1 ROOT** that is **narrow M-D, but relatively wide labiolingually.** The root may have a distal and/or lingual curvature, and **2 CANALS may be present** (if so, the labial canal is straighter). **Access opening for a mandibular central or lateral is a LONG OVAL**, with the greatest width placed incisogingivally, and the incisal extent very close to the incisal edge. **Pulpitis can cause referred pain to the MENTAL REGION OF THE MANDIBLE.**

MAXILLARY TEETH ROOT ANATOMY:
- **Maxillary Incisors & Canines**: ALL have **1 root, 1 canal, & a distal axial inclination**. Thus, when penetrating along the long axis of the tooth, the bur must be slightly angled toward the distal surface to **avoid perforation** of the mesial portion of the root.
  - **Maxillary Central Incisor**: **ALWAYS has 1 root & 1 canal.** The root is bulky with a slight distal axial inclination, but rarely has a dilacerations. The pulp chamber **access opening is OVAL-TRIANGULAR (it is somewhat triangular, as opposed to oval).** The triangle base will be the facial, and triangle apex is lingual. If it is not triangular, then it must be oval. **Pulpitis can cause referred pain to the FOREHEAD.**
  - **Maxillary Lateral Incisor**: is **MOST likely to have a curved root. It ALWAYS has 1 root with 1 canal.** The root is more slender than in the maxillary central incisor and often (55%) of the time has a distal and/or lingual curvature or dilacerations. The access opening is OVAL. **Pulpitis can cause referred pain to the FOREHEAD.**
  - **Maxillary Canine**-ALWAYS has 1 root & 1 canal, and is the LONGEST tooth in the maxillary arch. The **access opening is OVAL**. Pulpitis can cause referred pain to the NASOLABIAL AREA.

- **Maxillary 1st Premolar: ALMOST ALWAYS has 2 canals.** ~60% have 2 roots (1 B, 1 Palatal) each with 1 canal. The buccal & palatal roots can be completely separate, or twin projections rising from the root's middle 1/3 to the apex (this is more common). These 2 roots are usually equal in length from apex to cusp. However, the palatal root and canal may be wider.
  - ~40% of maxillary 1st premolars, only 1 root is present (usually with two separate canals). In cross section at the cervical line, the canal is shaped like a **FIGURE EIGHT (ELLIPSE).** The access is a **THIN OVAL**. Be careful not to perforate on the mesial (due to the mesial concavity).

- **Maxillary 2nd Premolar**: have a higher incidence of accessory canals (60%) than maxillary 1st premolars. A pulpitis of this tooth **MOST often refers PAIN to the TEMPORAL REGION** and sometimes **NASOLABIAL REGION.** If careful diagnosis does not reveal the affected tooth, other teeth and related anatomic structures become suspect. **Referred pain**-occurs when a pulpitis in one tooth causes pain in another area.
  - Usually (85%) have 1 root, while (15%) 2 separate roots exist (each with 1 canal). The access opening is also a **THIN OVAL** (exactly like maxillary 1st premolars).
  - When only 1 canal is present in a maxillary 1st or 2nd premolar, it is usually in the **CENTER of the access preparation**. If only 1 canal is found, but is not in the center of the tooth, it is probable than another canal is present. Overfilling either premolar may force gutta-percha material directly into the MAXILLARY SINUS.

- **Maxillary Molars**: have a **TRIANGLE** pulp chamber outline. The pulp chamber floor is formed by the buccal canals, and the apex is formed by the palatal canal. The line connecting the mesial & palatal canals is the longest. If a 4th canal exists, it is usually lingual to the orifice of the MB canal, and in the MB root. The 4th canal is more common than previously believed.

- **Maxillary 1st Molar**: its 3 canal orifices are arranged in a **TRIANGLE** shape. ~59% have **4th canal (ML)** with its orifice located just lingual to the MB canal orifice. **This 4th ML canal is in the MB root, and may join the MB canal or exit through a separate foramen**. If a lesion exists on the MB root prior to RCT and does not heal in the usual time frame (6-12 months) after treatment, it is most likely due to a missed ML canal.

NOTES

- **MB canal**: the **MB canal orifice is usually the MOST DIFFICULT to locate** because it is under the MB cusp and must be accessed from a distolingual position. It is the small canal that often splits into two canals, and may be calcified and difficult to instrument.
- **Palatal canal**: is the straightest, widest, and most tapering canal. The most common curvature of the palatal root is to the facial. **The U-SHAPED radiopacity commonly seen overlying the palatal root apex is most likely the ZYGOMATIC PROCESS of the** maxilla.
- **DB canal**: also a small, tapering canal, but its orifice has no direct relation to the DB cusp. The DB orifice is usually located by its relation to the MB orifice. The DB canal is found 2-3mm distal and slightly palatal to the MB canal orifice.

Important: nerve endings of **CN VII, IX, & X** are widely distributed in the **SUBNUCLEUS CAUDALIS of trigeminal nerve (CN V)**. A profuse, intermingling of these nerve fibers **creates potential of referred dental pain to many sites**.

Adjuncts to Endodontic Treatment:
- **Transplantation**-the transfer of a tooth from one alveolar socket to another in the same person or into another person. Transplanted teeth with partial root development have a better prognosis than fully developed roots. Intentional replantation is NOT a substitute for endodontic surgery if it can be done.

- **Orthodontic extrusion**-force controlled vertical tooth movement occlusally in the socket. Orthodontic extrusion indications: PRIOR to implant placement, untreatable subgingival pathoses (i.e. cervical caries, cervical fracture, periodontal defects, resorptive lesions, and perforations in the cervical area).

- To stabilize an intentionally replanted tooth, a very effective method is to ask the patient to close in centric occlusion for the rest of the day.

- A major disadvantage of endodontic implants is the lack of an apical seal.

- **Crown lengthening**-a procedure to apically position the gingival margin and/or to reduce cervical bone. Used to treat subgingival caries, perforations, and resorptions.

- **Root submersion**-involves resection of tooth roots 3mm below the alveolar crest, then cover with a mucoperiosteal flap. Submerged roots will prevent alveolar resorption and maintain better proprioception.
  - **Indications**: rampant caries, adverse periodontal conditions, repeated failure of prosthetic cases, and especially useful in medically compromised or handicapped patients requiring better denture control. Sometimes, root submersion is performed to avoid formation of an esthetic defect that may result after extraction.

THERMAL SENSITIVITY – the **EARLIEST** and **MOST COMMON** symptom of pulpal edema/inflamed pulp (acute pulpitis) is thermal sensitivity to hot and/or cold stimuli. Usually involves increased and persistent pain to cold.

- Best method to elicit the most accurate thermal response is to **INDIVIDUALLY ISOLATE the suspected teeth** with a rubber dam, then bathe each tooth in hot or cold water. All other methods may stimulate the tooth in only one section of one surface, thus are less accurate. Thermal tests may yield a false-negative in immature, recently traumatized teeth, or due to premedication with an analgesic.

- As caries enter dentin, it spreads laterally at the DEJ due to the increased organic content and involvement of many dentinal tubules. Tomes fibers-react, cause fatty degeneration and later decalcification (sclerosis).

- As caries progresses, dentin destruction is followed by bacterial invasion of the tubules and complete dentin destruction. Once odontoblasts are involved, pulpal changes occur (i.e. initially vascular dilation and local edema).

- The only reliable clinical evidence that secondary dentin has formed is DECREASED TOOTH SENSITIVITY (seen a few weeks after placing a filling). When dentinal tubules become completely calcified, dentin is insensitive.

Teeth conditions that usually DO NOT require endodontic treatment if managed properly because pulp remains vital:
1. **Cementoma (periapical cemental dysplasia)**-usually occurs in the **anterior region** of the **mandible**, starting as a radiolucent lesion that eventually calcifies. Cementoma **DOES NOT affect pulp vitality**.
2. **Traumatic bone cyst**-not a true cyst since there is no epithelial lining. Found mainly in young people and is **asymptomatic**. Appears as a radiolucency that **scallops around teeth** roots. **Teeth are usually vital**. No treatment.
3. **Globulomaxillary cyst**-a **developmental cyst** found at the junction of the globules and maxillary processes of the maxilla, between the **lateral incisor and canine roots**. This cyst arises from cells in a fissural line of bone. **Teeth are vital**.

Conditions that usually require Endodontic Treatment:
1. **Apical Scar**-a periapical granuloma, cyst, or abscess that heal with scar tissue. It's a well-circumscribed radiolucency resembling a granuloma. **Tooth is non-vital, so endodontic treatment is necessary**.
2. **Radicular Cyst**-usually occurs in a pre-existing granuloma, is rarely painful, and appears as an apex radiolucency of a **non-vital tooth**. **Endodontic treatment is necessary**.
3. **Chronic Dental Abscess**-often the cause of **a sinus tract in** the gingival tissue of children. It is often the result of a periapical granuloma, appearing as a **radiolucent area at the apex** of a non-vital tooth. A fistula is often found leading from an abscess cavity. Tooth pain stops upon drainage. **Endodontic treatment is necessary**.
4. **Chronic Periapical Granuloma**-asymptomatic, associated with a **non-vital tooth**, and the **MOST common sequelae of pulpitis. Endodontic treatment is necessary**.

PERIAPICAL ABSCESS – a condition that **results from a pulpal infection that extends through the apical foramen into the periapical tissues. MOST COMMON OF ALL DENTAL ABSCESSES**. It is a localized collection of pus in the alveolar bone at the root apex after pulpal death with the infection extending into the periapical tissue.
- FIRST SYMPTOM is **slight tooth tenderness** that later develops into a **severe throbbing pain** (acute abscess) with **swelling of the overlying mucosa**.
- Tooth will **NOT** respond to **EPT or cold tests**, but may respond to **heat**.
- **Emergency treatment**: establish **drainage** (ideally through the canal) and **prescribe antibiotics & analgesics** to relieve the acute symptoms, followed by conventional RCT at a later date.
- For endodontic infections that do **not** respond to penicillin, **clindamycin** is recommended as it produces high bone levels, and is effective against anaerobic bacteria, but must be used with caution due to the potential for pseudomembranous colitis.
- **Acute Osteomyelitis**-occurs in the jaws, **most commonly caused by a DENTAL INFECTION**. It is not a common disease, but is a **serious sequela of a periapical infection** that often results in a diffuse spread of infection throughout the MEDULLARY SPACES, with subsequent necrosis of a variable amount of bone.
  - **Acute or subacute osteomyelitis may involve the maxilla or mandible**. The disease usually remains fairly well-localized to the area of initial infection in the maxilla. In the mandible, bone involvement is more diffuse and widespread.
  - Clinically, the afflicted person has **severe pain, temperature/fever, and regional lymphadenopathy**. The teeth in the involved area are **loose and sore** making eating difficult, if not impossible.
  - **Radiographically**: AO progresses rapidly and demonstrates little radiographic evidence of its presence until it has developed for at least 1-2 weeks. At that time, **diffuse lytic changes in bone appear. A "moth-eaten" radiolucency is evident**.
  - **Treatment**: establish & maintain drainage, and prescribe antibiotics to prevent further spread and complications.

PERIODONTAL ABSCESS – an **acute abscess** that develops through the **periodontal pocket** that involves **alveolar bone loss, pocket formation, and periodontal pathologic conditions. Tooth is usually palpation & percussion positive, and responds to EPT (unlike the periapical abscess)**. Bacteria associated with the periodontal abscess are **gram (-) rods** (i.e. Capnocytophaga species, Vibrio-corroding organisms, Fusobacterium species).

NOTES

GINGIVAL ABSCESS – a **RARE abscess** that occurs when bacteria invade through a break in the gingival surface. Caused by mastication, oral hygiene procedures, or dental treatment.

CHRONIC APICAL ABSCESS **(SUPPURATIVE APICAL PERIODONTITIS)** – a long-standing, low-grade infection of the periapical bone with the **root canal being the source of the infection**. It is generally asymptomatic, and sometimes so painless that it may go undetected for years until revealed by an x-ray. **Treatment is conventional root canal therapy**.

- Chronic apical abscess may follow an acute alveolar abscess or unsatisfactory RCT. Radiographs reveal a diffuse radiolucency & PDL thickening. The tooth may be slightly loose, or tender to percussion.

- Chronic apical abscess is differentiated from cysts & granulomas because cysts & granulomas are well-defined radiolucencies.

PHOENIX ABSCESS (suppurative apical periodontitis = recrudescent abscess) – an **apical lesion (acute abscess) that develops as an acute exacerbation of a chronic apical abscess**. It develops as the granulomatous zone becomes contaminated or infected by root canal elements. Diagnosis is based on acute symptoms (pain to percussion) and radiographic examination (reveals a large periapical radiolucency).
- A massive invasion of pulpal contaminants **will result** in the formation of an **acute abscess (Phoenix abscess)**.

Important: 30%-50% of bone calcium must be altered before radiographic evidence of periapical breakdown occurs. This alteration occurs at the **junction between the cortical and cancellous bone**.

ACUTE APICAL/ALVEOLAR ABSCESS (AA) – a localized collection of pus inside alveolar bone at the root apex after pulpal death, with the infection extending into the periapical tissue. **FIRST SYMPTOM of AA may be slight tooth tenderness, that later develops into a SEVERE THROBBING PAIN to percussion with swelling of the overlying mucosa.**

- The tooth becomes more painful, elongated, and loose. At times, the pain may decrease or completely disappear. The patient may appear weak, irritable, and have a fever.

- AA diagnosis is based on history, exam, and radiographs. **An AA tooth will not respond to EPT or cold tests, but MAY respond to HEAT.**

- **Treatment**: establish drainage & debride the canal system of necrotic tissue to relieve the acute symptoms. At a later date, perform conventional RCT. (**Note**: if the abscess ruptures through the periosteum into soft tissue, the patient's symptoms will subside).

GRANULOMA – a **growth of granulomatous tissue continuous with the PDL due to pulpal death** with diffusion of toxic products into the periapical area. Is **usually asymptomatic**. Radiographically, a **well-defined area of rarefaction (radiolucency)** with some irregularities is evident. Clinically, the tooth is NOT sensitive.

CYST – inflammatory response of the periapex that develops from pre-existing granulomatous tissue (granuloma), characterized by a **central, fluid-filled, epithelium-lined cavity, surrounded by a granulomatous tissue & peripheral fibrous encapsulation**. Often associated with a chronically infected and potentially mobile tooth, but is **usually asymptomatic**.
- **Radiographically**: evident as a well-defined area of rarefaction (radiolucency) that is limited by a continuous radiopaque, sclerotic border of bone.

Important: a **granuloma or cyst** is ONLY differentially diagnosed by a HISTOLOGIC EXAMINATION.

COMBINED PERIODONTAL-ENDODONTIC LESION – endodontic treatment takes precedence over periodontal management. **Combined endodontic-periodontal therapy** is widely used because the anatomic and clinical connections b/t the pulp and periodontal structures are close & numerous. **In most combined endo-perio lesions, endodontic procedures are performed first, and when necessary, are followed by periodontal treatment**.

- **Ex:** If bone loss extends from the cemento-enamel junction (CEJ) to the tooth apex on a radiograph, probing depth are above normal all around the tooth, but at one point the probe drops precipitously to an even greater depth, and vitality test is negative. This **patient may require endodontic treatment followed by periodontic treatment**.

- In these cases, the value of precise pocket probing and correct appraisal of pulp vitality is crucial. In some doubtful cases, it is best to wait until after RCT is complete to see if spontaneous resolution (pocket closure and osseous fill-in) will occur before surgical periodontal procedures are begun.

- **Periodontal therapy is initiated first ONLY in the case of a primary periodontal lesion**, with subsequent secondary endodontic involvement.

- A common clinical finding of a periodontal problem is **PAIN to LATERAL PERCUSSION** on a tooth with a wide sulcular pocket.

- **Periodontic-Endodontic Abscess**-a combined lesion that usually shows radiographic involvement of the periodontium & apex of the involved tooth.

Probing Lesions:
1. **Conical-Shaped Probing Lesion**-a periodontal probing defect that cannot be managed by endodontic treatment alone that is typical of a periodontal problem. Periodontal Lesions characteristically show bone loss that starts at the crestal bone level and progresses apically. Thus, probing defect is conical-shaped. Periodontal lesions may not be amenable to RCT alone even if it is associated with a pulpless tooth. However, endodontic treatment must be completed PRIOR to treating the periodontal problem.
2. **Blow-Out (acute) Probing Lesion**-a clue for diagnosis is a non-vital (necrotic) pulp that can completely heal after RCT. A tooth with this lesion shows normal sulcus depth all around the tooth until the area of swelling is probed. At this point, the probe drops to a level near the root apex. Probing depths in all other areas are within normal limits.
3. **Narrow Sinus Tract Lesion**-probing reveals normal depths all around the tooth except at one very narrow area. Thus, the probe can pass down the root surface to some distance (sometimes to the apex). The tooth is pulpless (non-vital). Once RCT is complete, the lesion completely heals within one week. Another clue for diagnosis is a non-vital (necrotic) pulp.

REVERSIBLE PULPITIS (PULPAL HYPEREMIA = PULPAL INFLAMMATION) — most commonly caused by bacteria. Pain is not spontaneous, but requires an external irritant to evoke a painful response (i.e. cold, sweets). **Pains are SHARP & BRIEF, stopping when the irritant is removed.** Radiographs appear normal (may show deep caries or cavity preparation).

- Tooth is usually **percussion negative**, and with thermal tests, the **pulp responds more readily to cold** than to hot (the response leaves shortly after the irritant is removed).

- A short, painful response to cold suggest pulpal hyperemia. Pulpal hyperemia is an excessive accumulation of blood in the pulp due to vascular congestion. It is the engorgement of pulpal vessels with blood. Once the causative agent (i.e. bacteria or a restoration in hyperocclusion) is removed or adjusted, the pulp usually returns to normal.

- Pulpal hyperemia is congestion of blood within the pulp chamber caused by physical, chemical, or bacterial insult. After restoration placement, teeth often become hyperemic and sensitive to cold for a few days. **The pain is not spontaneous, and does not last after the stimulus is removed.** This short pain duration and low intensity is what distinguishes pulpal hyperemia from the pain of **acute pulpitis ("irreversible pulpitis")**.

- Pulpal hyperemia caused by bacterial insult is a limited inflammation of the pulp. The tooth can recover if the caries is eliminated by timely operative treatment.

- **Treatment**: usually a sedative filling or new restoration with a base.

NOTES

- Hyperemic teeth respond on a lower level of current on the EPT (electric pulp tester) than a normal tooth.

- The most effective way to reduce pulp injury during tooth preparation is to minimize dehydration of dentin.

IRREVERSIBLE PULPITIS ("ACUTE PULPITIS") – condition characterized by **SPONTANEOUS PAIN** with periods of cessation (intermittent in nature). Clinical symptoms severity varies as the inflammatory response increases. Pain varies from a mild & readily tolerated discomfort, to a severe, throbbing, and excruciating pain that is spontaneous, intermittent, and **LINGERS AFTER THE IRRITANT IS REMOVED**.

- Pain is usually not readily localized by the patient, but is diffuse in nature.

- Irreversible pulpitis is an acute inflammation of the pulp characterized by intermittent spasms of pain that becomes continuous. In the early stages, it may appear as a very severe hyperemia. As the condition continues, the pain is gnawing or dull-throbbing, and is generally increased by heat and relieved by cold.

- Lying down or bending over intensifies the pain because the overall increase in cephalic blood pressure is relayed to the confined pulp tissue.

- Tooth may be tender to percussion (tooth is usually percussion positive), heat may intensify the pain response, while cold may relieve it (in advanced stages). Usually HOT & COLD cause severe and lasting pain. Thus, thermal test is the best aid to diagnose an irreversible pulpitis.

- When the pulp becomes severely inflamed as indicated by a thermal stimulus producing pain that lasts long after the stimulus is removed (longer than 10 seconds), this suggests "irreversible pulpitis" and the pulp is unlikely to recover after removing the caries. Pulpal pain (spontaneous or elicited by an irritant) that lingers more than 10-15 seconds.

- Radiographs do NOT disclose periapical pathology.

- Sometimes it is hard to distinguish between reversible and irreversible pulpitis, in which case caries control (placing a temporary filling) is a conservative approach toward making the final diagnosis. If a tooth responds well to the temporary filling, the there is no need for RCT at this time.

- Treatment: RCT (complete pulp removal).

NECROTIC PULP (PULP DEATH) – may have no painful symptoms and does not respond to EPT at any current level, but the tooth sometimes responds to heat, but will not respond to cold. A tooth affected with a necrotic pulp may have no painful symptoms and may appear discolored. EPT is valuable because there will be no response at any current level.
- Treatment: RCT or extraction.

Significant Bacteroides species involved in pulpal-periradicular infection are **Porphyromonas & Prevotella** which received a separate genus (undergone taxonomic revision) due to their distinct characteristics. **Predominant bacterial species isolated from INFECTED ROOT CANALS** include:
- **Eubacterium, Peptostreptoccus, Fusobacterium, Porphyromonas, and Prevotella species**.
- Streptococcus species may not be as important in the progession of a carious lesion (leading to pulp exposure) as much as it is in the initiation of the lesion. Strict anaereobes play a major role in periapical pathoses.

Virulence Factors involved in periradicular pathosis:
- Lippolysaccharide (LPS)-found on the surface of gram (-) bacteria.
- Enzymes-neutralize antibodies and complement components.
- Extracellular vesicles-involved in bacterial adhesion, proteolytic activities, hemagglutination, and hemolysis.
- Fatty acids-affect chemotaxis and phagocytosis.

Vital pulp resists bacterial invasion. Even if vital pulp is exposed to microorganisms for 2 weeks, the bacterial penetration may extend no > 2mm into the pulp. In contrast, non-vital pulp is a fertile ground for bacterial growth and leads to necrosis.

Endodontic Therapy Contraindications:
1. non-restorable tooth OR non-strategic tooth (i.e. tooth not in occlusion).
2. tooth with insufficient periodontal support.
3. tooth with a vertical root fracture.
4. tooth with massive internal or external resorption.
5. tooth with a canal unsuitable for instrumentation or surgery (i.e. broken instruments, dentinal sclerosis, sharp dilacerations).

Any teeth not contraindicated are EXCELLENT candidates for successful endodontic therapy.

HEMOPHILIA – a medical condition that is **NOT a contraindication to conventional endodontic therapy**, but is strongly recommended that the dentist obtain clearance from the patient's physician before treatment.

Example of a Special Case: a previously traumatized tooth may show complete obliteration of the pulp chamber & canal, but the PDL may appear normal. The patient will be asymptomatic and the **tooth will not respond to pulp vitality testing. Treatment of choice: observe as long as the tooth remains asymptomatic & no periapical changes are evident**.

Restoring Endodontically Treated Teeth:
A major disadvantage of posts (dowels) is it does not reinforce the tooth structure, but WEAKENS IT.
- All posts designs are predisposed to leakage.
- At least 4mm of gutta-percha MUST remain to preserve the apical seal.
- Threaded screw posts may actually increase the chance of fracture. Thus, parallel-sided posts and tapered posts are preferred.
- Pins increase stresses and microfractures in dentin, thus should not be used.
- Cusps adjacent to lost marginal ridges should be restored with an ONLAY.

Restoration Options for Endodontically Treated Posterior Teeth: Endodontically treated posterior teeth are more prone to fracture than non-treated posterior teeth due MAINLY to destruction of coronal tooth structure and reduced structural integrity.
- **Restoration of occlusal opening only**: in rare instances, the access opening and caries destruction do not encroach on the cusps and marginal ridges. These teeth may be restored with an occlusal amalgam. However, a cuspal coverage restoration provides fracture protection
- **Onlays**: in most cases, it is required that root canal treated teeth be protected from fracture by a cusp-coverage restoration. **The minimum (most conservative) preparation is an onlay that covers cusps and marginal ridges**.
- **Crown**: a full-coverage crown is preferred when the remaining coronal tooth structure does not afford sufficient tooth structure for an onlay.
- **Crown with Post & Core**: to reinforce the treated tooth and provide suitable coronal tooth structure for an optimum crown preparation, a post & core is indicated. Be very careful when placing posts as perforations and vertical root fractures can occur.
- If performing a **pulp-chamber-retained amalgam**, you must **place amalgam 3mm** into each canal for retention.

NOTES

CHAPTER 8

ORAL PATHOLOGY TREATMENT PEARLS

Patient with bulging eyes (**Exopthalmos**), **weight loss**, and Grave's Disease is due to **Hyperthyroidism**.

Graves Disease signs/symptoms: skinny, weight loss.

Hypothyroidism: WEIGHT GAIN, dry hair, lower voice, feels cold.

Acute Adrenal Insufficiency (Addison's Disease): a patient on steroids might have an attack if not **supplemented by doubling the steroid dose** before dental treatment (due to their inability to produce extra cortisol in response to stress).

Ectodermal Dysplasia: reduced or missing teeth on a panorex.

Cleidocranial Dysplasia: patient has SUPERNUMERARY teeth (extra teeth).

Paget's Disease: can cause HYPERCEMENTOSIS of roots. Generalized skull and jaw enlargment, COTTON-WOOL appearance of bone. ↑ Alkaline Phosphatase

Hypercementosis: will follow the PDL on a PAX.

Cleft Lip: defective fusion of medial nasal process with maxillary process.

Cleft Palate: failure of palatal shelves to fuse BIFID UVULA.

Pierre Robin Syndrome: cleft palate, mand micrognathia, glossoptosis (airway obstruction).

Hypocalcified teeth: looks like white and brown spots on the teeth.

Fluorosis: CANNOT REVERSE (microabrasion and bleaching can improve esthetics), but cannot reverse the condition.

Flurosis can be caused by a patient living in a region where the fluoride content in the water is 4ppm (normal is 0.7ppm).

Amelogenesis Imperfecta: NO EMAMEL on the teeth on BWX or PAX.

Dentinogenesis Imperfecta: can see OBLITERATED PULP CHAMBERS on radiographs and teeth have a TRANSLUCENT or OPALESCENT HUE (grayish to bluish brown).

SYPHILLIS: funky molar development, **mulberry molars**, screwdriver-shaped incisors (Hutchinson incisors). Maxillary anteriors with central depressions.

Gemination (Twinning): incomplete formation of two teeth, common on incisors; see maxillary lateral.

Taurodontsm: bull-shaped crowns with shortened roots on a PAX or panorex.

If a man or woman is overweight, HYPERTENSION can be a contributing factor.

Tzanck Test: to diagnose **Acute Herpetic Gingivostomatitis** (small painfull ulcers that recur every 5-6 months with fever). Treatment is **palliative** with Lidocaine rinses and analgesics.

Major Aphthous Ulcers: are long-standing and heal with a scar. Can see on the lip and palate. Pemphigoid can also heal with a scar.

Mucocele on the lower lip: identify the mucocele. It is due to an injured salivery gland; treat with **excision**. INSIDE THE MUCOCELE IS SALIVA (MUCUS).

NOTES

- **Ranula on floor of mouth**: looks like a mucocele, but on the floor of the mouth. Treat by removing it via **SURGICAL EXCISION or marsupialize**.

- **Stenson's Duct**: carries saliva from the Parotid gland to the mouth on the cheek just behind the second molar. If there is a retrograde infection of the duct could be due to duct stones. Take a sialogram (x-ray of the salivary ducts and glands to see if stones exist). Can also palpate to see if saliva come out. If there is no calcification, it is a radiolucency on a radiograph.

- **Wharton's Duct**: a submandibular duct that can become calcified. If a stone is present, will look radiopaque on an occlusal film.

- **Occlusal Film**: used to detect a sialolith of a submandibular gland (Wharton's Duct).

- **Pleomorphic Adenoma**: the MOST COMMON SALIVARY NEOPLASM can see the lesion on the posterior palate. **PAINLESS SWELLING**. (slowly enlarging).

- **Lichen Planus**: shows white Whickman's Striae (Rectilinear Pattern) on the buccal mucosa. Treat with topical corticosteroids when symptomatic or erosive. If asymptomatic, **LEAVE IT ALONE**.

- **Fibrous Dysplasia**: "GROUND GLASS" appearance.

- A cyst can be seen on a panorex with a raised area on the sinus floor (maxillary left sinus).

- **Extravacation Cyst**: can present on inside of cheek with fluid-like blister Treatment is surgical removal.

- **Primordial Cyst (Developmental Odontogenic Cyst)** can see on a panorex even with all of the other third molars erupted (#17 area, but can be in any 3rd molar location).

- **Dentigerous Cyst**: MOST COMMON odontogenic cyst associated with the crown of an unerupted or partially erupted tooth (unilocular, well-defined margins and sclerotic borders and some root resorption). Frequent in posterior mandible.

- **Lateral Periodontal Cyst Treatment**: arises from PDL remnants. It is developmental, and not the result of infection or inflammation. **EXCISIONAL BIOPSY & ENUCLEATION**.

- PAX of mandibular anteriors with Periapical Cemental Dysplasia, all the teeth are VITAL. **REASSURE THE PATIENT, BUT DO NOT DO RCT**.

- **Stafne's Bone Cyst (Stafne Defect)**: a submandibular gland depression (indentation); asymptomiatic (unilocular radiolucency) below the mandibular canal in the posterior mandible between the molars and **ANGLE OF MANDIBLE** (almost a perfect circular radiolucency) NO TREATMENT. It's a developmental defect containing a portion of the submandibular gland. Also called a lingual salivary bone cavity.

- **Median Palatal Cyst**: can see on an occlusal film. Treatment: **Enucleation**.

- **Periapical film (PAX)** can show an extension of the maxillary sinus between the premolar and molars.

- Maxillary anterior regions reveals **midline radiopacity (look for a step)** may be due to TRAUMA.

- **Tongue**: trauma can show a flap area on the right close to the lateral border due to trauma that has now healed.

- **Lingual Varicosities**: blue/brown bumps or linear structures on the ventral tongue surface, and are often DUE TO AGEING.

- **Hemangioma Treatment**: watchful neglect.

Multiple Telangiectasias – look like little dilated blood vessels (telangiectasias) on the tongue

Median Rhomboid Glossitis: need to identify picture. Treat with NYSTATIN (due to Candida).
↳ dorsum of tongue w/ midline swelling posteriorly.

Hairy Tongue: looks nasty. Treat by taking the patient off of their medications, use mouthrinses, and improve oral hygiene (brush the tongue). → treat normally but no invasive procedures.

Oral Hairy Leukoplakia & AIDS: may need to **treat with antibiotics** if they are immunocompromised.

Kaposi's Sarcoma: oral manifestation in an AIDS patient; a malignant cancer of the lining of blood vessels on the **HARD PALATE**. May present as **purple lesions on the palate**. Provide **normal dental treatment, but no invasive procedures**.

Geographic Tongue (Migratory Glossitis): reassure the patient and leave alone. **NO TREATMENT**.

Fissured Tongue treatment: do nothing and reassure the patient.

Leukoplakia on the tongue or buccal mucosa must be **BIOPSIED**.

Asymptomatic finding on the tongue lateral border with a **5-year** history during which time it has **changed appearance repeatedly**. **Treatment**: REASSURANCE/NO TREATMENT.

A **keratotic, linear formation** on the tongue's lateral border has been present for about **2.5 years**. **Treatment**: **BIOPSY**.

Sickel Cell Anemia: can see on a PAX with radiolucent areas due to less striations in bone, decrease in trabeculae bone density, enlarged bone-marrow spaces, and stepladder appearance.

Midline Mandible Fracture: can see due an obvious step between teeth 24 & 25 on a panorex. Mandibular fractures can show a step down in the occlusal plane.

Burning Mouth Syndrome Etiology: idiopathic (unknown), nerves, or nutrition deficiency.

Lingual Tonsils (Adenoids): if enlarged when sick, it is NOT pathologic.

A younger teenager with swollen tonsils is an inflammatory condition.

Palatoglossus Muscle: to identify, it is the first pillar in front of the tonsils.

Pharyngeal Space on a Panorex is normal.

Cementoma (affects vital teeth): NO TREATMENT, JUST OBSERVE.

Condensing Osteitis (affects non-vital teeth): no radiolucent border, radiopacity is not separated from the apex, and clinical expansion is present. **Treatment**: ELIMINATE INFECTION SOURCE & INFLAMMATION.

Periapical Bone Scar: NO TREATMENT, JUST OBSERVE.

Periapical film of a mandibular first molar area with an irregular-shaped, periapical radiopacity. Treatment: **LEAVE ALONE**.

AMELOBLASTOMA: mandible has a SOAP-BUBBLE appearance due to multilocular radiolucencies.

A patient who had **Hepatitis A over year ago is okay to treat**. It resolves within a couple of weeks usually on its own.

Hepatitis A "Infectious" acquired from raw/steamed shellfish, contaminated water or food.

Hepatitis B: "serum" can be acute or chronic. Prolonged incubation 4-26 weeks.

NOTES

- **Hepatitis C**: caused by innoculations (serum, vaccination), IV drug use, blood transfusions.

- **Squamous Cell Carcinoma**: occurs on the **LOWER LIP** and **lateral tongue borders**. May have a crusted or cauliflower appearance.

- Patient comes in with hard palate swelling that has been there fore about 2 years. The patient tells you they had a similar lesion removed some years ago. **Treatment**: SURGICAL REMOVAL

- You see a swelling under the tongue on the floor of the mouth (ranula). **Treatment**: **SURGICAL REMOVAL**.

- Dense, firm ulcer with **INDURATED borders** is of 4 month duration, has been gradually increasing in size, and severely restricts tongue movement. **Treatment**: **PERFORM INCISIONAL BIOPSY**.

- You see a hard palate with a midline swelling present for several years. Patient is concerned about this swelling because there is a family history of carcinoma. **Treatment**: Leave alone and reassure the patient.

- **Basal Cell Carcinoma**: occurs on the face (might see under the eyes).

- Patient has a **RAISED LESION under the eye**, present for about 2 years. **Treatment**: Biopsy and Surgical Removal (Basal Cell Carcinoma).

- Nicotinic Stomatitis can be seen on the palate in a **PIPE SMOKER**.

- Picture of the palate with numerous small raised areas with central **RED DOTS** (nicotinic stomatitis) caused by **PIPE SMOKING**

- Palatal and muccobuccal fold lesions are often associated with tobacco (snuff).

- **Herpetic Stomatitis**-viral infection causing oral ulcers and inflammation. Mainly affects children (a child's first exposure to herpes virus). **Treatment**: **ACYCLOVIR**, liquid diet (cool, non-acidic drinks), and numbing medication (viscous lidocaine) rinse if severe pain.

- **Linea Alba**: no treatment, can be caused by cheek biting, dentures, orthodontic appliances, uneven teeth, and aggressive oral hygiene (benign hardening of the check mucosa due to excess keratin). **REMOVE THE IRRITANTS IS THE TREATMENT**.

- **Smokeless Tobacco Pouch Keratosis**:

- **Circumvallate Papillae**: largest, least numerous arranged in an inverted "v" shaped row at the back of the tongue (have taste buds).

- **Eagle Syndrome**: on a panorex view looks like a bone under the angle of the mandible. It is **ELONGATION** and calcification of the temporal **styloid process** at the back of the throat that occurs after a tonsillectomy or trauma. Carotid Artery Syndrome is elongation and mineralization of the styloid process that impinges carotid arteries and nerves. **Patient complains of unilateral neck pain when turning their head; possible sore throat, dysphagia**. **Treatment**: Mild Cases None except reassurance or local corticosteroids to relieve pain Severe Cases: surgical intra-oral excision of the process.

PRE-MEDICATION, DENTAL EMERGENCY, & MEDICAL HISTORY PRACTICE PEARLS

Penicillin Allergic Patient Pre-medication: Clindamycin or Erythromycin.

Non-Allergic Penicillin Patient Pre-medication: 2g Amoxicillin 1 hour prior to dental appt.

Hip/Joint Replacement Prophylaxis: first 2 years after surgery only.

Antibiotic prophylaxis is indicated for **RHEUMATIC HEART DISEASE** & patient with a history of bacterial endocarditis.

The dentist recommends antibiotic pre-medication for **dental procedures likely to cause bleeding**.

Tetracyclines & Oral Contraceptives: weaken the antibiotic's effectiveness.

A patient with history of **ACID REFLUX** and has mild dental pain, can prescribe Acetaminophen (Tylenol) for dental pain.

Gingival Hyperplasia: can be caused by Calcium Channel Blockers even after a few months. Treatment: have patient reduce or switch their medication. Last option is a gingivectomy.

LEUKEMIA symptoms include **increased WBC** above normal and gingival bleeding. Blood level example: RBC (2.2 million), Platelets (24,000), WBC (79,000). **Diagnose with COMPLETE BLOOD COUNTS and bone marrow examination.**

THROMBOCYTOPENIA patients have **LOW PLATELET COUNT (poor clotting)**. Normal platelet count is 150,000-450,000. **Below 50,000 per microliter is thrombocytopenia.**

ANEMIA: pale gums due to decreased RBC count (**normal RBC is 4.7-5.0 million**). Diagnose by a complete blood count test. 2 million RBC is a sign of anemia.

PT (Prothrombin Time or INR) is the test to evaluate blood coagulation (clotting) time and to monitor response to oral anti-coagulant therapy like **COUMARIN** & **LIVER DISEASE**.

If your patient is having a seizure, first action is to **PROTECT YOURSELF** AND THE PATIENT FROM **INJURING THEMSELVES** (clear the area, hold hands against the dental chair).

A patient taking Isoniazid (INH), Rifampin (RMP) or Pyrazinamide (PZA) (1st line anti-tuberculosis drugs), has **Tuberculosis**.

AIDS patient treatment: universal precautions, try to avoid invasive procedures, no treatment.

Dentist had a needlestick, have the patient do an **ELISA test** (enzyme-linked immunosorbent assay) "wet-lab" type analytic biochemistry to detect HIV antibodies (Ab).

Anaphylaxis Reaction/Shock: treat with EPI and steroids.

Medical history of a patient taking penicillin and has an allergic reaction on the lower lip. To treat, **APPLY TOPICAL STEROIDS** or maybe switch the antibiotic.

The first thing to do if a dental patient experiences **SYNCOPE** (fainting from hypotension) in the dental chair is place patient in the **TRENDELENBURG POSITION** (supine position). Feet higher than the head by 15-30 degrees to increase cerebral perfusion pressure. There is some debate about this though, and it is **NOT** recommended for hypovolemic shock.

NOTES

Anaphylactic Shock: place in supine position, O$_2$/ventilate manually, monitor vitals, 0.3-0.5ml EPI pen SC or IM.

 The major difference between syncope and severe anaphylactic shock is there can be **difficulty breathing** in anaphylactic shock.

Patient has **malaise, lethargy, itching** they may be having an allergic reaction give **BENEDRYL**.

 A 60-year old female taking **NAPROXENE**, one aspirin daily who is allergic to penicillin, is most likely taking the naproxene for **ARTHRITIS**. Do not make a precision attachment for her due to her lack of dexterity as the result of arthritis.

 Angioedema of the upper lip has been diagnosed as an **allergic reaction** with no other signs of allergy. Most appropriate treatment is oral administration of an antihistamine (**BENEDRYL**).

Albuterol: bronchodialator inhaler (relaxes muscles) for ASTHMA. Do not administer nitrous oxide to an asthmatic.

Promethazine: antihistamine to prevent motion sickness and as a sedative for insomnia when benzodiazepines are contraindicated. Can be used to treat allergic reactions. Common side effects: Tardive dyskinesia, xerostomia.

Propoxephine: analgesic for mild-to-moderate pain. DO NOT USE WITH KIDNEY (RENAL) FAILURE PATIENTS.

 If a patient has a kidney transplant, the patient may require antibiotics (stress dose) due to anti-rejection medications.

 A patient with KIDNEY DISEASE can prescribe TYLENOL (Acetaminophen), but NOT aspirin, advil, or naproxen.

If a stent was placed for kidney dialysis, there is no need for pre-medication. Patient's with a stent does not require premedication.

Triamterene & Spironlactone- a potassium (K+) sparing/conserving diuretics for hypertension and edema (Congestive Heart Failure-CHF). NOT USED FOR IMPAIRED RENAL FUNCTION PATIENTS.

Valium has metabolites for a long duration and binds to GABA receptors to cause inhibitory effects. Treats: benzodiazepine for anxiety, seizures, and insomnia.

 Follow ABC if a patient becomes **unconscious and unresponsive**: Activate EMS, check **A**irway, **B**reathing, & **C**irculation. 2010 guidelines changed to order to call 911, then CAB (compressions, then airway assessment, then breathing). 30 compressions: 2 breaths.

Norpace (Disopyramide Phosphate)-an anti-anginal & anti-arrhythmic agent.

MONA: morphine, oxygen, nitroglycerin, aspirin: priority treatment for angina.

If a patient is having an **MI (Myocardial Infarction/chest pain)**, administer anti-anginal drugs (**NITRO-GLYCERIN VASODILATOR**). Do not give if patient is taking VIAGRA or CIALIS as can cause severe drop in BP.

Patient is sitting in the dental chair with his hands on chest/heart, with a history of angina. **First thing to do is give the patient 0.4mg of nitroglycerine tablet**.

Angina Pectoris symptoms: chest discomfort (not pain), epigastrium area. Usually precipitated by exertion or stress. Nausea and vomiting can occur

A patient takes a nitroglycerine tablet with no effect by 5 minutes, you then give a second and third tablet and still nothing happens. **Patient is most likely having a MI (Myocardial Infarction)**.

MI Indications include: chest pain, pounding heart beat, left arm, jaw, neck pain, (NOT INDIGESTION or UPSET STOMACH). This is more a symptom of ANGINA.

Do not use a retraction cord that contains EPI for a crown patient who recently had a MI.

A MI (myocardial infarction) can produce **GI symptoms**, while syncope does not.

A patient on **steroids** will need **supplementation**.

Baby Bottle Syndrome: can cause rampant caries in a toddler/infant.

Xerostomia: can cause rampant decay due to lack of saliva to buffer acidic pH.

Tetracycline Stain Treatment: best to **LEAVE ALONE**, could do veneers.

Test the autoclave to ensure it is properly sterilizing by doing a **SPORE TEST** using **BIOLOGIC INDICATORS**  **WEEKLY**.

Change sodium hypochlorite DAILY

According to CDC regulations, you are NOT required to wash hands before and after removing gloves.

A standard cartridge (carpule) has 1.8 mL of 2% lidocaine (36mg)—the active ingredient, and 1:100,000 (0.018mg) of EPI (vasoconstrictor).

ORAL SURGERY TREATMENT PEARLS

A tooth with a **vertical root fracture** and **periapical radiolucency** should be **extracted**.

An **oroantral communication** can be treated with **flap surgery**.

A PAX or panorex of a **mesio-angular mandibular 3rd molar** impinging on the **2nd molar**, treatment is to **extract the 3rd molar**.

If you see a radiograph (PAX) with **facial swelling** due to a **wisdom tooth**, refer the patient to **OMS**. A patient with a **swollen face for 24 hours** send to the **OMS**.

A child with a **NECK SWELLING**: possibly related to a **mandibular 3rd molar** and **incision and drainage** (I & D).

Osteoradionecrosis can occur in the **mandible** (**posterior areas** are common).

Fibrinolytic Alveolar Osteitis (Dry Socket or Local Osteitis): **irrigate extraction site** and treat with **iodoform gauze and eugenol**. Patient returns **48-72 hours** after extraction with **pain** and **fetid odor**.

LIVER CLOT (JELLY CLOT): a **blood clot after extraction** (**post**-surgical sequela). **Remove** the liver clot with a curette, **apply pressure and reassess**.

If a **permanent** tooth is **avulsed**, **do not scrub clean** (destroys cells), put in **milk** of Hank's Balanced Salt Solution.

Traumatic Ulcer: can occur **after tooth extraction** or **poor-fitting dentures**.

Prophy teeth **BEFORE** an **extraction** to **reduce plaque and bacteria**, and allows **better healing** of tissue during **post** surgery healing.

A patient taking **ASPIRIN** when reviewing their **medical history** may have excessive **BLEEDING** following an extraction.

A patient taking **COUMADIN** requires a **tooth extraction**, must request **PT test** (INR)

A **recent extraction socket**. Patient **returns with pain** from the area of the extraction site (usually occurs 48-72 hours after extraction—also **bad taste**). **Treatment**: **syringe socket and pack idoform gauze + eugenol paste**.

You see a **large blood clot** in the area of **#31**. The patient had this tooth removed **several hours ago**. This is a **liver clot**. **Treatment**: **Have patient bite on gauze (pressure) and re-assess**.

PERIODONTIC TREATMENT PEARLS

After SRP, you should typically find a reduction in inflammation and 1-2mm probing depth (pocket reduction).

A 6-7mm pocket with continued BOP despite good oral hygiene and root planning would result from **RETAINED SUBGINGIVAL BACTERIA or CALCULUS**.

The best way to determine if a patient's periodontal condition is stable is there is **no increase in pocket depth**.

FURCATION LESIONS (involvement) and pocket depths are the most significant factors that influence the course of periodontal disease.

Best (initial and most effective) treatment for **ANUG** is **SRP (debridement)**.

ANUG can cause foul (bad) breath.

Stillman's Cleft (v-shaped) treatment is to SRP and place a gingival graft.

Common **goal of flap surgery:** access roots for debridement to allow pocket elimination.

Healing of **LONG JUNCTIONAL EPITHELIUM** occurs after raising a flap.

The normal width of keratinized gingiva the mandibular anterior region is 3-4mm.

Drugs like Naproxene, Penicillin, and Aspirin **DO NOT INCREASE POCKET DEPTH**. Tetracyclines (Arestin) can decrease pocket depth in conjunction with SRP.

Pocket Depth-the distance from the free gingival margin (FGM) to the CEJ of the tooth.

Furcation Involvement (Grade 1, 2, 3,4) : **Grade 4 has the worst prognosis:**

- **Grade 1:** treated with SRP only. ≤ 3mm depth.

- **Grade 2:** SRP followed by GTR (guided tissue regeneration) with bone graft and membrane barrier to prevent epithelial migration into the furcation and allow bone migration, differentiation, and maturation of the area. At least 3mm depth.

- **Grade III & IV:** success is limited; tunnelization is used to create a tunnel through the furcation to allow an interproximal brush to clean the furcation. > 2mm with Nabers probe. Grade II & IV furcation defect goes through the entire width of tooth so no bone is attached to the angle of the furcation.

- Grade I & II have an excellent prognosis. Grade III & IV have limited prognosis.

- **Goal of GTR:** uses barrier membranes to direct growth of new bone and gingival tissue in deficient areas to promote regeneration of the PDL, cemental attachment and alveolar bone. Used after extractions of bony defects.

NOTES

Interleukin (IL-1): a protein (cytokine) activated by macrophages and neutrophils that **produces periodontal inflammation**.

Occlusal trauma can contribute to periodontal disease by causing a widened PDL and bone resorption, and mobile teeth. Secondary occlusal trauma occurs when there is a pre-existing periodontal condition and trauma is placed on the teeth.

STAIN on the lingual surface of mandibular teeth is NOT primarily caused by periodontal disease, but extrinsic staining factors (diet, medication). **Pocket depth, furcation/bony lesions, and patient hygiene compliance** affect a periodontal prognosis.

To maintain gingival health when making a temporary crown, **UNDERCONTOUR** the temporary crown.

Patient returns to your office 4 weeks after SRP and still 4mm pockets present. **Treatment**: **SRP the area again**.

ENDODONTIC TREATMENT PEARLS

Pain on **RELEASE** of biting is a symptom of **ROOT FRACTURE SYNDROME**.

A tooth with a horizontal root fracture at the coronal third may need to be treated with by either reducing the fractured portion of the tooth and splinting it to adjacent teeth to immobilize the tooth or RCT.

Dentoalveolar fractures are caused by TRAUMA and can be treated with RCT.

Periapical of #9 with an existing crown has a fracture 1mm below the CEJ (above crest of bone). To treat, remove crown + RCT + post/core/crown and supraerupt the tooth with ortho to bring the marginal coronal.

If no endodontic or pulpal response eight hours after trauma. **Treatment**: nothing because that is a normal response right after trauma.

Did a recent RCT three months prior, you take a PAX and the lesion is getting smaller. Best treatment: **NONE, JUST FOLLOW-UP**.

Irreversible Pulpitis: spontaneous pain with intermittent periods, lingering thermal sensitivity, percussion pain, pain is diffuse (not localized), lying down or bending over intensifies the pain. **THERMAL COLD TEST IS BEST TO DIAGNOSE**. Pain may be increased by heat and relieved by cold.

ZINC PHOSPHATE is the **most irritating** base to the dental pulp.

Teeth that are traumatized will not pulp test accurately if testing immediately after the trauma.

Dowel (Post) in a canal: should be **1/3 the canal width**. Any wider may fracture the root. When using a round bur to make a dowel with **post width should be 1/3 the root diameter**.

When a root is 15mm from the CEJ, the post should be **10mm long (5mm from the apex)**.

A periapical film showing pulp stone calcifications will make endodontics more difficult.

Enamel pearls in the canal is a calcified circle on the radiograph.

Sodium Hypochlorite for endodontics is used from 0.5%-5.25% concentrations.

The major constituent of gutta percha is ZINC OXIDE. Gutta percha is an inert, polyterpene derived from trees.

Transillumination: laser transmits light through the tooth to diagnose cracked tooth syndrome.

A radiograph of an asymptomatic RCT tooth long-standing with a short obturation, the treatment is just observe.

Maxillary molar that is vital, but has a periapical infection/abscess (irreversible pulpitis).

ORTHODONTIC TREATMENT PEARLS

Generalized root blunting and root resorption on a panorex can be due to ORTHODONTIC TREATMENT. Root resorption can also be due to trauma.

The most significant finding when comparing pre and post orthodontic treatment panorex is ROOT RESORPTION.

A mesially inclined molar can be uprighted with an orothodontic FIXED appliance.

Patient with a missing lateral incisor, can try to close the space with an orthodontic FIXED appliance.

A Class I malocclusion with spacing, refer for an orthodontic consultation.

An orthodontic tipping device is used for TIPPING (root is tipped labially or lingually to correct the angle of the tooth crown).

DB cusp of mandibular 1st molar (#30 or #19) occludes in the central fossa maxillary first molar (#3 or #14)

Class III Malocclusion: a protruded mandible.

PAX related to space maintenance: if a premolar is almost erupted, then extract the primary molar. If a primary molar, but no premolar coming in, keep the primary molar; if a premolar is erupting incorrectly, and the primary molar has caries, extract the molar and guide the premolar with orthodontics.

Periapical of maxillary anterior region reveals an UNERUPTED permanent canine past due. Treatment: Extract the primary (deciduous) canine and orthodontics.

PROSTHODONTICS & RESTORATIVE TREATMENT PEARLS

- The order of selective grinding (occlusal adjustments) is centric, working, lateral (balancing), then protrusive movements.

- If there are occlusal discrepancies when the immediate denture is fitted, the dentist should do **SELECTIVE OCCLUSAL GRINDING**. The sequence of selective grinding is CO, working, balancing, then protrusive. (CO, W, B, P).

- A patient with a complete denture recently fitted complains of **CHEEK BITING**. To correct, grind down BUCCAL surfaces (cusps) of posterior **MANDIBULAR TEETH**

- Set HORIZONTAL condylar inclination (guidance) on an articulator by using a PROTRUSIVE inclination record/registration.

- The technique most appropriate for recording the jaw relation to determine HORIZONTAL CONDYLAR INCLINATIONS on a semi-adjustable articulator is WITH A PROTRUSIVE INTER-OCCLUSAL RECORD.

- The part of a denture that is cervical to a contact is the retentive arm on a buccal clasp.

- Reciprocal arm (clasp) functions to counteract the forces of the retentive arm.

- Circumferential Clasp (suprabulge or Akers Clasp) wraps around more than 180 degrees of the tooth and usually contact the tooth along the entire clasp surface.

- **RECIPROCAL ARM CLASP**: the arm should ideally be placed at or CORONAL to the maximum tooth convexity (height of contour). Reciprocal clasp functions to COUNTERBALANCE the forces of the retentive arm.

- **RETENTIVE ARM**: placed ideally at or APICAL to the maximum tooth convexity.

- **LINGUAL BAR**: a major RPD connector. Major connector should be 3mm from the free gingiva for both maxillary and mandibular RPDs.

- The impression material used for **IMMEDIATE DENTURES** or for remaining anterior teeth (after the posterior teeth have been extracted) is: **POLYSULFIDE RUBBER** (rubber base materials) for a complete denture.

- Material with the best 24 hour stability after impression is: POLYVINYLSILOXANE (PVS) because its greatest advantage is it has HIGH DIMENSIONAL STABILITY. Can be poured after 24hrs or next day.

- If a patient complains of difficulty swallowing with their denture, the problem is **INADEQUATE INTER-OCCLUSAL SPACE**.

- **Difficulty swallowing and painful throat** are most likely related to a new denture with overextended lingual flanges (lingual flanges are too long).

- Minimum BUCCAL/**FACIAL (LABIAL)** reduction for a PFM is 1.5mm.

- Minimum amount of unsupported porcelain on a crown is 2.0mm.

- The best way to communicate to the lab where to cut the teeth for an immediate denture is to remove the clinical crowns.

- A **soft reline** after an immediate denture can be done **ANYTIME** or maybe **1 month**.

- A **hard reline (lab reline)** is done **6 months** after an immediate denture is delivered.

- After relining an immediate denture, **REDUCE VERTICAL DIMENSION**.

- Trim immediate denture relining material **AT THE TIME OF EXTRACTIONS (SURGERY)**.

- Stages of Extractions for Immediate Dentures: posterior teeth first (leave premolars and anteriors). After 8 weeks, take the impressions to make the denture.

- The sequence of tooth extractions when doing an immediate denture is to remove the **posteriors (molars) first** and leave the **anterior** and **premolars** (which are extracted at the time of surgery) to **MAINTAIN VERTICAL DIMENSION** to make the **immediate denture**.

- When the impression is made and you see small projections of impression material from the extraction sites, **TRIM THE PROJECTIONS FLUSH WITH THE BONY RIDGE**.

- The initial step when constructing immediate dentures is to **extract all the posterior teeth** except the premolars and anteriors to **maintain vertical dimension**. Then wait two months (8 weeks) from the first extraction appointment until taking the impressions for the final denture.

- Use a **CUSTOM (individualized) TRAYS WITHOUT TOOTH STOPS** for a final impression for the denture as it gives the most predictable results.

- Extending a mandibular complete denture will provide increased capacity of underlying tissue to withstand physical stress.

- Best time to take an impression for an immediate denture after extracting the posterior teeth is **8 weeks (2 months)**.

- The minimal time interval between delivering an immediate denture and taking the impressions for the patient's **final denture** or **lab hard reline is SIX MONTHS**.

- After delivering a denture, tell the patient (give instructions) to **wear the dentures until the 24-hour adjustment appointment**.

- After the immediate denture is delivered, the denture should be removed **at the 24 hour recall (the following day) by the DENTIST**.

- The sequence of removing the denture after the teeth have been removed is **1 day, then 3 days, then 1 week**.

- Use an **OPEN HORSESHOE** palatal RPD framework for a large **TORUS PALATINUS**.

- If the surgical stent guide fits, but the immediate denture does not, use tissue conditioner and adjust the immediate denture until it fits.

- With an extraction site, the **tissue conditioner (impression material)** is trimmed **AT THE GINGIVAL TISSUE LEVEL**.

- If dentures do not seat at the delivery appointment, **use pressure indicating paste and adjust the high spots until the denture seats**.

NOTES

- A man with an **Epulis Fissuratum** under the denture is treated with **EXCISION & RELINE**. Epulis fissuratum is the **most likely tissue reaction due to long-term wearing** of an ill-fitting denture.

- After you take final impressions and give the **lab hard and soft tissue records**, you obtain those records from the **poured MODELS**.

- When adjusting complete dentures us the **BULL rule** (Buccal Cusps of Upper, Lingual Cusps of Lower).

- The **minimum undercut** for a clasp is **0.01 inch**.

- Purpose of **guide planes** on the tooth's proximal surface is to **aid in denture insertion**.

- **Modified Ridge Lap Pontic**: BEST (ideal) pontic design for **ANTERIOR TEETH**.

- **Hygienic Pontic**: best pontic design for **POSTERIORS**.

- The most likely cause of **PORCELAIN FRACTURING** on a bridge 6-x-x-x-x-11 (long span) is **BENDING OF METAL DUE TO THE LONG SPAN**.

- Temporary flipper placed three months ago when patient lost tooth in an accident The next step in treating this patient is to do **FULL TREATMENT PLANNING** to find the **best treatment sequence**.

- Panorex shows an edentulous patient with marked **pneumatization of both maxillary sinuses**. This is a new patient who wants a complete new set of dentures. To treat this patient, **MAKE THE DENTURES**.

- **CORONOID PROCESS** plays a role in **maxillary denture stability** as it can **DISLODGE THE DENTURE**.

- **Anti-hypertensive drugs** can affect **RETENTION & STABILITY** of complete dentures if there is tissue EDEMA retention can be lost. If anti-hypertensive drugs function by fluid loss (diuretics), too much fluid loss can also reduce retention.

- Main advantage of doing a **MARYLAND BRIDGE** vs. a **PFM** is it conserves tooth structure (less tooth reduction).

- Main disadvantage of a MARYLAND BRDIGE or RESIN-BONDED BRIDGE is **DEBONDING** (comes off).

- Disadvantages of a resin-bonded bridge: esthetics, rebonding, staining, tooth preparation, and cost.

- A **precision attachment** for a RPD is NOT indicated for a patient with poor manual dexterity (**arthritis patient**).

- Yellow or blue material is painted on the dies for a crown (die spacer) to **MAKE ROOM FOR THE CEMENT**.

- If unable or unsure which color to use to match the color for porcelain for denture teeth, use **LOW COLOR SATURATION & LESS GRAY**.

- To select proper denture teeth shade, **sit the patient upright, no light in patient's face** or on the teeth.

- The **LEAST important** factor in selecting **posterior teeth** for dentures is **AGE** The shape of the teeth ridge and size and incisal guidance are all important.

Do not use porcelain denture teeth that **oppose** natural teeth because the porcelain teeth will wear down the natural teeth.

The purpose of doing a tooth try-in when making immediate dentures is to check **CENTRIC OCCLUSION & CENTRIC RELATION (CONFIRM JAW RELATIONS)**.

Purpose of maxillary anterior teeth for a patient with a low lip line (you do not see the teeth when the denture is used) is for **SPEECH & LIP SUPPORT**.

A patient with a chromium cobalt RPD is going to be made, the most important concern if there is a mesially shifted third molar is **EXTRUSION OF THE TOOTH**, which will affect the denture support.

The best cement for bonding a PFM to the preparation is **ZINC PHOSPHATE**.

When bonding to enamel there is **CHEMICAL RETENTION**.

Use **35% or 37% PHOSPHORIC ACID** to etch when placing a composite restoration.

Use HF acid + silane before cemented an all porcelain crown or veneer to improve the bond strength.

If you detect Class V caries, check to see if it is generalized to the entire mouth before restoring the single lesion to determine if there is an greater underlying problem.

If a patient has a large diastema between 8 & 9, it may be too large to treat with a **HYBRID** composite restorations, may be able to do veneers. But may not be able to do anything.

Anterior tooth (#8) in with a fractured incisal angle can restore with **HYBRID** composite.

Overhanging restorations and bad crown margins can cause periodontal problems (gingivitis).

Facial surfaces of maxillary anterior teeth have cervical caries. **Treatment**: Class V composite restorations.

Gingival tissue around a crown margin (ex: #9) can be due to the margin being a plaque trap or rough porcelain.

If preparing a crown with a 2mm pocket, place the finish line 1mm under the gingival to maintain periodontal health.

The bevel angle on a porcelain crown should be 45-60 degrees. Anterior tooth crown preparation for a jacket crown is a **SHOULDER** with butt joint for porcelain thickness.

Sealants are most likely to come off due to **improperly isolating the tooth from saliva**.

Crown-to-Root Ratio: when considering an FPD the root surface area of the abutment teeth has to **equal or surpass** that of the teeth being replaced with pontics.

Main cause of cement debonding: saliva contamination, improper etching or mixing ratios.

RADIOGRAPHIC TREATMENT PEARLS

If a white bell curve in the center of the panorex, then the **thyroid collar** got in the way.

If earings are left in on a panorex, it creates **GHOST IMAGES**.

If white columns and teeth are different sizes on a panorex, then there was an **interruption during the panorex**.

Thryoid collar is used for intra-oral films but NOT for a panorex.

PAX **film is backwards** can tell by the bubble if a manual PAX was taken or look at the position of teeth.

SLOB Rule (Same Lingual Opposite Buccal): on periapical radiographs for RCT, roots are superimposed on each other, and require separation for proper identification and visualize lengths/anatomy. To properly identify the roots, shift the tubehead **mesially or distally**. The lingual or palatal root imaged will move in the same direction as the tubehead, and MB & DB roots will move the opposite direction that the tubehead cone was directed.

If a BWX is **BLURRY**, usually the **patient moved**.

RINN XCP-R Alignment System: helps give better radiographs because **more parallel and perpendicular alignment** and reduces DISTORTION and reduces the number of components needed for accurate positioning (can take can take anterior and posterior PAXs and BWXs with just the one ring system).

E-Speed Film gives patients the LEAST radiation exposure because it requires half the exposure time (faster) compared to traditional D-speed films.

Upon examination, the mandibular anterior teeth reveal a midline step, the first diagnostic step to check for a fracture is to **take a RADIOGRAPH**. The most diagnostic finding to check for a fracture is a **STEP**.

Positions of **Coronoid Process** & **Fractured Condyle** on a panorex or on a model.

TEST WITH CONFIDENCE!

THE ULTIMATE STUDY GUIDE FOR CONQUERING
ADEX/NERB DIAGNOSTIC SKILLS EXAMINATION (DSE) FOR DENTISTS

is available online at
www.dentalboardbusters.com